CliffsTestPrep™

GMAT® CAT (Computer-Adaptive Graduate Management Admission Test)

8th Edition

by

Jerry Bobrow, Ph.D.

Contributing Authors/Consultants

Allan Casson, Ph.D.

Jean Eggenschwiler, M.A.

Rajiv Rimal, Ph.D.

Peter Z Orton, Ph.D.

William A. Covino, Ph.D.

Michele Spence, M.A.

Harold Nathan, Ph.D.

David A. Kay, M.S.

Dale Johnson, M.A.

IDG Books Worldwide, Inc.
An International Data Group Company

Foster City, CA ◆ Chicago, IL ◆ Indianapolis, IN ◆ New York, NY

About the Author

Dr. Jerry Bobrow, Ph.D., is a national authority in the field of test preparation. As executive director of Bobrow Test Preparation Services, he has been administering the test preparation programs at over 25 California institutions for the past 27 years. Dr. Bobrow has authored over 30 national best-selling test preparation books, and his books and programs have assisted over two million test-takers. Each year, Dr. Bobrow personally lectures to thousands of students on preparing for graduate, college, and teacher credentialing exams.

Publisher's Acknowledgments

Editorial

Project Editor: Joan Friedman

Copy Editor: Corey Dalton, Janet M. Withers

Editorial Assistant: Carol Strickland

Production

Proofreader: Vicki Broyles

IDG Books Indianapolis Production Department

CliffsTestPrep™ GMAT® CAT, 8th Edition

Published by
IDG Books Worldwide, Inc.
An International Data Group Company
919 E. Hillsdale Blvd. Suite 400
Foster City, CA 94404
www.idgbooks.com (IDG Books Worldwide Web Site)
www.cliffsnotes.com (CliffsNotes Web Site)

Library of Congress Control Number: 00-105679

ISBN: 0-7645-8610-6

Printed in the United States of America

10 9 8 7 6 5 4 3 2 1

8X/SQ/QX/QQ/IN

Distributed in the United States by IDG Books Worldwide, Inc.

Distributed by CDG Books Canada Inc. for Canada; by Transworld Publishers Limited in the United Kingdom; by IDG Norge Books for Norway; by IDG Sweden Books for Sweden; by IDG Books Australia Publishing Corporation Pty. Ltd. for Australia and New Zealand; by TransQuest Publishers Pte Ltd. for Singapore, Malaysia, Thailand, Indonesia, and Hong Kong; by Gotop Information Inc. for Taiwan; by ICG Muse, Inc. for Japan; by Intersoft for South Africa; by Eyrolles for France; by International Thomson Publishing for Germany, Austria and Switzerland; by Distribuidora Cuspide for Argentina; by LR International for Brazil; by Galileo Libros for Chile; by Ediciones ZETA S.C.R. Ltda. for Peru; by WS Computer Publishing Corporation, Inc., for the Philippines; by Contemporanea de Ediciones for Venezuela; by Express Computer Distributors for the Caribbean and West Indies; by Micronesia Media Distributor, Inc. for Micronesia; by Chips Computadoras S.A. de C.V. for Mexico; by Editorial Norma de Panama S.A. for Panama; by American Bookshops for Finland.

For general information on IDG Books Worldwide's books in the U.S., please call our Consumer Customer Service department at 800-762-2974. For reseller information, including discounts and premium sales, please call our Reseller Customer Service department at 800-434-3422.

For information on where to purchase IDG Books Worldwide's books outside the U.S., please contact our International Sales department at 317-596-5530 or fax 317-572-4002.

For consumer information on foreign language translations, please contact our Customer Service department at 1-800-434-3422, fax 317-572-4002, or e-mail rights@idgbooks.com.

For information on licensing foreign or domestic rights, please phone +1-650-653-7098.

For sales inquiries and special prices for bulk quantities, please contact our Order Services department at 800-434-3422 or write to the address above.

For information on using IDG Books Worldwide's books in the classroom or for ordering examination copies, please contact our Educational Sales department at 800-434-2086 or fax 317-572-4005.

For press review copies, author interviews, or other publicity information, please contact our Public Relations department at 650-653-7000 or fax 650-653-7500.

For authorization to photocopy items for corporate, personal, or educational use, please contact Copyright Clearance Center, 222 Rosewood Drive, Danvers, MA 01923, or fax 978-750-4470.

Trademarks: GMAT is a registered trademark of Graduate Management Admission Council. Cliffs, CliffsTestPrep, CliffsNote-a-Day, CliffsNotes, and all related logos and trade dress are registered trademarks or trademarks of IDG Books Worldwide, Inc., in the United States and other countries. All other trademarks are the property of their respective owners. IDG Books Worldwide is not associated with any product or vendor mentioned in this book.

 is a registered trademark under exclusive license to IDG Books Worldwide, Inc., from International Data Group, Inc.

Author's Acknowledgments

I would like to thank former Cliffs Notes Editor Michele Spence for her meticulous editing of the original manuscript and Joan Friedman and the IDG editorial staff for reviewing and editing this newest edition of my work.

I would also like to extend my sincere appreciation to the following authors and publications for permission to use excerpts from their fine writings:

Dr. Albert Upton, *Design for Thinking,* Stanford University Press.

Sy Montgomery, "Sharks," *Los Angeles Times,* February 23, 1991, p. B-3.

And finally, I would like to thank my wife Susan, daughter Jennifer (22), and sons Adam (19) and Jonathan (15) for their patience, moral support, and comic relief.

Table of Contents

PART I: INTRODUCTION TO THE GMAT CAT: THE COMPUTER-ADAPTIVE GRADUATE MANAGEMENT ADMISSION TEST

PART II: ANALYSIS OF EXAM AREAS

PART III: FULL-LENGTH GMAT CAT PRACTICE TEST

PART IV: ANOTHER PRACTICE TEST

Preface

Many students are needlessly afraid of the computer-adaptive GMAT.
Although the delivery system and format are different from those of the paper-and-pencil test, the types of questions are still the same. So don't be concerned about the computer-adaptive GMAT; *be prepared!*

Better scores result from thorough preparation. Because this new-format exam adapts to your ability level, you must use your study time more effectively than ever before to get thorough preparation and raise your level. You need the most comprehensive test preparation guide available to give you that extra edge. It must be complete, direct, precise, and easy to use, giving you all the information you need to do your best on the GMAT CAT.

In keeping with the fine tradition of Cliffs Notes, this guide was developed by leading experts in the field of test preparation as part of a series to specifically meet these standards. The testing strategies, techniques, and materials have been researched, tested, and evaluated and are presently used at GMAT CAT preparation programs at many leading colleges and universities. This guide features the Bobrow Test Preparation Services approach, which focuses on a careful **analysis of each exam area** followed by **strategies, techniques, and practice problems** categorized by level of difficulty to help you maximize your score. Taking, reviewing, charting, and analyzing a specially designed **simulation computer-adaptive type GMAT** will give you invaluable insight into the GMAT CAT as well as outstanding test practice. All tests and practice problems have answers and complete explanations.

Special introductory sections are included featuring **an overview of the computerized test-taking process** and a **Patterned Plan of Attack** for each type of question. A **math review** with diagnostic pretests in **arithmetic, algebra, and geometry** is also included.

This guide was written to give you the edge in doing your best by maximizing your effort in a minimum amount of time. If you take the time to follow the **Study Guide Checklist** in this book, you will get the best preparation possible.

Study Guide Checklist

❑ 1. Read the new GMAT CAT Information Bulletin.

❑ 2. Become familiar with the Format of the Test and the General Description, page 3.

❑ 3. Familiarize yourself with the answers to the Questions Commonly Asked about the Computer-Adaptive GMAT (GMAT CAT), page 5.

❑ 4. Review Taking the GMAT CAT: An Overview of the Process, beginning on page 9.

❑ 5. Learn the Test-Taking Strategies for the new CAT, page 15.

❑ 6. Carefully read Part II, Analysis of Exam Areas, beginning on page 21.

❑ 7. Work the practice problems arranged by levels of difficulty in each area.

❑ 8. Carefully read the answers and explanations for these practice problems.

❑ 9. Strictly observing time allotments, work the problems as directed in the Full-Length GMAT CAT Practice Test, beginning on page 255.

❑ 10. Check all your results.

❑ 11. Chart and analyze your results, pages 345–352.

❑ 12. Carefully read the answers and explanations for the problems you worked.

❑ 13. Return to the simulated computer-adaptive test and work all the level 1 problems — 4-1, 5-1, 6-1, 7-1, and so on.

❑ 14. Review the answer to each problem after you work it.

❑ 15. After attempting and reviewing the simpler problems, work all the level 2 problems, that is 4-2, 5-2, 6-2, 7-2, and so on.

❑ 16. Review the answer to each problem after you work it.

❑ 17. In the same manner, work and review the answers to the level 3 problems, then the level 4 problems, and then the level 5 problems.

❑ 18. Carefully reread Part II, Analysis of Exam Areas, beginning on page 21.

❑ 19. Strictly observing time allotments, take the second Full-Length GMAT CAT Practice Test in this book, beginning on page 391.

❑ 20. Check all your results.

❑ 21. Chart and analyze your results, pages 417–418.

❑ 22. Carefully read the answers and explanations for these practice problems.

❑ 23. Review Taking the GMAT CAT: An Overview of the Process, beginning on page 9.

❑ 24. Go over Final Preparations on page 433.

PART I

INTRODUCTION TO THE GMAT CAT: THE COMPUTER-ADAPTIVE GRADUATE MANAGEMENT ADMISSION TEST

GENERAL DESCRIPTION

The GMAT CAT lasts approximately three and a half hours and is composed of two 30-minute analytical writing responses, a 75-minute quantitative section, and a 75-minute verbal section.

- **Analytical Writing Assessment:** You will type two essay responses on topics provided. One response will be an analysis of an issue, and the other will be an analysis of an argument.

- **Quantitative:** This section contains 37 multiple-choice questions. Data Sufficiency and Problem Solving questions are intermingled.

  - Data Sufficiency: Each question requires you to decide how much of the mathematical data provided is sufficient for answering a question.

  - Problem Solving: You will solve general math and word-type problems.

- **Verbal:** This section contains 41 multiple-choice questions. Sentence Correction, Reading Comprehension, and Critical Reasoning questions are intermingled.

  - Sentence Correction: You will demonstrate your knowledge of correct and effective English expression.

  - Reading Comprehension: You will answer questions after reading passages about a variety of subjects.

  - Critical Reasoning: You will derive logical conclusions and relationships from a variety of situations and passages.

These sections measure your general knowledge background, not specific knowledge from any particular course or courses. No formal background in business or management is required.

The analytical writing responses are scored from 0 to 6, and the multiple-choice questions are scored from 200 to 800. The average score on multiple-choice questions is about 480. Two subscores are also generated: a quantitative score ranging from 0 to 60 (with an average score of approximately 28), and a verbal score ranging from 0 to 60 (with an average score of approximately 27).

Format of the Test		
Test Section	**Minutes**	**Number of Questions**
Analytical Writing Assessment (not computer-adaptive, responses are typed)		
Analysis of an Issue	**30**	**1**
Analysis of an Argument	**30**	**1**
Optional five-minute break		
Quantitative Section (computer-adaptive)	**75**	**37**
Problem Solving and Data Sufficiency (intermingled)		
Optional five-minute break		
Verbal Section (computer-adaptive)	**75**	**41**
Sentence Correction, Reading Comprehension, Critical Reasoning (intermingled)		

Tutorials for simple word processing for the Analytical Writing Assessment and for the quantitative and verbal sections will be available for review before the test sections are administered.

Note: The format of the test and the way results are scored are subject to change.

QUESTIONS COMMONLY ASKED ABOUT THE COMPUTER-ADAPTIVE GMAT (GMAT CAT)

Q: **Who administers the GMAT CAT?**

A: The GMAT CAT is written and administered by Educational Testing Service (ETS). The Graduate Management Admission Council (GMAC), made up of representatives from 113 graduate schools of management, serves as an advisor to ETS.

Q: **When is the computer-adaptive GMAT given?**

A: The computer-adaptive GMAT is offered six days each week for three weeks each month. Testing center hours may vary.

Q: **How do I schedule my GMAT CAT appointment?**

A: You can schedule (or reschedule) an appointment by calling your local testing center or a toll-free number. Phone numbers and a complete list of testing centers are in the GMAT information bulletin and on the GMAT Web site.

Q: **When should I schedule my appointment?**

A: Carefully check your graduate school admission deadlines to guide you in scheduling your appointment. Allow at least two weeks for your test results to be scored and sent to you. You may schedule your appointment just a few days before taking the test, but you should schedule early to get preferred dates, times, and locations.

Q: **Where do I take the GMAT CAT?**

A: There are approximately 400 computer-based testing centers. Testing centers are located at Sylvan Learning Centers, at colleges and universities, and at ETS field service offices.

Q: **Can I take the GMAT CAT more than once?**

A: Yes. You may take the exam once per calendar month. For example, if you take your first GMAT any time in January, then you can take the test again any time in February or later. Be aware that in addition to your latest score, your two most recent test scores since October 1992 will also appear on your score report.

Q: What is a computer-adaptive GMAT?

A: Only the Quantitative and Verbal sections of the test are computer-adaptive; the Analytical Writing Assessment requires you to type your responses into the computer. In the computer-adaptive sections, the screen displays one multiple-choice question at a time. The first question in each section is of medium difficulty. Each subsequent question varies in difficulty based on your responses to the previous questions. The questions displayed are chosen from a large pool of questions that have been categorized by level of difficulty and content. As the level of questions adjusts to your ability level, you will get more questions that are within your range. This "adaptive" system ultimately determines your level of ability. You must answer each question displayed. After you have answered a question and moved on to the next screen, you cannot go back to the previous question.

Q: What will the test center be like?

A: The conditions at the test center should be quiet and private, since the tests are administered individually at separate testing stations.

Q: Can I use scratch paper on the test?

A: You will be given scratch paper at the testing site. Use the scratch paper to your advantage to brainstorm essay ideas, outline your responses, sketch diagrams, do calculations, and so on.

Q: Will there be any breaks during the test?

A: Yes, two. You will have the opportunity to take a five-minute break after the essay section, and again between the quantitative and verbal sections.

Q: Should I guess on the GMAT CAT?

A: Yes. If you get stuck on a question or simply don't know the answer, guess. The computer-adaptive GMAT requires that you answer every question.

Q: What should I bring to the test center?

A: A valid photo-bearing ID, your score recipient information, your authorization voucher (if you requested one from ETS), and some sharpened pencils for scratch work on the scratch paper provided.

Q: How long does it take to get my scores?

A: For the multiple-choice sections (quantitative and verbal), you can see your scores as soon as you complete the exam. Your official score report, including the Analytical Writing Assessment scores, will be mailed about two weeks after your test date. At the testing site, you can designate the schools that are to receive your scores.

Q: Are the scores for the computer-based GMAT comparable to those of the paper-based GMAT?

A: GMAC and ETS research indicates that the scores are comparable.

Q: **Will accommodations be made for test-takers with disabilities?**

A: Yes. All centers should be equipped with appropriate devices to aid test-takers with disabilities, such as wheelchair access and screen magnification. Check with your center to make sure that the proper accommodations are available.

Q: **What computer skills are necessary for the GMAT CAT?**

A: The GMAT CAT is preceded by a tutorial program that starts with the very basics, so minimal computer skills are required. The tutorials will cover using the simple word-processing program, using a mouse, entering and confirming a response, changing a response, accessing the "help" function, and moving to the next question. The "help" function will be available throughout the test in case you have questions or need assistance.

Q: **How should I prepare for the GMAT CAT?**

A: Preparing well for the GMAT CAT requires following a careful plan:

1. Make sure that you are familiar with and understand each type of question you will encounter.

2. Understand and become comfortable with the format of the new exam and the computer delivery system. (Learn to use a simple word processor, a mouse, and so on.)

3. Review the subject matter—math, grammar, and analytical writing skills.

4. Practice, practice, practice.

Q: **How is my GMAT score used?**

A: The GMAT is used as part of an assessment of your probable success in graduate business school. Other factors, such as undergraduate grades, interviews, and letters of recommendation, also figure into this assessment. The importance of GMAT scores varies from institution to institution, so you should contact the graduate schools to which you are applying for further information.

Q: **Can I get more information about the test?**

A: Yes. Contact ETS by phone, fax, e-mail, or mail at:

GMAT
Educational Testing Service
P.O. Box 6103
Princeton, NJ 08541-6103
Phone: (609) 771-7330
Fax: (609) 883-4349
E-mail: gmat@ets.org
Internet: www.gmat.org

TAKING THE GMAT CAT: AN OVERVIEW OF THE PROCESS

Test Center Procedure

Be sure to arrive at the test center at least 30 minutes before your scheduled time. Don't be late! When you arrive at the test center, you will be checked in. Be sure to have

- a valid photo-bearing ID
- your score recipient information
- your authorization voucher (if you requested one from ETS)

After you have checked in, you will be assigned a seat. You will receive some scratch paper, and you may request more during the test. After you hear the general instructions and preliminary procedures for the test, you will be given time to work through the interactive tutorials. After the tutorials, you begin the actual GMAT.

The first section is the Analytical Writing Assessment. You will have 30 minutes to respond to the first topic by entering your response on the computer through the word-processing program. You will then have 30 minutes to respond to the second topic in the same manner. Following this hour of testing, you can take a 5-minute break if you choose.

Next, you will have 75 minutes for a multiple-choice section. You will enter all answers on the computer by using a mouse. Following this 75 minutes of testing, you will have the opportunity to take a 5-minute break.

Finally, you will have 75 minutes for the second multiple-choice section. You will enter all answers on the computer by using a mouse.

During the exam, if you have a problem with the computer, need additional scratch paper, or wish to speak to an administrator for any reason, raise your hand to get his or her attention.

Using the Interactive Tutorials

Many test takers are needlessly afraid of a computerized exam. You should understand that the testing company has gone to great lengths to make sure that the computerized test is easy to use, even for the computer novice. The test makers have included very basic tutorials to make sure that you are comfortable working with the computer. Take advantage of these tutorials; work through them slowly.

The interactive tutorials explain and let you try the simple word-processing program that you'll use for the two essay questions and the basic functions for the multiple-choice questions. You'll have plenty of time to become familiar with the computer before the test begins.

The Answer-Selection and Word-Processing Tutorial

One tutorial explains and reviews the simple word-processing program you will use for the two essay questions and the method by which you select answers in the multiple-choice sections. This tutorial carefully explains and lets you try the various word-processing functions; it also lets you practice selecting an answer oval and changing answers on multiple-choice questions.

Typing Essays

The basic typing keyboard is used for the essays, and the functions include the following:

Movement arrows move the cursor left, right, up, or down:

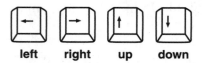

left   **right**   **up**   **down**

Movement keys

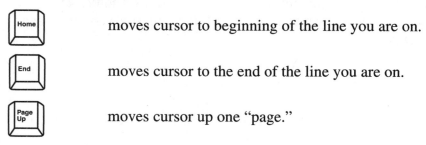

Home   moves cursor to beginning of the line you are on.

End   moves cursor to the end of the line you are on.

Page Up   moves cursor up one "page."

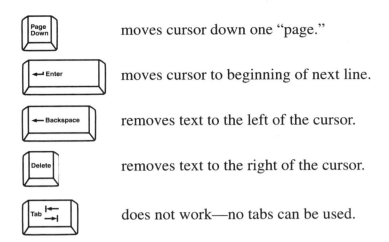

moves cursor down one "page."

moves cursor to beginning of next line.

removes text to the left of the cursor.

removes text to the right of the cursor.

does not work—no tabs can be used.

Simple editing (these icons appear on the right side of the screen)

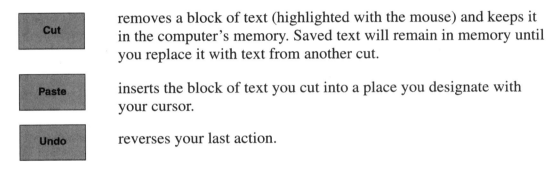

removes a block of text (highlighted with the mouse) and keeps it in the computer's memory. Saved text will remain in memory until you replace it with text from another cut.

inserts the block of text you cut into a place you designate with your cursor.

reverses your last action.

Reviewing and practicing each of the above functions on a basic word-processing program before you go to take the test will be helpful.

The screen for the essays is similar to this:

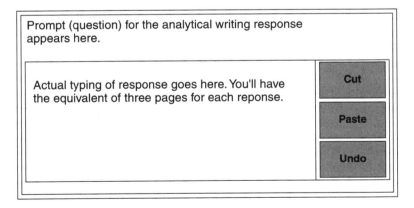

Selecting an Answer

You use your mouse to select your answer choice in the multiple-choice sections simply by moving the onscreen arrow to the oval in front of your answer choice and clicking (pressing a button on) the mouse. At that time, the oval will become blackened, showing your choice. For example,

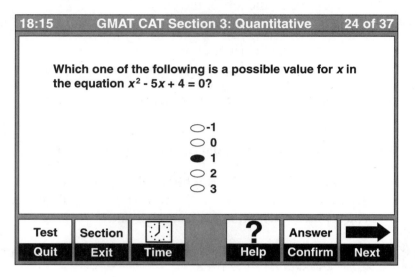

Notice the time display in the upper left corner of the screen, which indicates how much time remains for this section of the test. The number of the problem you are on and the total number of problems in the section are displayed in the upper right corner.

The Functions Tutorials

These tutorials review using a mouse, using the testing tools, and scrolling through long passages or graphs.

Using a Mouse

You use a mouse to enter your answer choice or input other information. Simply move the arrow to your selection by moving the mouse to the appropriate position and clicking (pressing) the left button on the mouse. The tail (cord) of the mouse should always be pointing away from you, and your fingers should be close to the buttons.

Using the Screen Tools

The following illustration shows the bottom part of the screen, on which the various tools are displayed.

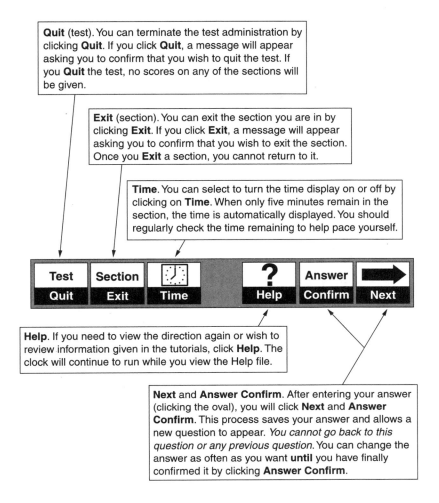

Quit (test). You can terminate the test administration by clicking **Quit**. If you click **Quit**, a message will appear asking you to confirm that you wish to quit the test. If you **Quit** the test, no scores on any of the sections will be given.

Exit (section). You can exit the section you are in by clicking **Exit**. If you click **Exit**, a message will appear asking you to confirm that you wish to exit the section. Once you **Exit** a section, you cannot return to it.

Time. You can select to turn the time display on or off by clicking on **Time**. When only five minutes remain in the section, the time is automatically displayed. You should regularly check the time remaining to help pace yourself.

Help. If you need to view the direction again or wish to review information given in the tutorials, click **Help**. The clock will continue to run while you view the Help file.

Next and **Answer Confirm**. After entering your answer (clicking the oval), you will click **Next** and **Answer Confirm**. This process saves your answer and allows a new question to appear. *You cannot go back to this question or any previous question.* You can change the answer as often as you want **until** you have finally confirmed it by clicking **Answer Confirm**.

Note: If a tool is gray (not dark), it will not work. You can use only the tools that appear dark onscreen.

Using the Scroll Bar

If a passage is too long to fit on the screen or if there is too much information in a graph or chart to fit on the screen, a scroll bar will appear alongside the passage or graph (which is usually shown on the left side of the screen). The scrolling portion of the screen is called a *scrolling pane.* The scroll bar is used to move (scroll) the information on the scrolling pane up and down. It allows you to bring information onscreen that was not shown previously. The information in the scrolling pane will not move horizontally. In the following screen, notice the scroll bar, the arrow in the scroll bar, and the status bar (the gray area with white letters) at the top of the scrolling pane.

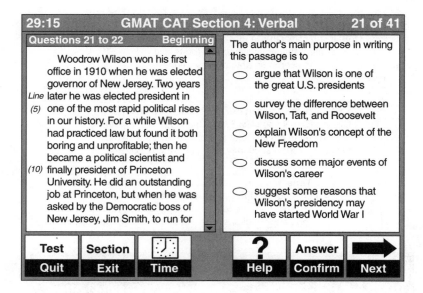

By clicking the arrows in the scroll bar, you can move the information up or down by a line. By clicking between an arrow and the box, you can move the information up or down the page in larger increments. Holding the mouse button down on an arrow makes the lines scroll very quickly.

The status bar indicates whether you are at the beginning or end of a passage or whether more text is available. The messages in the bar help you to keep track of where you are when you are scrolling.

If you are even slightly familiar with a Macintosh or PC Windows system, you will probably be very comfortable with the GMAT computerized format.

Scratch Paper

Before you start the exam, you will be given scratch paper. It is important that you use this scratch paper to its maximum benefit. When you do mathematical computations, you can list wrong answers, take notes, and redraw diagrams on the scratch paper. These and other strategies are discussed in the following chapter.

TEST-TAKING STRATEGIES: THE APPROACH

Don't Get Stuck

Many people who take standardized exams don't get the score they could achieve because they spend too much time dwelling on a single question, leaving insufficient time to answer other questions they could get right. Don't let this happen to you. Never spend more than a minute and a half to two minutes on any one question. With sufficient practice, you will almost automatically know when a problem is taking too long. If this happens, try to eliminate some choices, and then take a guess. *The key is not to get stuck!*

Eliminate Wrong Answers

Eliminate answer choices from consideration when possible. Because you can't mark on the computer screen, use your scratch paper to help you keep track of choices you've eliminated. You may wish to simply list answer choices and mark them out as follows. **Note:** You would use the markings A, B, C, D, and E to signify only the *order* of the choices given; no letters will appear next to your choices onscreen.

A̶
B
C̶
D
E̶

You may wish to use question marks to signify possible answers as follows:

A̶
? B
C̶
? D
E̶

Either of these methods can help you avoid reconsidering those choices already eliminated and can help you narrow down your possible answers. Remember to keep this marking system very simple.

Working from Multiple-Multiple-Choice Answers

You may encounter a few questions of the multiple-multiple-choice type. This type of question gives you answers marked with roman numerals (I, II, III) and then asks you if one, two, or possibly all three of the choices are correct answers. This type of question can appear in the Problem Solving, Reading Comprehension, or Critical Reasoning areas. Following is an example in the form of a Problem Solving question:

Which of the following are equations with the only solution $x = 6$?

$$\text{I.} \quad x^2 - 36 = 0$$

$$\text{II.} \quad x^2 - 7x + 6 = 0$$

$$\text{III.} \quad x + 5 = 3x - 7$$

   A. I only

   B. II only

   C. III only

   D. I and III only

   E. I, II, and III

A good strategy for this question type is to try to answer one of the roman numeral choices quickly. On your scratch paper, write

I
II
III
A
B
C
D
E

Then place a **T** or **F** by the numeral (for true or false), review the choices, and eliminate possibilities. In the example, since I, $x^2 - 36 = 0$, gives you an answer of 6 and −6 (that is, $x^2 = 36$ gives $x = 6$ or $x = -6$), it is false. Immediately place an **F** by roman numeral I and eliminate any answer choices that include I.

F I
II
III
~~A~~
B
C
~~D~~
~~E~~

Now you know that the answer must be **B** or **C**, since you've eliminated choices **A, D,** and **E** because they contain I. You can now focus on either equation II or equation III, since only one of them can be true. Working with equation II gives

$x^2 - 7x + 6 = 0$

$(x - 1)(x - 6) = 0$

$x - 1 = 0; x - 6 = 0$

$x = 1; x = 6$

So II is not true. Therefore, the answer must be **C,** III only. To finish the example, working III gives the following answer. (But remember that there's no need to work it in the exam because you've eliminated all the other answers.)

$$x + 5 = 3x - 7$$

$$
\begin{array}{rcl}
x + 5 &=& 3x - 7 \\
-5 & & -5 \\
\hline
x &=& 3x - 12 \\
-3x & & -3x \\
\hline
-2x &=& -12 \\
\dfrac{-2x}{-2} &=& \dfrac{-12}{-2}
\end{array}
$$

So $x = 6$, and **C** is your answer.

PART II

ANALYSIS OF EXAM AREAS

THE ANALYTICAL WRITING ASSESSMENT

Introduction

The Analytical Writing Assessment section requires you to write two prose responses with a time limit of 30 minutes for each. You will receive two types of questions: (1) an analysis of an issue, which presents an issue you must discuss, and (2) an analysis of an argument, which presents an argument you must analyze.

Because the GMAT is now computerized, you will enter your response to each of the analytical writing questions into the computer through a very simple word-processing system. Prior to starting the test, a tutorial will carefully walk you through using the word processor. This word processing program includes the basic typing keyboard functions including Cut, Paste, and Undo. It also includes the Home, End, Backspace, Delete, Page Up, Page Down, and Enter keys. The program does not allow you to use tabs, however.

You receive the equivalent of three pages to type each response, as well as scratch paper for prewriting, outlining, notes, and so forth. The prompt (question) for each type of response appears at the top of the page, and you type your response in the writing box below.

The screen is similar to this:

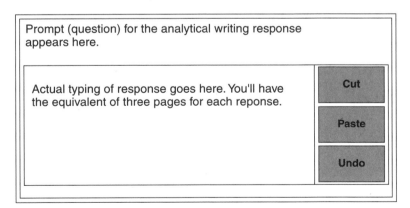

The GMAT information bulletin and the GMAT Web site will prepublish a list of possible analytical writing prompts, so checking this information carefully is important. You should take advantage of the information given and write practice responses to some of the prepublished essay prompts.

Ability Tested

This section tests your ability to think critically, to analyze issues and features of arguments, and to communicate complex ideas.

Basic Skills Necessary

You should possess good college-level writing, reading, and reasoning skills. You should be able to express your ideas in correct, clear, concise, and persuasive language.

Directions

Analysis of an Issue

This section requires you to analyze and explain your views on a given issue. Consider many points of view as you develop your own position on the issue. No right or wrong answers exist for the question.

The actual directions will read something like this: "Do you agree or disagree with the given statement? Support your point of view with reasons and/or examples from your own experience, observations, or reading."

Read the statement and directions carefully. Make any notes or do any prewriting (clustering, outlining, and so forth) on your scratch paper. Then type your response into the computer.

Analysis of an Argument

This section requires you to critique a given argument. Some possible approaches to this section include questioning underlying assumptions, finding alternative explanations or counterexamples, and delineating evidence to strengthen or weaken the argument.

The actual directions will read something like this: "Write an essay in which you discuss how convincing you find the given argument. Your essay should consider the argument's line of reasoning and how well it uses evidence. You may wish to discuss any doubtful assumptions and how other possible explanations could affect the argument's conclusions. Your essay may also consider how one could make the argument more persuasive and its conclusion more convincing."

Read the argument and directions carefully. Make any notes or do any prewriting (clustering, outlining, and so forth) on your scratch paper. Then type your response into the computer.

Scoring the Analytical Writing Section

Teachers skilled in the evaluation of writing holistically score the two responses. They concern themselves with the overall quality of the responses—the command of logic, clarity, and cogency—not with minor errors of spelling or grammar.

The scoring guides for each section (which follow) were developed by categorizing responses written during the development of this section of the GMAT, rather than from a preconceived notion of what responses should be like. Each of the two responses receives a score ranging from 0 (lowest) to 6 (highest) by two readers who are each unaware of the other's score. If the two scores differ by more than two points, a third reader grades the response. If the third reader's score matches one of the other readers, the answer receives that score. If the third reader's score falls between the two differing scores, the answer receives the average of the three grades. The scores of the issue analysis response and the argument analysis response are averaged, resulting in the final Analytical Writing Assessment score (a single grade ranging from 0 to 6).

Again, the quality of thought and the writing skill determine the response scores. In the scoring of the analysis of an issue, a well-written, thoughtful response will receive a high score regardless of what side of the issue the writer chooses. A minor spelling error or a small error in grammar will not affect the final score. In the scoring of the analysis of an argument, the content of the response weighs more heavily than the quality of the writing. Readers reward students for what they do well.

Analyzing the Scores

Grading the Analysis of an Issue Response

Because you must write your response in a limited period of time, graders do not allow minor errors of grammar or mechanics to affect your score. A response that receives a 6 is not, necessarily, errorless, but it is superior in content.

Score of 6: Excellent

The following qualities characterize these responses:

- coverage of all the tasks required by the exam question
- an understanding of the complexity of the issue
- cogent reasoning and logical development of a position
- relevant persuasive supporting details
- superior organization
- superior command of standard written English

Score of 5: Good

The following qualities characterize these responses:

- coverage of all the tasks required by the exam question
- clear reasoning and development of a position
- use of well-chosen supporting evidence
- good organization
- good handling of standard written English

Score of 4: Competent

The following qualities characterize these responses:

- coverage of all the tasks
- development of a position
- adequately reasoned and supported arguments
- competent organization
- adequate handling of standard written English

Score of 3: Limited

The following qualities characterize these responses:

- failure to fully understand the issue and develop a position
- failure to respond to all the assigned tasks
- failure to use supporting details
- numerous minor errors in grammar or mechanics
- less than adequate use of standard written English

Score of 2: Weak

These responses compound the deficiencies of responses in the 3 range. They likely fail to present a position on the issue or fail to employ supporting detail. Also, they likely include incompetent organization, grammar, diction, and mechanics.

Score of 1: Poor

These responses compound the deficiencies of the responses in the 2 range. They display an inability to deal with the topic and write standard English prose. They are often unacceptably brief.

Score of 0

Wholly off-topic responses receive a score of zero.

Score of NR

If you provide no response, you receive a score of NR.

Grading the Analysis of an Argument Response

Because you must write your response in a limited period of time, graders do not allow minor errors of grammar or mechanics to affect your score. A response that receives a 6 is not, necessarily, errorless, but it is superior in content.

Score of 6: Excellent

The following qualities characterize these responses:

- thorough coverage of all the tasks required by the exam question
- careful analysis of the important features of the argument
- cogent reasoning and logical development
- relevant supporting details of the critique
- superior organization
- superior command of standard written English

Score of 5: Good

The following qualities characterize these responses:

- good coverage of all the tasks required by the exam question
- good analysis of the important features of the argument
- clear reasoning and development
- use of supporting evidence of the critique
- good organization
- good handling of standard written English

Score of 4: Competent

The following qualities characterize these responses:

- some coverage of the tasks required by the exam question
- competent analysis of the important features of the argument
- adequately reasoned and supported points of the critique
- competent organization
- adequate handling of standard written English

Score of 3: Limited

The following qualities characterize these responses:

- failure to respond to all of the assigned tasks
- failure to understand or to analyze the important features of the argument
- failure to use supporting details of the critique
- numerous minor errors in grammar or mechanics
- less than adequate use of standard written English

Score of 2: Weak

Most 2 responses fail to analyze the argument and instead present, in place of critique, the writer's ideas about the topic. These papers are often well written but wholly lacking in analysis of an argument.

Other 2 responses compound the deficiencies of responses in the 3 range. They likely misunderstand the main features of the argument, fail to present an analysis, and fail to employ supporting detail. The organization, grammar, diction, and mechanics are likely incompetent.

Score of 1: Poor

These responses compound the deficiencies in the 2 range. They display an inability to respond to the topic and write standard English prose. They are often unacceptably brief.

Score of 0

Wholly off-topic responses receive a score of zero.

Score of NR

If you provide no response, you receive a score of NR.

Suggested Approach with Samples

Again, the Analytical Writing Assessment presents you with two distinct tasks: (1) analyze an issue and (2) analyze an argument. To analyze an issue, the test asks you to take a position on the given issue and to support your position with relevant details or examples. To analyze an argument, the test asks you analyze the weaknesses of a given argument. In explaining your point of view you must analyze failures of the reasoning in the argument itself and in its use of evidence or support.

Analysis of an Issue

For any timed writing task, you should envision three steps leading to the finished product:

1. Preparing to write (prewriting)
2. Writing
3. Proofreading (editing)

Preparing to Write

Note time and space constraints.

Before you begin analyzing the topic itself, you should make yourself aware of the amount of time allotted for the assignment as well as the space available. For the Analytical Writing Assessment, you receive thirty minutes to write each response. You will have the equivalent of three pages to complete your response. Use the provided scratch paper to organize your writing before you begin inputting your response.

Carefully read the topic.

Next, read and understand the topic. Giving too little time and attention to this task is a major mistake. Remember that if you address the topic incorrectly, or even partially, your score drops significantly, no matter how well you organize, support, and write the response. Therefore, you must spend adequate time carefully reading and understanding the topic and its exact requirements.

Pay special attention to key words in the directions, like *describe, compare, explain,* and *contrast.* Be aware that *or* requires a choice. For example, "Present your opinions for or against . . ." means take one point of view, not both. Be careful to assess completely all the tasks required. You may find reading the topic several times helpful, focusing on the key words or tasks.

Be sure to discriminate between required and optional tasks. If the instructions use the word *may*, you may omit that task or a part of it.

Plan by brainstorming and organizing.

Remembering, inventing, and organizing information at short notice can be difficult unless you are prepared with an effective technique. Writing your response immediately after reading the topic often results in a poorly organized, haphazard response. Take time to organize your thoughts on paper before writing.

Brainstorming

The process of creating and accumulating ideas, examples, and illustrations is called "brainstorming." Brainstorming simply entails jotting down on scratch paper as many thoughts, ideas, and possibilities as you can remember, invent, or otherwise bring to mind to address the topic. Neatness, order, and spelling do not matter at this point.

Organizing

After generating as many illustrations as you can within the time allotted, assess these ideas. Remember that development relies on specific examples: Decide which examples best enable you to support your points. Eliminate (cross out) those you don't wish to use, and number those you'll want to address in your response. Add any notes regarding more specific details or new thoughts that come to mind. However, don't worry about developing everything completely, because only you use these planning notes. Your time will be better spent developing these points in your writing and not in your notes.

Writing

Opening Paragraph

A strong opening paragraph provides an essential component for a well-developed response. One easy-to-master, yet extremely effective, type of introduction is a GENERALIZE-FOCUS-SURVEY structure. In this three- to four-sentence paragraph, the first sentence generalizes about the given topic, the second sentence focuses on what you have chosen to discuss, and the last one or two sentences survey the particulars you intend to present.

An effective first paragraph tells your reader what to expect in the body of the response. The GENERALIZE-FOCUS-SURVEY paragraph points toward the specifics you will discuss and suggests the order in which you will discuss them.

Body

Writing the body of the response involves presenting specific details and examples that relate to the aspects you introduced in the first paragraph. The body may consist of one longer paragraph or several shorter paragraphs. If you choose to break your discussion into several paragraphs, make sure that each paragraph consists of at least three sentences. Very short paragraphs may make your response appear insubstantial and scattered.

Be realistic about how much you can write. Your readers do not give more credit for longer responses. Although they want you to support your points adequately, they understand that you must write concisely to finish in time.

Providing at least one substantial example, or "for instance," is important for each aspect you discuss in the body of your response.

Conclusion

As you prepare to write the conclusion, you should pay special attention to time. Having a formal conclusion to your response is unnecessary, but a conclusion may function to (1) complete your response to the question, (2) add information that you failed to introduce earlier, or (3) point toward the future.

Proofreading

Always allow a few minutes to proofread your response for errors in grammar, usage, and spelling.

One Approach: The "Why" Format

One good way to approach a question that asks you to explain, analyze, or evaluate is to use a "why" format. You build a "why" response around a thesis sentence. The thesis sentence begins with your opinion followed by the word *because* and then a list of the most important reasons the opinion is valid, reasonable, or well founded.

The "why" format could look like this:

Paragraph	"Why" Response Format
1	Introduction: Thesis Sentence
2	Reason 1
3	Reason 2
4	Reason 3
5	Conclusion

Each paragraph should contain at least three to five sentences. The introduction invites the reader to read on. Your reasons (three are often sufficient) should give examples or evidence to support each reason. Your concluding paragraph summarizes your reasons and restates the thesis statement.

Sample: Analysis of an Issue

Read the following question and the sample analysis that follows, looking for the strengths of the writer's response and considering how you would approach the same topic.

> More than half of the Americans recently surveyed expressed approval of the use of flogging to punish young offenders guilty of crimes such as vandalism. Opponents of flogging argue that the punishment is cruel and barbaric and that it leaves both physical and psychological scars.
>
> Do you believe that flogging should be used in this country? Explain your position with support from your observations, readings, and/or experience.

Sample Analysis of an Issue Response

In light of the disturbing increase in crime in our cities and suburbs in recent years, many Americans have expressed an interest in the use of flogging to punish young offenders guilty of crimes such as vandalism. I am opposed to the use of flogging as punishment based on humanitarian, psychological, and moral grounds.

While I share the frustration of other law-abiding citizens who are trying to stem the tide of senseless destruction of personal property, I believe that flogging is a cruel and uncivilized form of punishment that has no place in our country. The public infliction of painful physical punishment was banished from civilized countries years ago with the disappearance of the stocks, pillories, and public whippings. As witnessed in the case of the American teenager who was sentenced to a caning for vandalism in Singapore, most civilized countries around the world objected vehemently to the severity and barbarism of this form of punishment for a nonviolent crime.

On psychological grounds, inflicting physical punishment to teach a lesson has been frowned upon for years by child psychologists and behavioral experts. Spankings, beltings, and beatings are all considered forms of abuse and have been proved to have only very negative affects on behavior. Studies have also supported the conclusion that violence begets violence, and it would seem very probable that the use of flogging to punish a young person who committed vandalism may well lead to a more violent expression of anger next time. The troubled individual whose antisocial behavior was directed toward property may well be incited to take his anger out in a physically violent way against people after being subjected to such treatment.

Finally, on moral grounds, we need to make the distinction between crimes against persons and crimes against property. In terms of the Biblical injunction of "an eye for an eye, a tooth for a tooth," inflicting physical injury on an offender who committed damage to property is hardly equitable. What is the lesson we are trying to teach? In the 1970s, the movie "A Clockwork Orange" dealt with the issue of violent crime in a futuristic setting and society's increasingly cruel methods of "rehabilitation." It left the viewer questioning which was more barbaric, the crime or the punishment?

In conclusion, we must continue to search for ways to reduce the incidence of crimes against property as well as persons, but we must above all keep sight of our humanity. Flogging is not the answer.

Evaluation of Analysis of an Issue Response

This excellent analysis would probably receive a score of 6. The writer takes a stand and develops it with apt examples, referring to current events, a psychological film, and personal attitudes. Though writing a five-paragraph response is *not* necessary, this one shows you how easily and effectively you can organize such a response. The introductory paragraph lists three grounds of opposition (humanitarian, psychological, and moral), and each of the next three paragraphs develops one of these. The final paragraph sums up the argument. The response is gracefully written and syntactically varied. (The last paragraph, for example, plays a long sentence against a short one.) Though its mechanics are not perfect (*affects* in the third paragraph should be *effects*), the writer's command of standard written English is first-rate.

A PATTERNED PLAN OF ATTACK
Analysis of an Issue

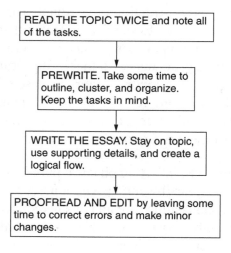

READ THE TOPIC TWICE and note all of the tasks.

PREWRITE. Take some time to outline, cluster, and organize. Keep the tasks in mind.

WRITE THE ESSAY. Stay on topic, use supporting details, and create a logical flow.

PROOFREAD AND EDIT by leaving some time to correct errors and make minor changes.

Analysis of an Argument

In the analysis of an argument section, your analysis plays a more important role than your style. In fact, you may use the "bullet format"—you might use asterisks (*) or dashes (—) preceding each of your points—and still score in the upper half of the scale if your analysis is cogent. You will score even better if you combine the "bullet format" with conventional prose paragraphs.

The argument you must analyze will never be strong. Do not waste your time trying to find something good to say about it. Common errors in the argument's line of reasoning likely resemble one or more of the following:

- Assuming because *x* happened before *y,* that *x* was the cause of *y.* (Post hoc, ergo propter hoc—after that, therefore because of that.) For example, "Last night there was a full moon, and this morning my cat was sick. Therefore, a full moon makes my cat sick."

- Drawing a conclusion from a failure to respond or act—assuming, for example, that because no hostile response existed, the response was favorable.

- Trusting a survey without looking at complete information about the people questioned and the questions asked.

The weakest responses are usually those in which students write about the subject of the quotation (how a restaurant should be run, why television advertising is a good idea, why student fees should be reduced) but never analyze the weakness in the reasoning of the argument. Even very well-written responses that fail to analyze the argument receive low scores, while essays in broken but understandable English with twice as many errors in grammar and spelling that do explain the flaws in reasoning receive scores in the upper half of the six-point scale.

Sample: Analysis of an Argument

Read the following sample question and the two student responses. Then decide which of the two gives a better answer.

> The following announcement appeared in an East-West Bus Line company memorandum:
>
> "Beginning on June 1, the East-West Bus Company will no longer run buses on any of its interstate routes on Saturdays and Sundays. A survey of the riders on the Boston-New York route taken over a ten-day period in November showed that more than 95% of the passengers do not use the buses on weekends. This reduction in the schedule will allow the company to continue to increase its return to stockholders with a minimum of inconvenience to the bus-riding public."
>
> Write an essay in which you discuss how convincing you find this argument. Your essay should consider the argument's line of reasoning and how well it uses evidence. You may wish to discuss any doubtful assumptions and how other possible explanations could affect its conclusions. Your essay may also consider how the argument could be made more persuasive and its conclusion more convincing.

Sample Analysis of an Argument Response 1

The revealing phrase in this announcement is "increase its return to stock-holders." Just where does the bus company think its real primary responsibility lies? To the stockholders or to the bus-riding public? The stockholders are probably well-heeled men who are used to flying first-class to their travel destinations, or riding in their BMWs and Cadillacs. Meanwhile, the people who cannot afford to fly and take the bus because it is less costly and expensive, who have to take buses to get to work or to see their families and loved ones, will have to find a new way to travel or be unable to travel at all.

Too many firms see only "the bottom line," and forget their responsibility to the general public at large. Did it ever occur to them that there are several airlines that run shuttle services between Boston and New York, so if the buses stop running, there is still no problem getting from one city to the other. But what bothers them is that the weekend bus service is not a big money-maker. What the argument needs is more concern with the public who ride on buses and less worry about the profits of the "fat cats."

Sample Analysis of an Argument Response 2

The argument is weak for several reasons.

—we don't know when the ten days in November were. Over Thanksgiving weekend?

—where else are routes of bus company?

—how does number of riders on Boston-New York compare with other routes?

—how many riders didn't read or take survey?

—how much profit and loss are made in company on weekend?

The announcement is weak argument because it doesn't tell enough about the survey. If the survey was taken on Thanksgiving week there were probably no riders on Thursday. Anyway, we don't know if more people ride in November or in July. And we don't know other routs of this company. Maybe some of them are in hard to get to places like Montana or Oregon unlike Boston-New York.

Before we can judge argument, we should know what the survey asked and who on the bus took the survey. Did all people on the bus take the survey. Or did just some of them? What if more peole didn't take the survey than did take it? Without knowing more about the survey, we cant accept the argument. The evidence is to uncertain to trust.

Evaluation of Analysis of an Argument Responses

The first of these two responses would receive a score of 2, rescued from the lowest possible grade by its competent prose and the glimmer of recognition that the Boston-New York route may not represent all routes. The second response would receive a 5, in recognition of its perception of a number of the weaknesses in the argument. The flaws in the writing would prevent it from receiving the highest score.

Another Sample: Analysis of an Argument

The following appeared as a letter to the editor of a large city newspaper:

"The Department of Public Works should install the extra-bright street lighting fixtures throughout the city. Since these lights were put in place in the Belmont Hill section, the number of arrests in that neighborhood has been greatly reduced. The cost of the new lighting will quickly be paid for by large savings in the police, court, and prison budgets."

Write an essay in which you discuss how convincing you find this argument. Your essay should consider its line of reasoning and how well it uses evidence. You may wish to discuss any doubtful assumptions and how other possible explanations could affect its conclusions. Your essay may also consider how the argument could be made more persuasive and its conclusion more convincing.

Sample Analysis of an Argument Response

This argument contends that the new brighter street lights in one section of the city has led to a large reduction in the number of arrests in that area, and that the use of these lights elsewhere throughout the city would have the same crime-reducing effect. The costs of the new lighting, the argument claims, would be regained by savings in the police, court, and prison budgets.

The first (and probably the most important) questionable assumption of this argument is that the reduction in crime is a consequence of the new street lighting. But this idea is unsupported. We do not know by how much crime has been reduced, or what kind of crimes, or even if the crimes were committed at night when increased visibility would be a factor. Streetlights cannot affect white-collar crime.

Further we know only that the number of arrests has declined, but we do not know how this statistic is related to better lighting. Have other factors contributed to the reduced arrest-rate? Was policing in the area increased? Did the decline take place at a time of year when heavy snows kept people indoors, or longer days made better lighting less important?

The so-called reduction has occurred in the Belmont Hill area. Has there been a decline elsewhere in the city where no new lighting has been installed? Did Belmont Hill have a high crime rate before? Is it densely or sparsely populated? Do its features resemble those of the rest of the city? Without information of this sort, we cannot judge the practicality of putting new lights throughout the city.

Finally, with no specific information about just what kind of arrests have been reduced and by how much, and with no specific information about the actual cost of the lights and the cost of policing, we cannot begin to estimate what the real cost of the new lighting would be. The argument needs far more specific detail about the nature of the district, the nature and the number of the crimes that have been reduced, and crucially, the causative connection between better lighting and increased citizen safety.

Evaluation of Analysis of an Argument Response

An essay like this would probably receive the highest score. It summarizes the line of reasoning of the argument accurately, and it specifically identifies several of its weaknesses. The paragraphs are coherent, the organization is clear, and the writer supports the analysis with cogent detail. The writing is controlled and varied, and though it is not flawless (see the minor agreement error of "has" for "have" in the first sentence), the command of standard written English is superior.

A PATTERNED PLAN OF ATTACK
Analysis of an Argument

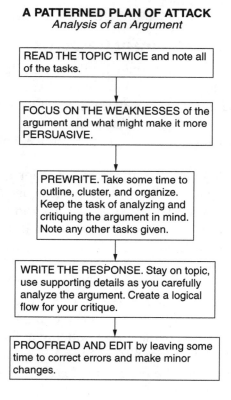

READ THE TOPIC TWICE and note all of the tasks.

FOCUS ON THE WEAKNESSES of the argument and what might make it more PERSUASIVE.

PREWRITE. Take some time to outline, cluster, and organize. Keep the task of analyzing and critiquing the argument in mind. Note any other tasks given.

WRITE THE RESPONSE. Stay on topic, use supporting details as you carefully analyze the argument. Create a logical flow for your critique.

PROOFREAD AND EDIT by leaving some time to correct errors and make minor changes.

Extra Practice Topics

In addition to the topics and questions provided in the practice test, here are samples of topics for practicing Analytical Writing Assessment responses. Limit your time on each to 30 minutes to simulate the actual examination. Find someone skilled in writing to evaluate your responses using the checklist and grading scale following these extra practice topics. Remember, because you must write your responses in a limited time period, minor errors of grammar or mechanics will not affect your scores.

Analysis of an Issue Questions

1. "Some environmentalists believe that wood-burning stoves are among the best ways to conserve natural resources and protect the environment. But in many parts of the world, wood is in short supply, some wooded areas house animals, and wood smoke may be more harmful to air quality than emissions from fossil fuels like coal or oil."

   Which of these positions do you prefer? Explain your choice with support from your personal experience or knowledge of the issues.

2. "Violence is the unavoidable consequence of the Western idea of manhood: winning at all costs, physical supremacy, the primacy of work, the suppression of sensitivity."

   Do you agree with this position? Support your view from your reading and/or your observations.

3. "The result of tuition raises in state colleges is a better education. Classes are no longer overcrowded, and a far higher percentage of the entering first-year students complete their degrees in four years or fewer."

   Do you believe the benefits of higher tuition in state colleges outweigh the disadvantages? Make your opinion clear with specific support drawn from your observations or readings.

4. "A company's long-term success depends upon customer satisfaction and service."

   Do you agree or disagree with this statement? Support your point of view with reasons and/or examples from your own experience, observations, or reading.

5. "The ends justify the means."

   Explain what this famous quote means and discuss to what extent you agree or disagree with it. Use specific reasons and examples from your own experience, observations, or reading to support your view.

6. "Individuals are responsible for protecting our environment, not the local, state, or federal governments."

   Do you agree or disagree with this opinion? Support your point of view with reasons and/or examples from your own experience, observations, or reading.

7. "It's not what happens to you that's important, but how you deal with it."

   Do you agree or disagree with the statement above? Support your point of view with reasons and/or examples from your own experience, observations, or reading.

8. "The Internet should not be regulated as that would encroach upon our rights of free speech."

   Do you agree or disagree with this statement? Support your point of view with reasons and/or examples from your own experience, observations, or reading.

9. "Overcrowding is the main problem in our schools today. Smaller class sizes would solve most of our educational problems."

   Do you think that the view expressed above is accurate? Explain your opinion by using reasons and examples based on your own experience, observations, and reading.

10. "Experience should teach us to be most on our guard to protect liberty when the government's purposes are beneficent. The greatest dangers to liberty lurk in insidious encroachment by men of zeal, well-meaning but without understanding."

    Are "men of zeal" a threat to liberty? Write a response in which you explain your position for or against this position. Support your case with information from your reading or experience.

Analysis of an Argument Questions

1. The following appeared in the editorial pages of a national news magazine:

"A nationwide survey conducted in 1990 found that fifty percent of high school seniors had experimented with drugs at least once, while a survey in 1992 found that the number had increased to fifty-five percent. The results of the 1994 survey are unavailable, but we can infer that by 1995, at least sixty percent of the teen-age population had experimented with drugs at least once."

Write an essay in which you discuss how convincing you find this argument. Your essay should consider its line of reasoning and how well it uses evidence. You may wish to discuss any doubtful assumptions and how other possible explanations could affect its conclusions. Your essay may also consider how the argument could be made more persuasive and its conclusion more convincing.

2. The following appeared as part of an editorial in a local newspaper:

"The notion that American voters do not turn out on election day can be believed no longer. In the most recent state by-elections, a contest in which no important national office was at stake, over sixty percent of the registered voters cast ballots on the referenda and bond measures. The participation by the electorate is up almost twenty percent over last year's totals and makes clear that the days of the low election turnout are over for good."

Write an essay in which you discuss how convincing you find this argument. Your essay should consider its line of reasoning and how well it uses evidence. You may wish to discuss any doubtful assumptions and how other possible explanations could affect its conclusions. Your essay may also consider how the argument could be made more persuasive and its conclusion more convincing.

3. The following appeared in the minutes of a school board meeting:

"In the three months since metal detectors and random locker searches were introduced at Ben Franklin High School, no serious weapons incidents have been reported. Consequently, despite the high costs, all of the junior high and high schools in the city must have metal detectors at all entrances and random locker searches throughout the school term. To protect the safety of our students, no cost is too high."

Write an essay in which you discuss how convincing you find this argument. Your essay should consider its line of reasoning and how well it uses evidence. You may wish to discuss any doubtful assumptions and how other possible explanations could affect its conclusions. Your essay may also consider how the argument could be made more persuasive and its conclusion more convincing.

4. The following is part of a memorandum from a government subcommittee:

"In keeping with its concern for a more equitable distribution of the tax burden, the Subcommittee on Taxation has proposed the elimination of all taxes on capital gains and, to replace this revenue, a one half of one percent tax on all domestic electrical use charges to be collected by the local utility companies. The income from this tax will be almost the same as the income now generated by the twenty-eight percent tax on capital gains, but it will be distributed more fairly over a much wider population."

Write an essay in which you discuss how convincing you find this argument. Your essay should consider its line of reasoning and how well it uses evidence. You may wish to discuss any doubtful assumptions and how other possible explanations could affect its conclusions. Your essay may also consider how the argument could be made more persuasive and its conclusion more convincing.

5. The following announcement was made by the regents of a state university:

"Beginning in the fall of next year, the public colleges and universities in the state system will no longer offer remedial courses in mathematics and English. These courses should be unnecessary for students in the state university system. Few of the private colleges in the state offer remedial education classes. In any event, they are readily available at lower cost at junior colleges throughout the state. The savings in classroom space and instructors' wages will allow greater expenditure on the research programs that are central to the university's well-being."

Write an essay in which you discuss how convincing you find this argument. Your essay should consider its line of reasoning and how well it uses evidence. You may wish to discuss any doubtful assumptions and how other possible explanations could affect its conclusions. Your essay may also consider how the argument could be made more persuasive and its conclusion more convincing.

6. The following appeared in a letter to a news magazine:

"The increased political pressure to restrict violence and sexual topics in television and film has, ironically, only increased their frequency. There is now far more graphic violence, and language is more unrestrained than in the films and television programs of ten years ago. Studies show that the number of deaths per hour shown in prime-time television has more than doubled, and the incidence of obscene language is also greater. The increase in violent crime, especially among teenagers, is the direct consequence of degenerate cinema and television."

Write an essay in which you discuss how convincing you find this argument. Your essay should consider its line of reasoning and how well it uses evidence. You may wish to discuss any doubtful assumptions and how other possible explanations could affect its conclusions. Your essay may also consider how the argument could be made more persuasive and its conclusion more convincing.

7. The following appeared in the annual report of a large retail grocery company:

"Since the merger of Happy Stores with Thrifty Shopper Markets, the profits of both companies have risen, and customer satisfaction is higher than ever. There have been far fewer complaints about the reduced availability of many national brands than had been expected, and less than twenty percent of the customers interviewed in selected stores have expressed dissatisfaction with the merger. This increased customer satisfaction has produced increased profits for the company."

Write an essay in which you discuss how convincing you find this argument. Your essay should consider its line of reasoning and how well it uses evidence. You may wish to discuss any doubtful assumptions and how other possible explanations could affect its conclusions. Your essay may also consider how the argument could be made more persuasive and its conclusion more convincing.

8. The following appeared in a pamphlet issued by the makers of a weight-loss herbal remedy:

"The value of regular exercise in reducing the number of fatal heart attacks has been greatly overestimated. In southern California, where exercising to look beautiful is an obsession, there are more fatal heart attacks per capita than in many other regions of the country. In Los Angeles County, the number of fatalities is especially high."

Write an essay in which you discuss how convincing you find this argument. Your essay should consider its line of reasoning and how well it uses evidence. You may wish to discuss any doubtful assumptions and how other possible explanations could affect its conclusions. Your essay may also consider how the argument could be made more persuasive and its conclusion more convincing.

9. The following appeared in an environmentalist newsletter:

"The passage of new laws to insure that no oil leases for off-shore American waters can be sold is essential. The Gulf of Alaska has not yet recovered from the oil tanker disaster of twenty years ago, and on both the Atlantic and Pacific coasts, commercial fisheries continue to decline. If we are to preserve the beauty, safety, and commercial viability of our coastlines, all off-shore drilling must be terminated."

Write an essay in which you discuss how convincing you find this argument. Your essay should consider its line of reasoning and how well it uses evidence. You may wish to discuss any doubtful assumptions and how other possible explanations could affect its conclusions. Your essay may also consider how the argument could be made more persuasive and its conclusion more convincing.

10. The following appeared in a vegetarian newsletter:

"A scientific study sponsored by the American Vegetarian Association has shown that men and women who eat a larger than average portion of vegetables at meals each day live longer than those who eat only average-sized servings. Further, the consumption of vegetables is higher now than it was ten years ago. Consequently, Americans are living longer and healthier lives."

Write an essay in which you discuss how convincing you find this argument. Your essay should consider its line of reasoning and how well it uses evidence. You may wish to discuss any doubtful assumptions and how other possible explanations could affect its conclusions. Your essay may also consider how the argument could be made more persuasive and its conclusion more convincing.

Response Scoring Checklist

Use the following checklists to analyze your essays.

Analysis of an Issue

Questions	Completely	Partially	No
1. Does the response focus on the assigned topic and cover all of the tasks?			
2. Does the response show an understanding of the complexity of the issue?			
3. Does the response show cogent reasoning and logical position development?			
4. Are there sufficient relevant persuasive supporting details?			
5. Is the response well organized?			
6. Does the response show a command of standard written English?			

Analysis of an Argument

Questions	Completely	Partially	No
1. Does the response focus on the assigned topic and cover all of the tasks?			
2. Does the response carefully analyze the important weaknesses of the argument?			
3. Does the response show cogent reasoning and logical development?			
4. Are there sufficient relevant supporting details of the critique?			
5. Is the response well organized?			
6. Does the response show a command of standard written English?			

THE QUANTITATIVE SECTION

The computer-adaptive GMAT gives you 75 minutes to answer 37 quantitative questions. This section is composed of both Problem Solving and Data Sufficiency questions, and the question types are intermingled. The first question you see will be of medium difficulty. If you get that question right, the computer will offer you a slightly more difficult question next. If you answer the first question incorrectly, the computer will offer you a slightly less difficult question next. The computer will continue to adapt the level of questions you receive based on your responses to all the previous questions.

You will use the scratch paper provided to work through each question, and you will record your answers on the computer screen by clicking your mouse on the appropriate ovals. You will not be allowed to go back to a previous question, so be sure to answer each question to the best of your ability before moving on to the next question.

To assist you in understanding explanations and to direct your attention to different questions and answer choices, this book assigns each question a number and each answer choice a letter. **Note that on the actual exam, questions will not be numbered and answer choices will not be lettered.**

Introduction to Problem Solving

Problem Solving questions are mostly word problems. Occasionally, questions refer to a graph or chart.

Ability Tested

Problem Solving questions test your ability to solve mathematical problems involving arithmetic, algebra, and geometry and word problems by using problem-solving insight, logic, and applications of basic skills.

Basic Skills Necessary

The basic skills necessary to do well on this section include high school arithmetic, algebra, and intuitive geometry—no formal trigonometry or calculus is necessary. The exam tests these skills as well as logical insight into problem-solving situations.

Directions

Solve each problem in this section by using the information given and your own mathematical calculations. Then select the correct answer of the five choices given. Use your scratch paper for any necessary calculations.

Note: Some problems may be accompanied by figures or diagrams. These figures are drawn as accurately as possible except when a specific problem states that the figure is not drawn to scale. Each figure will provide information useful in solving one or more problems. Unless otherwise stated or indicated, all figures lie in a plane.

All numbers used are real numbers.

Analysis

All scratchwork should be done on the paper given at the test; get used to referring to the computer screen as you do your calculations and drawings. You are looking for the *one* correct answer; therefore, although other answers may be close, there is never more than one right answer.

Suggested Approach with Samples

Always carefully focus on what you are looking for to ensure that you are answering the right question.

Samples

> **1.** If $x + 6 = 9$ then $3x + 1 =$
>
> **A.** 3
>
> **B.** 9
>
> **C.** 10
>
> **D.** 34
>
> **E.** 46

You should first recognize that $3x + 1$ is the part of the question you are solving for. Solving for x in the first part of the question tells you that $x = 3$. Substituting that information into $3x + 1$ gives $3(3) + 1$, or 10. The most common mistake with this type of question is to solve for x, which is 3, and mistakenly choose **A** as your answer. But remember, you are solving for $3x + 1$, not just x. You should also notice that most of the other choices offered would be possible answers if you made simple mistakes. The correct answer is **C**. *Make sure that you are answering the right question.*

2. An employee's annual salary was increased $15,000. If her new annual salary now equals $90,000, what was the percent increase?

    A. 15%

    B. 16⅔%

    C. 20%

    D. 22%

    E. 24%

Focus on what you are looking for. In this case, you need to calculate *percent increase.*

Percent increase equals change divided by starting point. If the employee's salary was increased $15,000 to reach a total of $90,000, then the starting salary was $90,000 - 15,000 = 75,000$. Therefore, percent increase $= 15,000/75,000 = \frac{1}{5} = 20\%$. The correct answer is **C.**

Pulling information out of the word problem structure can often give you a better look at what you are working with and help you gain additional insight into the problem. Organize this information on your scratch paper.

Sample

3. If a mixture is ³⁄₇ alcohol by volume and ⁴⁄₇ water by volume, what is the ratio of the volume of alcohol to the volume of water in this mixture?

    A. $\frac{3}{7}$

    B. $\frac{4}{7}$

    C. $\frac{3}{4}$

    D. $\frac{4}{3}$

    E. $\frac{7}{4}$

First pull out what you are looking for: "ratio of the volume of alcohol to the volume of water." Rewrite it as $A{:}W$ and then into its working form: A/W. Next, pull out the volumes of each substance; $A = \frac{3}{7}$ and $W = \frac{4}{7}$. Now you can figure the answer by inspection or substitution. Divide $\frac{3}{7}$ by $\frac{4}{7}$. To do so, invert the bottom fraction and multiply the two to get $\frac{3}{7} \times \frac{7}{4} = \frac{3}{4}$. The ratio of the volume of alcohol to the volume of water is 3 to 4. The correct answer is **C.**

When pulling out information, actually write out the numbers and/or letters on your scratch paper, putting them into some helpful form and eliminating some of the wording. Sometimes combining terms, performing simple operations, or simplifying the problem in some other way will give you insight and make the problem easier to solve.

Sample

4. Which of the following is equal to $\frac{1}{5}$ of 0.02 percent?

    A. 0.4

    B. 0.04

    C. 0.004

    D. 0.0004

    E. 0.00004

Simplifying this problem first means changing $\frac{1}{5}$ to .2. Next change 0.02 percent to 0.0002 (because $.02 \times .01 = 0.0002$).

Now that you have simplified the problem, simply multiply $.2 \times 0.0002$, which gives 0.00004. The correct answer is **E.**

If you immediately recognize the method or proper formula to solve the problem, then go ahead and do the work. Otherwise, simplify the information in order to identify the problem-solving strategy. Work forward.

Sample

5. Which of the following numbers is between $\frac{1}{3}$ and $\frac{1}{4}$?

    A. .45

    B. .35

    C. .29

    D. .22

    E. .20

You should focus on "between $\frac{1}{3}$ and $\frac{1}{4}$." If you know that $\frac{1}{3}$ is .333 and $\frac{1}{4}$ is .25, you have insight into the problem and should simply work it forward. Since .29 is the only number between .333 and .25, the correct answer is **C.** By the way, a quick peek at the answer choices would tip you off that you should work in decimals.

If you don't immediately recognize a method or formula, or if using the method or formula would take a great deal of time, try working backward from the answers. Since the answers are usually given in ascending or descending order, almost always start by plugging in choice **C** first. Then you'll know whether to go up or down with your next try. (Sometimes you might want to plug in one of the simple answers first.)

Samples

6. If $\frac{x}{2} + \frac{3}{4} = 1\frac{1}{4}$, what is the value of x?

    A. −2

    B. −1

    C. 0

    D. 1

    E. 2

You should first focus on "value of x." If you've forgotten how to solve this kind of equation, work backward by plugging in answers. Start with choice **C**; plug in 0.

$$\frac{0}{2} + \frac{3}{4} \neq 1\frac{1}{4}$$

Since this answer is too small, try choice **D,** a larger number. Plugging in 1 gives

$$\frac{1}{2} + \frac{3}{4} = 1\frac{1}{4}$$
$$\frac{2}{4} + \frac{3}{4} = 1\frac{1}{4}$$
$$\frac{5}{4} = 1\frac{1}{4}$$

This answer is true, so **D** is the correct answer. *Working from the answers is a valuable technique.*

7. What is the greatest common factor of the numbers 18, 24, and 30?

    A. 2

    B. 3

    C. 4

    D. 6

    E. 12

The largest number that divides evenly into 18, 24, and 30 is 6. You could work from the answers to solve this problem. Instead of starting with the middle answer, in this situation you should start with the largest answer choice because you're looking for the *greatest* common factor. The correct answer is **D.**

If you do not immediately recognize a method or formula to solve the problem, look for a reasonable approach and then work from the answer choices. A reasonable approach requires understanding the exact information the question asks you to look for.

Samples

> **8.** Barney can mow the lawn in 5 hours, and Fred can mow the lawn in 4 hours. How long will it take them to mow the lawn together?
>
> **A.** 5 hours
>
> **B.** $4\frac{1}{2}$ hours
>
> **C.** 4 hours
>
> **D.** $2\frac{2}{9}$ hours
>
> **E.** 1 hour

Suppose that you are unfamiliar with the type of equation for this problem. Try the "reasonable" method. Since Fred can mow the lawn in 4 hours by himself, he will take less than 4 hours if Barney helps him. Therefore, choices **A, B,** and **C** are not sensible. Taking this method a little farther, suppose that Barney could also mow the lawn in 4 hours. Then together it would take Barney and Fred 2 hours. But since Barney is a little slower than this, the total time should be more than 2 hours. The correct answer is **D,** $2\frac{2}{9}$ hours.

Using the equation for this problem would give the following calculation:

$$\tfrac{1}{5} + \tfrac{1}{4} = \tfrac{1}{x}$$

In 1 hour, Barney could do $\frac{1}{5}$ of the job, and in 1 hour, Fred could do $\frac{1}{4}$ of the job. The unknown $\frac{1}{x}$ is the part of the job they could do together in one hour. Now, to solve this, you calculate as follows:

$$\tfrac{4}{20} + \tfrac{5}{20} = \tfrac{1}{x}$$

$$\tfrac{9}{20} = \tfrac{1}{x}$$

Cross multiplying gives $9x = 20$; therefore, $x = \frac{20}{9}$, or $2\frac{2}{9}$.

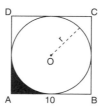

9. Circle *O* is inscribed in square *ABCD* as shown above. The area of the shaded region is approximately

    A. 10

    B. 25

    C. 30

    D. 50

    E. 75

Using a reasonable approach, you would first find the area of the square: $10 \times 10 = 100$. Then divide the square into four equal sections as follows:

Since a quarter of the square is 25, then the shaded region must be much less than 25. The only possible answer is choice **A.**

Another approach to this problem would be to first find the area of the square: $10 \times 10 = 100$. Then subtract the approximate area of the circle: $A = \pi(r^2) \cong 3(5^2)$ $= 3(25) = 75$. Therefore, the total area inside the square but outside the circle is approximately 25. One quarter of that area is shaded. Therefore, 25/4 is approximately the shaded area. The closest answer is **A.**

> **Substituting numbers for variables can often be an aid to understanding a problem. Remember to substitute simple numbers, because you have to do the work.**

Sample

10. If $x > 1$, which of the following decreases as x decreases?

$$\text{I.} \quad x + x^2$$

$$\text{II.} \quad 2x^2 - x$$

$$\text{III.} \quad \frac{1}{x + 1}$$

A. I only

B. II only

C. III only

D. I and II only

E. II and III only

This problem is most easily solved by taking each situation and substituting simple numbers.

However, in the I equation, $x + x^2$, you should recognize that this expression will decrease as x decreases.

Trying $x = 2$ gives $2 + (2)^2$, which equals 6.

Now trying $x = 3$ gives $3 + (3)^2 = 12$.

Notice that choices **B, C,** and **E** are already eliminated because they do not contain I. You should also realize that now you need to try only the values in II; since III is not paired with I as a possible choice, III cannot be one of the answers.

Trying $x = 2$ in the expression $2x^2 - x$ gives $2(2)^2 - 2$, or $2(4) - 2$, which leaves 6.

Now trying $x = 3$ gives $2(3)^2 - 3$, or $2(9) - 3 = 18 - 3 = 15$. This expression also decreases as x decreases. Therefore, the correct answer is choice **D.** Once again, notice that III was not even attempted because it was not one of the possible choices.

Some problems may deal with percent or percent change. If you don't see a simple method for working the problem, try using values of 10 or 100 and see what you get.

Sample

> **11.** A corporation triples its annual bonus to 50 of its employees. What percent of the employees' new bonus is the increase?
>
> **A.** 50%
>
> **B.** 66⅔%
>
> **C.** 100%
>
> **D.** 200%
>
> **E.** 300%

Let's use $100 for the normal bonus. If the annual bonus was normally $100, tripled it would now be $300. Therefore, the increase ($200) is ⅔ of the new bonus ($300). Two-thirds is 66⅔%. The correct answer is **B.**

Sketching diagrams or simple pictures can also be very helpful because the diagram may tip off either a simple solution or a method for solving the problem.

Samples

> **12.** What is the maximum number of pieces of birthday cake of size 4" by 4" that can be cut from a cake 20" by 20"?
>
> **A.** 5
>
> **B.** 10
>
> **C.** 16
>
> **D.** 20
>
> **E.** 25

Sketching the cake and marking the sketch as follows makes this a fairly simple problem.

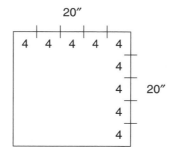

Notice that five pieces of cake will fit along each side; therefore, $5 \times 5 = 25$. The correct answer is **E.** Finding the total area of the cake and dividing it by the area of one of the 4×4 pieces would also give you the correct answer, but beware of this method because it may not work if the pieces do not fit evenly into the original area.

---

13. If P lies on $\overarc{ON}$ such that $\overarc{OP} = 2\overarc{PN}$ and Q lies on $\overarc{OP}$ such that $\overarc{OQ} = \overarc{QP}$, what is the relationship of $\overarc{OQ}$ to $\overarc{PN}$?

    A. ⅓

    B. ½

    C. 1

    D. ²⁄₁

    E. ³⁄₁

A sketch would look like this:

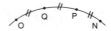

It is evident that $\overarc{OQ} = \overarc{PN}$, so the ratio is ¹⁄₁, or 1. Or you could assign values on $\overarc{ON}$ such that $\overarc{OP} = 2\overarc{PN}$: $\overarc{OP}$ could equal 2, and $\overarc{PN}$ could equal 1. If Q lies on $\overarc{OP}$ such that $\overarc{OQ} = \overarc{QP}$, then $\overarc{OP}$ (2) is divided in half. So $\overarc{OQ} = 1$, and $\overarc{QP} = 1$. So the relationship of $\overarc{OQ}$ to $\overarc{PN}$ is 1 to 1. The correct answer is **C.**

> **Redrawing and marking in diagrams on your scratch paper as you read them can save you valuable time. Marking can also give you insight into how to solve a problem because you will have the complete picture clearly in front of you.**

Samples

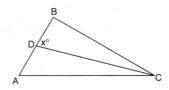

14. In the triangle, $\overline{CD}$ is an angle bisector, angle *ACD* is 30°, and angle *ABC* is a right angle. What is the measurement of angle *x* in degrees?

    A. 80°

    B. 75°

    C. 60°

    D. 45°

    E. 30°

After redrawing the diagram on your scratch paper, you should read the problem and mark as follows:

"In the triangle, $\overline{CD}$ is an angle bisector" *(stop and mark in the drawing)*, "angle *ACD* is 30°" *(stop and mark in the drawing)*, "and angle *ABC* is a right angle" *(stop and mark in the drawing)*. "What is the measurement of angle *x* in degrees?" *(Stop and mark in or circle what you are looking for in the drawing.)*

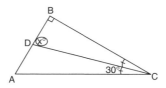

With the drawing marked in, it is evident that since angle *ACD* is 30°, angle *BCD* is also 30° because they are formed by an angle bisector (which divides an angle into two equal parts). Since angle *ABC* is 90° (a right angle) and *BCD* is 30°, then angle *x* is 60° because there are 180° in a triangle; $180 - (90 + 30) = 60$. The correct answer is **C.** *After redrawing the diagrams on your scratch paper, always mark in the diagrams as you read their descriptions and information about them. This includes what you are looking for.*

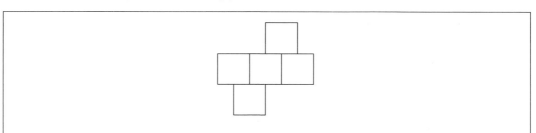

15. If each square in the preceding figure has a side of length 3, what is the perimeter?

    A. 12

    B. 14

    C. 21

    D. 30

    E. 36

Redraw and mark in the information given.

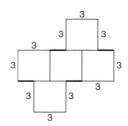

We now have a calculation for the perimeter: 30 *plus* the darkened parts. Now look carefully at the top two darkened parts. They will add up to 3. (Notice how the top square may slide over to illustrate that fact.)

The same is true for the bottom darkened parts. They will add to 3.

Thus, the total perimeter is 30 + 6 = 36, choice **E**.

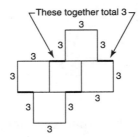

> If it appears that extensive calculations are going to be necessary to solve a problem, check to see how far apart the choices are, and then approximate. The reason for checking the answers first is to give you a guide for how freely you can approximate.

Sample

---

16. The value for (0.889 × 55)/9.97 to the nearest tenth is

   A. 0.5

   B. 4.63

   C. 4.9

   D. 7.7

   E. 49.1

Before starting any computations, take a glance at the answers to see how far apart they are. Notice that the only close answers are choices **B** and **C**, but **B** is not possible, since it is to the nearest hundredth, not tenth. Now, making some quick approximations, $0.889 \cong 1$ and $9.97 \cong 10$, leaves the problem in this form:

$$\frac{1 \times 55}{10} = {}^{55}/_{10} = 5.5$$

The closest answer is **C;** therefore, it is the correct answer. Notice that choices **A** and **E** are not reasonable.

> Some problems may not ask you to solve for a numerical answer or even an answer including variables. Rather, you may be asked to set up the equation or expression without doing any solving. A quick glance at the answer choices will help you know what is expected.

Sample

> **17.** Rick is three times as old as Maria, and Maria is four years older than Leah. If Leah is z years old, what is Rick's age in terms of z?
>
>   **A.** $3z + 4$
>
>   **B.** $3z - 12$
>
>   **C.** $3z + 12$
>
>   **D.** $(z + 4)/3$
>
>   **E.** $(z - 4)/3$

The correct answer is **C,** because

$$z = \text{Leah's age}$$
$$z + 4 = \text{Maria's age}$$
$$3(z + 4) = \text{Rick's age}$$
$$\text{or } 3z + 12 = \text{Rick's age}$$

In some problems, you may be given special symbols that you are unfamiliar with. Don't let these special symbols alarm you. They typically represent an operation or combination of operations that you are familiar with. Look for the definition of the special symbol or how it is used.

Sample

> **18.** If $\odot$ is a binary operation such that a $\odot$ b is defined as $\dfrac{a^2 - b^2}{a^2 + b^2}$, then what is the value of $3 \odot 2$?
>
>   **A.** $^{-5}/_{13}$
>
>   **B.** $^{1}/_{13}$
>
>   **C.** $^{1}/_{5}$
>
>   **D.** $^{5}/_{13}$
>
>   **E.** 1

The correct answer is **D.** The value of a $\odot$ b =

$$\frac{a^2 - b^2}{a^2 + b^2}$$

Simply replacing a with 3 and b with 2 gives

$$\frac{3^2 - 2^2}{3^2 + 2^2} = \frac{9 - 4}{9 + 4} = \frac{5}{13}$$

The correct answer is **D.**

A PATTERNED PLAN OF ATTACK
Problem Solving (Multiple-Choice)

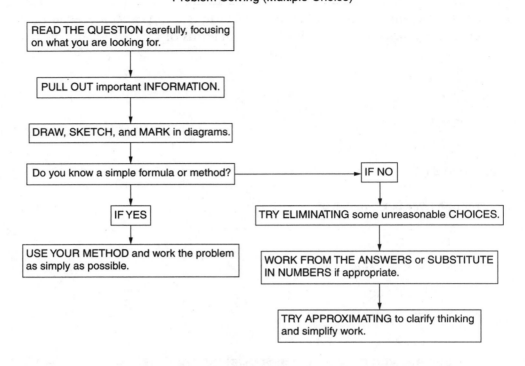

READ THE QUESTION carefully, focusing on what you are looking for.

PULL OUT important INFORMATION.

DRAW, SKETCH, and MARK in diagrams.

Do you know a simple formula or method? → IF NO

IF YES

USE YOUR METHOD and work the problem as simply as possible.

TRY ELIMINATING some unreasonable CHOICES.

WORK FROM THE ANSWERS or SUBSTITUTE IN NUMBERS if appropriate.

TRY APPROXIMATING to clarify thinking and simplify work.

ALWAYS MAKE SURE YOUR ANSWER IS REASONABLE.

Practice Problem Solving Questions

Easy to Moderate

1. What percent of 60 is 80?

    A. $133\frac{1}{3}$

    B. 75

    C. 60

    D. $33\frac{1}{3}$

    E. 25

2. On a map, 1 centimeter represents 35 kilometers. Two cities 245 kilometers apart would be separated on the map by how many centimeters?

    A. 5

    B. 7

    C. 9

    D. 210

    E. 280

3. Harriet planned to complete a certain task on Wednesday, January 1, but because of illness the completion date was postponed 48 days. On which day of the week in February was the task completed?

    A. Monday

    B. Tuesday

    C. Wednesday

    D. Thursday

    E. Friday

4. How many combinations are possible if a person has 4 sport jackets, 5 shirts, and 3 pairs of slacks?

    A. 4

    B. 5

    C. 12

    D. 60

    E. 120

5. John received a 10% raise each month for three consecutive months. What was his salary after the three raises if his starting salary was $1,000 per month?

    A. $1,248

    B. $1,300

    C. $1,331

    D. $1,410

    E. $1,463

6. Printer A and Printer B can each print $\frac{1}{4}$ page per second. How long will it take both printers working together to print 100 pages?

    A. 25 seconds

    B. 50 seconds

    C. 100 seconds

    D. 200 seconds

    E. 400 seconds

7. If the quantity $(p - 5)$ is 5 times the quantity $(q - 5)$, then what is the relationship between p and q?

   A. $p = 5q + 30$

   B. $p = 5q - 30$

   C. $5p = q + 20$

   D. $p = 5q$

   E. $p = 5q - 20$

8. If $x = 6$ and $y = -2$, what is the value of $(x - 2y)^y$?

   A. -100

   B. 0.01

   C. 0.25

   D.   4

   E.   8

9. If $x > 0$, which of the following is equal to $\sqrt{72x^5}$?

   A. $36\sqrt{2x^5}$

   B. $36x\sqrt{2x}$

   C. $18x^2\sqrt{2x}$

   D. $6x^2\sqrt{2x}$

   E. $6x\sqrt{2x^2}$

10. A strip of ribbon is cut into three smaller strips in the ratio 2:3:5. If the shortest of the three strips is 30 inches in length, what was the length, in inches, of the ribbon before it was cut?

   A.   60

   B.   75

   C.   90

   D. 120

   E. 150

11. In the number line shown above, point P is midway between A and B. Point Q is midway between C and D. What is the distance between points P and Q?

   A. $3/7$

   B. $4/7$

   C. $6/7$

   D. $17/7$

   E. $18/7$

12. A girl runs k miles in n hours. How many miles will she run in x hours at the same rate?

   A. knx

   B. k/n

   C. kx/n

   D. kx

   E. kn/x

13. If $ax + by = c$, then $b =$

   A. $\dfrac{c}{y} - ax$

   B. $c - ax - y$

   C. $\dfrac{c}{ax} - y$

   D. $\dfrac{c - ax}{y}$

   E. $\dfrac{ax - c}{y}$

14. What is the total surface area in square meters of a rectangular solid whose length is 7 meters, width is 6 meters, and depth is 3 meters?

A. 32m^2

B. 81m^2

C. 126m^2

D. 162m^2

E. 252m^2

15. If $\frac{1}{3} + \frac{1}{2} + \frac{1}{x} = 4$, then $x =$

A. $\frac{18}{5}$

B. $\frac{19}{6}$

C. $\frac{24}{11}$

D. $\frac{6}{19}$

E. $\frac{5}{18}$

16. If two numbers have only the number 1 as a common divisor, then they are called "relatively prime." Which of the following are NOT relatively prime?

I.   3

II. 4

III. 7

IV. 12

A. I and II, I and III

B. I and IV, II and IV

C. II and III, II and IV

D. II and IV, III and IV

E. I and II, I and IV

Average

17. If 5 machines can produce 20 units in 10 hours, how long would it take 20 machines to produce 100 units?

A. 50 hours

B. 40 hours

C. 12.5 hours

D. 12 hours

E. 8 hours

18. Pete has some apples. He sold 40% more than he ate. If he sold 70 apples, how many did he eat?

A. 90

B. 50

C. 42

D. 28

E. 6

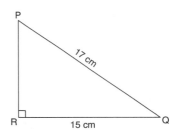

19. What is the perimeter of right triangle *PQR*?

A. 8 cm

B. 40 cm

C. 41 cm

D. 42 cm

E. 64 cm

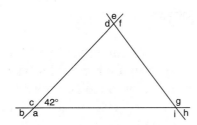

20. In the figure above, what is the sum of the nine angles labeled with letters?

    A. 138°

    B. 378°

    C. 678°

    D. 900°

    E. It cannot be determined from the information given.

21. Approximately how many cubic feet of water are needed to fill a circular swimming pool that is 50 feet across and 8 feet deep?

    A. 400

    B. 6,000

    C. 16,000

    D. 20,000

    E. 42,000

22. Dividing by $^3/_8$ and then multiplying by $^5/_6$ is the same as dividing by what number?

    A. $3^1/_5$

    B. $^{16}/_5$

    C. $^{20}/_9$

    D. $^9/_{20}$

    E. $^5/_{16}$

23. At an elementary school, 70% of the faculty members are women and 60% of the faculty members are married. If $^2/_3$ of the men are single, what fraction of the women are married?

    A. $^5/_7$

    B. $^7/_{10}$

    C. $^1/_3$

    D. $^7/_{30}$

    E. $^5/_{70}$

24. At a party, there were five times as many females as males. There were three times as many adults as children. Which of the following could NOT be the number of people at the party?

    A. 384

    B. 258

    C. 216

    D. 120

    E. 72

25. The Arnolds purchased 550 square feet of Kentucky Gem sod at $1.89 per square foot and 270 square feet of Zelzea Blue sod at $1.38 per square foot. What was the approximate average price per square foot paid for all the sod?

    A. $1.63

    B. $1.64

    C. $1.68

    D. $1.72

    E. $1.76

26. While traveling from city A to city B, Sharon and Andy average 50 miles per hour. For the return trip, they average 40 miles per hour. What was their average speed for the round trip?

A. 45 mph

B. More than 45 mph

C. Less than 45 mph

D. More than 50 mph

E. It cannot be determined from the information given.

27. If $g < 0$ and $f \neq 0$, which of these four expressions must have a positive sign?

I. gf

II. $g^2 f$

III. gf^2

IV. $(gf)^2$

A. IV only

B. I and III only

C. I and IV only

D. II and III only

E. II and IV only

28. If $x = y + y^2$, and y is a negative integer, when y decreases in value, then x

A. increases in value

B. fluctuates

C. decreases in value

D. remains the same

E. decreases in constant increments

29. If m and n are integers and $\sqrt{mn} = 10$, which of the following cannot be a value of $m + n$?

A. 25

B. 29

C. 50

D. 52

E. 101

30. The three digits of a number add up to 11. The number is divisible by 5. The leftmost digit is double the middle digit. What is the product of the three digits?

A. 40

B. 72

C. 78

D. 88

E. 125

31. Which is closest to 1?

A. $\dfrac{3}{3 + 0.03}$

B. $\dfrac{3}{(3 + 0.03)^2}$

C. $\dfrac{3}{3 + 0.3}$

D. $\dfrac{3}{3 + (0.03)^2}$

E. $\dfrac{3}{(3 + 0.3)^2}$

32. The smallest of three consecutive even integers is 40 less than three times the largest. What is the largest of these integers?

A. 14

B. 17

C. 18

D. 19

E. 20

63

Above Average to Difficult

33. In ten years, David will be four times as old as Aaron. Twenty years ago, David was twice as old as Ellen. If David is seven years older than Ellen, how old is Aaron?

    A. 1–5

    B. 6–10

    C. 11–15

    D. 16–20

    E. 21–25

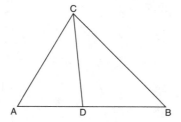

34. In the figure, $AB = BC$, $CD = BD$, and angle $CAD = 70°$. Therefore, what is the measure of angle ADC?

    A. 50

    B. 60

    C. 70

    D. 80

    E. 85

35. Two airplanes take off from one airfield at noon. One flies due east at 200 miles per hour while the other flies directly northeast at 283 miles per hour. Approximately how many miles apart are the airplanes at 2 p.m.?

    A. 166

    B. 332

    C. 400

    D. 483

    E. 566

36. A square, with perimeter 16, is inscribed in a circle. What is the area of the circle?

    A. 4π

    B. 8π

    C. 12π

    D. 16π

    E. 32π

37. Approximately how many revolutions will be made by a car tire with a 14-inch diameter if the car travels ½ mile?

    A. 120

    B. 180

    C. 360

    D. 720

    E. 1,440

38. If a man travels f miles an hour for t hours and r miles an hour for s hours, what is his average rate in miles per hour for the entire distance traveled?

    A. $ft + rs$

    B. $\dfrac{ft + rs}{2}$

    C. $\dfrac{f}{t} + \dfrac{r}{s}$

    D. $\dfrac{ft + rs}{t + s}$

    E. $\dfrac{ft + rs}{t - s}$

39. The greatest common factor of two positive integers is X. The least common multiple of these two integers is Y. If one of the integers is Z, what is the other?

A. XY/Z

B. $XZ + YZ$

C. $X/Z + Y$

D. $X + Y/Z$

E. $X + Z/Y$

40. Given the exponential quantities $m = 8^5$ and $n = 2^{12}$, what is the quotient m/n?

A. 6^{-7}

B. 7^{-6}

C. 6

D. 8

E. 16

41. What is the area of a square that has a diagonal of length $\sqrt{10}$?

A. 5

B. 10

C. 20

D. 40

E. 45

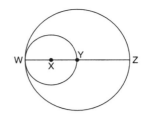

42. In the figure, X and Y are the centers of the two circles. If the area of the larger circle is 144π, what is the area of the smaller circle?

A. 72π

B. 36π

C. 24π

D. 12π

E. It cannot be determined from the information given.

43. The length of a rectangle is decreased by 15% and its width is increased by 40%. Does the area of the rectangle decrease or increase and by what percent?

A. Decreases by 19%

B. Decreases by 25%

C. Increases by 6%

D. Increases by 19%

E. Increases by 25%

44. A prize of $600 is to be distributed among 20 winners, each of whom must be awarded at least $20. If $\frac{2}{5}$ of the prize will be distributed to $\frac{3}{5}$ of the winners, what is the greatest possible individual award?

A. $ 20

B. $ 25

C. $200

D. $220

E. $300

45. If electricity costs x cents per kilowatt hour for the first 30 kilowatt hours and y cents per kilowatt hour for each additional kilowatt hour, what is the cost of z kilowatt hours ($z > 30$)?

   A. $30(x - y) + yz$

   B. $30y - 30x + yz$

   C. $30(x - y + z)$

   D. $(z - 30)x + 30y$

   E. $30x + (y - 30)z$

46. A right circular cylinder has a diameter of 20, as shown in the figure. If its height is 100, then its total surface area in square inches is approximately

   A.   600

   B.   3,000

   C.   6,000

   D.   6,600

   E.   30,000

47. If the @ of an integer is defined as the product of its cube root and its square root, then the @ of N equals 50% of N for which of the following?

   A.   1

   B.   64

   C.   100

   D.   144

   E. 1,000,000

48. Macey is three times as old as Mike. In eight years, she will be twice as old as Mike. How old was Macey three years ago?

   A.   5

   B.   8

   C. 21

   D. 24

   E. 30

49. If a, b, and c are consecutive positive odd integers, not necessarily in that order, which of the following must be true?

   I. $a + b > c$

   II. $bc > a$

   III. $(a + c)^2 > b$

   A.   I only

   B.   II only

   C.   III only

   D.   I and II only

   E.   I and III only

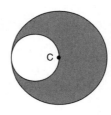

50. In the figure above, point C is the center of the larger circle. What is the ratio of the area of the shaded crescent to the area of the small circle?

   A. 2

   B. 2.4

   C. 3

   D. 3.25

   E. 4

51. If *x, y,* and *z* are consecutive positive integers greater than 1, not necessarily in that order, then which of the following is (are) true?

  I. $x > z$

  II. $x + y > z$

  III. $yz > xz$

  IV. $xy > y + z$

  A. I only

  B. II only

  C. II and III only

  D. II and IV only

  E. III and IV only

52. An empty fuel tank is filled with brand Z gasoline. When the tank is half empty, it is filled with brand Y gasoline. When the tank is half empty again, it is filled with brand Z gasoline. When the tank is half empty again, it is filled with brand Y gasoline. At this time, what percent of the gasoline in the tank is brand Z?

  A. 50%

  B. 40%

  C. 37.5%

  D. 33⅓%

  E. 25%

53. Forty percent of the employees of Company A are females, and 60% of Company B are females. If 30 female employees move from Company B to Company A, making the number of female employees of each of the two companies equal, and if the total number of employees in each company is equal, how many total male employees are there in Companies A and B together?

  A. 400

  B. 300

  C. 200

  D. 100

  E. 50

Answers and Explanations for the Practice Problem Solving Questions

Easy to Moderate

  1. A. One method for approaching this problem is:

$$\frac{\text{is number}}{\text{of number}} = \frac{\text{percent}}{100}$$

$$\frac{80}{60} = \frac{x}{100}$$

Cross-multiplying gives $60x = 8,000$.

Divide by 60: $x = \frac{8,000}{60}$

Then $x = 133\frac{1}{3}\%.$

Another method requires making an equation by replacing "what percent" with $x/100$, "of" by times $(\cdot)$ and "is" by equals $(=)$, giving the equation

$$\frac{x}{100} \cdot 60 = 80$$

Simplifying gives $\frac{3}{5}x = 80$.

Multiply by $\frac{5}{3}$: $\left(\frac{5}{3}\right)\left(\frac{3}{5}\right)x = 80\left(\frac{5}{3}\right).$

$$x = \frac{400}{3}$$

Then $x = 133\frac{1}{3}\%.$

2. **B.** Solve by setting up a proportion:

   If 1 cm = 35 km,

   then x cm = 245 km

   and $\frac{1}{x} = \frac{35}{245}$

   $35x = 245$

   $\frac{35x}{35} = \frac{245}{35}$

   $x = 7$

3. **B.** Forty-eight days late is one day shy of exactly 7 weeks (7 weeks × 7 days/week = 49 days). If the job were finished in 49 days, then it would have been complete on the same day, Wednesday. But since 48 days is one day less than 7 weeks, it was completed one day earlier than Wednesday: Tuesday.

4. **D.** Because each of the 4 sport jackets may be worn with 5 different shirts, we have 20 possible combinations. These may be worn with each of the 3 pairs of slacks for a total of 60 possible combinations. Stated simply, $5 \times 4 \times 3 = 60$ possible combinations. Notice that answers **A** and **B** are not reasonable.

5. **C.** To calculate,

   10% of 1,000 is 100. $(1,000 + 100) = 1,100$

   10% of 1,100 is 110. $(1,100 + 110) = 1,210$

   10% of 1,210 is 121. $(1,210 + 121) = 1,331$

6. **D.** Because each printer can print ¼ page per second, working together, they can print ¼ + ¼ = ½ page per second. Hence, to print 1 page, they will take 2 seconds. And, to print 100 pages, they will take $100 \times 2 = 200$ seconds.

7. **E.** If $p - 5$ is 5 times $q - 5$, we can write:

   $p - 5 = 5(q - 5)$

   or $p = 5q - 25 + 5$

   or $p = 5q - 20.$

8. B. Substituting for x and y, the expression is:

$$(6 - 2(-2))^{-2}$$
$$= (6 + 4)^{-2} = (10)^{-2}$$
$$= \frac{1}{(10)^2} = \frac{1}{100} = 0.01$$

9. D. Simplify the problem as follows: $\sqrt{72x^5} = \sqrt{36 \cdot 2 \cdot x^4 \cdot x}$. Since the $\sqrt{36}$ is 6, and $\sqrt{x^4}$ is x^2, then $\sqrt{36 \cdot 2 \cdot x^4 \cdot x} = 6x^2\sqrt{2x}$. You could also work from the answers.

10. E. The shortest strip is in the ratio to the length of the ribbon as:

$$\frac{2}{1 + 3 + 5} = \frac{2}{10} = \frac{1}{5}$$

That is, 30 inches is ⅕ of the total length of the strip, which means the total length of the strip is $30 \times 5 = 150$ inches.

11. E. Each tick mark is ³⁄₇ unit wide. Point P is 3.5 tick marks away from 0 and point Q is 2.5 tick marks away from 0. Therefore, the total distance between P and Q is $2.5 + 3.5 = 6$ tick marks. Since each tick mark is ³⁄₇ unit, total distance is $6 \times \frac{3}{7} = \frac{18}{7}$.

12. C. Distance = rate × time:

$$d = rt$$
$$k = rn$$
$$r = \frac{k}{n} \text{ miles per hour}$$
$$d = \frac{k}{n}(x) = \frac{kx}{n}$$

13. D.
$$ax + by = c$$
$$\frac{-ax \qquad\quad -ax}{by = c - ax}$$
$$\frac{by}{y} = \frac{c - ax}{y}$$
$$b = \frac{c - ax}{y}$$

14. D. A rectangular solid consists of six rectangular faces. This one in particular has two 7×6, two 6×3, and two 7×3 rectangles with areas of 42, 18, and 21, respectively. Hence the total surface area will be $2(42) + 2(18) + 2(21) = 84 + 36 + 42 = 162$ square meters.

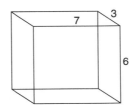

15. D. Multiplying the equation $\frac{1}{3} + \frac{1}{2} + \frac{1}{x} = 4$ by common denominator $6x$, we get $\frac{6x}{3} + \frac{6x}{2} + \frac{6x}{x} = 4(6x)$. Reducing, we get:

$$2x + 3x + 6 = 24x$$

$$5x + 6 = 24x$$

$$6 = 19x$$

$$\frac{6}{19} = x$$

16. B. Checking each possible pair of numbers for common divisions:

$$\left.\begin{array}{ll} \text{I.} & 3 \\ \text{II.} & 4 \end{array}\right\} \begin{array}{l}\text{Only common divisor 1}\\ \text{These are relatively prime}\end{array}$$

$$\left.\begin{array}{ll} \text{I.} & 3 \\ \text{III.} & 7 \end{array}\right\} \begin{array}{l}\text{Only common divisor 1}\\ \text{These are relatively prime}\end{array}$$

$$\left.\begin{array}{ll} \text{I.} & 3 \\ \text{IV.} & 12 \end{array}\right\} \begin{array}{l}\text{Common divisors are 1 and 3}\\ \text{These are } not \text{ relatively prime}\end{array}$$

Because I and IV are *not* relatively prime, check the choices to see which include I and IV. Notice that I and II are only in choices **B** and **E;** therefore, those are the two possible choices. A closer look eliminates choice **E** because I and II have numbers that are relatively prime. For good measure, check II and IV:

$$\left.\begin{array}{ll} \text{II.} & 4 \\ \text{IV.} & 12 \end{array}\right\} \begin{array}{l}\text{Common divisors are 1 and 4}\\ \text{These are } not \text{ relatively prime}\end{array}$$

Therefore, I and IV, and II and IV are not relatively prime, giving the correct answer of **B.**

Average

17. C. If 5 machines can produce 20 units in 10 hours, then 20 machines can produce 80 units in 10 hours. Since 100 is 25% more than 80, the correct answer is 25% more than 10, or 12.5 hours.

18. B. Let x = number of apples Peter ate. Thus $x + 0.4x = 1.4x$ is the number of apples Peter sold. Thus $1.4x = 70$; $x = 70/1.4$, or 50. Notice that answers **A, D,** and **E** are not reasonable.

19. B. The third side of the right triangle can be found using the Pythagorean theorem.

$$a^2 + b^2 = c^2$$

$$a^2 + (15)^2 = (17)^2$$

$$a^2 + 225 = 289$$

$$a^2 = 64$$

$$a = 8$$

The perimeter is the sum of the three sides of the triangle.

$$8 + 15 + 17 = 40 \text{ cm}$$

20. **D.** The four angles around each point of intersection sum to 360°, a complete revolution. The twelve angles in the figure must sum to $3 \times 360° = 1{,}080°$. Three of the angles are the interior angles of a triangle, so the nine lettered angles equal $1{,}080° - 180° = 900°$. The 42° angle is merely a distraction.

21. **C.** The volume of the swimming pool equals its area times its depth. The circular area has a radius of 25 feet.

    $$V = \pi r^2 h = 3.14(25)^2(8) = 15{,}700$$

    That volume is closest to choice **C**.

22. **D.** Dividing by a number is the same as multiplying by its inverse, and vice versa. Thus multiplying by $\frac{5}{6}$ is the same as dividing by $\frac{6}{5}$. Thus the answer is $(\frac{3}{8})(\frac{6}{5}) = \frac{18}{40} = \frac{9}{20}$.

23. **A.** Suppose that there are 100 faculty members at the school. If 70% of them are women, then 30% of them are men. We then have 70 women and 30 men. If $\frac{2}{3}$ of the men are single, then $\frac{1}{3}$ of $30 = 10$ men who are married. 60% or 60 teachers are married. If 10 are men, then 50 are women. Therefore, the fraction of women who are married is $\frac{50}{70}$, or $\frac{5}{7}$.

24. **B.** From the first sentence, we see that the total number of persons at the party must be divisible by 6 (5:1). From the second sentence, the total must be divisible by 4 (3:1). Thus the total must be a number divisible by both 6 and 4; such a number would be divisible by 12. The only number given that is not divisible by 12 is 258.

25. **D.** Notice that approximately 2 square feet of Kentucky Gem sod was purchased for every 1 square foot of Zelzea Blue. Therefore, the problem may be simplified by using a simple 2 to 1 ratio. Find the average as follows:

    $$\begin{array}{ll} 2\,\text{square feet} @ \$1.89 = & \$3.78 \\ \underline{1\,\text{square foot} @ \$1.38 =} & \underline{1.38} \\ 3\,\text{square feet} & \$5.16 \end{array}$$

    Dividing \$5.16 by 3 = \$1.72 per square foot.

26. **C.** Since more time was spent traveling at 40 mph, the average will be closer to 40 than to 50.

27. **A.** Since g is negative and f may be negative, it is necessary to square each of the two parameters to be assured of obtaining a positive expression. Note that $(gf)^2 = g^2f^2$.

28. **A.** Substituting small negative integers is the most effective method for this problem.

    $$\begin{aligned} \text{Let } y &= -1 \\ \text{then } x &= -1 + (-1)^2 \\ x &= -1 + 1 \\ x &= 0 \\ \text{Let } y &= -2 \\ \text{then } x &= -2 + (-2)^2 \\ x &= -2 + 4 \\ x &= 2 \end{aligned}$$

    Therefore, x increases in value.

29. **C.** $\sqrt{mn} = 10$, $mn = 100$, and the possible values for m and n would be as follows: 1 and 100, 2 and 50, 4 and 25, 5 and 20, 10 and 10. Since none of these combinations yield $m + n = 50$, choice **C** is correct.

30. **A.** Since the number is divisible by 5, it must end with a 0 or a 5. Because the first digit is double the second, the first two digits of the number must be 21, 42, 63, or 84. The only combination that adds to 11 is 425. The product of those digits is $4 \times 2 \times 5 = 40$.

31. **D.** Note that choices **B** and **E** are approximately equal to $3/(3)^2$ or 1/3. For the remaining choices, the fraction closest to 1 will be the fraction whose denominator has the *least* value added to 3. Choice **D** has the smallest value, 0.0009, added to 3. Note: $(0.03)^2 = 0.0009$.

32. **C.** Set the three consecutive even integers equal to x, $x + 2$, and $x + 4$. The equation: $x = 3(x + 4) - 40$, $x = 3x + 12 - 40$, $-2x = -28$. Thus $x = 14$. But that is the smallest of the three integers. Thus 18 is the largest.

Above Average to Difficult

33. **A.** The solution to this problem can be seen through the following grid. The sequence of the solution is indicated by the arrows.

	20 years ago	now	in 10 years
David	4x - 30 ←	4x - 10 ←	4x
Ellen	2x - 15 →	2x + 5	
Aaron		x - 10 ←	x

$$4x - 10 = (2x + 5) + 7$$
$$4x - 10 = 2x + 12$$
$$2x = 22$$
$$x = 11$$

Therefore, Aaron is now $x - 10 = 1$.

34. **D.** Since $AB = BC$, angle CAD is equal to angle ACB (isosceles triangle ABC). Thus angle ACB is also 70°. This makes angle B equal to 40° (180° in a triangle). Also, angle BCD equals 40° (same reason as above). Thus angle ADC equals 80° (external angle theorem: External angle of a triangle is equal to the sum of the opposite two angles).

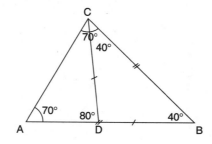

35. C. It is helpful to sketch a map of the positions, as shown following. You should know that the northeast direction is 45° north of east, bisecting the north and east directions. After two hours the airplanes are at the arrowheads on the map. Since $566 \cong 400\sqrt{2}$, they are at two corners of a 45° right triangle. At that time, the airplanes are approximately 400 miles apart.

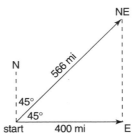

36. B. In the square *ABCD,* each side is 4, because the perimeter is 16. Then by the Pythagorean theorem, $d = 4\sqrt{2}$.

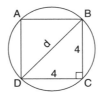

$$4^2 + 4^2 = d^2$$
$$16 + 16 = d^2$$
$$32 = d^2$$
$$\sqrt{32} = d$$

Simplifying,

$$d = \sqrt{32}$$
$$d = \sqrt{16 \times 2}$$
$$d = \sqrt{16} \times \sqrt{2}$$
$$d = 4\sqrt{2}$$

The radius is

$$r = {}^d\!/_2$$
$$r = \frac{4\sqrt{2}}{2}$$
$$r = 2\sqrt{2}$$

The area of the circle is

$$= \pi r^2$$
$$= \pi\left(2\sqrt{2}\right)^2$$
$$= \pi \times 4 \times 2$$
$$= 8\pi$$

Thus **B** is correct. If you recognize *DBC* as a 45°-45°-90° triangle with side ratios $1:1:1\sqrt{2}$, you can quickly find *d* by $4:4:4\sqrt{2}$.

37. D. First calculate the circumference of the circle using the equation $C = \pi d$ (or $C = 2\pi r$). $C = (^{22}/_7)14 = 44$. The circumference is 44 inches. Now change ½ mile to feet (2,640) to inches, $2,640 \times 12 = 31,680$. Dividing 31,680 by 44 = 720 revolutions.

38. D. Average rate is total distance (found by multiplying rate times time and adding $ft + rs$) divided by total time $(t + s)$; therefore, the average rate is

$$\frac{ft + rs}{t + s}$$

39. A. The product of the LCM and GCF of two numbers is the same as the product of the two original numbers. Thus the answer is *XY/Z*.

40. D. Exponential quantities can be readily divided (or multiplied) if they have the same base. To convert m from base-8 to base-2, consider that $8 = 2^3$. Therefore, $m = 8^5 = (2^3)^5 = 2^{15}$.

$$\frac{m}{n} = \frac{2^{15}}{2^{12}} = 2^3 = 8$$

If two exponential quantities have the same base, they may be divided by subtracting the exponent of the denominator from the exponent of the numerator.

41. A. From the relationship that exists in a right triangle, we see that the sides of the square must equal the square root of 5. Thus the area of the square is 5.

42. B. Area of the larger circle = 144π. Since area = πr^2, then

$$\pi r^2 = 144\pi$$
$$r^2 = 144$$
$$r = 12$$

Radius of larger circle = 12

Diameter of smaller circle = 12

Radius of smaller circle = 6

Area of smaller circle = πr^2, or $\pi 6^2$, or 36π

43. D. Let $85\%L$ represent a 15% decrease in length. Then $140\%W$ represents a 40% increase in width. The new rectangle will have

$$\text{area} = (\text{new length})(\text{new width})$$
$$= (85\%L)(140\%W)$$
$$= \frac{\overset{17}{\cancel{85}}}{\underset{20}{\cancel{100}}} L \cdot \frac{\overset{7}{\cancel{140}}}{\underset{5}{\cancel{100}}} W$$
$$= \frac{119}{100} LW$$
$$= 119\%LW$$

The old rectangle has area $100\%LW$. Thus, the new rectangle has area 19% *greater* than the original 100%.

44. D. If ⅖ of the prize (⅖ of $600 = $240) is distributed to ⅗ of the winners (⅗ of 20 is 12 winners), this indicates that each of those 12 winners will receive the minimum of $20.

That leaves $360 to be divided among 8 remaining winners. If 7 of those winners receive the minimum $20 (total $140), then the eighth winner would receive all the remaining prize money, $360 − $140 = $220.

45. **A.** From the given information, it costs 30x for the first 30 kilowatt hours. Thus $z - 30$ kilowatt hours remain at y cents per kilowatt hour. Thus $30x + (z - 30)y = (30x) - (30y) + yz = 30(x - y) + yz$.

46. **D.** To find the total surface area of a right circular cylinder, you must find not only the area of the "barrel" portion but also the area of the top and bottom circles. The area of the "barrel" portion equals the circumference of either the top or bottom circle times the height. $C = \pi d \cong 3 \times 20 = 60$. Thus the area of the "barrel" $= C \times h = 60 \times 100 = 6,000$. Now to find the *total* surface area, add the areas of both top and bottom circles, or $2 \times \pi r^2 \cong 2 \times 3 \times 10^2 = 600$. Therefore, the total surface area $\cong 6,000 + 600 = 6,600$.

47. **B.** Working from the answer choices, the @ of $64 = 4 \times 8 = 32$, which is 50% of 64.

48. **C.** Let x be Mike's age. Thus $3x$ is Macey's age. Thus $3x + 8 = 2(x + 8)$, $3x + 8 = 2x + 16$. Thus $x = 8$. Therefore, $3x = 24$. Thus Macey is 24 and 3 years ago was 21.

Notice you could also work from the answers.

49. **C.** The positive odd integers a, b, and c could be 1, 3, and 5. Option I is not necessarily true: $1 + 3$ is not greater than 5. Option II is not necessarily true: 1×3 is not greater than 5. Only option III must be true: the square of the sum of any two of the integers will be greater than the third integer.

50. **C.** The radius of the large circle equals the diameter of the small circle so the radius of the large circle is twice the radius of the small circle. Area is proportional to the square of the radius, so the large circle has an area $2^2 = 4$ that of the small circle. If the small circle is ¼ of the large circle, then the crescent area is ¾ of the large circle. The crescent and small circle are in the ratio (¾)/(¼) = 3.

51. **B.** Adding any two of three consecutive positive integers greater than 1 will always be greater than the other integer; therefore, II is true. The others cannot be determined, as they depend on the values and/or the order of x, y, and z.

52. **C.** We can tabulate the data:

	Part of tank brand Z	Part of tank brand Y
after first fill up	1	0
before second fill up	¹/₂	0
after second fill up	¹/₂	¹/₂
before third fill up	¹/₄	¹/₄
after third fill up	³/₄	¹/₄
before fourth fill up	³/₈	¹/₈
after fourth fill up	³/₈	⁵/₈

Since the tank is now full, ⅜, or 37.5%, is brand Z.

53. B. Try a simple number of total employees and see what happens. If the total employees for Company A is 100, then 40 are female and 60 are male. Then Company B has 60 females and 40 males. If 30 female employees move from Company B to A, then there are 70 in A and 30 in B. They are not equal. Next try 200. Then Company A has 80 females and 120 males, while Company B has 120 females and 80 males. Try 300. If A has 300, then 120 are female, and 180 are male, and B has 180 female and 120 male. If 30 females from Company B join Company A, then each company has 150 females, so each company must have 150 males for a total of 300.

Introduction to Data Sufficiency

Data Sufficiency questions do not necessarily require you to calculate a specific mathematical answer; they require that you recognize if a specific problem could be answered using the information provided. These problems usually take less time than Problem Solving questions.

Ability Tested

Data Sufficiency questions test your ability to analyze a problem, to recognize relevant or irrelevant information in determining the solution of that problem, and to determine when you have sufficient information to solve that problem.

Basic Skills Necessary

Correctly answering these questions requires competence in high school arithmetic, algebra, and intuitive geometry. Mathematical insight and problem-solving skills are also necessary. No advanced mathematics is required.

Directions

Each of the problems below consists of a question and two statements, labeled (1) and (2), in which certain data are given. You must decide whether the data given in the statements is *sufficient* to answer the question. Using the data given in the statements plus your knowledge of mathematics and everyday facts (such as the number of days in July or the meaning of *counterclockwise*), you are to choose answer

> **A** if statement (1) ALONE is sufficient, but statement (2) alone is not sufficient to answer the question asked;
>
> **B** if statement (2) ALONE is sufficient, but statement (1) alone is not sufficient to answer the question asked;
>
> **C** if both statements (1) and (2) TOGETHER are sufficient to answer the question asked, but NEITHER statement ALONE is sufficient;
>
> **D** if EACH statement ALONE is sufficient to answer the question asked;
>
> **E** if statements (1) and (2) TOGETHER are NOT sufficient to answer the question asked, and additional data specific to the problem are needed.

Remember that on the actual exam the statements will not be lettered. You will simply choose the oval of the correct statement.

Analysis

The purpose here is to determine whether information given is sufficient to answer the question; therefore, do not solve the problem unless it is absolutely necessary.

The memory aid 12TEN will simplify the directions, making it easier to avoid reading them again for every question. 12TEN stands for:

1 *First* statement alone is sufficient, not the second. CHOOSE **A.**

2 *Second* statement alone is sufficient, not the first. CHOOSE **B.**

T *Together* is the only way the statements are sufficient. CHOOSE **C.**

E *Either* statement alone is sufficient. CHOOSE **D.**

N *Neither* statement, together or alone, is sufficient. CHOOSE **E.**

Remember: one, two, together, either, neither, or 12TEN. (*Note:* Either means choose answer **D,** not **E.**)

Because of the structure of this type of question, you should always be able to eliminate some of the choices. If statement (1) ALONE is sufficient to answer the question, then the answer *must* be **A** or **D.** If statement (1) ALONE is *not* sufficient to answer the question, then the answer *must* be **B, C,** or **E.** If statements (1) and (2) ALONE are not sufficient, then the answer *must* be **C** or **E.**

If statements (1) or (2) ALONE *are* sufficient, then you *never* try them TOGETHER.

Sometimes geometric figures are included; they should be used only for positional value. Do not try to measure them, because they are not necessarily drawn to scale.

Suggested Approach With Samples

Note that on the exam the answer choices will appear at the bottom of the screen for each question.

Quickly decide what is the necessary basic information to answer the question. Then see if the data supplies that information.

Samples

1. What is the area of circle O?

(1) The circumference is 12π.

(2) The diameter is 12.

A. Statement (1) ALONE is sufficient, but statement (2) alone is not sufficient.

B. Statement (2) ALONE is sufficient, but statement (1) alone is not sufficient.

C. BOTH statements (1) and (2) TOGETHER are sufficient, but NEITHER statement ALONE is sufficient.

D. EACH statement ALONE is sufficient.

E. Statements (1) and (2) TOGETHER are NOT sufficient.

To find the area of a circle, it is necessary to have the radius. (1) gives enough information to find the radius by substituting into the circumference formula, $C = 2\pi r$, and getting $12\pi = 2\pi r$. Then simply solve for r, which is 6. Thus the area is 36π. None of this solving is necessary, only knowing that you need the radius and can find it from the information given. (2) also gives enough information to find the radius; therefore, the answer is **D**, either will be sufficient.

---

2. If $2x + 3y = 15$, then what is the value of x?

(1) $y = x + 2$

(2) y is a prime number less than 7.

To solve for two variables, you need two equations containing those variables or information that will give you a value for one of the variables.

The first bit of data gives you that second equation, so you now have two equations containing the two variables. You can find a value for x.

The second bit of data does not give you a value for y, it simply limits it to 2, 3, or 5. So you cannot solve for a value of x. The correct answer is **A**.

---

3. What is the value of x?

(1) $3x + 12 = 36$

(2) $5x + 3y = 16$

This problem is most easily solved by inspecting the first bit of data and quickly noticing that (1) is enough to answer the question (one variable, one equation, solvable). (2) does not answer the question.

This can also be determined by inspection (two variables, one equation, not solvable for a single value). The correct answer is **A**, yet no actual solving needs to be done.

> **4.** Sarah purchased an antique lamp and immediately took it to an appraiser. The appraiser told her that the lamp was a fair purchase and was worth what she had paid for it. Five years later, Sarah had the lamp appraised again, and the increase in value was substantial. What was the percent increase in value compared to Sarah's original purchase price?
>
> (1) Sarah's original purchase price was $200.
>
> (2) The new appraised value was $700.

To find the percent increase you would use the following equation:

$$\frac{\text{difference}}{\text{starting point}} \times 100 = \% \text{ increase}$$

or in this case,

$$\frac{\text{new appraised value} - \text{original purchase price}}{\text{original purchase price}} \times 100 = \% \text{ increase}$$

So it is evident that you need both statements to answer the question. The correct answer is **C.** No actual solving was done.

Use a simple marking system on your scratch paper to assist you in making your decision.

Samples

> **5.** What is the average height of Tom, Bob, and Luke?
>
> (1) Bob is 4 inches shorter than Luke, and Tom is 4 inches taller than Luke.
>
> (2) Luke is 5 feet 6 inches tall.

Write a (1) and (2) on your scratch paper to represent the data given. (1) is not sufficient, since no actual height is given; therefore mark a slash through (1). Note that the answer is immediately narrowed to **B, C,** or **E.** (2) by itself is also not sufficient, as the other two, Tom and Bob, aren't mentioned; therefore, a slash should be made through (2). Notice that the answer is now narrowed to **C** or **E.** The markings on your paper should look as follows:

(1)
(2)

Now trying them together, they are sufficient. The answer is **C.** In marking the data, if you are in doubt whether it is sufficient or not, put a question mark by the data and try the next bit of data. Don't waste time trying one bit of data for more than about 30 seconds.

6. The symbol θ represents a binary operation such as addition, subtraction, multiplication, or division. What is the value of 4 θ 5?

(1) $a \theta b = \frac{a+b}{b}$

(2) $2 \theta 3 = \frac{5}{3}$

Since (1) gives you an actual definition for the operation, you could simply substitute in the numbers and get a value for 4 θ 5.

$$4 \theta 5 = \frac{4+5}{5} = \frac{9}{5}$$

So if you put a (1) and (2) on your scratch paper, you should have circled (1). The answer will now be either **A** or **D.**

(2) looks like it might work, but the sample that is given does not really show you what the operation θ means.

θ could mean $\frac{a+b}{b}$ or θ could mean $\frac{3b-2a}{b}$. So the correct answer is **A.**

Don't read in specialized knowledge; use only the information given and general or common knowledge.

Sample

7. What is the runner's average speed in running around the track?

(1) One lap took 49 seconds.

(2) He ran 5 seconds faster than his previous best time.

Someone familiar with track and field would quickly assume that one lap is the standard 440 yards and would then *incorrectly answer* **A.** This sort of assumption cannot be made because it is from specialized knowledge in the area and therefore is not general knowledge. The correct answer is **E,** as the distance around the track is not given in either bit of data.

If a geometric figure is involved in the question, redraw the figure on your scratch paper, mark the figure with the information given, and circle what you are looking for.

Samples

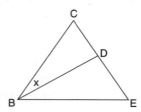

8. In the equilateral triangle above, what is the measure of angle x?

   (1) $\overline{BD}$ is a median.

   (2) Angle BDE is 90°.

After redrawing the figure, notice the markings from the information given:

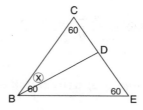

Mark in information given in data (1) as you read it, but *remember to erase that information before you try data* (2). (1) If $\overline{BD}$ is a median in an equilateral triangle, then it is also an angle bisector, making angle x equal to 30°. (Once again, the answer is not necessary, just the knowledge that it could be found.) (2) also gives enough information because if angle BDE is 90°, then angle BDC is 90°, and angle x is 30°, as there are 180° in a triangle. Redrawing and marking the diagram makes the problem easier to solve.

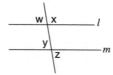

9. If l and m are parallel in the figure above, which is greater: $x + y$ or $w + z$?

   (1) $\angle x$ is not a right angle

   (2) $\angle y = 50°$

Once you are given the information that the lines are parallel, then you could redraw and mark the figure as follows:

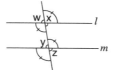

Statement (1) does not give you enough information to answer the question, because x could be greater than or less than 90 degrees.

Now use statement (2), $\angle y = 50°$, to fill in the figure as follows:

Since 180 degrees comprise a straight line, you could fill in the complete figure:

Since you now know the measure of all of the angles, you could answer the question. The correct answer is **C**. By the way, $x + y$ is greater than $w + z$, since $130 + 50$ is greater than $50 + 50$.

If a geometric diagram is discussed, but no figure is given, draw a simple diagram on your scratch paper.

Samples

> **10.** If the legs of a trapezoid are equal, what is the area?
>
> (1) The smaller base is 8 inches and the legs are 6 inches.
>
> (2) The height is 5 inches.

Drawing the diagram helps give important insight into what is needed to answer the question.

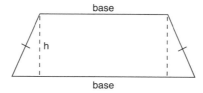

Now consider what is needed to find the area—the length of each base and the height, since the area formula is $\frac{1}{2}h(b_1 + b_2)$, or $h(b_1 + b_2)/2$.

(1) does not give sufficient information to find the larger base or the height. (2), by itself, does not give enough information to find the bases. (1) and (2) together give enough information to find the bases and the height. The answer is **C.** The Pythagorean theorem would be necessary to find the length of the difference between the smaller and larger bases. Adding this difference to the length of the shorter base would give the longer base. You now have the necessary information. Notice the markings on the diagram below, to assist you in deciding what you have to work with.

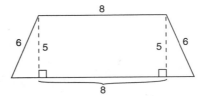

---

11. What is the length of the edge of a cube?

    (1) The surface area of the cube equals 54 square inches.

    (2) The volume of the cube is 27 cubic inches.

Again, first draw the diagram. In this case, draw a cube.

Now consider the first bit of data. If the surface area of a cube is 54 square inches, could you find the length of an edge? Since there are 6 equal faces on a cube, then $54 \div 6 = 9$ gives the area of one face. Since each face is a square with an area of the 9, then the edge must be 3. So (1) is sufficient to answer the question. The answer is now **A** or **D.**

Next consider the second bit of data. If the volume of a cube is 27 cubic inches, could you find the length of an edge? Since the volume of a cube is length × width × height (or the edge cubed since all the dimensions are the same), then what number cubed is 27? Since 3 cubed is 27, the edge must be 3. So (2) is also sufficient to answer the question. The correct answer is **D;** either statement (1) or (2) is sufficient.

Remember, you do not need to do all of the work to find the answer, just know if you have enough information to find the answer. Pulling out information can be valuable in setting up the problem.

Samples

> **12.** Phil took four tests in his chemistry class. His average score after the first three tests was 85%. After his fourth test, Phil's overall average dropped. What score did he get on his fourth test?
>
> (1) The average score of Phil's first two tests was 90%.
>
> (2) After Phil's fourth test, his overall average was 80%.

Pulling out information will help you set up the following:

$$\text{Let } w = \text{first test}$$

$$x = \text{second test}$$

$$y = \text{third test}$$

$$z = \text{fourth test}$$

$$\text{then } \frac{w + x + y}{3} = 85$$

$$\text{and } \frac{w + x + y + z}{4} = ?$$

Given these two equations, knowing the average of the first two scores (1) will make it possible to find the score of the third test but will not answer the question. You still know nothing about the fourth score or its effect on the average.

(2) says that the overall average after the fourth test is 80%. Using the first equation, the total for the first three tests was 3×85, or 255. You could use the second equation, replacing $w + x + y$ with 255, and solve as follows:

$$\frac{255 + z}{4} = 80$$

$$255 + z = 320$$

$$z = 320\text{-}255$$

$$z = 65$$

So z is 65%. Statement (2) is enough to answer the question, so the correct answer is **B**.

> **13.** Ten colored marbles are placed in a bowl. Each of the marbles is one of three colors—blue, red, or green. How many of the ten marbles are green?
>
> (1) The probability of selecting a red marble from the bowl is 1 out of 5.
>
> (2) The probability of selecting a blue marble is twice that of selecting a red marble.

You could have pulled out information and set up the following:

$$B \quad R \quad G$$
$$? + ? + x = 10$$

The first bit of data gives you the information that 2 of the marbles are red, because $\frac{1}{5} = \frac{2}{10}$. But that is not enough information to answer the question.

The second bit of data alone gives you no information that is helpful in answering the question. But together, you can answer the question. If 2 out of 10 marbles are red, and twice that number are blue, then 4 marbles are blue. Therefore, 4 of the marbles must be green to total 10 marbles. The correct answer is **C.**

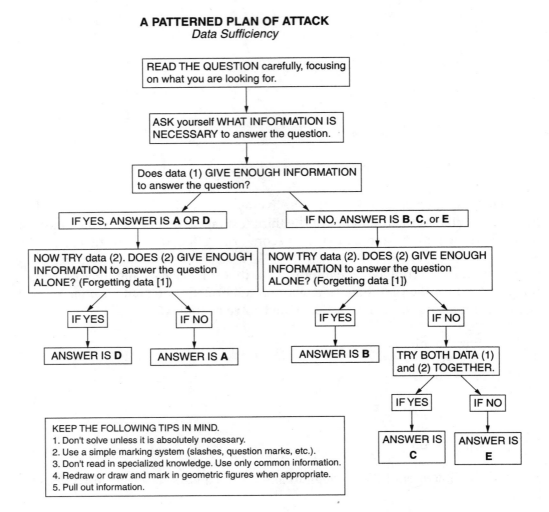

A PATTERNED PLAN OF ATTACK
Data Sufficiency

READ THE QUESTION carefully, focusing on what you are looking for.

ASK yourself WHAT INFORMATION IS NECESSARY to answer the question.

Does data (1) GIVE ENOUGH INFORMATION to answer the question?

IF YES, ANSWER IS **A** OR **D**

IF NO, ANSWER IS **B**, **C**, or **E**

NOW TRY data (2). DOES (2) GIVE ENOUGH INFORMATION to answer the question ALONE? (Forgetting data [1])

IF YES — ANSWER IS **D**

IF NO — ANSWER IS **A**

NOW TRY data (2). DOES (2) GIVE ENOUGH INFORMATION to answer the question ALONE? (Forgetting data [1])

IF YES — ANSWER IS **B**

IF NO — TRY BOTH DATA (1) and (2) TOGETHER.

IF YES — ANSWER IS **C**

IF NO — ANSWER IS **E**

KEEP THE FOLLOWING TIPS IN MIND.
1. Don't solve unless it is absolutely necessary.
2. Use a simple marking system (slashes, question marks, etc.).
3. Don't read in specialized knowledge. Use only common information.
4. Redraw or draw and mark in geometric figures when appropriate.
5. Pull out information.

Practice Data Sufficiency Questions

Easy to Moderate

For each question, select one of the following answer choices:

A. Statement (1) ALONE is sufficient, but statement (2) alone is not sufficient.

B. Statement (2) ALONE is sufficient, but statement (1) alone is not sufficient.

C. BOTH statements (1) and (2) TOGETHER are sufficient, but NEITHER statement ALONE is sufficient.

D. EACH statement ALONE is sufficient.

E. Statements (1) and (2) TOGETHER are NOT sufficient.

1. Who is the tallest of four men?

   (1) Jim is shorter than Steve.

   (2) Mark and Steve are shorter than Walter.

2. Does $A = C$?

   (1) $A \neq B$

   (2) $B \neq C$

3. Which is more expensive, a peach or a plum?

   (1) A dozen plums cost $1.79.

   (2) Peaches are 69¢ a pound.

4. What is the distance from Chicago to Miami?

   (1) A 550 mph turbojet takes $3\frac{1}{4}$ hours for the flight.

   (2) The jet consumes 3 gallons of fuel per mile.

5. In the equation $3a - 7b + 14 = 0$, what is the value of b?

   (1) $a = b$

   (2) $a = 3$

6. What is the area of a circular garden?

   (1) The circumference is 314 feet.

   (2) The radius is 50 feet.

7. How far is Sacramento from Los Angeles?

   (1) A car that obtains 28 miles per gallon drove the distance on exactly one tank of gasoline.

   (2) Another car averaged 50 miles per hour and arrived in 8 hours.

Average

8. What was the percentage increase of Mr. Doolittle's rent?

   (1) His rent was raised $45.

   (2) He now pays $315 per month.

9. What is the numerical value of the ratio n/m?

   (1) $mn = 14$

   (2) $m = 6n$

10. How many brothers does David have?

   (1) His parents have seven surviving children.

   (2) He has twice as many sisters as brothers.

11. Is x greater than y?

   (1) $(x - y) > 0$

   (2) $x^2 < y^2$

12. What is the interest rate on a savings account?

   (1) The saver collected $42 in simple interest over several months.

   (2) There was $1,680 in the account initially.

13. Which is the smallest of three numbers that average 7?

   (1) One of the numbers is 4.

   (2) One of the numbers is 6.

14. How many Mondays are in December of a particular year?

   (1) There are four Tuesdays that December.

   (2) There are four Saturdays that December.

15. Students took a test and received either A's, B's, C's, D's, or F's. If 30% of the class got A's or B's, and 50% got C's or D's, how many students got F's?

   (1) 10 students received B's.

   (2) There was a total of 40 students in the class.

16. Were more new sports cars or new sedans purchased in Wichita during the years 1985 through 1995?

   (1) In the years 1985 through 1995, one fourth of the population of Wichita purchased new sedans.

   (2) In the years 1985 through 1995, one third of the population of Wichita purchased new sports cars.

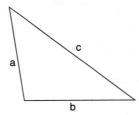

17. What is the length of side c?

   (1) $a = 6$

   (2) $b = 7$

18. Is x greater than y?

   (1) $x = \sqrt{3}$

   (2) y is a prime number.

Above Average to Difficult

19. What is the value of *j* if *h* is *k*% of *j*?

   (1) *h* is 25% of 40.

   (2) $k = 20$

20. Eloise's aquarium contains six tropical fish. If the largest fish is 4 ounces heavier than the smallest fish, how heavy is the smallest fish?

   (1) If the largest fish were 6 ounces heavier, it would weigh twice as much as the smallest fish.

   (2) The six fish average 14 ounces in weight.

21. Otto and his wife, Anna, leave home at 1 p.m. and bicycle in different directions. How far apart are they at 4 p.m.?

   (1) Otto rides at 12 mph westward for two hours and then stops.

   (2) Anna rides at 10 mph southward for one hour and then rides westward at the same speed for three hours.

22. How long is the diagonal through the center of a particular cube?

   (1) A diagonal across one face is 4.24 centimeters.

   (2) The surface area of the cube is 54 square centimeters.

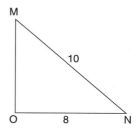

23. What is the perimeter of triangle *MNO*?

   (1) The area of triangle *MNO* is 24.

   (2) Angle *MON* equals 90°.

24. A hexagonal playing field is composed of six equilateral triangles, each the same size. If one player controls each triangle, how much area is controlled by all six players?

   (1) One edge of one triangle equals 15 feet.

   (2) The perimeter of one triangular region equals 45 feet.

25. What is the value of $(u + v)$?

   (1) $2w - 7 = 0$

   (2) $u + v - 3w = 11$

Answers and Explanations for the Practice Data Sufficiency Questions

Easy to Moderate

1. **C.** From both statements, Jim must also be shorter than Walter, who is taller than any of the other men.

2. **E.** The relationship between two quantities is uncertain given merely that each is unequal to a third quantity.

3. **E.** The first statement enables us to find the cost of one plum. But without the weight of one peach, we cannot use (2) to find the cost of a peach.

4. **A.** Distance equals rate times time. Statement (1) tells us the rate and time. Multiplying 550 by $3\frac{1}{4}$ yields a distance of 1,788 miles.

5. **D.** Either statement transforms the equation so there is only one unknown, which therefore could be found:

   (1) $3b - 7b + 14 = 0$

   (2) $9 - 7b + 14 = 0$

6. **D.** The area can be calculated from $A = \pi r^2$ if we know the radius, which is given in the second statement. The first statement gives the circumference, from which the radius may be found by $r = C/2\pi$.

7. **B.** Statement (1) lacks the capacity of the tank. But from (2) and the formula $d = rt$, you can compute the distance to be 400 miles.

Average

8. **C.** His initial rent was $315 - $45 = $270, so the increase was 45 divided by 270 equals 16.7%.

9. **B.** Statement (1) reveals a product, not a quotient. However, dividing both sides of equation (2) by $6/m$ demonstrates that $n/m = 1/6$.

10. **C.** From the first statement, David has six sisters and brothers (he is the seventh child). Combining that piece of data with the second statement, he must have four sisters and two brothers.

11. **A.** Inequality (1) informs us that x exceeds y, whether positive, zero, or negative. Inequality (2) does not tell us so much, because the sign of the numbers is masked by the squaring.

12. **E.** Simple interest equals principal times rate times time. We are not told the length of time the money was in the account.

13. C. With both statements, we know that the third number must exceed 7, so the smallest number is 4. But with the first statement alone, all we know is $4 + x + y = 3 \times 7$, and one of the unknown numbers could be less than 4.

14. C. You must know that December has 31 days. (For the GMAT, you should know the number of days in each month of the year.) Therefore, December has 4 weeks and 3 extra days. For the 7 days of the week, 4 occur 4 times and the other 3 occur 5 times. Since there are only 2 days between Saturday (statement 2) and Tuesday (statement 1), there must be 4 Sundays and Mondays that month.

15. B. Since a total of 80% received A's, B's, C's, and D's, then 20% received F's. 20% of 40 (the total given in statement 2) = 8 students. The first statement does not help because we don't know how many students received A's.

16. E. Neither of the statements gives definitive information about the number of new sedans or the number of new sports cars purchased. For example, although one fourth of the population may have purchased new sedans, the members of that fraction of the population may have each purchased several new sedans, bringing the number of new sedans purchased above the number of new sports cars purchased.

17. E. The Pythagorean theorem, $a^2 + b^2 = c^2$, can be employed only for a triangle known to have a right angle.

18. C. The smallest prime is 2, which exceeds $\sqrt{3}$ (approximately 1.73). Consequently, x is less than y.

Above Average to Difficult

19. C. From statement (1), we find $h = 10$. From (2), $k = 20$. Then the question translates to: The number 10 is 20% of what number j? Because $10 = 0.2j$, then j = 10/0.2 = 50.

20. A. From statement (1), the following equation may be derived:

$L + 6 = 2S$

From the information given in the question, the following equation may be derived:

$L = S + 4$

Using simultaneous equations, we may solve for both S and L. Notice that statement (2) tells nothing about the individual weight of any fish.

21. C. Because the compass directions are at right angles, the distance can be computed by using the Pythagorean theorem, providing that Otto's and Anna's positions at 4 p.m. are known. Otto will be 24 miles west of the origin. Anna will be 10 miles south and 4 miles east at 4 p.m. It is helpful to sketch a map in a problem involving positions.

22. D. The diagonal through the center of a cube, from one corner to the opposite corner, may be found with the Pythagorean theorem providing that the length of the cube's edge is known. Statement (1) implies that the edge is $4.24/\sqrt{2}$ centimeters. Moreover, since the surface area (2) has 6 faces, each face has an area of $54/6 = 9$ cm², and so the edge is $\sqrt{9} = 3$ cm.

23. **D.** Since statement (1) tells us that the area of triangle *MNO* is 24, its height must be 6. Note that side *MO* will be the height because 6-8-10 is a Pythagorean triple. Thus we can find the perimeter. Using statement (2), we know that triangle *MON* is a right triangle and can use the Pythagorean theorem to find the third side.

24. **D.** Given the edge (*N*) of an equilateral triangle, one can determine its height ($N\sqrt{3}/2$) and therefore its area. So one can determine the area of all six equilateral triangular regions, each of the same size.

25. **C.** From the first statement, $w = 3\frac{1}{2}$. Substituting that into (2) yields $u + v - 3 \times 3\frac{1}{2} = 11$, which can be solved for $(u + v) = 21\frac{1}{2}$.

Introduction to Graphs and Charts

Graphs and charts appear in the quantitative section of the exam.

Ability Tested

You will need to understand and to derive information from graphs, charts, and tables. Many of the problems require brief calculations based on the data, so your mathematical ability is also tested.

Basic Skills Necessary

The mathematics associated with diagrammatic interpretation does not go beyond high-school level. Your familiarity with a wide range of chart and graph types will help you feel comfortable with these problems and read the data accurately.

Directions

You are given data represented in chart or graph form. Following each set of data are questions based on that data. Select the best answer to each question by referring to the appropriate chart or graph, and mark your choice on the screen. Use only the given or implied information to determine your answer.

Analysis

Remember that you are looking for the best answer, not necessarily the perfect answer. Often, graph questions ask you for an approximate answer; if this happens, don't forget to round off numbers to make your work easier.

Use only the information given; never "read into" the information on a graph.

Suggested Approach with Samples

Here are some helpful strategies for extracting accurate information, followed by some sample graph questions.

> **Skim the question and quickly examine the whole graph before starting to work the problem; this sort of pre-reading will tell you what to look for.**

> Sometimes the answer to a question is available in supplementary information given with a graph (heading, scale factors, legends, etc.). Be sure to read this information.

> Look for the obvious: dramatic trends, high points, low points, etc. Obvious information often leads directly to an answer.

> You may need to scroll the graph to see all of the information it contains.

Charts and Tables

Charts and tables are often used to give an organized picture of information, or data. Be sure that you understand *what is given*. Column headings and line items give the important information. These titles give the numbers meaning.

First, pay special attention to what information is given in the chart. The following chart shows the number of "Burger Sales for the Week of August 8–14." The days of the week are given along the left side of the chart. The number of *hamburgers* for each day is given in one column and the number of *cheeseburgers* in the other column.

Samples

Questions 1–3 refer to the following chart.

Burger Sales for the Week of August 8–14		
Day	**Hamburgers**	**Cheeseburgers**
Sunday	120	92
Monday	85	80
Tuesday	77	70
Wednesday	74	71
Thursday	75	72
Friday	91	88
Saturday	111	112

1. On which day were the most burgers sold (hamburgers and cheeseburgers)?

    A. Sunday

    B. Monday

    C. Friday

    D. Saturday

    E. Tuesday

The answer is **D.** To answer this question, you must understand the chart and do some simple computation. Working from the answers is probably the easiest method.

    A. Sunday: $120 + 92 = 212$

    B. Monday: $85 + 80 = 165$

    C. Friday: $91 + 88 = 179$

    D. Saturday: $111 + 112 = 223$

    E. Tuesday: $77 + 70 = 147$

Another method is to *approximate* the answers.

2. On how many days were more hamburgers sold than cheeseburgers?

    A. 7

    B. 6

    C. 5

    D. 4

    E. 3

The answer is **B.** To answer this question, you must compare the sales for each day. Hamburgers outsold cheeseburgers every day except Saturday.

3. If the pattern of sales continues,

    A. the weekend days will have the fewest number of burger sales next week.

    B. the cheeseburgers will outsell hamburgers next week.

    C. generally, when hamburger sales go up, cheeseburger sales will go up.

    D. hamburgers will be less expensive than cheeseburgers.

    E. more customers will buy hamburgers than cheeseburgers next Saturday.

The answer is **C**. To answer this question, you must notice one of the trends. Most days that hamburger sales go up, cheeseburger sales go up (with the exception of Saturday to Sunday).

Graphs

Information may be displayed in many ways. The three basic types of graphs you should know are bar graphs, line graphs, and pie graphs (or pie charts).

Bar Graphs

Bar graphs convert the information in a chart into separate bars or columns. Some graphs list numbers along one edge and places, dates, people, or things (individual categories) along another edge. Always try to determine the *relationship* between the columns in a graph or chart.

Samples

Question 4 refers to the following graph.

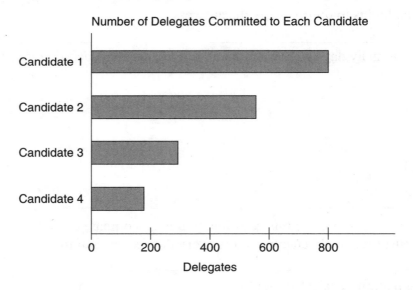

Number of Delegates Committed to Each Candidate

4. Candidate 1 has approximately how many more delegates committed than does Candidate 2?

   A. 150

   B. 200

   C. 250

   D. 400

   E. 450

The answer is **C.** To understand this question, you must be able to read the bar graph and make comparisons. Notice that the graph shows the "Number of Delegates Committed to Each Candidate," with the numbers given along the bottom of the graph in increases of 200. The candidates are listed along the left side. Candidate 1 has approximately 800 delegates (possibly a few more). The bar graph for Candidate 2 stops about three quarters of the way between 400 and 600. Now, consider that halfway between 400 and 600 would be 500. So Candidate 2 is about 550.

$$800 - 550 = 250$$

Questions 5–7 refer to the following graph.

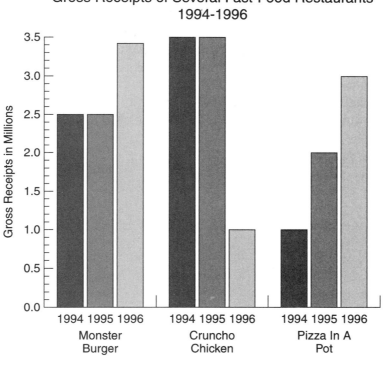

Gross Receipts of Several Fast-Food Restaurants
1994-1996

5. The 1994–1996 gross receipts of Monster Burger exceeded those of Pizza In A Pot by approximately how much?

   A.   0.2 million

   B.   2 million

   C.   8.2 million

   D.   8.4 million

   E.   17 million

Here we have multiple bars representing each fast-food category; each single bar stands for the receipts from a single year.

You may be tempted to write out the numbers as you do your arithmetic (3.5 million = 3,5000,000). This is unnecessary, as it often is when working with graphs that use large numbers. All measurements are given in millions, and adding zeros does not add precision to the numbers.

The answer is **B.** Referring to the Monster Burger bars, we see that gross receipts are as follows: 1994 = 2.5, 1995 = 2.5, 1996 = 3.4. (If you have trouble seeing how the bars line up with the numbers, you might want to use a piece of scratch paper against the screen as a straightedge to determine a number such as this last one.) Totaling the receipts for all three years, we get 8.4.

Referring to the Pizza In A Pot bars, we see that gross receipts are as follows: 1994 = 1, 1995 = 2.1, 1996 = 3. (Don't designate numbers beyond the nearest tenth, because the graph numbers and the answer choices prescribe no greater accuracy than this.) Totaling the receipts for all three years, we get 6.1.

So Monster Burger exceeds Pizza In A Pot by 2.3 million. The answer that best approximates this figure is **B.**

---

6. From 1995 to 1996, the percent increase in receipts for Pizza In A Pot exceeded the percent increase for Monster Burger by approximately how much?

   A.   0%

   B.   2%

   C.   10%

   D.   15%

   E.   43%

The answer is **C.** Graph questions on the GRE may ask you to calculate percent increase or percent decrease. The formula for figuring either of these is the same:

$$\frac{\text{amount of the change}}{\text{starting amount}\,(\text{follows the word } from)}$$

In this case, we may first calculate the percent increase for Monster Burger.

   Gross receipts in 1995 = 2.5

   Gross receipts in 1996 = 3.4

   Amount of the change = 0.9

   The 1995 amount is the starting amount.

   $\dfrac{\text{amount of the change}}{\text{starting amount}} = \dfrac{0.9}{2.5} = 0.36 = 36\%$

The percent increase for Pizza In A Pot is:

Gross receipts in 1995 = 2.1

Gross receipts in 1996 = 3

Amount of the change = 0.9

$$\frac{\text{amount of the change}}{\text{starting amount}} = \frac{0.9}{2.1} \cong 0.428 \cong 43\%$$

So Pizza In A Pot exceeds Monster Burger by 7% (43% compared to 36%). The answer that best approximates this figure is **C.**

---

7. The 1996 decline in Cruncho Chicken's receipts may be attributed to

    A.   an increase in the popularity of burgers.

    B.   an increase in the popularity of pizza.

    C.   a decrease in the demand for chicken.

    D.   a predictable slump attributable to the increase in terrorist activity.

    E.   It cannot be determined from the information given.

The answer is **E.** Never use information that you know is not given. In this case, the multiple factors which could cause a decline in receipts are not represented by the graph. All choices except **E** require you to speculate beyond the information given.

Line Graphs

Line graphs convert data into points on a grid. These points are then connected to show a relationship between the items, dates, times, etc. Notice the slopes of lines connecting the points. These lines will show increases and decreases. The sharper the slope *upward*, the greater the *increase*. The sharper the slope *downward*, the greater the *decrease*. Line graphs can show trends, or changes, in data over a period of time.

Samples

Questions 8 and 9 refer to the following graph.

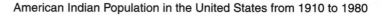

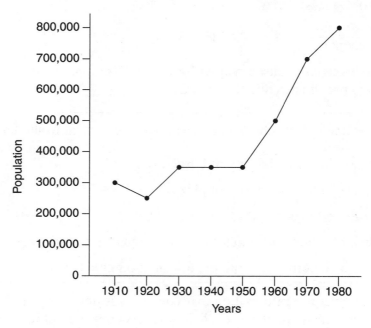

American Indian Population in the United States from 1910 to 1980

8. In which of the following years were there about 500,000 American Indians?

A.   1940

B.   1950

C.   1960

D.   1970

E.   1975

The answer is **C.** The information along the left side of the graph shows the number of Indians in increases of 100,000. The bottom of the graph shows the years from 1910 to 1980. The graph shows that in 1960 there were about 500,000 American Indians in the United States. Using the edge of your answer sheet like a ruler will help you see that the dot in the 1960 column lines up with 500,000 on the left.

9. During which of the following time periods was there a decrease in the American Indian population?

    A. 1910 to 1920

    B. 1920 to 1930

    C. 1930 to 1940

    D. 1960 to 1970

    E. 1970 to 1980

The answer is **A.** The slope of the line goes *down* from 1910 to 1920, so there must have been a decrease in that period. If you read the actual numbers, you will notice a decrease from 300,000 to 250,000.

Questions 10–12 refer to the following graph.

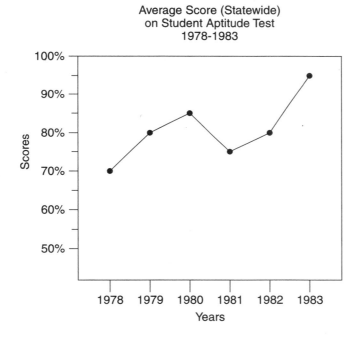

10. Between which two years was the greatest rise in average test scores?

    A. 1978 and 1979

    B. 1979 and 1980

    C. 1980 and 1981

    D. 1981 and 1982

    E. 1982 and 1983

The answer is **E.** The most efficient way to compute greatest rise is to locate the *steepest* upward slope on the chart. Note that the steepest climb is between 1982 and 1983. Therefore choice **E** indicates the greatest rise in average test scores.

---

11. In which year was the average score approximately 85%?

   A. 1978

   B. 1979

   C. 1980

   D. 1981

   E. 1982

The answer is **C.** According to the graph, the average test score was approximately 85% in 1980. When you must read the graph for a precise measurement, it may be helpful to use your answer sheet as a straight edge to more accurately compare points with the grid marks along the side.

---

12. Approximately what was the highest score achieved statewide on the test?

   A. 80%

   B. 85%

   C. 90%

   D. 97%

   E. cannot be determined

The answer is **E.** The first thing you should do when confronted with a graph or chart is read its title to understand what the graph is telling you. In this case the graph is relating information about *average scores*. It tells you nothing about the *highest* score achieved. Thus **E** is the correct answer.

Circle Graphs (Pie Charts)

A circle graph, or pie chart, shows the relationship between the whole circle (100%) and the various slices that represent portions of that circle. The larger the slice, the higher the percentage of the circle it represents.

Samples

Questions 13–15 refer to the following graph.

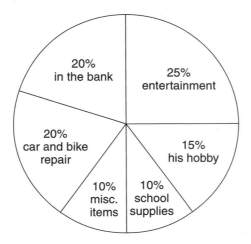

How John Spends His Monthly Paycheck

---

13. John spends one-fourth of his monthly paycheck on

   A. his hobby

   B. car and bike repairs

   C. entertainment

   D. school supplies

   E. his bank account

The answer is **C.** To answer this question, you must be able to read the graph and apply some simple math. Notice how the information is given in the graph. Each item is given along with the percent of money spent on that item. Since one quarter is the same as 25%, entertainment is the one you are looking for.

---

14. If John receives $100 in this month's paycheck, how much will he put in the bank?

   A. $ 2

   B. $20

   C. $35

   D. $60

   E. $80

The answer is **B.** To answer this question, you must again read the graph carefully and apply some simple math. John puts 20% of his income in the bank. Twenty percent of $100 is $20. So he will put $20 in the bank.

15. The ratio of the amount of money John spends on his hobby to the amount he puts in the bank is

- **A.** ½
- **B.** ⅝
- **C.** ⅔
- **D.** ¾
- **E.** ⅞

The answer is **D.** To answer this question, you must use the information in the graph to make a ratio.

$$\frac{\text{his hobby}}{\text{in the bank}} = \frac{15\%}{20\%} = \frac{15}{20} = \frac{3}{4}$$

Notice that the ratio of 15% to 20% reduces to ¾.

Questions 16–18 refer to the following graphs.

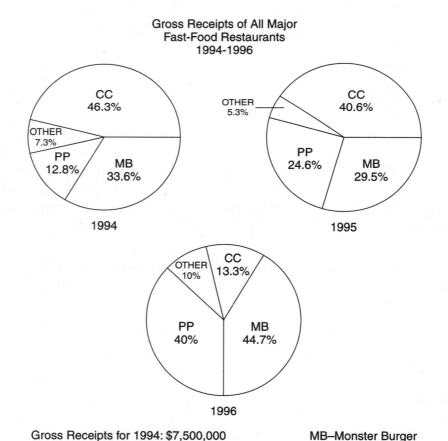

Gross Receipts of All Major
Fast-Food Restaurants
1994-1996

Gross Receipts for 1994: $7,500,000
Gross Receipts for 1995: $8,550,000
Gross Receipts for 1996: $8,100,000

MB–Monster Burger
CC–Cruncho Chicken
PP–Pizza In A Pot

16. The gross receipts for 1994 are approximately what percentage of the gross receipts for all three years?

   A. 30%

   B. 46.3%

   C. 46.7%

   D. 50%

   E. It cannot be determined from the information given.

The answer is **A.** You can solve this problem without referring to the graphs; the necessary information is available in the list of gross receipts below the graphs. Don't write out all the zeros when calculating with these large figures; brief figures are easier to work with.

    Gross receipts for 1994 = 7.5 million.

    Gross receipts for all three years = 7.5 + 8.6 + 8.1 = 24.2 million.

    $7.5/24.2 = 31\%$

The answer that best approximates 31% is 30%, **A.** Notice that even without doing the calculations, you may approximate 30% by realizing that the gross receipts for any one year are about a third of the total.

17. Over all three years, the average percentage of gross receipts for Cruncho Chicken exceeds the average percentage of gross receipts for Pizza In A Pot by approximately how much?

   A. 53%

   B. 30%

   C. 23%

   D. 8%

   E. 4%

The answer is **D.** To calculate the average percentage for Cruncho Chicken, add the percentages for each year and divide by 3.

    46.3 + 40.6 + 13.3 = 100.2 ÷ 3 = 33.4%

Do the same for Pizza In A Pot.

    12.8 + 24.6 + 40 = 77.4 ÷ 3 = 25.8%

Cruncho Chicken exceeds Pizza In A Pot by 33.4 − 25.8 = 7.6%. The answer **D,** 8%, best approximates this figure.

18. The gross receipts earned by other restaurants in 1996 amount to precisely how much?

    A. $1,810,650

    B. $ 810,000

    C. $ 547,500

    D. $ 453,150

    E. $ 405,000

The answer is **B.** In 1996, other restaurants earned precisely 10%. 10% of $8,100,000 equals $810,000.

A PATTERNED PLAN OF ATTACK
Graphs and Charts

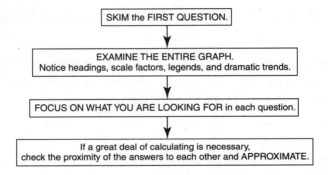

SKIM the FIRST QUESTION.

EXAMINE THE ENTIRE GRAPH.
Notice headings, scale factors, legends, and dramatic trends.

FOCUS ON WHAT YOU ARE LOOKING FOR in each question.

If a great deal of calculating is necessary,
check the proximity of the answers to each other and APPROXIMATE.

Practice Graphs and Chart Problems

Set 1

Questions 1–5 refer to the following graphs.

AVERAGE FAMILY'S EXPENSES

1970
Average Income $12,000

1975
Average Income $16,000

1. For the year in which the average family's housing expenses were $3,000, what were the average family's medical expenses?

 A. $ 600

 B. $1,000

 C. $1,200

 D. $1,920

 E. $2,400

2. What was the approximate ratio of income spent on housing in 1970 to income spent on housing in 1975?

 A. 4 to 17

 B. 3 to 5

 C. 25 to 32

 D. 1 to 1

 E. 3 to 2

3. What was the percent increase from 1970 to 1975 in the percentage spent on food and drink?

 A. 4%

 B. 18%

 C. 22%

 D. 40%

 E. 50%

4. How much more did the average family spend on entertainment in 1975 than in 1970?

 A. $4,000

 B. $1,120

 C. $ 870

 D. $ 400

 E. $ 280

5. Which of the following statements about the average family's expenses can be inferred from the graph?

 I. More money was put into savings in 1970 than in 1975.

 II. More money was spent for food and drink in 1975 than for food and drink in 1970.

 III. More money was spent in 1975 for "other" expenses than for "other" expenses in 1970.

 A. I only

 B. II only

 C. III only

 D. II and III only

 E. I, II, and III

Set 2

Questions 6–10 refer to the following graphs.

BASEBALL CARD PRICES FOR SELECTED 1956 SERIES
PRICES REALIZED AT START OF 1991 SEASON

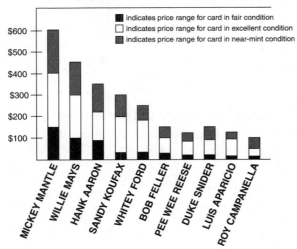

PRICE FLUCTUATION DURING SEASON OF 5 SELECTED 1956 CARDS

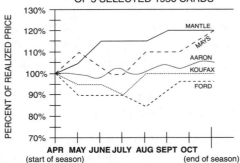

6. At the start of the 1991 season, the price range realized for a 1956 Bob Feller card in excellent condition was

A. $100 to $200

B. $100 to $150

C. $50 to $100

D. $30 to $100

E. $0 to $30

7. The price range realized in September for a near-mint-condition Mickey Mantle card was

A. $150 to $400

B. $400 to $600

C. $440 to $660

D. $480 to $720

E. $600 to $800

8. At the start of the season, which of the following cards had the greatest ratio of near-mint-condition range to excellent condition range?

A. Willie Mays

B. Whitey Ford

C. Bob Feller

D. Duke Snider

E. Roy Campanella

9. What was the difference in price realized anytime during the 1991 season between the highest-priced excellent-condition Willie Mays card and the highest-priced near-mint-condition Hank Aaron card?

A. $ 7.50

B. $10.00

C. $12.50

D. $30.00

E. $60.00

10. Which of the following can be inferred from the graphs above?

   I.   Any price realized during the 1991 season for a near-mint-condition Sandy Koufax card would be enough to purchase one each of fair-condition cards of Whitey Ford, Bob Feller, Pee Wee Reese, Duke Snider, Luis Aparicio, and Roy Campanella.

   II.   The 1990 end-of-season price for a near-mint-condition Whitey Ford was less than its start-of-season price.

   III.   The highest price realized during the 1991 season for an excellent-condition Bob Feller is less than the lowest price realized during the 1991 season for a near-mint-condition Pee Wee Reese.

   A. I only

   B. II only

   C. III only

   D. I and II only

   E. II and III only

Set 3

Questions 11–15 refer to the graph below.

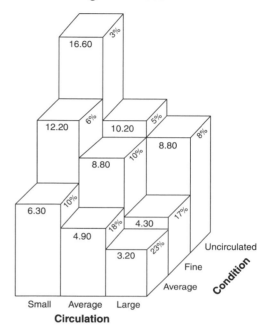

U.S. Indian Head Nickels Average Retail Cost

Percentages indicate percent of total coins available for sale.

Other numbers indicate average price of each coin.

11. Which of the following coin classifications represents the most coins?

   A. large circulation

   B. average circulation

   C. average condition

   D. fine condition

   E. small circulation

12. If 10,000 uncirculated coins were available for sale, what would be the average cost per coin?

    A. $9.01–$9.50

    B. $9.51–$10.00

    C. $10.01–$10.50

    D. $10.51–$11.00

    E. $11.01–$11.50

13. If 20,000 total coins are available for sale, how many of them would be from coins of average circulation?

    A. 3,500–5,000

    B. 5,001–6,500

    C. 6,501–8,000

    D. 8,001–9,500

    E. 9,501–11,000

14. If a coin collector who once collected only fine condition coins were to now collect both uncirculated and fine condition coins, the number of coins now available for her collection would represent an increase of approximately what percent over the number of coins formerly available?

    A. 16%

    B. 27%

    C. 33%

    D. 48%

    E. 66%

15. If 100 total coins are available for sale, how much more would a collector pay for all the average circulation coins of fine condition than for all the small circulation coins of average condition?

    A. $15

    B. $25

    C. $35

    D. $63

    E. $88

Answers and Explanations for the Graphs and Charts Practice Problems

Set 1

1. **C.** In 1970, housing was 25% of $12,000, or $3,000. In that same year, medical expenses were 10% of $12,000, or $1,200.

2. **B.** In 1970, income spent on housing was 25% of $12,000, or $3,000. In 1975, income spent on housing was 32% of $16,000, or $5,120. The ratio is 3,000 to 5,120, or approximately 3 to 5.

3. **C.** There was an increase from 18% to 22%. That is a 4% increase. A 4% increase from 18% is a 22% increase in the percent spent on food and drink.

4. **E.** In 1975, entertainment was 7% of $16,000, or $1,120. In 1970, entertainment was 7% of $12,000, or $840. So $280 more was spent on entertainment in 1975 than in 1970.

5. **B.** II only. Statement I cannot be inferred from the graph: Savings in 1970 were 5% of $12,000, or $600, whereas savings in 1975 were 4% of $16,000, or $640. Statement II can be inferred from the graph: Expenses for food and drink were a larger percentage of a larger total in 1975 than the corresponding figures in 1970. Statement III cannot be inferred from the graph: In 1970, "other" expenses comprised 35% of $12,000, or $4,200. In 1975, "other" expenses comprised 23% of $16,000, or $3,680.

Set 2

6. **D.** The range for excellent condition (white part of the bar) for Bob Feller's card extends from $30 to $100.

7. **D.** In September, a Mantle card realized 120% of its start-of-season price. The price range at the start of season for a near-mint Mantle card was $400 to $600. Therefore, increasing its range by 20% would indicate a new range of $480 to $720.

8. **E.** Roy Campanella had a greater range for near-mint condition ($50 to $100, or a range of $50) compared to the range for excellent condition ($20 to $50, or $30). Campanella is the only card whose near-mint-condition range exceeded its excellent-condition range.

9. **A.** An excellent-condition Willie Mays card had a top price of $300 at the start of the season and realized 120% of its price at the end of the season. So its highest price for such a condition card was $360. A near-mint-condition Hank Aaron card started the season with a top price of $350 and reached 105% of its price in October, or $367.50. So the difference in highest prices of these condition cards was $750.

10. A. I is true. At its lowest price, a near-mint Sandy Koufax card realized 90% (in July) of $200, or $180. The top prices for fair-condition cards of Whitey Ford, Bob Feller, Pee Wee Reese, Duke Snider, Luis Aparicio, and Roy Campanella were $50, $30, $25, $20, and $20, respectively, which equals $170.

II is false. No information is given about end-of-season 1990 prices.

III is false. The highest price realized for an excellent-condition Bob Feller was $100, whereas the lowest price for a near-mint-condition Pee Wee Reese was under $100.

Set 3

11. C. Adding the percentages, the large circulation coins represent (23% + 17% + 8%) 48%, while the average condition coins represent (23% + 18% + 10%) 51%.

12. D. The number of coins is irrelevant. Because 3%, 5%, and 8% add up to 16%, we have the following:

$16.60 \times 3\%$ plus $10.20 \times 5\%$ plus $8.80 \times 8\% = 1.712$, and $1.712 \div .16 = 10.70$, which is the average price.

13. C. There are (5% + 10% + 18%) 33% in this category. Thirty-three percent of 20,000 is 6,600.

14. D. The coin collector previously collected only fine condition coins, or a total of $17 + 10 + 6 = 33\%$ of the coins available for sale. Now the collector collecting both fine and uncirculated adds another 16% (3 + 5 + 8) of the coins available for sale. Percent increase is found by dividing the change (in this case 16%) by the starting point (in this case 33%): $16 \div 33$ is approximately 48%.

15. B. Average circulation coins of fine condition represent 10% of the total of 100, or 10 coins, at $8.80 each, for a total price of $88. Small circulation coins of average condition represent 10% of the total of 100, or 10 coins, at $6.30 each, or a total price of $63. Therefore a collector would pay $25 more for all the average circulation coins of fine condition than for all the small circulation coins of average condition.

BASIC MATH REVIEW

The following pages are designed to give you an intensive review of some of the basic skills used on the GMAT Quantitative section: arithmetic, algebra, geometry, axioms, properties of numbers, terms, and simple statistics. Before you begin the diagnostic review tests, it would be wise to become familiar with basic mathematics terminology, formulas, and general mathematical information, which are covered first in this chapter. Then proceed to the arithmetic diagnostic test, which you should take to spot your weak areas. Then use the arithmetic review that follows to strengthen those areas.

After reviewing the arithmetic, take the algebra diagnostic test and once again use the review that follows to strengthen your weak areas. Next, take the geometry diagnostic test and carefully read the complete geometry review.

Even if you are strong in arithmetic, algebra, and geometry, you may wish to skim the topic headings in each area to refresh your memory of important concepts. If you are weak in math, you should read through the complete review.

Symbols, Terminology, Formulas, and General Mathematical Information

Common Math Symbols and Terms

Symbol References:

$=$	is equal to
$\neq$	is not equal to
$>$	is greater than
$<$	is less than
$\geq$	is greater than or equal to
$\leq$	is less than or equal to
$\parallel$	is parallel to
$\perp$	is perpendicular to

Natural numbers—the counting numbers: 1, 2, 3, . . .

Whole numbers—the counting numbers beginning with zero: 0, 1, 2, 3, . . .

Integers—positive and negative whole numbers and zero: . . . –3, –2, –1, 0, 1, 2, . . .

Odd numbers—numbers not divisible by 2: 1, 3, 5, 7, . . .

Even numbers—numbers divisible by 2: 0, 2, 4, 6, . . .

Prime number—number divisible by only 1 and itself: 2, 3, 5, 7, 11, 13, . . .

Composite number—number divisible by more than just 1 and itself: 4, 6, 8, 9, 10, 12, 14, 15, . . . (0 and 1 are neither prime nor composite)

Squares—the results when numbers are multiplied by themselves: $2 \times 2 = 4$; $3 \times 3 = 9$. Examples of squares are 1, 4, 9, 16, 25, 36, . . .

Cubes—the results when numbers are multiplied by themselves twice: $2 \times 2 \times 2 = 8$; $3 \times 3 \times 3 = 27$. Examples of cubes are 1, 8, 27, 64 . . .

Math Formulas

Triangle	Perimeter $= s_1 + s_2 + s_3$
	Area $= \frac{1}{2}bh$
Square	Perimeter $= 4s$
	Area $= s \times s$, or s^2
Rectangle	Perimeter $= 2(b + h)$, or $2b + 2h$
	Area $= bh$, or lw
Parallelogram	Perimeter $= 2(l + w)$, or $2l + 2w$
	Area $= bh$
Trapezoid	Perimeter $= b_1 + b_2 + s_1 + s_2$
	Area $= \frac{1}{2}h(b_1 + b_2)$, or $h\frac{b_1 + b_2}{2}$
Circle	Circumference $= 2\pi r$, or πd
	Area $= \pi r^2$

Cube	Volume $= s \cdot s \cdot s = s^3$
	Surface area $= s \cdot s \cdot 6$
Rectangular Prism	Volume $= l \cdot w \cdot h$
	Surface area $= 2(lw) + 2(lh) + 2(wh)$
Right triangles	$a^2 + b^2 = c^2$: The sum of the square of the legs of a right triangle equals the square of the hypotenuse. This is known as the **Pythagorean theorem.**

Important Equivalents

$\frac{1}{100} = .01 = 1\%$ $\frac{1}{3} = .33\frac{1}{3} = 33\frac{1}{3}\%$

$\frac{1}{10} = .1 = .10 = 10\%$ $\frac{2}{3} = .66\frac{2}{3} = 66\frac{2}{3}\%$

$\frac{1}{5} = \frac{2}{10} = .2 = .20 = 20\%$ $\frac{1}{8} = .125 = .12\frac{1}{2} = 12\frac{1}{2}\%$

$\frac{3}{10} = .3 = .30 = 30\%$ $\frac{3}{8} = .375 = .37\frac{1}{2} = 37\frac{1}{2}\%$

$\frac{2}{5} = \frac{4}{10} = .4 = .40 = 40\%$ $\frac{5}{8} = .625 = .62\frac{1}{2} = 62\frac{1}{2}\%$

$\frac{1}{2} = \frac{5}{10} = .5 = .50 = 50\%$ $\frac{7}{8} = .875 = .87\frac{1}{2} = 87\frac{1}{2}\%$

$\frac{3}{5} = \frac{6}{10} = .6 = .60 = 60\%$ $\frac{1}{6} = .16\frac{2}{3} = 16\frac{2}{3}\%$

$\frac{7}{10} = .7 = .70 = 70\%$ $\frac{5}{6} = .83\frac{1}{3} = 83\frac{1}{3}\%$

$\frac{4}{5} = \frac{8}{10} = .8 = .80 = 80\%$ $1 = 1.00 = 100\%$

$\frac{9}{10} = .9 = .90 = 90\%$ $2 = 2.00 = 200\%$

$\frac{1}{4} = \frac{25}{100} = .25 = 25\%$ $3\frac{1}{2} = 3.5 = 3.50 = 350\%$

$\frac{3}{4} = \frac{75}{100} = .75 = 75\%$

Measures

Customary System, or English System

Length

12 inches (in) = 1 foot (ft)

3 feet = 1 yard (yd)

36 inches = 1 yard

1,760 yards = 1 mile (mi)

5,280 feet = 1 mile

Area

144 square inches (sq in) = 1 square foot (sq ft)

9 square feet = 1 square yard (sq yd)

Weight

16 ounces (oz) = 1 pound (lb)

2,000 pounds = 1 ton (T)

Capacity

2 cups = 1 pint (pt)

2 pints = 1 quart (qt)

4 quarts = 1 gallon (gal)

4 pecks = 1 bushel

Time

365 days = 1 year

52 weeks = 1 year

10 years = 1 decade

100 years = 1 century

Metric System, or The International System of Units

Length—meter

Kilometer (km) = 1,000 meters (m)

Hectometer (hm) = 100 meters

Dekameter (dam) = 10 meters

10 decimeters (dm) = 1 meter

100 centimeters (cm) = 1 meter

1,000 millimeters (mm) = 1 meter

Volume—liter

1,000 milliliters (ml or mL) = 1 liter (l or L)

1,000 liters = 1 kiloliter (kl or kL)

Mass—gram

1,000 milligrams (mg) = 1 gram (g)

1,000 grams = 1 kilogram (kg)

1,000 kilograms = 1 metric ton (t)

Some approximations

One meter is a little more than a yard.

One kilometer is about .6 mile.

One kilogram is about 2.2 pounds.

One liter is slightly more than a quart.

Math Words and Phrases

Words that signal an operation:

Addition

- Sum
- Total
- Plus
- Increase
- More than
- Greater than

Subtraction

- Difference
- Less
- Decreased
- Reduced
- Fewer
- Have left

Multiplication

- Or
- Product
- Times
- At (sometimes)
- Total (sometimes)

Division

- Quotient
- Divisor
- Dividend
- Ratio
- Parts

Mathematical Properties and Basic Statistics

Some Properties (Axioms) of Addition

Commutative means that the *order* does not make any difference.

$2 + 3 = 3 + 2$

$a + b = b + a$

Note: Commutative does *not* hold for subtraction.

$3 - 1 \neq 1 - 3$

$a - b \neq b - a$

Associative means that the *grouping* does not make any difference.

$(2 + 3) + 4 = 2 + (3 + 4)$

$(a + b) + c = a + (b + c)$

The grouping has changed (parentheses moved), but the sides are still equal.

Note: Associative does *not* hold for subtraction.

$4 - (3 - 1) \neq (4 - 3) - 1$

$a - (b - c) \neq (a - b) - c$

The *identity element* for addition is 0. Any number added to 0 gives the original number.

$3 + 0 = 3$

$a + 0 = a$

The *additive inverse* is the opposite (negative) of the number. Any number plus its additive inverse equals 0 (the identity).

$3 + (-3) = 0$; therefore, 3 and -3 are inverses

$-2 + 2 = 0$; therefore, -2 and 2 are inverses

$a + (-a) = 0$; therefore, a and $-a$ are inverses

Some Properties (Axioms) of Multiplication

Commutative means that the order does not make any difference.

$2 \times 3 = 3 \times 2$

$a \times b = b \times a$

Note: Commutative does *not* hold for division.

$2 \div 4 \neq 4 \div 2$

Associative means that the grouping does not make any difference.

$(2 \times 3) \times 4 = 2 \times (3 \times 4)$

$(a \times b) \times c = a \times (b \times c)$

The grouping has changed (parentheses moved), but the sides are still equal.

Note: Associative does *not* hold for division.

$(8 \div 4) \div 2 \neq 8 \div (4 \div 2)$

The identity element for multiplication is 1. Any number multiplied by 1 gives the original number.

$3 \times 1 = 3$

$a \times 1 = a$

The multiplicative inverse is the reciprocal of the number. Any number multiplied by its reciprocal equals 1.

$2 \times \frac{1}{2} = 1$; therefore, 2 and $\frac{1}{2}$ are inverses

$a \times \frac{1}{a} = 1$; therefore, a and $\frac{1}{a}$ are inverses

A Property of Two Operations

The distributive property is the process of distributing the number on the outside of the parentheses to each number on the inside.

$2(3 + 4) = 2(3) + 2(4)$

$a(b + c) = a(b) + a(c)$

119

Note: You cannot use the distributive property with only one operation.

$3(4 \times 5 \times 6) \neq 3(4) \times 3(5) \times 3(6)$

$a(bcd) \neq a(b) \times a(c) \times a(d)$ or $(ab)(ac)(ad)$

Some Basic Terms in Statistics

To find the arithmetic *mean,* or average, simply total the numbers and divide by the number of numbers.

Find the arithmetic mean of 3, 5, 6, 7, and 9. The total is $3 + 5 + 6 + 7 + 9 = 30$. Then divide 30 by 5, giving a mean, or average, of 6.

To find the *mode,* look for the most frequently occurring score or measure.

Find the mode of these scores: 3, 5, 5, 5, 6, 7. The mode is 5, since it appears most. If there are two modes, distribution of scores is called *bimodal.*

To find the *median,* arrange the scores or numbers in order by size. Then find the middle score or number.

Find the median of these scores: 2, 5, 7, 3, 6. First arrange them in order by size: 7, 6, 5, 3, 2. The middle score is 5; therefore, the median is 5. If the number of scores is even, take the average of the two middle scores. Find the median of these scores: 2, 5, 7, 4, 3, 6. First arrange them in order by size: 7, 6, 5, 4, 3, 2. The two middle numbers are 4 and 5; therefore, the median is 4½.

The *range* of a group of scores or numbers is calculated by subtracting the smallest from the largest.

Find the range of the scores, 3, 2, 7, 9, 12. The range is $12 - 2 = 10$.

Arithmetic Diagnostic Test

Questions

1. $6 = \frac{?}{4}$

2. Change $5\frac{3}{4}$ to an improper fraction.

3. Change $\frac{32}{6}$ to a whole number or mixed number in lowest terms.

4. $\frac{2}{5} + \frac{3}{5} =$

5. $\frac{1}{3} + \frac{1}{4} + \frac{1}{2} =$

6. $1\frac{3}{8} + 2\frac{5}{6} =$

7. $\frac{7}{9} - \frac{5}{9} =$

8. $11 - \frac{2}{3} =$

9. $6\frac{1}{4} - 3\frac{3}{4} =$

10. $\frac{1}{6} \times \frac{1}{6} =$

11. $2\frac{3}{8} \times 1\frac{5}{6} =$

12. $\frac{1}{4} \div \frac{3}{2} =$

13. $2\frac{3}{7} \div 1\frac{1}{4} =$

14. $.07 + 1.2 + .471 =$

15. $.45 - .003 =$

16. $\$78.24 - \$31.68 =$

17. $.5 \times .5 =$

18. $8.001 \times 2.3 =$

19. $.7\sqrt{.147}$

20. $.002\sqrt{12}$

21. $\frac{1}{3}$ of $\$7.20 =$

22. Circle the larger number: 7.9 or 4.35.

23. 39 out of 100 means:

24. Change 4% to a decimal.

25. 46% of 58 =

26. Change .009 to a percent.

27. Change 12.5% to a fraction.

28. Change $\frac{3}{8}$ to a percent.

29. Is 93 prime?

30. What is the percent increase in a rise in temperature from 80° to 100°?

31. Average 0, 8, and 10.

32. $8^2 =$

33. Approximate $\sqrt{30}$.

Answers

1. 24
2. $^{23}/_{4}$
3. $5^{2}/_{6}$ or $5^{1}/_{3}$
4. $^{5}/_{5}$ or 1
5. $^{13}/_{12}$ or $1^{1}/_{12}$
6. $4^{5}/_{24}$
7. $^{2}/_{9}$
8. $10^{1}/_{3}$
9. $2^{3}/_{4}$ or $2^{1}/_{2}$
10. $^{1}/_{36}$
11. $^{209}/_{48}$ or $4^{17}/_{48}$
12. $^{1}/_{6}$
13. $^{68}/_{35}$ or $1^{33}/_{35}$
14. 1.741
15. .447
16. $46.56
17. .25
18. 18.4023
19. .21
20. 6,000
21. $2.40
22. 7.9
23. 39% or $^{39}/_{100}$
24. .04
25. 26.68
26. .9% or $^{9}/_{10}$%
27. $^{125}/_{1000}$ or $^{1}/_{8}$
28. 37.5% or $37^{1}/_{2}$%
29. No
30. 25%
31. 6
32. 64
33. 5.5 or $5^{1}/_{2}$

Arithmetic Review

Rounding Off

To round off any number:

1. Underline the place value to which you're rounding off.

2. Look to the immediate right (one place) of your underlined place value.

3. Identify the number (the one to the right). If it is 5 or higher, round your underlined place value up 1. If the number (the one to the right) is 4 or less, leave your underlined place value as it is and change all the other numbers to its right to zeros. For example:

Round to the nearest thousandth:

345,678 becomes 346,000

928,499 becomes 928,000

This works with decimals as well. Round to the nearest hundredth:

3.4<u>6</u>78 becomes 3.47

298,435.0<u>8</u>3 becomes 298,435.08

Place Value

Each position in any number has *place value.* For instance, in the number 485, 4 is in the hundreds place, 8 is in the tens place, and 5 is in the ones place. Thus, place value is as follows:

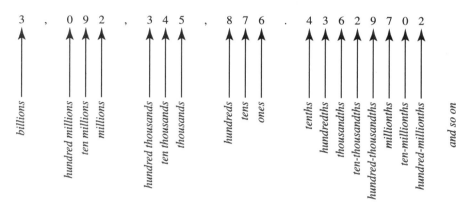

Fractions

Fractions consist of two numbers: a *numerator* (which is above the line) and a *denominator* (which is below the line).

$\frac{1}{2}$ numerator / denominator or numerator ½ denominator

The denominator lets us know the number of equal parts into which something is divided. The numerator tells us how many of these equal parts are contained in the fraction. Thus, if the fraction is ³⁄₅ of a pie, then the denominator 5 tells us that the pie has been divided into 5 equal parts, of which 3 (numerator) are in the fraction.

Sometimes it helps to think of the dividing line (in the middle of a fraction) as meaning "out of." In other words, ³⁄₅ would also mean 3 "out of" 5 equal pieces from the whole pie.

Common Fractions and Improper Fractions

A fraction like ³⁄₅, where the numerator is smaller than the denominator, is less than one. This kind of fraction is called a *common fraction.*

But sometimes a fraction may represent more than one. This is when the numerator is larger than the denominator. Thus, $^{12}/_7$ is more than one. This is called an *improper fraction.*

Mixed Numbers

When a term contains both a whole number (such as 3, 8, or 25) and a fraction (such as ½, ¼, or ¾), it is called a *mixed number.* For instance, 5¼ and 290¾ are both mixed numbers.

To change an improper fraction to a mixed number, you divide the denominator into the numerator. For example:

$$\frac{18}{5} = 3\tfrac{3}{5} \qquad 5\overline{)18}$$

To change a mixed number to an improper fraction, you multiply the denominator times the whole number, add in the numerator, and put the total over the original denominator. For example:

$$4\tfrac{1}{2} = \tfrac{9}{2} \qquad 2 \times 4 + 1 = 9$$

Reducing Fractions

A fraction must be reduced to *lowest terms.* This is done by dividing both the numerator and the denominator by the largest number that will divide evenly into both. For example, $^{14}/_{16}$ is reduced by dividing both terms by 2, thus giving us $^7/_8$. Likewise, $^{20}/_{25}$ is reduced to $^4/_5$ by dividing both numerator and denominator by 5.

Adding Fractions

To add fractions, you must first change all denominators to their *lowest common denominator* (LCD)—the lowest number that can be divided evenly by all the denominators in the problem. When you have all the denominators the same, you may add fractions by simply adding the numerators (the denominator remains the same). For example:

$$\frac{3}{8} = \frac{3}{8}$$
$$+\frac{1}{2} = \frac{4}{8}$$
$$\frac{7}{8}$$

one-half is changed to four-eights

$$\frac{1}{4} = \frac{3}{12}$$
$$+\frac{1}{3} = \frac{4}{12}$$
$$\frac{7}{12}$$

change both fractions to LCD of 12

In the first example, we changed the $\frac{1}{2}$ to $\frac{4}{8}$ because 8 is the lowest common denominator, and then we added the numerators 3 and 4 to get $\frac{7}{8}$.

In the second example, we had to change both fractions to get the lowest common denominator of 12, and then we added the numerators to get $\frac{7}{12}$. Of course, if the denominators are already the same, just add the numerators. For example:

$$\frac{6}{11} + \frac{3}{11} = \frac{9}{11}$$

Adding Mixed Numbers

To add mixed numbers, the same rule (find the LCD) applies, but make sure that you always add the whole number to get your final answer. For example:

$$
\begin{aligned}
2\frac{1}{2} &= 2\frac{2}{4} \quad \longleftarrow \left\{ \begin{array}{l} \text{change one-half} \\ \text{to two-fourths} \end{array} \right. \\
+\ 3\frac{1}{4} &= 3\frac{1}{4} \\
\hline
&\ \ 5\frac{3}{4} \\
&\quad \nwarrow \underline{\qquad} \left\{ \begin{array}{l} \text{remember to add} \\ \text{the whole numbers} \end{array} \right.
\end{aligned}
$$

Subtracting Fractions

To subtract fractions, the same rule (find the LCD) applies, except that you subtract the numerators. For example:

$$
\begin{array}{ll}
\frac{7}{8} = \frac{7}{8} & \qquad \frac{3}{4} = \frac{9}{12} \\
-\frac{1}{4} = \frac{2}{8} & \qquad -\frac{1}{3} = \frac{4}{12} \\
\hline
\quad \frac{5}{8} & \qquad \quad \frac{5}{12}
\end{array}
$$

Subtracting Mixed Numbers

When you subtract mixed numbers, sometimes you may have to "borrow" from the whole number, just like you sometimes borrow from the next column when subtracting ordinary numbers. For example:

$$
\begin{array}{ll}
6\overset{4}{\cancel{5}}\overset{11}{1} & \quad \overset{3\frac{6}{6}}{\cancel{4}}\frac{1}{6} \\
-\ 129 & \quad -\ 2\frac{5}{6} \\
\hline
\ \ 522 & \quad \ 1\frac{2}{6} = 1\frac{1}{3}
\end{array}
$$

you borrowed 1   you borrowed one in
from the 10's   the form $\frac{6}{6}$ from
column   the 1's column

To subtract a mixed number from a whole number, you have to "borrow" from the whole number. For example:

$$6 \quad = 5\tfrac{5}{5} \quad \longleftarrow \begin{cases} \text{borrow one in the form of} \\ \tfrac{5}{5} \text{ from the 6} \end{cases}$$
$$\underline{-3\tfrac{1}{5} \; = 3\tfrac{1}{5}}$$
$$2\tfrac{4}{5}$$
$$\longleftarrow \underline{\qquad} \begin{cases} \text{remember to subtract the} \\ \text{remaining whole numbers} \end{cases}$$

Multiplying Fractions

Simply multiply the numerators; then multiply the denominators. Reduce to lowest terms if necessary. For example:

$$\tfrac{2}{3} \times \tfrac{5}{12} = \tfrac{10}{36} \quad \text{reduce } \tfrac{10}{36} \text{ to } \tfrac{5}{18}$$

This answer has to be reduced because it wasn't in lowest terms.

Canceling when multiplying fractions: You could first have "canceled." That would have eliminated the need to reduce your answer. To cancel, find a number that divides evenly into one numerator and one denominator. In this case, 2 will divide evenly into 2 in the numerator (it goes in one time) and 12 in the denominator (it goes in 6 times). Thus:

$$\frac{\overset{1}{\cancel{2}}}{3} \times \frac{5}{\underset{6}{\cancel{12}}} =$$

Now that you've canceled, you can multiply out as you did before.

$$\frac{\overset{1}{\cancel{2}}}{3} \times \frac{5}{\underset{6}{\cancel{12}}} = \frac{5}{8}$$

Remember, you may cancel only when *multiplying* fractions.

Multiplying Mixed Numbers

To multiply mixed numbers, first change any mixed number to an improper fraction. Then multiply as previously shown. To change mixed numbers to improper fractions:

1. Multiply the whole number by the denominator of the fraction.
2. Add this to the numerator of the fraction.
3. This is now your numerator.
4. The denominator remains the same.

$$3\tfrac{1}{3} \times 2\tfrac{1}{4} = \tfrac{10}{3} \times \tfrac{9}{4} = \tfrac{90}{12} = 7\tfrac{6}{12} = 7\tfrac{1}{2}$$

Then change the answer, if in improper form, back to a mixed number and reduce if necessary.

Dividing Fractions

To divide fractions, invert (turn upside down) the second fraction and multiply. Then reduce if necessary. For example:

$$\frac{1}{6} \div \frac{1}{5} = \frac{1}{6} \times \frac{5}{1} = \frac{5}{6} \qquad \frac{1}{6} \div \frac{1}{3} = \frac{1}{6} \times \frac{3}{1} = \frac{1}{2}$$

Simplifying Fractions

If either numerator or denominator consists of several numbers, these numbers must be combined into one number. Then reduce if necessary. For example:

$$\frac{28+14}{26+17} = \frac{42}{43} \text{ or}$$

$$\frac{\frac{1}{4}+\frac{1}{2}}{\frac{1}{3}+\frac{1}{4}} = \frac{\frac{1}{4}+\frac{2}{4}}{\frac{4}{12}+\frac{3}{12}} = \frac{\frac{3}{4}}{\frac{7}{12}} = \frac{3}{4} \times \frac{12}{7} = \frac{36}{28} = \frac{9}{7} = 1\frac{2}{7}$$

Decimals

Fractions may also be written in decimal form by using a symbol called a *decimal point*. All numbers to the left of the decimal point are whole numbers. All numbers to the right of the decimal point are fractions with denominators of only 10, 100, 1,000, 10,000, and so on, as follows:

$$.6 \;\; = \;\; \frac{6}{10} \;\; = \frac{3}{5} \qquad .0007 = \frac{7}{10,000}$$

$$.7 \;\; = \;\; \frac{7}{10} \qquad\qquad .00007 = \frac{7}{100,000}$$

$$.07 \;\; = \;\; \frac{7}{100} \qquad\qquad .25 = \frac{25}{100} = \frac{1}{4}$$

$$.007 = \frac{7}{1,000}$$

Adding and Subtracting Decimals

To add or subtract decimals, just line up the decimal points and then add or subtract in the same manner you would add or subtract regular numbers. For example:

$$23.6 + 1.75 + 300.002 = \begin{array}{r} 23.6 \\ 1.75 \\ \underline{300.002} \\ 325.352 \end{array}$$

Adding in zeros can make the problem easier to work:

$$
\begin{array}{r}
23.600 \\
1.750 \\
\underline{300.002} \\
325.352
\end{array}
$$

$$
54.26 - 1.1 =
\begin{array}{r}
54.26 \\
\underline{-\,1.10} \\
53.16
\end{array}
$$

and

$$
78.9 - 37.43 =
\begin{array}{r}
78.\overset{8}{\cancel{9}}{}^{1}0 \\
\underline{-37.43} \\
41.47
\end{array}
$$

Whole numbers can have decimal points to their right. For example:

$$
17 - 8.43 =
\begin{array}{r}
1\overset{6}{7}.\overset{9}{\cancel{0}}{}^{1}0 \\
\underline{-\ 8.43} \\
8.57
\end{array}
$$

Multiplying Decimals

To multiply decimals, just multiply as usual. Then count the total number of digits above the line which are to the right of all decimal points. Place your decimal point in your answer so there is the same number of digits to the right of it as there was above the line. For example:

$$
\begin{array}{r}
40.012 \\
\times\quad 3.1 \\
\hline
40012 \\
\underline{120036\quad} \\
124.0372
\end{array}
$$

40.012 ← 3 digits { total of 4 digits above the line that are to the right of the decimal point

3.1 ← 1 digit

124.0372 ← 4 digits { decimal point placed so there is same number of digits to the right of the decimal point

Dividing Decimals

Dividing decimals is the same as dividing other numbers, except that if the divisor (the number you're dividing by) has a decimal, move it to the right as many places as necessary until it is a whole number. Then move the decimal point in the dividend (the number being divided into) the same number of places. Sometimes you may have to add zeros to the dividend (the number inside the division sign).

$$1.27 \overline{)5.} = 125 \overline{\smash{)}500.}^{4.}$$

or

$$0.002 \overline{)26.} = 2 \overline{\smash{)}26000.}^{13000.}$$

Conversions

Changing Decimals to Percents

To change decimals to percents:

1. Move the decimal point two places to the right.
2. Insert a percent sign.

    $.75 = 75\%$ $.05 = 5\%$

Changing Percents to Decimals

To change percents to decimals:

1. Eliminate the percent sign.
2. Move the decimal point two places to the left. (Sometimes adding zeros will be necessary.)

    $75\% = .75$ $5\% = .05$

    $23\% = .23$ $.2\% = .002$

Changing Fractions to Percents

To change a fraction to a percent:

1. Multiply by 100.
2. Insert a percent sign.

    $\frac{1}{2} = (\frac{1}{2}) \times 100 = \frac{100}{2} = 50\%$

    $\frac{2}{5} = (\frac{2}{5}) \times 100 = \frac{200}{5} = 40\%$

Changing Percents to Fractions

To change percents to fractions:

1. Divide the percent by 100.
2. Eliminate the percent sign.
3. Reduce if necessary.

$$60\% = {}^{60}\!/_{100} = {}^{3}\!/_{5} \qquad 13\% = {}^{13}\!/_{100}$$

Changing Fractions to Decimals

To change a fraction to a decimal, simply do what the operation says. In other words, ${}^{13}\!/_{20}$ means 13 divided by 20. So do just that (insert decimal points and zeros accordingly):

$$20\overline{)13.00} = .65 \qquad {}^{5}\!/_{8} = 8\overline{)5.00} = .625$$

Changing Decimals to Fractions

To change a decimal to a fraction:

1. Move the decimal point two places to the right.
2. Put that number over 100.
3. Reduce if necessary.

$$.65 = {}^{65}\!/_{100} = {}^{13}\!/_{20}$$

$$.05 = {}^{5}\!/_{100} = {}^{1}\!/_{20}$$

$$.75 = {}^{75}\!/_{100} = {}^{3}\!/_{4}$$

Read it: .8

Write it: ${}^{8}\!/_{10}$

Reduce it: ${}^{4}\!/_{5}$

Percents

Finding Percent of a Number

To determine percent of a number, change the percent to a fraction or decimal (whichever is easier for you) and multiply. Remember, the word "of" means multiply.

What is 20% of 80?

$(^{20}/_{100}) \times 80 = {}^{1600}/_{100} = 16$ or $.20 \times 80 = 16.00 = 16$

What is 12% of 50?

$(^{12}/_{100}) \times 50 = {}^{600}/_{100} = 6$ or $.12 \times 50 = 6.00 = 6$

What is ½% of 18?

$\frac{\frac{1}{2}}{100} \times 18 = (1/200) \times 18 = 18/200 = 9/100$ or $.005 \times 18 = .09$

Other Applications of Percent

Turn the question word-for-word into an equation. For "what" substitute the letter x; for "is" substitute an *equal sign*; for "of" substitute a *multiplication sign*. Change percents to decimals or fractions, whichever you find easier. Then solve the equation.

18 is what percent of 90?

$18 = x(90)$

$18/90 = x$

$1/5 = x$

$20\% = x$

10 is 50% of what number?

$10 = .50(x)$

$10/.50 = x$

$20 = x$

What is 15% of 60?

$x = (15/100) \times 60 = 90/10 = 9$

or $.15(60) = 9$

Percentage Increase or Decrease

To find the *percentage change* (increase or decrease), use this formula:

$$\frac{\text{change}}{\text{starting point}} \times 100 = \text{percentage change}$$

For example:

What is the percentage decrease of a $500 item on sale for $400?

Change: $500 - 400 = 100$

$$\frac{change}{starting\ point} \times 100 = \frac{100}{500} \times 100 = \frac{1}{5} \times 100 = 20\% \text{ decrease}$$

What is the percentage increase of Jon's salary if it went from $150 a month to $200 a month?

Change: $200 - 150 = 50$

$$\frac{change}{starting\ point} \times 100 = \frac{50}{150} \times 100 = \frac{1}{3} \times 100 = 33\frac{1}{3}\% \text{ increase}$$

Prime Numbers

A *prime number* is a number that can be evenly divided by only itself and 1. For example, 19 is a prime number because it can be evenly divided only by 19 and 1, but 21 is not a prime number because 21 can be evenly divided by other numbers (3 and 7).

The only even prime number is 2; thereafter any even number may be divided evenly by 2. Zero and 1 are *not* prime numbers. The first ten prime numbers are 2, 3, 5, 7, 11, 13, 17, 19, 23, and 29.

Arithmetic Mean, or Average

To find the *average* of a group of numbers:

1. Add them up.

2. Divide by the number of items you added.

For example: What is the average of 10, 20, 35, 40, and 45?

$$10 + 20 + 35 + 40 + 45 = 150$$

$$150 \div 5 = 30$$

The average is 30.

What is the average of 0, 12, 18, 20, 31, and 45?

$$0 + 12 + 18 + 20 + 31 + 45 = 126$$

$$126 \div 6 = 21$$

The average is 21.

What is the average of 25, 27, 27, and 27?

$$25 + 27 + 27 + 27 = 106$$

$$106 \div 4 = 26\tfrac{1}{2}$$

The average is $26\tfrac{1}{2}$

Median

A *median* is simply the middle number of a list of numbers after it has been written in order. (If the list contains an even number of items, average the two middle numbers to get the median.) For example, in the following list—3, 4, 6, 9, 21, 24, 56—the number 9 is the median.

Mode

The *mode* is simply the number most frequently listed in a group of numbers. For example, in the following group—5, 9, 7, 3, 9, 4, 6, 9, 7, 9, 2—the mode is 9 because it appears more often than any other number.

Squares and Square Roots

To *square* a number, just multiply it by itself. For example, 6 squared (written 6^2) is 6×6 or 36. 36 is called a perfect square (the square of a whole number). Any exponent means to multiply by itself that many times. For example:

$$5^3 = 5 \times 5 \times 5 = 125$$

$$8^2 = 8 \times 8 = 64$$

Remember, $x^1 = x$ and $x^0 = 1$ when x is any number (other than 0).

Following is a list of some perfect squares:

$1^2 = 1$	$7^2 = 49$
$2^2 = 4$	$8^2 = 64$
$3^2 = 9$	$9^2 = 81$
$4^2 = 16$	$10^2 = 100$
$5^2 = 25$	$11^2 = 121$
$6^2 = 36$	$12^2 = 144$

Square roots of nonperfect squares can be approximated. Two approximations you may wish to remember are:

$$\sqrt{2} \cong 1.4$$

$$\sqrt{3} \cong 1.7$$

To find the *square root* of a number, you want to find some number that when multiplied by itself gives you the original number. In other words, to find the square root of 25, you want to find the number that when multiplied by itself gives you 25. The square root of 25, then, is 5. The symbol for square root is $\sqrt{}$. Following is a list of perfect (whole number) square roots:

$\sqrt{1} = 1$	$\sqrt{36} = 6$
$\sqrt{4} = 2$	$\sqrt{49} = 7$
$\sqrt{9} = 3$	$\sqrt{64} = 8$
$\sqrt{16} = 4$	$\sqrt{81} = 9$
$\sqrt{25} = 5$	$\sqrt{100} = 10$

Square Root Rules

Two numbers multiplied under a radical (square root) sign equal the product of the two square roots. For example:

$$\sqrt{(4)(25)} = \sqrt{4} \times \sqrt{25} = 2 \times 5 = 10 \text{ or } \sqrt{100} = 10$$

and likewise with division:

$$\sqrt{\frac{64}{4}} = \frac{\sqrt{64}}{\sqrt{4}} = \frac{8}{2} = 4 \text{ or } \sqrt{16} = 4$$

Addition and subtraction, however, are different. The numbers must be combined under the radical before any computation of square roots may be done. For example:

$$\sqrt{10+6} = \sqrt{16} = 4 \qquad \sqrt{10+6} \text{ does } not \text{ equal } [\neq] \sqrt{10} + \sqrt{6}$$

$$\sqrt{93-12} = \sqrt{81} = 9$$

Approximating Square Roots

To find a square root which will not be a whole number, you should approximate. For example:

Approximate $\sqrt{57}$

Because $\sqrt{57}$ is between $\sqrt{49}$ and $\sqrt{64}$, it will fall somewhere between 7 and 8. And because 57 is just about halfway between 49 and 64, $\sqrt{51}$ is therefore approximately 7½.

Approximate $\sqrt{83}$

$$\frac{9}{\sqrt{81}} < \sqrt{83} < \frac{10}{\sqrt{100}}$$

Since $\sqrt{83}$ is slightly more than $\sqrt{81}$ (whose square root is 9), then $\sqrt{83}$ is a little more than 9. Since 83 is only two steps up from the nearest perfect square (81) and 17 steps to the next perfect square (100), then 83 is ²⁄₁₉ of the way to 100.

$$^2\!/_{19} \cong {}^2\!/_{20} \cong {}^1\!/_{10} = .1$$

Therefore, $\sqrt{83} \cong 9.1$

Simplifying Square Roots

To simplify numbers under a radical (square root sign):

1. Factor the number to two numbers, one (or more) of which is a perfect square.
2. Take the square root of the perfect square(s).
3. Leave the others under the $\sqrt{}$.

Simplify $\sqrt{75}$

$$\sqrt{75} = \sqrt{25 \times 3} = \sqrt{25} \times \sqrt{3} = 5\sqrt{3}$$

Simplify $\sqrt{200}$

$$\sqrt{200} = \sqrt{100 \times 2} = \sqrt{100} \times \sqrt{2} = 10\sqrt{2}$$

Simplify $\sqrt{900}$

$$\sqrt{900} = \sqrt{100 \times 9} = \sqrt{100} \times \sqrt{9} = 10 \times 3 = 30$$

Signed Numbers (Positive Numbers and Negative Numbers)

On a number line, numbers to the right of 0 are positive. Numbers to the left of 0 are negative, as follows:

Given any two numbers on a number line, the one on the right is always larger, regardless of its sign (positive or negative).

Adding Signed Numbers

When adding two numbers with the same sign (either both positive or both negative), add the numbers and keep the same sign. For example:

$$
\begin{array}{r} +5 \\ ++7 \\ \hline +12 \end{array}
\qquad
\begin{array}{r} -8 \\ +-3 \\ \hline -11 \end{array}
$$

When adding two numbers with different signs (one positive and one negative), subtract the numbers and keep the sign from the larger one. For example:

$$
\begin{array}{r} +5 \\ +-7 \\ \hline -2 \end{array}
\qquad
\begin{array}{r} -59 \\ ++72 \\ \hline +13 \end{array}
$$

Subtracting Signed Numbers

To subtract positive and/or negative numbers, just change the sign of the number being subtracted and then add. For example:

$$
\begin{array}{r} +12 \\ -+4 \\ \hline \end{array}
\quad
\begin{array}{r} +12 \\ +-4 \\ \hline +8 \end{array}
\quad
\begin{array}{r} -19 \\ -+6 \\ \hline \end{array}
\quad
\begin{array}{r} -19 \\ +-6 \\ \hline -25 \end{array}
$$

$$
\begin{array}{r} -14 \\ --4 \\ \hline \end{array}
\quad
\begin{array}{r} -14 \\ ++4 \\ \hline -10 \end{array}
\quad
\begin{array}{r} +20 \\ --3 \\ \hline \end{array}
\quad
\begin{array}{r} +20 \\ ++3 \\ \hline +23 \end{array}
$$

Multiplying and Dividing Signed Numbers

To multiply or divide signed numbers, treat them just like regular numbers but remember this rule: An odd number of negative signs will produce a negative answer; an even number of negative signs will produce a positive answer. For example:

$$(-3)(+8)(-5)(-1)(-2) = +240$$

$$(-3)(+8)(-1)(-2) = -48$$

$$\frac{-64}{-2} = +32$$

$$\frac{-64}{2} = -32$$

Parentheses

Parentheses are used to group numbers. Everything inside parentheses must be done before any other operations. For example:

$$6 - (-3 + a - 2b + c) =$$

$$6 + (+3 - a + 2b - c) =$$

$$6 + 3 - a + 2b - c = 9 - a + 2b - c$$

Order of Operations

If multiplication, division, powers, addition, parentheses, and so on, are all contained in one problem, the order of operations is as follows:

1. parentheses
2. powers and square roots

3. multiplication ⎫
4. division ⎭ whichever comes first, left to right

5. addition ⎫
6. subtraction ⎭ whichever comes first, left to right

For example:

$$10 - 3 \times 6 + 10^2 + (6 + 1) \times 4 =$$

$$10 - 3 \times 6 + 10^2 + (7) \times 4 = \text{ (parentheses first)}$$

$$10 - 3 \times 6 + 100 + (7) \times 4 = \text{ (powers next)}$$

$$10 - 18 + 100 + 28 = \text{ (multiplication)}$$

$$-8 + 100 + 28 = \text{ (addition/subtraction, left to right)}$$

$$92 + 28 = 120$$

An easy way to remember the order of operations after parentheses is: *Please My Dear Aunt Sarah* (*Powers, Multiplication, Division, Addition, Subtraction*).

Algebra Diagnostic Test

Questions

1. Solve for x: $x + 5 = 17$

2. Solve for x: $4x + 9 = 21$

3. Solve for x: $5x + 7 = 3x - 9$

4. Solve for x: $mx - n = y$

5. Solve for x: $\frac{r}{x} = \frac{s}{t}$

6. Solve for y: $\frac{3}{7} = \frac{y}{8}$

7. Evaluate: $3x^2 + 5y + 7$ if $x = -2$ and $y = 3$

8. Simplify: $8xy^2 + 3xy + 4xy^2 - 2xy =$

9. Simplify: $6x^2(4x^3y) =$

10. Simplify: $(5x + 2z) + (3x - 4z) =$

11. Simplify: $(4x - 7z) - (3x - 4z) =$

12. Factor: $ab + ac$

13. Factor: $x^2 - 5x - 14$

14. Solve: $x^2 + 7x = -10$

15. Solve for x: $2x + 3 \le 11$

16. Solve for x: $3x + 4 \ge 5x - 8$

Answers

1. $x = 12$

2. $x = 3$

3. $x = -8$

4. $x = (y + n)/m$

5. $x = \frac{rt}{s}$

6. $y = {}^{24}\!/_7$ or $3\,{}^3\!/_7$

7. 34

8. $12xy^2 + xy$

9. $24x^5y$

10. $8x - 2z$

11. $x - 3z$

12. $a(b + c)$

13. $(x - 7)(x + 2)$

14. $x = -2$ or $x = -5$

15. $x \le 4$

16. $x \le 6$

Algebra Review

Equations

An *equation* is a relationship between numbers and/or symbols. It helps to remember that an equation is like a balance scale, with the equal sign (=) being the fulcrum, or center. Thus, if you do the *same thing to both sides* of the equal sign (say, add 5 to each side), the equation will still be balanced. To solve the equation $x - 5 = 23$, you must get x by itself on one side; therefore, add 5 to both sides:

$$x - 5 = 23$$
$$\underline{+5 \quad +5}$$
$$x = 28$$

In the same manner, you may subtract, multiply, or divide *both* sides of an equation by the same (nonzero) number, and the equation will not change. Sometimes you may have to use more than one step to solve for an unknown. For example:

$$3x + 4 = 19$$

Subtract 4 from both sides to get the $3x$ by itself on one side:

$$3x + 4 = 19$$
$$\underline{-4 \quad -4}$$
$$3x \quad = 15$$

Then divide both sides by 3 to get x:

$$\frac{3x}{3} = \frac{15}{3}$$
$$x = 5$$

Remember: Solving an equation requires using opposite operations until the letter is on a side by itself (for addition, subtract; for multiplication, divide; and so on).

Understood Multiplying

When two or more letters, or a number and letters, are written next to each other, they are understood to be multiplied. Thus, $8x$ means 8 times x. Or ab means a times b. Or $18ab$ means 18 times a times b.

Parentheses also represent multiplication. Thus, $(a)b$ means a times b. A raised dot also means multiplication. Thus, $6 \cdot 5$ means 6 times 5.

Literal Equations

Literal equations have no numbers, only symbols (letters). For example:

Solve for Q: $QP - X = Y$

First add X to both sides:

$$QP - X = Y$$
$$\underline{\quad +X \qquad +X}$$
$$QP \qquad = Y + X$$

Then divide both sides by P:

$$\frac{QP}{P} = \frac{Y+X}{P}$$

$$Q = \frac{Y+X}{P}$$

Again opposite operations were used to isolate Q.

Cross Multiplying

Solve for x: $\quad \dfrac{b}{x} = \dfrac{p}{q}$

To solve this equation quickly, you cross multiply. To cross multiply:

1. Bring the denominators up next to the opposite side numerators.
2. Multiply.

$$\frac{b}{x} = \frac{p}{q}$$

$$bq = px$$

Then divide both sides by p to get x alone:

$$\frac{bq}{p} = \frac{px}{p}$$

$$\frac{bq}{p} = x \ \text{ or } \ x = \frac{bq}{p}$$

Cross multiplying can be used only when the format is two fractions separated by an equal sign.

Proportions

Proportions are written as two fractions equal to each other.

Solve this proportion for x: $\quad \dfrac{p}{q} = \dfrac{x}{y}$

This is read "*p* is to *q* as *x* is to *y*." Cross multiply and solve:

$$py = xq$$

$$\frac{py}{q} = \frac{xq}{q}$$

$$\frac{py}{q} = x \ \text{ or } \ x = \frac{py}{q}$$

Evaluating Expressions

To *evaluate* an expression, just insert the value for the unknowns and do the arithmetic. For example:

Evaluate: $2x^2 + 3y + 6$ if $x = 2$ and $y = 9$

$$2(2^2) + 3(9) + 6 =$$

$$2(4) + 27 + 6 =$$

$$8 + 27 + 6 = 41$$

Monomials and Polynomials

A *monomial* is an algebraic expression that consists of only one term. For instance, $9x$, $4a^2$, and $3mpxz^2$ are all monomials.

A *polynomial* consists of two or more terms; $x + y$, $y^2 - x^2$, and $x^2 + 3x + 5y^2$ are all polynomials.

Adding and Subtracting Monomials

To add or subtract monomials, follow the same rules as with regular signed numbers, provided that the terms are alike:

$$\begin{array}{r} 15x^2yz \\ -18x^2yz \\ \hline -\ 3x^2yz \end{array} \qquad 3x + 2x = 5x$$

Multiplying and Dividing Monomials

To multiply monomials, add the exponents of the same terms:

$$(x^3)(x^4) = x^7$$

$$(x^2y)(x^3y^2) = x^5y^3$$

$$-4(m^2n)(-3m^4n^3) = 12m^6n^4 \text{ (multiply numbers)}$$

To divide monomials, subtract the exponents of the like terms:

$$\frac{y^{15}}{y^4} = y^{11} \qquad \frac{x^5 y^2}{x^3 y} = x^2 y \qquad \frac{36a^4 b^6}{-9ab} = -4a^3 b^5$$

Remember: x is the same as x^1.

Adding and Subtracting Polynomials

To add or subtract polynomials, just arrange like terms in columns and then add or subtract:

$$
\begin{array}{l}
\quad\ a^2 + ab + b^2 \\
\text{Add:}\ \ \underline{3a^2 + 4ab - 2b^2} \\
\quad\ 4a^2 + 5ab - b^2
\end{array}
$$

$$
\begin{array}{lll}
 & a^2 + b^2 & \rightarrow \quad\ a^2 + b^2 \\
\text{Subtract:} & \underline{(-)\,2a^2 - b^2} & \underline{+-\,2a^2 + b^2} \\
 & & \quad\ -a^2 + 2b^2
\end{array}
$$

Multiplying Polynomials

To multiply polynomials, multiply each term in one polynomial by each term in the other polynomials. Then simplify if necessary:

$$(3x + a)(2x - 2a) =$$

$$
\begin{array}{llll}
\quad\ 2x - 2a & & 23 \\
\underline{\times\ 3x +\ a} & & \underline{\times 19} \\
\quad +2ax - 2a^2 & \text{similar to} & \ \ 207 \\
\underline{6x^2 - 6ax} & & \underline{\ \ 23} \\
6x^2 - 4ax - 2a^2 & & \ \ 437
\end{array}
$$

Factoring

To *factor* means to find two or more quantities whose product equals the original quantity.

Factoring out a common factor

Factor: $2y^3 - 6y$

1. Find the largest common monomial factor of each term.

2. Divide the original polynomial by this factor to obtain the second factor. (The second factor will be a polynomial.)

   For example:

   $2y^3 - 6y = 2y(y^2 - 3)$

   $x^5 - 4x^3 + x^2 = x^2(x^3 - 4x + 1)$

Factoring the difference between two squares

Factor: $x^2 - 144$

1. Find the square root of the first term and the square root of the second term.

2. Express your answer as the product of the sum of the quantities from step 1 times the difference of those quantities.

   For example:

   $x^2 - 144 = (x + 12)(x - 12)$

   $a^2 - b^2 = (a + b)(a - b)$

   Note: $x^2 + 144$ is *not* factorable.

Factoring Polynomials That Have Three Terms: $Ax^2 + Bx + C$

To factor polynomials that have three terms, of the form $Ax^2 + B + C$,

1. Check to see if you can monomial factor (factor out common terms). Then if A = 1 (that is, the first term is simply x^2), use double parentheses and factor the first term. Place these factors in the left sides of the parentheses. For example, $(x \quad)(x \quad)$.

2. Factor the last term, and place the factors in the right sides of the parentheses.

To decide on the signs of the numbers, do the following:

   If the sign of the last term is negative

   1. Find two numbers whose product is the last term and whose *difference* is the *coefficient* (number in front) of the middle term.

   2. Give the larger of these two numbers the sign of the middle term, and give the *opposite* sign to the other factor.

- If the sign of the last term is *positive*

  1. Find two numbers whose product is the last term and whose *sum* is the coefficient of the middle term.

  2. Give both factors the sign of the middle term.

For example:

1. Factor $x^2 - 3x - 10$

First check to see if you can *monomial factor* (factor out common terms). Because this is not possible, use double parentheses and factor the first terms as follows: $(x \quad)(x \quad)$. Next, factor the last term (10) into 2 times 5. (Using the information above, 5 must take the negative sign and 2 must take the positive sign because they will then total the coefficient of the middle term, which is -3). Add the proper signs, leaving

$$(x - 5)(x + 2)$$

Multiply the *means* (inner terms) and *extremes* (outer terms) to check your work.

$$(x - 5)(x + 2)$$
$$-5x$$
$$\underline{+ 2x}$$
$$- 3x \text{ (which is the middle term)}$$

To completely check, multiply the factors together.

$$\begin{array}{r} x - 5 \\ \times \quad x + 2 \\ \hline + 2x - 10 \\ x^2 - 5x \quad\quad \\ \hline x^2 - 3x + 10 \end{array}$$

2. Factor $x^2 + 8x + 15$

$$(x + 3)(x + 5)$$

Notice that $3 \times 5 = 15$ and $3 + 5 = 8$, the coefficient of the middle term. Also note that the signs of both factors are +, the sign of the middle term. To check your work:

$$(x + 3)(x + 5)$$
$$+ 3x$$
$$\underline{+ 5x}$$
$$+ 8x \text{ (the middle term)}$$

If, however, $A \neq 1$ (that is, the first term has a coefficient — for example, $4x^2 + 5x + 1$), then additional trial and error will be necessary.

3. Factor $4x^2 + 5x + 1$

$(2x +\quad)(2x +\quad)$ might work for the first term. But when 1's are used as factors to get the last term — $(2x + 1)(2x + 1)$ — the middle term comes out as $\underline{4}x$ instead of $5x$.

$$\begin{array}{c} (2x + 1)(2x + 1) \\ + 2x \\ \underline{+ 2x} \\ + 4x \end{array}$$

Therefore, try $(4x +\quad)(x +\quad)$. This time, using 1's as factors to get the last terms gives $(4x + 1)(x + 1)$. Checking for the middle term,

$$\begin{array}{c} (4x + 1)(x + 1) \\ + 1x \\ \underline{+ 4x} \\ + 5x \end{array}$$

Therefore, $4x^2 + 5x + 1 = (4x + 1)(x + 1)$.

4. Factor $5x^3 + 6x^2 + x$

Factoring out an x leaves $\quad x(5x^2 + 6x + 1)$

Now, factor as usual giving $\quad x(5x + 1)(x + 1)$

To check your work,

$$\begin{array}{c} (5x + 1)(x + 1) \\ + 1x \quad \text{(the middle term} \\ \underline{+ 5x} \quad \text{after x was} \\ + 6x \quad \text{factored out)} \end{array}$$

Solving Quadratic Equations

A *quadratic equation* is an equation that could be written as $Ax^2 + Bx + C = 0$. To solve a quadratic equation,

1. Put all terms on one side of the equal sign, leaving zero on the other side.

2. Factor.

3. Set each factor equal to zero.

4. Solve each of these equations.

5. Check by inserting your answer in the original equation.

For example:

1. Solve $x^2 - 6x = 16$

Following the steps, $x^2 - 6x = 16$ becomes $x^2 - 6x - 16 = 0$.

Factoring, $(x - 8)(x + 2) = 0$

$$x - 8 = 0 \qquad or \qquad x + 2 = 0$$

$$x = 8 \qquad\qquad x = -2$$

To check, $8^2 - 6(8) = 16 \qquad or \quad (-2)^2 - 6(-2) = 16$

$$64 - 48 = 16 \qquad\qquad 4 + 12 = 16$$

$$16 = 16 \qquad\qquad 16 = 16$$

Both values 8 and −2 are solutions to the original equation.

2. Solve $y^2 = -6y - 5$

Setting all terms equal to zero,

$$y^2 + 6y + 5 = 0$$

Factoring, $(y + 5)(y + 1) = 0$

Setting each factor to 0,

$$y + 5 = 0 \qquad\qquad or \qquad y + 1 = 0$$

$$y = -5 \qquad\qquad\qquad y = -1$$

To check, $(-5)^2 = -6(-5) - 5 \qquad or \qquad (-1)^2 = -6(-1) - 5$

$$25 = 30 - 5 \qquad\qquad\qquad 1 = 6 - 5$$

$$25 = 25 \qquad\qquad\qquad 1 = 1$$

A quadratic with a term missing is called an *incomplete quadratic*.

3. Solve $x^2 - 16 = 0$

Factoring, $(x + 4)(x - 4) = 0$

$$x + 4 = 0 \qquad or \qquad x - 4 = 0$$

$$x = -4 \qquad\qquad\qquad x = 4$$

To check, $(-4)^2 - 16 = 0 \qquad or \qquad (4)^2 - 16 = 0$

$$16 - 16 = 0 \qquad\qquad\qquad 16 - 16 = 0$$

$$0 = 0 \qquad\qquad\qquad\qquad 0 = 0$$

4. Solve $x^2 + 6x = 0$

Factoring, $x(x + 6) = 0$

$$x = 0 \qquad or \qquad x + 6 = 0$$

$$x = 0 \qquad\qquad\qquad x = -6$$

To check, $(0)^2 + 6(0) = 0 \qquad or \qquad (-6)^2 + 6(-6) = 0$

$$0 + 0 = 0 \qquad\qquad\qquad 36 + (-36) = 0$$

$$0 = 0 \qquad\qquad\qquad\qquad 0 = 0$$

Inequalities

An *inequality* is a statement in which the relationships are not equal. Instead of using an equal sign (=) as in an equation, we use > (greater than) and < (less than), or ≥ (greater than or equal to) and ≤ (less than or equal to).

When working with inequalities, treat them exactly like equations, EXCEPT: If you multiply or divide both sides by a negative number, you must *reverse* the direction of the sign. For example:

Solve for x: $2x + 4 > 6$

$$2x + 4 > 6$$

$$\underline{\quad -4 \quad -4 \quad}$$

$$2x \quad\; > 2$$

$$\frac{2x}{2} > \frac{2}{2}$$

$$x > 1$$

Solve for x: $-7x > 14$ (divided by -7 and reverse the sign)

$$\frac{-7x}{-7} < \frac{14}{-7}$$

$$x < -2$$

$3x + 2 \geq 5x - 10$ becomes $-2x \geq -12$ by opposite operations. Divide both sides by -2 and reverse the sign.

$$\frac{-2x}{-2} \leq \frac{-12}{-2}$$

$$x \leq 6$$

Geometry Diagnostic Test

Questions

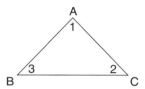

1. Name any angle of this triangle three different ways.

2. A(n) _____ angle measures less than 90 degrees.

3. A(n) _____ angle measures 90 degrees.

4. A(n) _____ angle measures more than 90 degrees.

5. A(n) _____ angle measures 180 degrees.

6. Two angles are complementary when their sum is _____.

7. Two angles are supplementary when their sum is _____.

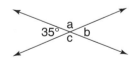

8. In the above diagram, find the measures of $\angle a$, $\angle b$, and $\angle c$.

9. Lines that stay the same distance apart and never meet are called _____ lines.

10. Lines that meet to form 90 degree angles are called _____ lines.

11. A(n) _____ triangle has three equal sides. Therefore, each interior angle measures _____.

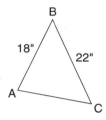

12. In the above triangle, AC must be smaller than _____ inches.

13. In the above triangle, which angle is smaller, $\angle A$ or $\angle C$?

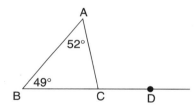

14. What is the measure of $\angle ACD$ above?

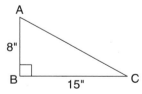

15. What is the length of AC above?

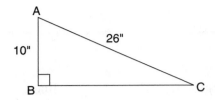

16. What is the length of *BC* above?

17. Name each of the following polygons:

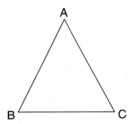

A. $AB = BC = AC$

$\angle A = \angle B = \angle C = 60°$

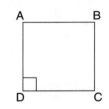

B. $AB = BC = CD = AD$

$\angle A = \angle B = \angle C = \angle D = 90°$

C. $\overline{AB} \parallel \overline{DC}$

$AB = DC$

$\overline{AD} \parallel \overline{BC}$

$AD = BC$

$\angle A = \angle C$

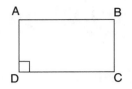

D. $AB = DC$

$AD = BC$

$\angle A = \angle B = \angle C = \angle D = 90°$

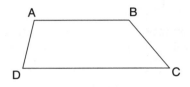

E. $\overline{AB} \parallel \overline{DC}$

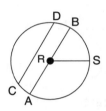

18. Fill in the blanks for circle *R* above:

A. $\overline{RS}$ is called the _____.

B. $\overline{AB}$ is called the _____.

C. $\overline{CD}$ is called a _____.

19. Find the area and circumference for the above circle ($\pi \cong 22/7$):

A. area =

B. circumference =

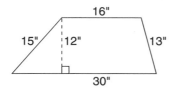

20. Find the area and perimeter of the above figure:

    A. area =

    B. perimeter =

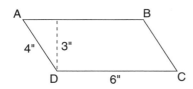

21. Find the area and perimeter of the above figure (*ABCD* is a parallelogram):

    A. area =

    B. perimeter =

22. Find the volume of the above figure if $V = (\pi r^2)h$. (Use 3.14 for π):

23. What is the surface area and volume of the above cube?

    A. surface area =

    B. volume =

Answers

1. $\angle 3$, $\angle CBA$, $\angle ABC$, $\angle B$

   $\angle 1$, $\angle BAC$, $\angle CAB$, $\angle A$

   $\angle 2$, $\angle ACB$, $\angle BCA$, $\angle C$

2. acute

3. right

4. obtuse

5. straight

6. $90°$

7. $180°$

8. $a = 145°$

   $b = 35°$

   $c = 145°$

   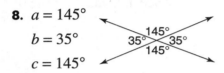

9. parallel

10. perpendicular

11. equilateral, $60°$

12. 40 inches. Since $AB + BC = 40$ inches, then $AC < AB + BC$ and $AC < 40$ inches

13. $\angle C$ must be the smaller angle, because it is opposite the shorter side AB.

14. $\angle ACD = 101°$

15. $AC = 17$ inches

16. Since $\triangle ABC$ is a right triangle, use the Pythagorean theorem:

    $$a^2 + b^2 = c^2$$
    $$10^2 + b^2 = 26^2$$
    $$100 + b^2 = 676$$
    $$b^2 = 576$$
    $$b = 24"$$

17. **A.** equilateral triangle

    B. square

    C. parallelogram

    D. rectangle

    E. trapezoid

18. **A.** radius

    B. diameter

    C. chord

19. **A.** area $= \pi r^2$

    $= \pi(7^2)$

    $= {}^{22}\!/_7(7)(7)$

    $= 154$ square inches

    B. circumference $= \pi d$

    $= \pi(14)$ ($d = 14"$, because $r = 7"$)

    $= {}^{22}\!/_7(14)$

    $= 22(2)$

    $= 44$ inches

20. **A.** area $= \frac{1}{2}(a + b)h$

    $= \frac{1}{2}(16 + 30)12$

    $= \frac{1}{2}(46)12$

    $= 23(12)$

    $= 276$ square inches

    B. perimeter $= 16 + 13 + 30 + 15 = 74$ inches

21. **A.** area $= bh$

    $= 6(3)$

    $= 18$ square inches

    B. perimeter $= 6 + 4 + 6 + 4 = 20$ inches

22. volume $= (\pi r^2)h$

    $= (\pi \cdot 10^2)(12)$

    $= 3.14(100)(12)$

    $= 314(12)$

    $= 3{,}768$ cubic inches

23. **A.** All six surfaces have an area of 4×4, or 16 square inches, because each surface is a square. Therefore, $16(6) = 96$ square inches in the surface area.

    B. Volume $=$ side $\times$ side $\times$ side, or $4^3 = 64$ cubic inches.

Geometry Review

Plane geometry is the study of shapes and figures in two dimensions (the plane).

Solid geometry is the study of shapes and figures in three dimensions.

A *point* is the most fundamental idea in geometry. It is represented by a dot and named by a capital letter.

Lines

A straight *line* is the shortest distance between two points. It continues forever in both directions. A line consists of an infinite number of points. It is named by any two points on the line. The symbol $\leftrightarrow$ written on top of the two letters is used to denote that line.

This is line *AB*:

It is written: $\overleftrightarrow{AB}$

A line may also be named by one small letter. The symbol would not be used.

This is line *l*:

A *line segment* is a piece of a line. A line segment has two endpoints. It is named by its two endpoints. The symbol — written on top of the two letters is used to denote that line segment.

This is line segment *CD*:

It is written: $\overline{CD}$

Note that it is a piece of $\overleftrightarrow{AB}$

A *ray* has only one endpoint and continues forever in one direction. A ray could be thought of as a half-line. It is named by the letter of its endpoint and any other point on the ray. The symbol $\rightarrow$ written on top of the two letters is used to denote that ray.

This is ray *AB*:

It is written: $\overrightarrow{AB}$

This is ray *BC*:

It is written: $\overrightarrow{BC}$ or $\overleftarrow{CB}$

Note that the direction of the symbol is the direction of the ray.

Angles

An *angle* is formed by two rays that start from the same point. That point is called the *vertex*; the rays are called the *sides* of the angle. An angle is measured in degrees. The degrees indicate the size of the angle, from one side to the other.

In the diagram, the angle is formed by rays *AB* and *AC*. *A* is the vertex.

$\overrightarrow{AB}$ or $\overrightarrow{AC}$ are the sides of the angle.

The symbol ∠ is used to denote an angle.

An angle can be named in *various* ways.

1. By the letter of the vertex—therefore, the angle above could be named ∠*A*.

2. By the number (or small letter) in its interior—therefore, the angle above could be named ∠1.

3. By the letters of the three points that formed it—therefore, the angle above could be named ∠*BAC*, or ∠*CAB*. The center letter is always the letter of the vertex.

Types of Angles

Adjacent angles are any angles that share a common side and a common vertex.

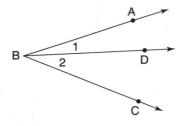

In the diagram, ∠1 and ∠2 are adjacent angles.

A *right angle* has a measure of 90°. The symbol ∟ in the interior of an angle designates the fact that a right angle is formed.

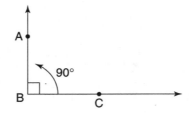

In the diagram, ∠*ABC* is a right angle.

Any angle whose measure is less than 90° is called an *acute angle*.

In the diagram, ∠*b* is acute.

Any angle whose measure is larger than 90° but smaller than 180° is called an *obtuse angle*.

In the diagram, ∠4 is an obtuse angle.

A *straight angle* has a measure of 180°.

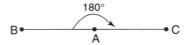

In the diagram, ∠BAC is a straight angle (also called a line).

Two angles whose sum is 90° are called *complementary angles*.

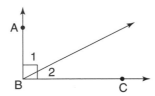

In the diagram, because ∠*ABC* is a right angle, ∠1 + ∠2 = 90°.

Therefore, ∠1 and ∠2 are complementary angles. If ∠1 = 55°, its complement, ∠2, would be: 90° − 55° = 35°.

Two angles whose sum is 180° are called *supplementary angles*. Two adjacent angles that form a straight line are supplementary.

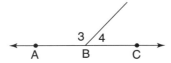

In the diagram, since ∠*ABC* is a straight angle, ∠3 + ∠4 = 180°.

Therefore, ∠3 and ∠4 are supplementary angles. If ∠3 = 122°, its supplement, ∠4, would be: 180° − 122° = 58°.

A ray from the vertex of an angle that divides the angle into two equal pieces is called an *angle bisector.*

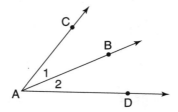

In the diagram, $\overrightarrow{AB}$ is the angle bisector of $\angle$CAD.

Therefore, $\angle 1 = \angle 2$.

If two straight lines intersect, they do so at a point. Four angles are formed. Those angles opposite each other are called *vertical angles.* Those angles sharing a common side and a common vertex are, again, *adjacent angles.* Vertical angles are always equal.

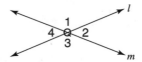

In the diagram, line *l* and line *m* intersect at point *Q.* $\angle 1$, $\angle 2$, $\angle 3$, and $\angle 4$ are formed.

$$\left.\begin{array}{l} \angle 1 \text{ and } \angle 3 \\ \angle 2 \text{ and } \angle 4 \end{array}\right\} \text{ are vertical angles}$$

$$\left.\begin{array}{l} \angle 1 \text{ and } \angle 2 \\ \angle 2 \text{ and } \angle 3 \\ \angle 3 \text{ and } \angle 4 \\ \angle 1 \text{ and } \angle 4 \end{array}\right\} \text{ are adjacent angles}$$

$$\text{Therefore, } \begin{array}{l} \angle 1 = \angle 3 \\ \angle 2 = \angle 4 \end{array}$$

Types of Lines

Two or more lines that cross each other at a point are called *intersecting lines.* That point would be on each of those lines.

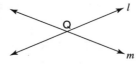

In the diagram, lines *l* and *m* intersect at Q.

Two lines that meet to form right angles (90°) are called *perpendicular lines.* The symbol $\perp$ is used to denote perpendicular lines.

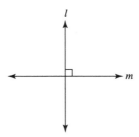

In the diagram, line $l \perp$ line m.

Two or more lines that remain the same distance apart at all times are called *parallel lines*. Parallel lines never meet. The symbol ‖ is used to denote parallel lines.

In the diagram, $l \parallel m$.

Polygons

Closed shapes or figures with three or more sides are called *polygons*. (*Poly* means "many"; *gon* means "sides"; thus, *polygon* means "many sides.")

Triangles

This section deals with those polygons having the fewest number of sides. A *triangle* is a three-sided polygon. It has three angles in its interior. The sum of these angles is *always* 180°. The symbol for triangle is Δ. A triangle is named by all three letters of its vertices.

This is ΔABC:

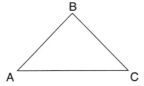

There are various types of triangles:

- A triangle having all three sides equal (meaning all three sides having the same length) is called an *equilateral triangle*.

- A triangle having two sides equal is called an *isosceles triangle*.

- A triangle having none of its sides equal is called a *scalene triangle*.

- A triangle having a right (90°) angle in its interior is called a *right triangle*.

Facts about Triangles

Every triangle has a base (bottom side) and a height (or altitude). Every height is the *perpendicular* (forms right angles) distance from a vertex to its opposite side (the base).

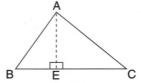

In this diagram of $\triangle ABC$, $\overline{BC}$ is the base, and $\overline{AE}$ is the height. $\overline{AE} \perp \overline{BC}$.

Every triangle has a median. The median is the line segment drawn from a vertex to the midpoint of the opposite side.

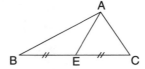

In this diagram of $\triangle ABC$, E is the midpoint of $\overline{BC}$. Therefore, $\overline{BE} = \overline{EC}$. $\overline{AE}$ is the median of ABC.

In an equilateral triangle, all three sides are equal, and all three angles are equal. If all three angles are equal and their sum is 180°, the following must be true:

$$x + x + x = 180°$$
$$3x = 180°$$
$$x = 60°$$

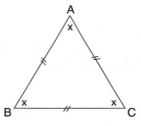

Every angle of an equilateral triangle always has a measure of 60°.

In any triangle, the longest side is always opposite from the largest angle. Likewise, the shortest side is always opposite from the smallest angle. In a right triangle, the longest side will always be opposite from the right angle, as the right angle will be the largest angle in the triangle.

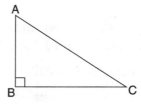

$\overline{AC}$ is the longest side of right $\triangle ABC$.

The sum of the lengths of any two sides of a triangle must be larger than the length of the third side.

In the diagram of $\triangle ABC$:

$$AB + BC > AC$$

$$AB + AC > BC$$

$$AC + BC > AB$$

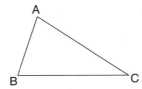

If one side of a triangle is extended, the exterior angle formed by that extension is equal to the sum of the other two interior angles.

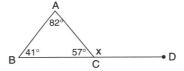

In the diagram of $\triangle ABC$, side BC is extended to D. $\angle ACD$ is the exterior angle formed.

$$\angle x = \angle y + \angle z$$

$$x = 82° + 41°$$

$$x = 123°$$

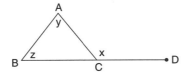

Pythagorean Theorem

In any right triangle, the relationship between the lengths of the sides is stated by the Pythagorean theorem.

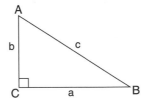

The parts of a right triangle are:

$\angle C$ is the right angle.

The side opposite the right angle is called the *hypotenuse* (side c). (The hypotenuse will always be the longest side.) The other two sides are called the *legs* (sides a and b).

The three lengths a, b, and c will always be numbers such that:

$$a^2 + b^2 = c^2$$

For example:

If $a = 3$, $b = 4$, and $c = 5$,

$$a^2 + b^2 = c^2$$

$$3^2 + 4^2 = 5^2$$

$$9 + 16 = 25$$

$$25 = 25$$

Therefore, 3-4-5 is called a Pythagorean triple. There are other values for a, b, and c that will always work. Some are: 1-1-$\sqrt{2}$, 5-12-13, and 8-15-17. Any multiple of one of these triples will also work. For example, if we multiply the 3-4-5, we determine that 6-8-10, 9-12-15, and 15-20-25 are also Pythagorean triples.

If perfect squares are known, the lengths of these sides can be determined easily. A knowledge of the use of algebraic equations can also be used to determine the lengths of the sides.

For example:

$$a^2 + b^2 = c^2$$

$$x^2 + 10^2 = 15^2$$

$$x^2 + 100 = 225$$

$$x^2 = 125$$

$$x = \sqrt{125}$$

$$= \sqrt{25} \times \sqrt{5}$$

$$= 5\sqrt{5}$$

Quadrilaterals

A polygon having four sides is called a *quadrilateral.* There are four angles in its interior. The sum of these interior angles will always be 360°. A quadrilateral is named by using the four letters of its vertices.

This is quadrilateral *ABCD*.

Types of Quadrilaterals

The *square* has four equal sides and four right angles.

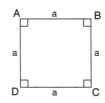

The *rectangle* has opposite sides that are equal and four right angles.

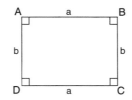

The *parallelogram* has opposite sides equal and parallel, opposite angles equal, and consecutive angles supplementary. Every parallelogram has a height.

$$\angle A = \angle C$$

$$\angle B = \angle D$$

$$\angle A + \angle B = 180°$$

$$\angle A + \angle D = 180°$$

$$\angle B + \angle C = 180°$$

$$\angle C + \angle D = 180°$$

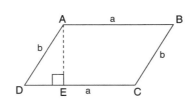

$\overline{AE}$ is the height of the parallelogram, $\overline{AB}\|\overline{CD}$, and $\overline{AD}\|\overline{BC}$.

The *rhombus* is a parallelogram with four equal sides. A rhombus has a height. $\overline{BE}$ is the height.

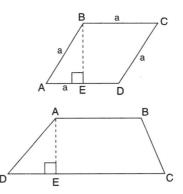

The *trapezoid* has only one pair of parallel sides. A trapezoid has a height. $\overline{AE}$ is the height. $\overline{AB}\|\overline{DC}$

Other Polygons

- The *pentagon* is a five-sided polygon.
- The *hexagon* is a six-sided polygon.
- The *octagon* is an eight-sided polygon.
- The *nonagon* is a nine-sided polygon.
- The *decagon* is a ten-sided polygon.

Facts about Polygons

Regular means all sides have the same length and all angles have the same measure. A regular three-sided polygon is the equilateral triangle. A regular four-sided polygon is the square. There are no other special names. Other polygons will just be described as regular, if they are. For example, a regular five-sided polygon is called a regular pentagon. A regular six-sided polygon is called a regular hexagon.

Perimeter

Perimeter means the total distance all the way around the outside of any polygon. The perimeter of any polygon can be determined by adding up the lengths of all the sides. The total distance around will be the sum of all sides of the polygon. No special formulas are really necessary.

Area

Area (*A*) means the amount of space inside the polygon. The formulas for each area are as follows:

Triangle: $A = \frac{1}{2}bh$

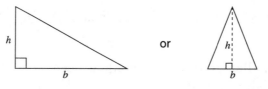

For example:

$A = \frac{1}{2}bh$

$A = \frac{1}{2}(24)(18) = 216$ sq in

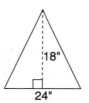

Square or rectangle: $A = lw$

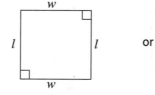 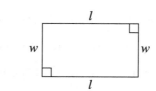

For example:

$$A = l(w) = 4(4) = 16 \text{ sq in}$$

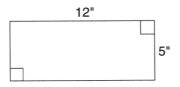

$$A = l(w) = 12(5) = 60 \text{ sq in}$$

Parallelogram: $A = bh$

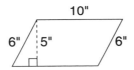

For example:

$$A = b(h)$$

$$A = 10(5) = 50 \text{ sq in}$$

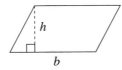

Trapezoid: $A = \frac{1}{2}(a + b)h$

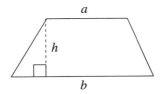

For example:

$$A = \frac{1}{2}(a + b)h$$

$$A = \frac{1}{2}(8 + 12)7$$

$$= \frac{1}{2}(20)7 = 70 \text{ sq in}$$

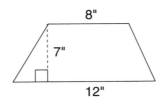

Circles

A closed shape whose side is formed by one curved line all points of which are equidistant from the center point is called a *circle*. Circles are named by the letter of their center point.

This is circle *M*. *M* is the center point, since it is the same distance away from any point on the circle.

Parts of a Circle

The *radius* is the distance from the center to any point on the circle. In any circle, all radii (plural) are the same length.

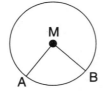

$\overline{MA}$ is a radius.

$\overline{MB}$ is a radius.

The *diameter* of a circle is the distance across the circle, through the center. In any circle, all diameters are the same length. Each diameter is two radii.

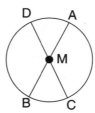

$\overline{AB}$ is a diameter.

$\overline{CD}$ is a diameter.

A *chord* of a circle is a line segment whose end points lie on the circle itself.

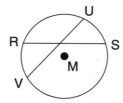

$\overline{RS}$ is a chord.

$\overline{UV}$ is a chord.

The diameter is the longest chord in any circle.

An *arc* is the distance between any two points *on* the circle itself. An arc is a piece of the circle. The symbol ⌢ is used to denote an arc. It is written on top of the two endpoints that form the arc. Arcs are measured in degrees. There are 360° around the circle.

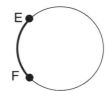

This is $\overset{\frown}{EF}$.

Minor $\overset{\frown}{EF}$ is the shorter distance between E and F.

Major $\overset{\frown}{EF}$ is the longer distance between E and F.

When $\overset{\frown}{EF}$ is written, the minor arc is assumed.

Circumference and Area

Circumference is the distance around the circle. Since there are no sides to add up, a formula is needed. π (pi) is a Greek letter that represents a specific number. In fractional or decimal form, the commonly used approximations are: $\pi \cong 3.14$ or $\pi \cong {}^{22}\!/_7$.

The formula for circumference is: $C = \pi d$ or $C = 2\pi r$.

For example:

In circle M, $d = 8$, since $r = 4$.

$C = \pi d$

$\quad = \pi(8)$

$\quad = 3.14(8)$

$\quad = 25.12$ inches

The *area* of a circle can be determined by: $A = \pi r^2$.

For example:

In circle M, $r = 5$, since $d = 10$.

$A = \pi(r^2)$

$\quad = \pi(5^2)$

$\quad = 3.14(25)$

$\quad = 78.5$ sq in

Volume

In three dimensions, additional facts can be determined about shapes. *Volume* refers to the capacity to hold. The formula for volume of each shape is different.

> **The volume of any prism (a three-dimensional shape having many sides, but two bases) can be determined by: Volume (V) = (area of base)(height of prism).**

Specifically for a rectangular solid:

$$V = (lw)(h)$$

$$= lwh$$

Specifically for a cylinder (circular bases):

$$V = (\pi r^2)h$$

$$= \pi r^2 h$$

Volume is labeled "cubic" units.

Surface Area

The *surface area* of a three-dimensional solid is the area of all of the surfaces that form the solid. Find the area of each surface, and then add up those areas. The surface area of a rectangular solid can be found by adding up the areas of all six surfaces. For example:

The surface area of this prism is:

top	$18 \times 6 = 108$
bottom	$18 \times 6 = 108$
left side	$6 \times 4 = 24$
right side	$6 \times 4 = 24$
front	$18 \times 4 = 72$
back	$18 \times 4 = \underline{72}$
	408 sq in

Basic Coordinate Geometry Review

Coordinate Graphs (*x-y* Graphs)

A *coordinate graph* is formed by two perpendicular number lines. These lines are called *coordinate axes*. The horizontal axis is called the *x-axis* or the *abscissa*. The vertical line is called the *y-axis* or the ordinate. The point at which the two lines intersect is called the *origin* and is represented by the coordinates (0, 0), often marked simply *O*.

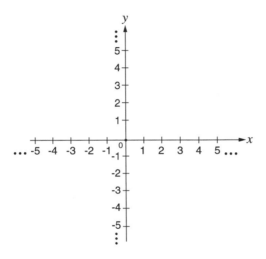

Each point on a coordinate graph is located by an ordered pair of numbers called *coordinates*. Notice the placement of points on the graph below and the coordinates, or ordered pairs, that show their location. Numbers are not usually written on the *x* and *y* axes.

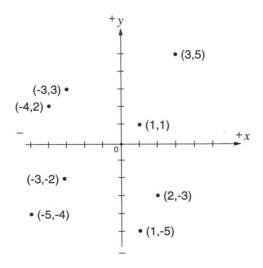

Also notice that on the *x*-axis, the numbers to the right of 0 are positive and to the left of 0 are negative. On the *y*-axis, numbers above 0 are positive and numbers below 0 are negative. The first number in the ordered pair is called the *x-coordinate* and shows how far to the right or left of 0 the point is. The second number is called the *y-coordinate* and shows how far up or down the point is from 0. The coordinates, or ordered pairs, are shown as (*x, y*). The order of these numbers is very important, as the point (3, 2) is different from the point (2, 3). Also, don't combine the ordered pair of numbers, because they refer to different directions.

The coordinate graph is divided into four quarters called *quadrants*. These quadrants are labeled as follows.

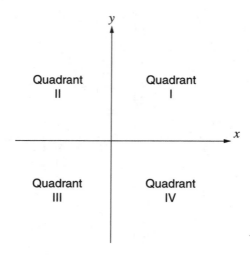

You can see that

- In quadrant I, *x* is always positive and *y* is always positive.
- In quadrant II, *x* is always negative and *y* is always positive.
- In quadrant III, *x* is always negative and *y* is always negative.
- In quadrant IV, *x* is always positive and *y* is always negative.

Sample Questions

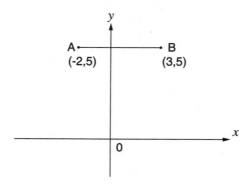

1. What is the length of *AB* in the graph above?

    A. 3

    B. 4

    C. $4\frac{1}{2}$

    D. 5

    E. $5\frac{1}{2}$

The correct answer is **D.** Because the coordinates of the points are $(-2, 5)$ and $(3, 5)$, the first, or *x*, coordinate will tip you off to the distance of each point from the *y*-axis. The distance to point *B* from the *y*-axis is 3, and the distance to point *A* from the *y*-axis is 2. $(-2$ is 2 in the negative direction.) So $3 + 2$ gives a length of 5.

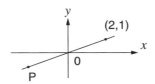

2. In the coordinate graph above, if the line passes through the origin, which of the following could be the coordinates of point *P*?

    A. $(1, 1)$

    B. $(-1, 0)$

    C. $(-1, 1)$

    D. $(-2, 0)$

    E. $(-2, -1)$

The correct answer is **E.** In this particular problem only choice **E** is reasonable. Since point *P* is in the third quadrant, both coordinates must be negative. From the slope of the line you could see that $(-2, -1)$ would lie on it.

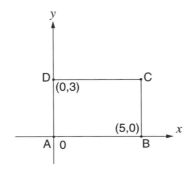

3. What is the area of rectangle *ABCD* in the graph above?

    A. 3

    B. 5

    C. 8

    D. 15

    E. 16

The correct answer is **D**. The formula for the area of a rectangle is base × height. Since point *A* is at (0, 0) and point *B* is at (5, 0), the base is 5. Because point *D* is at (0, 3), the height is 3, so the area is $5 \times 3 = 15$.

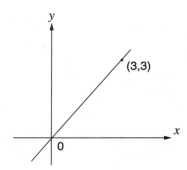

4. What is the slope of the line that passes through the origin (0, 0) and (3, 3) in the graph above?

    A. 0

    B. 1

    C. 2

    D. 3

    E. 6

The correct answer is B. The slope is the rise/run, or the change in *y* over the change in *x*. From the graph, you can see that if the line goes up 3, it also goes 3 to the right. 3/3 = 1. You could also use the slope formula.

$$\text{slope} = \frac{(y_2 - y_1)}{(x_2 - x_1)} = \frac{3 - 0}{3 - 0} = \frac{3}{3} = 1$$

So the slope is 1.

Practice Basic Coordinate Geometry Questions

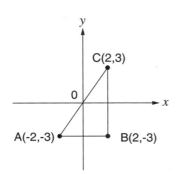

1. What is the area of $\triangle ABC$ in the preceding figure?

   A. 3

   B. 6

   C. 12

   D. 18

   E. 24

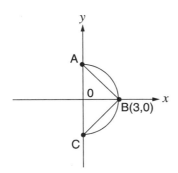

2. In the preceding figure, what is the perimeter of $\triangle ABC$ inscribed within the semicircle with center O?

   A. 9

   B. $6 + 3\sqrt{2}$

   C. $9 + 3\sqrt{3}$

   D. $6 + 6\sqrt{2}$

   E. $12\sqrt{2}$

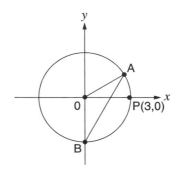

3. In the preceding figure, circle O has its center at the origin. If $\angle AOP = 30°$, what is the area of $\triangle OAB$?

   A. $\sqrt{3}$

   B. $\dfrac{9\sqrt{3}}{4}$

   C. $3\sqrt{2}$

   D. $3\sqrt{3}$

   E. 9

Answers

1. C. The area of a triangle is $\frac{1}{2} \times$ base $\times$ height.

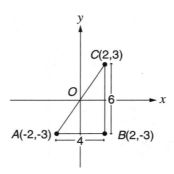

Base AB of the triangle is 4 units (because from A to the y-axis is 2 units and from the y-axis to B is another 2 units). Height BC of the triangle is 6 units (3 units from B to the x-axis and another 3 units to C). Note that $\angle B$ is a right angle. So

$$\text{area of triangle} = \frac{1}{2} \times 4 \times 6$$
$$= \frac{1}{2} \times 24$$
$$= 12$$

2. D. To find the perimeter of the triangle, you need the lengths of the three sides. You know that radius OB is 3 units long. Then OA and OC are each 3 units because they are also radii. Therefore, side AC of the triangle is 6 units.

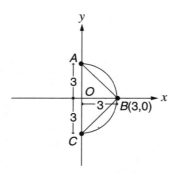

In triangle AOB, you know that OA is 3 and OB is 3. From the Pythagorean theorem,

$$a^2 + b^2 = c^2$$
$$(OA)^2 + (OB)^2 = (AB)^2$$
$$3^2 + 3^2 = (AB)^2$$
$$9 + 9 = (AB)^2$$
$$18 = (AB)^2$$
$$\sqrt{18} = AB$$
$$\sqrt{9 \times 2} = AB$$
$$3\sqrt{2} = AB$$

(If you spotted that triangle *AOB* is an isosceles right triangle with sides in the ratio $1:1:\sqrt{2}$, you wouldn't have needed to use the Pythagorean theorem.)

By symmetry, you know that $AB = CB$. So $CB = 3\sqrt{2}$ and

$$\text{perimeter} = CA + AB + CB$$
$$= 6 + 3\sqrt{2} + 3\sqrt{2}$$
$$= 6 + 6\sqrt{2}$$

3. **B.** To find the area of $\triangle OAB$, you need its base and its height. You can take side *OB* as the base of the triangle. Because *OP* is 3 (you know this from the coordinates of *P*), and *OP* is the radius of the circle, *OB* is also 3 (because *OB* is another radius). So the base of the triangle is 3. You now need its height.

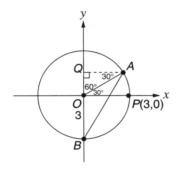

To find the height of the triangle, you can project its base *OB* to point *Q*. Then *AQ* is the height of the triangle. Note that because $\angle AOP$ is 30°, $\angle QOA$ must be $90° - 30° = 60°$. And because *OA* is also a radius, it is 3. So now you know $\triangle OQA$ is a 30°–60°–90° right triangle in which

$$\angle AQO = 90°$$
$$\angle QOA = 60°$$
$$\angle OAQ = 30°$$

In a triangle, the three corresponding sides are in the ratio 1, $\sqrt{3}$, and 2, respectively. In $\triangle OAQ$, side *OA*, which is opposite the 90° angle, is 3, which is ³⁄₂ times 2. Then side *AQ*, which is opposite the 60° angle, should be ³⁄₂ times $\sqrt{3}$. That is, the height of $\triangle OAB$ is $\frac{3}{2}\sqrt{3}$.

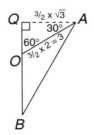

Then the area of $\triangle OAB = \frac{1}{2}$ (base × height)

$$= \frac{1}{2}\left(3 \times \frac{3}{2}\sqrt{3}\right)$$

$$= \frac{1}{2}\left(\frac{9}{2}\sqrt{3}\right)$$

$$= \frac{9\sqrt{3}}{4}$$

THE VERBAL SECTION

Prior to starting the exam, you will be carefully walked through a very basic tutorial program explaining how to use the computer for this exam. The computer-adaptive GMAT gives you 75 minutes to answer 41 verbal questions. These questions are composed of Reading Comprehension, Sentence Correction, and Critical Reasoning, with the question types intermingled throughout the section.

You are given a medium-difficulty question to start with, and then the computer will adapt the level of questions you receive based on your responses to all the previous questions. Although you can take notes or do work on the scratch paper provided, you record all of your answers on the computer screen by using a mouse to click on the appropriate ovals. You are not allowed to go back to a previous question, but you are allowed to review a passage if it applies to a series of questions. Always fill in an answer choice before you attempt to move to the next question.

In this book—to assist you in understanding explanations and to direct your attention to different questions and answer choices—each question is given a number, and letters have been used instead of ovals next to the answer choices. **Note that on the actual exam, questions do not have numbers next to them and there are no letters assigned to answer choices.**

Introduction to Reading Comprehension

Reading Comprehension typically consists of a passage of about 200 to 400 words followed by three or four questions based on the passage.

Ability Tested

This question type tests your ability to understand, interpret, and analyze reading passages on a variety of topics. Passages are generally taken from the following categories:

- **Biological science:** passages about botany, medicine, or zoology
- **Physical science:** passages about chemistry, physics, or astronomy
- **Humanities:** passages about art, literature, music, folklore, or philosophy
- **Social studies:** passages about history, government, economics, or sociology

The questions will frequently ask you to recognize or evaluate

- the main idea, main point, or possible title of the passage.
- information that is directly stated in the passage.
- information that is implied, suggested, or can be inferred.
- applications of the author's opinions or ideas.
- the way the author develops and presents the passage.
- the style or tone of the passage.

Basic Skills Necessary

Students who have read widely and know how to read, analyze, and interpret stated and implied information efficiently tend to do well on this section.

Directions

Each passage is followed by questions based on its content. After reading a passage, choose the best answer to each question and select the corresponding oval on the screen. Answer all questions about the passage on the basis of what is *stated* or *implied* in that passage. You may refer back to the passage.

Analysis

- You should answer questions using only the information given or implied in a passage. Do not consider outside information, even if it seems more accurate than the given information.
- You are looking for the best answer, so be sure to read all the choices.
- If you don't know the answer, try to eliminate some choices; then take an educated guess.
- Since you may refer back to the passage, don't try to memorize everything in the passage. Read the passage focusing on the main point or purpose and the structure of the passage.
- The complete passage may not fit on the screen, so make sure you are comfortable with the method of scrolling on the screen.
- Each passage contains numbered lines for reference, which assist you in finding a particular spot.

Suggested Approach with Samples

Samples

Suppose the first question were as follows:

> **1.** The author's main purpose in writing this passage is to
>
> **A.**
>
> **B.**
>
> **C.**
>
> **D.**
>
> **E.**

Five answer options would be provided. Now you know to focus on the author's main purpose as you read the passage. Do not spend time reading the answer choices when you preread the first question. Preread the question only, focus on the key word(s), and then read the passage.

Now suppose the first question were as follows:

> **1.** The author implies which of the following about the New Jersey progressives?
>
> **A.**
>
> **B.**
>
> **C.**
>
> **D.**
>
> **E.**

As you preread the question, your focus should be on the words "author implies . . . about New Jersey progressives." This phrase tells you to watch for what the author is saying "between the lines" about New Jersey progressives. Again preread the question only, not the choices. **Remember:** You can only preread the first question to each passage given.

As you read the following passage, focus on what the author is really saying or what point the author is trying to make. Also pay attention to how the passage is put together—that is, the structure.

Questions 1–5

Woodrow Wilson won his first office in 1910 when he was elected governor of New Jersey. Two years later, he was elected president in one of the most rapid political rises in our history. For a while, Wilson had practiced law but found it both boring and unprofitable; then he became a political scientist and
(5)   finally president of Princeton University. He did an outstanding job at Princeton, but when he was asked by the Democratic boss of New Jersey, Jim Smith, to run for governor, Wilson readily accepted because his position at Princeton was becoming untenable.

Until 1910, Wilson seemed to be a conservative Democrat in the Grover
(10) Cleveland tradition. He had denounced Bryan in 1896 and had voted for the National Democratic candidate who supported gold. In fact, when the Democratic machine first pushed Wilson's nomination in 1912, the young New Jersey progressives wanted no part of him. Wilson later assured them that he would champion the progressive cause, and so they decided to work
(15) for his election. It is easy to accuse Wilson of political expediency, but it is entirely possible that by 1912 he had changed his views as had countless other Americans. While governor of New Jersey, he carried out his election pledges by enacting an impressive list of reforms.

Wilson secured the Democratic nomination on the 46th ballot. In the cam-
(20) paign, Wilson emerged as the middle-of-the-road candidate—between the conservative William H. Taft and the more radical Theodore Roosevelt. Wilson called his program the New Freedom, which he said was the restoration of free competition as it had existed before the growth of the trusts. In contrast, Theodore Roosevelt was advocating a New Nationalism, which
(25) seemed to call for massive federal intervention in the economic life of the nation. Wilson felt that the trusts should be destroyed, but he made a distinction between a trust and legitimately successful big business. Theodore Roosevelt, on the other hand, accepted the trusts as inevitable but said that the government should regulate them by establishing a new regulatory agency.

On the paper and pencil GMAT given a few years ago, you could read actively by marking (circling, underlining, and so on) important items in the passage. But since you cannot mark on the computerized GMAT, you need to focus on the main point(s) and the structure. Knowing the structure can help you go back into the passage and find things quickly.

Always look for the main point of the passage. There are many ways to ask about the main point of a passage. What is the main idea? What is the best title? What is the author's purpose?

Sample

> **1.** The author's main purpose in writing this passage is to
>
>   **A.** argue that Wilson is one of the great U.S. presidents.
>
>   **B.** survey the difference between Wilson, Taft, and Roosevelt.
>
>   **C.** explain Wilson's concept of the New Freedom.
>
>   **D.** discuss some major events of Wilson's career.
>
>   **E.** suggest reasons that Wilson's presidency may have started World War I.

The best answer is **D.** Choices **A** and **E** are irrelevant to the information in the passage, and choices **B** and **C** mention secondary purposes rather than the primary one.

Some information is not directly stated in the passage but can be gleaned by reading between the lines. This implied information can be valuable in answering some questions, such as the following.

Sample

> **2.** The author implies which of the following about the New Jersey progressives?
>
>   **A.** They did not support Wilson after he was governor.
>
>   **B.** They were not conservative Democrats.
>
>   **C.** They were more interested in political expediency than in political causes or reforms.
>
>   **D.** Along with Wilson, they were supporters of Bryan in 1896.
>
>   **E.** They particularly admired Wilson's experience as president of Princeton University.

The best choice is **B.** In the second paragraph, Wilson's decision to champion the progressive cause after 1912 is contrasted with his earlier career, when he seemed to be a conservative Democrat. Thus, you may conclude that the progressives, whom Wilson finally joined, were not conservative Democrats as Wilson was earlier in his career. Choices **A** and **D** contradict information in the paragraph, while choices **C** and **E** are not suggested by any information given in the passage.

> **Watch for important conclusions or information that might support a conclusion.**

Sample

> **3.** The passage supports which of the following conclusions about the progress of Wilson's political career?
>
> **A.** Few politicians have progressed so rapidly toward the attainment of higher office.
>
> **B.** Failures late in his career caused him to be regarded as a president who regressed instead of progressed.
>
> **C.** Wilson encountered little opposition once he determined to seek the presidency.
>
> **D.** The League of Nations marked the end of Wilson's reputation as a strong leader.
>
> **E.** Wilson's political allies were Bryan and Taft.

The best choice is **A.** The second sentence in paragraph one explicitly states that Wilson "was elected president in one of the most rapid political rises in our history."

> **Understand the meaning and possible reason for using certain words or phrases in the passage. And take advantage of the line numbers given.**

Sample

> **4.** In the statement "Wilson readily accepted because his position at Princeton was becoming untenable" (lines 7–8), the meaning of untenable is probably which of the following?
>
> **A.** unlikely to last for years
>
> **B.** filled with considerably less tension
>
> **C.** difficult to maintain or continue
>
> **D.** filled with achievement that would appeal to voters
>
> **E.** something he did not have a tenacious desire to continue

The best choice is **C.** On any reading comprehension test, keep alert to the positive and negative connotations of words and phrases in each passage as well as in the questions themselves. In the case of *untenable,* the prefix *un–* suggests that the word has a negative connotation. The context in which the word occurs does as well. Wilson *left* his position at Princeton; therefore, you may conclude that the position was somehow unappealing. Only two of the answer choices, **C** and **E,** provide a negative definition. Although choice **E** may attract your attention because *tenacious* looks similar to *tenable,* the correct choice is **C,** which is the conventional definition of *untenable.*

Your answer choice must be supported by information either stated or implied in the passage. Eliminate those choices that the passage does not support.

Sample

> **5.** According to the passage, which of the following was probably true about the presidential campaign of 1912?
>
> **A.** Woodrow Wilson won the election by an overwhelming majority.
>
> **B.** The inexperience of Theodore Roosevelt accounted for his radical position.
>
> **C.** Wilson was unable to attract two thirds of the votes but won anyway.
>
> **D.** There were three nominated candidates for the presidency.
>
> **E.** Wilson's New Freedom did not represent Democratic interests.

The best choice is **D.** Choices **A, B,** and **C** contain information that the passage does not address. You may eliminate them as irrelevant. Choice **E** contradicts the fact that Wilson was a Democratic candidate. The discussion of Taft and Roosevelt as the candidates who finally ran against Wilson for the presidency supports choice **D.**

Questions 6–7

The fact that bacteria are capable of chemical communication first emerged from investigations into marine bacteria able to glow in the dark. In 1970 Kenneth H. Nealson and John Woodland Hastings of Harvard University observed that luminous bacteria in culture do not glow at a constant intensity. In
(5) fact, they emit no light until the population reaches a high density.

Nealson and Hastings knew the light resulted from chemical reactions catalyzed by the enzyme luciferase. They postulated that this enzyme was ultimately controlled not by some mechanism inside each bacterial cell but by a molecular messenger that traveled between cells. Once inside target cells, the
(10) messenger, which the researchers called autoinducer, could induce expression of the genes' coding for luciferase and for the other proteins involved in light production; that is, autoinducer could stimulate synthesis of the encoded proteins and, thus, of light. Their theory met with skepticism at first but has since been confirmed and expanded.

Read all the choices because you are looking for the best answer given.

Sample

> **6.** According to the passage, Nealson and Woodland's research was instrumental in indicating that
>
>   **A.** bacteria communicate through molecular messengers that travel between cells.
>
>   **B.** luminous bacteria glow not at a constant density but at various densities.
>
>   **C.** bacteria are genetically coded by the autoinducer.
>
>   **D.** the molecular messenger luciferase causes bacteria to glow at high densities.
>
>   **E.** the autoinducer, not the enzyme luciferase as was previously believed, produces the luminosity of certain marine bacteria.

The best choice is **A.** Although the research focused on marine bacteria that glow, its broader significance is that it shows the chemical communication between bacteria. Choice **B** is the observation that led to the theory but is not the best answer. Choice **C** is inaccurate; an autoinducer does not code genes but induces their expression. Choice **D** is also incorrect; the molecular messenger that causes bacteria to glow is not the enzyme luciferase. Choice **E** might seem correct at first reading, but although the autoinducer allows the expression of the light-producing enzymes such as luciferase, it doesn't produce light itself.

Some questions deal with a specific detail in the passage. Know where to locate this detail.

Sample

> **7.** Which of the following are characteristics of the autoinducer involved in light production by marine bacteria?
>
>   I.   It catalyzes chemical reactions in bacterial cells.
>
>   II.   It stimulates synthesis of certain proteins.
>
>   III.   It acts as a messenger between enzymes and bacteria.
>
>   **A.** I and II only
>
>   **B.** II and III only
>
>   **C.** II only
>
>   **D.** III only
>
>   **E.** I, II, and III

The best choice is **C.** Only II is correct (line 12). Luciferase, not the autoinducer, catalyzes the reactions that cause light, making I incorrect (line 7). III is incorrect because the autoinducer acts as a messenger between bacteria cells (line 9), not between enzymes and bacteria.

Question 8–9

History gives a cruel experience of human nature, in showing how exactly the regard due to the life, possessions, and entire earthly happiness of any class of persons, was measured by what they had the power of enforcing; how all who made any resistance to authorities that had arms in their hands,
(5) however dreadful might be the provocation, had not only the law of force but all other laws, and all the notions of social obligation against them; and in the eyes of those whom they resisted, were not only guilty of crime, but of the worst of all crimes, deserving the most cruel chastisement which human beings could inflict. The first small vestige of a feeling of obligation in a supe-
(10) rior to acknowledge any right in inferiors began when he had been induced, for convenience, to make some promise to them. Though these promises, even when sanctioned by the most solemn oaths, were for many ages revoked or violated on the most trifling provocation or temptation, it is probable that this, except by persons of still worse than average morality, was seldom done
(15) without some twinges of conscience.

Notice what the author is *stating* and what the author is *implying*.

Sample

> **8.** The author implies that laws are based on
>
> **A.** the necessity of protecting the weakest members of a society.
>
> **B.** the interests of those in a society who possess the most power.
>
> **C.** the notions of social obligation that are passed from generation to generation.
>
> **D.** promises made to those without power by those with the most power.
>
> **E.** the belief that "earthly happiness" is the right of everyone in society, including those who resist authority.

The best choice is **B.** The author makes it clear that the person with the most power has "not only the law of force but all other laws" behind him, implying that the law itself exists to protect the interests of the powerful. Choices **A** and **E** are incorrect; in fact, the passage suggests the contrary. Choice **C** is also inaccurate; "all the notions of social obligation" support the powerful, according to the passage. Choice **D** might be tempting, but according to the author, promises are made only for the convenience of the powerful; laws are made to protect their interests.

> **Try to recognize the tone and purpose of the passage. Would the author agree or disagree with something?**

Sample

9. The author of this passage would be most likely to agree with which of the following statements?

   A. In order to prevent chaos in a society, authority must be strong and unquestioned.

   B. All men, whether weak or strong, desire justice in their dealings with others.

   C. Social obligation is the most important factor ensuring protection of the weak by the strong.

   D. Rights are granted to those without power when to do so will benefit those with power.

   E. In the past, when rights have been granted to people, only the most extreme circumstances have led to their being rescinded.

The best choice is **D.** According to the passage, the rights of the weak were acknowledged only when the strong were induced to do so for their own convenience (lines 9–11). Choice **A** is irrelevant; the author doesn't advocate strong, unquestioned authority, but only defines what he or she sees as the realistic situation. Choice **B** is incorrect; the author states that the powerful are concerned with their own interests, not with justice. Choice **C** is also incorrect; notions of social obligation are, like laws, based on the needs of the powerful. Choice **E** is refuted in the passage; the author states that rights have been "revoked or violated on the most trifling provocation."

Questions 10–13

As the Moorish states in all parts of Spain fell into progressive political, military, and literary decadence, the atmosphere of the established Christian centers became increasingly more favorable to an intensive and varied literary development. The growth of cities had produced a comparatively urban and
(5) cultured population with sufficient leisure and security to find time for literary entertainment. The growth of commerce had brought Spaniards into contact with other societies that had developed original and stimulating literary traditions. The growth of a recognized and responsible central government, following the definitive unification of Castile and León under Ferdinand III
(10) early in the thirteenth century, had provided a court or central cultural focus toward which men of literary ability could gravitate. The growing self-awareness of the writer as a unique creative personality, from the anonymity of the *cantares de gesta* to the tentative identification we see in the poetry of Berceo, to intense and affirmative individualism of the later *mester de*

(15) *clerecía* in Juan Ruiz and López de Ayala, demands an ever broader field in which to realize and fulfill itself. In obedience to this sort of aesthetic need and nurtured on the expanding possibilities of a settled and prospering society, the fifteenth century represents a period of great fecundity in the development and widening of literary genres.

(20) The medieval *cantar de gesta,* which had so magnificently served the needs of a society of embattled warriors, undergoes a major change, possibly through the influence of the *mester de clerecía.* In the new society there was neither time, place, nor public for the recitation of the long and usually complex epic poems, but the great deeds, the great heroes still held their magic

(25) for the general public. These survive in a new poetic form, the *romances.* The anonymous *romances* are short poems of regular meter and assonance which capture an intense and dramatic moment—of sorrow, of defeat, of parting, of return—in simple and direct language. They are generally fragmentary, combining lyricism and narration taken from the dramatic high points of the

(30) epics. Some critics have thought that the oldest *romances* represent a survival of the raw material from which the long *cantares* grew, but the more generally accepted opinion is that they represent the opposite process; as the old *cantares* fell into oblivion, the best moments and the most stirring passages were conserved and polished and given new life.

(35) Supporting this view is the fact that the earliest *romances* go back only to the middle of the fourteenth century, a time in which the *cantares* were in a period of final decadence and the oldest epic poems already forgotten. They share the realism and directness of the *cantares,* and also the greater polish and lyricism of the *mester de clerecía.* Some thousands of them have been

(40) collected and not all relate to the material of the Spanish epics.

> **Be careful to spot the word "EXCEPT" in a question.**

Sample

> **10.** According to the passage, all of the following probably contributed to increasing the number of literary genres in fifteenth-century Spain EXCEPT
>
> **A.** growth of Spanish cities.
>
> **B.** Spaniards' increased contact with other societies.
>
> **C.** conflicts between the Moorish and Christian states.
>
> **D.** unification of Castile and León.
>
> **E.** a change in the writer's view of himself.

The best choice is **C.** The passage indicates that more literary genres developed in Spain because the Christian states provided a "settled and prospering society" (line 17)—not because of conflicts between Moors and Christians. Choices **A, B, D,** and **E** are all mentioned as contributing to the developing literary climate in fifteenth-century Spain.

Use an elimination strategy. That is, immediately eliminate answers that are irrelevant, not addressed, or just wrong. Do not consider them again.

Sample

> **11.** The passage implies that
>
> **A.** the *cantares* focus on heroic deeds associated with war, whereas the *romances* are concerned with peace.
>
> **B.** the authors of *romances* were well-educated, recognized writers.
>
> **C.** the influence of Moorish culture on the *romance* was less strong than it was on the *cantares*.
>
> **D.** the *romances* probably influenced the *mester de clerecía*.
>
> **E.** the *cantares* were often recited to audiences.

The best choice is **E.** The implication in lines 22–24 is that the *cantares* were more often recited in public than read in private. Choice **A** is incorrect. The *romances* combine lyricism with narration taken from the dramatic high points of the epics; nothing suggests that they are concerned with peace rather than war. Notice that defeat is mentioned as one of the moments captured by *romances*. Eliminate choice **A.** Choice **B** is contradicted in line 26, where the *romances* are characterized as anonymous. Eliminate choice **B.** The passage does not refer to Moorish influence on any of the genres, so choice **C** can be eliminated. Choice **D** is a reversal of what the passage suggests (lines 20–22). Eliminate choice **D.** Although only choice **E** remains, you need to read it anyway to make sure that it is correct and that you have not misread one of the other choices.

Some questions ask you to reason from the information given.

Sample

> **12.** According to the passage, the theory that the *romances* come from the same raw material as the *cantares* is questionable because
>
> **A.** *romances* came into being only after the decline of the *cantares*.
>
> **B.** the subject matter of *romances* is the lives of everyday people rather than the lives of heroes.
>
> **C.** *romances* are more lyrical and complex than *cantares*.
>
> **D.** the *cantares* were unavailable to the writers of the *romances*.
>
> **E.** foreign influences are prevalent in the *romances* but not in the *cantares*.

The best choice is **A.** According to the author, the *cantares* were in a period of "final decadence" at the time the *romances* were born, so it is unlikely that they came from the same raw material. Choice **B** is incorrect; the subject matter of *romances* was not the lives of everyday people. In lines 23–24 the *cantares* are described as "usually complex," whereas in line 28 the *romances* are characterized as written in "simple and direct" language, making choice **C** also a bad choice. Since the subject matter of *romances* often derives from the epics, choice **D** is also incorrect. Foreign influences on the genres, choice **E,** are not addressed in the passage.

> **Realize what you can and can't infer from the passage. Watch for answers that are too general or too specific.**

Sample

---

13. From the passage the reader can infer that

   A. before the fifteenth century most Spaniards were illiterate.

   B. the *cantar* was the only literary genre in Spain before 1600.

   C. the decline of the Moorish states in Spain resulted in the destruction of much early Spanish literature.

   D. fifteenth-century Spanish culture benefited from outside influences.

   E. the *mester de clerecía* were more popular than the *cantares*.

The best choice is **D.** The author cites Spaniards' contact with other societies as a positive influence on Spain's literary development (lines 6–8). The statements in both choices **A** and **B** are far too sweeping, based on information in the passage. Choice **C** is not mentioned or implied, and nothing suggests that the *mester de clerecía* were more popular than the epics, choice **E.**

Other Important Strategies

- As you read, also watch for names, definitions, places, and numbers, but do not try to memorize the passage.

- Make sure that the answer you select really answers the question. Some good or true answers are not correct.

- Don't get stuck on the passage or any one question.

Practice Reading Comprehension Passages and Questions

Questions 1–8

The railroads played a key role in the settlement of the West. They provided relatively easy access to the region for the first time, and they also actively re-
(5) cruited farmers to settle there. The railroads are criticized for their part in settling the West too rapidly, with its resultant economic unrest. Of course there were abuses connected with building
(10) and operating the railroads, but it must be pointed out that they performed a useful service in extending the frontier and helping to achieve national unity.

The real tragedy of the rapid settlement
(15) of the Great Plains was the shameful way in which the American Indians were treated. Threatened with the destruction of their whole mode of life, the Indians fought back savagely. Justice
(20) was almost entirely on the Indians' side. The land was clearly theirs; frequently their title was legally certified by a treaty negotiated with the federal government. The Indians, however, lacked
(25) the military force and the political power to protect this right. Not only did white men encroach upon the Indians' hunting grounds, but they rapidly destroyed the Indians' principal means of
(30) subsistence—the buffalo. By 1869, the railroads had cut the herd in half, and by the middle of the 1880s, both the southern and northern herd were eliminated. The white man frequently killed the buf-
(35) falo merely for sport, leaving the valuable carcass to rot in the sun.

The plains Indians were considered different from the Indians encountered by the English colonists on the Atlantic
(40) coast. Mounted on horses, typical plains Indians were fierce warriors who could shoot arrows with surprising accuracy while galloping at top speed. Although they quickly adapted themselves to the
(45) use of the rifle, the Indians were not equal to the firepower of the United States Army and thus were doomed to defeat.

Theoretically, at least, the government
(50) tried to be fair to the Indians, but all too often the Indian agents were either too indifferent or corrupt to carry out the government's promises conscientiously. The army frequently ignored the Indian
(55) Bureau and failed to coordinate its policies with the civilians who were nominally in charge of Indian affairs. The settlers hated and feared the Indians and wanted them exterminated. This bar-
(60) baric attitude is certainly not excusable, but it is understandable in the context of the time.

1. The author's attitude toward the treatment of American Indians by whites is one of

   A. qualified regret.

   B. violent anger.

   C. strong disapproval.

   D. objective indifference.

   E. unfair bias.

2. The author implies which of the following about the forces at work during the settlement of the Great Plains?

   A. The federal government represented the moral use of law.

   B. Justice was overcome by military firepower.

   C. Attempts by the government to be fair were rejected by the Indians.

   D. The settlers' hatred and fear was offset by the Indians' attempts at kindness.

   E. The Indians and the white settlers shared a sporting interest in the hunting of buffalo.

3. Which of the following is concrete evidence that the white settlers did not need the buffalo for their own subsistence, as did the Indians?

   A. More than half of the great buffalo herd had disappeared by 1869.

   B. Nearly 15 million buffalo were killed within 20 years.

   C. Buffalo carcasses were left rotting in the sun by whites.

   D. The railroad brought necessary food and supplies to the white settlers from the East.

   E. The white settlers had their own hunting grounds separate from the Indians'.

4. What is the point of the comparison between the plains Indians and the Indians encountered on the Atlantic coast?

   A. The Atlantic coast Indians were not as abused by white settlers.

   B. Because they were considerably better warriors than the Atlantic coast Indians, the plains Indians were a match for the United States military.

   C. If Indians such as those on the Atlantic coast had populated the plains, there would have been no bloodshed of the white settlement.

   D. The Indians encountered by English colonists posed no violent threat to the colonists.

   E. The Atlantic coast Indians were unfamiliar with horses.

5. Which of the following characteristics of the passage suggests that the abuse of the Indians is a more significant topic for the author than the beneficial role of the railroads?

   A. the statement that the railroads "are criticized for their part in settling the West too rapidly" (lines 3–4)

   B. the amount of discussion devoted to the abuse of the Indians

   C. the reliance on statistical details in both the first and second paragraphs

   D. the mention of the plains Indians' ability to fight

   E. the perception that the achievement of national unity was one of the services that the railroad performed

6. The author of the passage would most likely disagree that

    A. the United States government's policies toward the American Indians were shameful.

    B. the land that the Indians fought to retain belonged to them.

    C. numerous abuses were among the results of the railroads' rapid spread westward.

    D. some American Indian tribes used sophisticated weapons brought by settlers.

    E. the United States army could not be considered a friend of the American Indian.

7. It can be inferred from the passage that the purpose of the Indian Bureau was to

    A. try Indians who violated the laws of the new territory.

    B. establish reservations where the peaceful American Indians would live.

    C. assist with Indian affairs and policies of the government regarding the American Indian.

    D. bring to justice white settlers who treated the Indians in a savage or unlawful manner.

    E. assist the Indians in learning a new method of procuring food to rely less on buffalo meat.

8. All of the following are presented as overt enemies of the Indians EXCEPT the

    A. railroads.

    B. white hunters.

    C. army.

    D. Indian agents.

    E. western settlers.

Questions 9–12

If you make a marked increase in the amount of light falling upon the normal eye, you observe an immediate adjustment of the iris to reduce the size of the
(5) pupil. This is called an unconditioned response, and the increased light is called an unconditioned stimulus. Now, if you make numerous trials taking care to sound a buzzer whenever the light is
(10) increased, the iris can be "taught," that is to say, conditioned, to reduce the pupil at the sound of the buzzer alone. This learned response is called a conditioned response and the sound of the
(15) buzzer, a conditioned stimulus.

Now symbols are our most important conditioned stimuli, and successful communication depends upon complementary conditioning, or complemen-
(20) tary experience. Just as we find ourselves shouting at listeners who do not speak our language, so by a similar irrational impulse we assume that those with whom we attempt to communicate
(25) are equipped with complementary sets of conditioned responses to our own common stock of symbols. It is easy to see the stupidity of expecting one who does not speak English to converse with
(30) you in English. It is not so easy to realize that one who does speak English may not have been conditioned to operate with the same set of senses for the familiar terms common to your vocabu-
(35) lary and his.

9. The primary purpose of the passage is to

   A. define an aspect of a topic.

   B. reconcile differing theories.

   C. propose a topic for investigation.

   D. solve a puzzle.

   E. analyze a phenomenon.

10. Which of the following may be best described as an unconditioned stimulus?

   A. an unanswered telephone ringing in an empty office

   B. a whistle that blows at five o'clock every weekday

   C. a shoelace that breaks in two

   D. a match that burns the finger of a careless pipe smoker

   E. an alarm clock that rings at midnight

11. Applying information from the passage, we may conclude that a child who begins feeling hungry as the school lunch bell rings each day may be exhibiting

   A. an awareness of time.

   B. a complementary structure.

   C. a conditioned response.

   D. an unconditioned stimulus.

   E. a conditioned appetite.

12. The passage suggests that those who speak English attempting to communicate with those who do not speak English are

   A. bound to fail completely.

   B. still dependent upon complementary responses to common symbols.

   C. likely to be more successful if they raise their voice.

   D. likely to be able to communicate where there are familiar words common to both speakers' vocabularies.

   E. subject to the limitations of third-party translations.

Questions 13–16

   Let us consider a hypothetical pair of communicants, utterer and interpreter, from the operation point of view. We shall assume that our utterer has six
(5) hats: red, blue, yellow, black, gray, and white. If the rods and cones (the tiny end organs packed together on what corresponds to the sensitive films in the stereoscopic or double-lens camera) of
(10) the retinae of his eyes are not defective, he will be able to see that the six hats differ even though they are of the same shape and material. If we reduce the light so that he can barely see, the white
(15) and the yellow will seem to be the same. But as the light grows stronger he will be able to see that the red, blue, and yellow affect him differently from black, gray, and white. He now has sufficient
(20) experience (remember, this is all grossly oversimplified) to conceive of color and shade. But he can also distinguish the red hat from the blue and yellow hats, the yellow from the blue and red, and so
(25) forth. He is thus ready for the concepts

red, blue, and yellow if, for example, we provide him with a red feather, a blue feather, and a yellow feather. Indeed, he may have the human impulse to deco-
(30) rate the hat with the corresponding feather. And if the feathers seem to have more in common with the white hat than the color hats have in common with the white hat, he can see that his concept of
(35) shade will determine the difference be-tween the two reds, the two blues, or the two yellows, and he will have need of the concepts of light and dark. And as we increase the number of shades, he
(40) will require relation concepts like those expressed in the suffixes –er and –est. By repeating the conventional symbols "hat" and "red" with the red hat, he con-ditions the sound of the words to the
(45) sight of the hat. If he sees that the rela-tion of each feather to its hat is similar to the other two, he has need of a rela-tion concept like the one expressed by the preposition "in," and he is thus pre-
(50) pared to say to himself "light red feather in dark red hat." Now in the dark he is not able to tell one hat or one feather from another, but in the middle of a moonless night he is able to think "red
(55) feather in red hat" simply by uttering the appropriate symbols to himself. And with his human impulse to try new com-binations, he can even think, "yellow feather in blue hat" without ever having
(60) seen them thus combined.

13. By discussing the different effects of reduced and increased light, the author is

   I. pointing to a limitation in the de-pendence on perception by sight.

   II. preparing to discuss the concepts of light and dark.

   III. laying the ground for the distinc-tion between what can be seen and what can be thought.

A. III only

B. I and II only

C. I and III only

D. II and III only

E. I, II, and III

14. Of the following, the most plausible criticism that could be directed at the "hats" example is that it is

A. too difficult to follow.

B. irrelevant.

C. too hypothetical.

D. too dependent on the esoteric language.

E. unreasonable.

15. According to the passage, the acquisition of symbols allows us not only to communicate, but also to

A. argue logically.

B. imagine.

C. respond to unconditioned stimuli.

D. respond to conditioned stimuli.

E. decorate hats.

16. The passage is most relevant to which of the following areas of study?

A. aesthetics of logic

B. literature and history

C. sociology

D. linguistics and psychology

E. anthropology

Questions 17–24

Many people seem to think that science fiction is typified by the covers of some of the old pulp magazines; the Bug-Eyed Monster, embodying every trait and fea-
(5) ture that most people find repulsive, is about to grab, and presumably ravish, a sweet, blonde, curvaceous, scantily-clad Earth girl. This is unfortunate because it demeans and degrades a worthwhile and
(10) even important literary endeavor. In contrast to this unwarranted stereotype, science fiction rarely emphasizes sex, and when it does, it is more discreet than other contemporary fiction. Instead, the
(15) basic interest of science fiction lies in the relation between man and his technology and between man and the universe. Science fiction is a literature of change and a literature of the future, and
(20) while it would be foolish to claim that science fiction is a major literary genre at this time, the aspects of human life that it considers make it well worth reading and studying—for no other literary
(25) form does quite the same things.

What is science fiction? It is a literary subgenre which postulates a change (for human beings) from conditions as we know them and follows the implications
(30) of these changes to a conclusion. That science fiction is a literary subgenre is a point that is often overlooked. Specifically, science fiction is either a short story or a novel. There are only a
(35) few poems and plays which could be called science fiction, with Karel Capek's *RUR* being the only play that is well known. To say that science fiction is a subgenre of prose fiction is to say
(40) that it has all the basic characteristics and serves the same basic functions in much the same way as prose fiction in general. Everything that can be said about prose fiction, in general, applies

(45) to science fiction. Every piece of science fiction, whether short story or novel, must have a narrator, a story, a plot, a setting, characters, language, and theme. And like any prose, the
(50) themes of science are concerned with interpreting man's nature and experience in relation to the world around him. Themes in science fiction are constructed and presented in exactly the
(55) same ways that themes are dealt with in any other kind of fiction. They are the result of a particular combination of narrator, story, plot, character, setting, and language. In short, the reasons for read-
(60) ing and enjoying science fiction, and the ways of studying and analyzing it, are basically the same as they would be for any other story or novel.

17. Although few examples of science fiction written before 1900 exist, you can infer that it has been most popular in the twentieth century because

   A. with the growth of literacy, the size of the reading public has increased.

   B. competition from television and film has created a demand for more exciting fiction.

   C. science fiction is easier to understand than other kinds of fiction.

   D. the increased importance of technology in our lives has given science fiction an increased relevance.

   E. other media have captured the large audience that read novels in the nineteenth century.

18. According to the definition in the passage, a fictional work that places human beings in a prehistoric world inhabited by dinosaurs

    A. cannot properly be called science fiction because it does not deal with the future.

    B. cannot properly be called science fiction because it does not deal with technology.

    C. can properly be called science fiction because it is prose fiction.

    D. can properly be called science fiction because it places people in an environment different from the one we know.

    E. can properly be called science fiction because it deals with humans' relation to the world around them.

19. Science fiction is called a literary subgenre because

    A. it is not important enough to be a literary genre.

    B. it cannot be made into dramatic presentation.

    C. it has its limits.

    D. it shares characteristics with other types of prose fiction.

    E. to call it a "genre" would subject it to literary jargon.

20. From the passage, you can infer that science fiction films based upon ideas that have originally appeared in other media are chiefly adaptations of

    A. short stories.

    B. plays.

    C. novels.

    D. poems.

    E. folk tales.

21. The author believes that, when compared to other literary genres, science fiction is

    A. deficient in its use of narrators.

    B. unable to be adapted to drama.

    C. a minor but worthwhile kind of fiction.

    D. more concerned with plot than with theme.

    E. in need of a unique literary approach if it is to be properly understood.

22. The emphasis on theme in the second paragraph of the passage suggests that the author regards which of the following as an especially important reason for reading science fiction?

    A. the discovery of meaning

    B. the display of character

    C. the beauty of language

    D. the psychological complexity

    E. the interest of setting

23. One implication of the final sentence in the passage is that

   A. the reader should turn next to commentaries on general fiction.

   B. there is no reason for any reader not to like science fiction.

   C. the reader should compare other novels and stories to science fiction.

   D. there are reasons for enjoying science fiction.

   E. those who can appreciate other prose fiction can appreciate science fiction.

24. An appropriate title for this passage would be

   A. On the Inaccuracies of Pulp Magazines

   B. Man and the Universe

   C. Toward a Definition of Science Fiction

   D. A Type of Prose Fiction

   E. Beyond the Bug-Eyed Monster

Questions 25–31

Let us take the terms "subjective" and "objective" and see if we can make up our minds what we mean by them in a statement like this: "Philosophers and
(5) artists are subjective; scientists, objective." First, the two terms make up a semantic pair. The one has no meaning without the other. We may define each by antonym with the other. We may de-
(10) fine them by synonym by translating the last syllable and say that "subjective" pertains to a subject, and "objective" pertains to an object. By operation analysis we may say that subjects per-
(15) ceive or conceive objects in the process of knowing. The word "knowing" reminds us that we are talking about the central nervous system and should waste no time in examining our terms
(20) for their sensory, affective, and logical components. The terms are primarily logical. What, then, is the basic logical relation that establishes whatever meaning they have? What goes on in the
(25) world when a poet is being subjective, and how does it differ from what goes on when a scientist is being objective?

When the poet sings "Drink to me only with thine eyes," he is responding im-
(30) mediately or in retrospect to an object, his beloved, outside himself; but he is fundamentally concerned with the sensations and emotions which that object stimulates in him; and whether the ob-
(35) ject justifies his praise in the opinion of others, or indeed whether there actually is such an object, is quite irrelevant to his purpose, which is the weaving of a beautiful pattern of sound and imagery
(40) into a richly affective concept of feminine loveliness. This is to be subjective.

Now the scientist is primarily concerned with the identity and continuity of the external object that stimulates his re-
(45) sponse. It need not seem absurd to locate the Eiffel Tower, or Everest, or the Grand Canyon, for that matter, in the mind because it is so perfectly obvious that they can exist as the Eiffel Tower,
(50) Everest, or the Grand Canyon nowhere else. Perhaps we can move a little closer to our definition of "objective" by suggesting a distinction between an object and thing. Let us define object as the ex-
(55) ternal cause of a thing. Whether objects "exist" is obviously not discussable, for the word "object" as used here must necessarily stand not for a thing but for a hypothesis. There is, for example,
(60) no way of telling whether objects are

195

singular or plural, whether one should say the stimulus of the Eiffel Tower experience or the stimuli of the Eiffel Tower experience. If then, it is impossi-
(65) ble even for the scientist to escape the essential subjectivity of his sensations, generalizations, and deductions, what do we mean by calling him objective?

25. Which of the following is NOT a semantic pair?

    A. chaos/order

    B. fact/fiction

    C. sitting/standing

    D. light/darkness

    E. virtue/vice

26. Which of the following pairs best exemplifies the subjective/objective opposition as defined by the passage?

    A. art/philosophy

    B. knower/known

    C. object/thing

    D. stimulus/stimuli

    E. emotion/sensation

27. The passage refers to "Drink to me only with thine eyes" (lines 28–29) primarily in order to

    A. suggest the affective powers of sound and imagery.

    B. exemplify the objective.

    C. exemplify the subjective.

    D. demonstrate how art can bestow universal significance on an object.

    E. illustrate the difference between literal and metaphorical language.

28. Given the content of the first and second paragraphs, the reader expects that the third paragraph will

    A. explain how the scientist is objective.

    B. define the identity and conformity of external objects.

    C. analyze what it is to be subjective.

    D. discriminate between an object and a thing.

    E. explore the implications of objectivity.

29. According to the passage, "objectivity" depends on the assumption that

    A. discrete objects exist external to the mind.

    B. one's vocation in life should be logical.

    C. subjectivity is a cognitive weakness.

    D. science is a viable discipline.

    E. the Eiffel Tower is a singular stimulus, not a diffuse experience.

30. Faced with this statement, "What you see is just in your head," the author of the passage would be likely to

    A. strongly disagree.

    B. agree that the statement is probably true.

    C. argue against the appropriateness of the word "just."

    D. assume that the person making the statement is not a scientist.

    E. argue that what is seen cannot be located outside or inside the mind.

31. According to the definitions of the third paragraph, which of the following is (are) true of an object?

    I. The reality of an object is hypothetical.

    II. Whether objects are plural or singular is uncertain.

    III. An object is the external cause of a thing.

    A. III only

    B. I and II only

    C. I and III only

    D. II and III only

    E. I, II, and III

Questions 32–35

As Augustine contemplates his own nature as well as that of his fellow men, he sees wickedness and corruption on every hand. Man is a sinful creature and
(5) there is nothing that is wholly good about him. The cause is to be found in original sin, which mankind inherited from Adam. If Adam is regarded as a particular human being, it would make
(10) no sense at all to blame his descendants for the mistakes that he made. But Adam is interpreted to mean the universal man rather than a particular individual. Since the universal necessarily
(15) includes all of the particulars belonging to the class, they are involved in whatever the universal does.

The total corruption of human nature as taught by Augustine did not mean that
(20) man is incapable of doing any good deeds. It meant that each part of his nature is infected with an evil tendency. In contrast to the Greek notion of a good mind and an evil body, he held that both
(25) mind and body had been made corrupt as a result of the fall. This corruption is made manifest in the lusts of the flesh and also in the activities of the mind. So
(30) far as the mind is concerned, the evil tendency is present in both the intellect and in the will. In the intellect, it is expressed in the sin of pride, and in the will, there is the inclination to follow
(35) that which is pleasant at the moment rather than to obey the demands of reason.

32. According to the passage, in order for modern man to be guilty of original sin,

    A. he must be corrupt in both mind and body.

    B. he must be guilty of intellectual and physical errors.

    C. Adam must be regarded as a unique human being.

    D. Adam must be regarded as the universal man.

    E. Adam must be regarded as responsible for Eve's fall.

33. Which of the following is a logical inference from this passage?

    A. The earlier in history a man is born, the more sinful he is likely to be.

    B. The later in history a man is born, the more sinful he is likely to be.

    C. Augustine would not agree with the phrase "as innocent as a newborn child."

    D. Augustine would agree that animals inherit original sin from Adam.

    E. At birth, a female is less guilty of sin than a male.

34. Which of the following would Augustine be most likely to regard as a consequence of the infected will?

   A. pride on one's ancestry

   B. envy of another's wisdom

   C. overeating

   D. vanity about one's appearance

   E. temper tantrums

35. According to the passage, the Greek idea of *man* differs from Augustine's because it believed that

   A. man is incapable of performing good deeds.

   B. man possesses an evil body but a good mind.

   C. corruption proceeds from the infected will.

   D. man possesses a good body and a good mind.

   E. man is incapable of following the dictates of reason.

Questions 36–39

Laboratory evidence indicates that life originated through chemical reactions in the primordial mixture (water, hydrogen, ammonia, and hydrogen cyanide) which
(5) blanketed the earth at its formation. These reactions were brought about by the heat, pressure, and radiation conditions then prevailing. One suggestion is that nucleosides and amino acids were
(10) formed from the primordial mixture, and the nucleosides produced nucleotides which produced the nucleic acids (DNA, the common denominator of all living things, and RNA). The amino acids be-
(15) came polymerized (chemically joined) into proteins, including enzymes, and lipids were formed from fatty acids and glycerol-like molecules. The final step appears to have been the gradual accu-
(20) mulation of DNA, RNA, proteins, lipids, and enzymes into a vital mass which began to grow, divide, and multiply.

The evolution of the various forms of life from this biochemical mass must not
(25) be considered a linear progression. Rather, the fossil record suggests an analogy between evolution and a bush whose branches go every which way. Like branches, some evolutionary lines
(30) simply end, and others branch again. Many biologists believe the pattern to have been as follows: bacteria emerged first and from them branched viruses, red algae, blue-green algae, and green
(35) flagellates. From the latter branched green algae, from which higher plants evolved, and colorless rhizoflagellates, from which diatoms, molds, sponges, and protozoa evolved. From ciliated
(40) protozoa (ciliophora) evolved multinucleate (syncytial) flatworms. These branched into five lines, one of which leads to the echinoderms and chordates. The remaining lines lead to most of the
(45) other phyla of the animal kingdom.

36. From the language of the first paragraph, it can be assumed that

   I. some scientists do not accept the theories of the origin of life the passage presents.

   II. the reactions that produced life required a unique combination of heat, pressure, and radiation.

   III. some living forms are without DNA.

   A. I only

   B. I and II only

C. I and III only

D. II and III only

E. I, II, and III

37. Which of the following best expresses the analogy between evolution and a bush?

A. species : evolution ::
bush : branching

B. species : branching ::
bush : evolution

C. evolution : species ::
bush : branched viruses

D. evolution : species ::
bush : branches

E. evolution : species ::
branches : bush

38. Which of the following can we infer to be the least highly evolved?

A. green algae

B. blue-green algae

C. molds

D. flatworms

E. ciliated protozoa

39. According to the passage, the evolutionary line of sponges in its proper order is

A. bacteria–viruses–green algae–sponges.

B. bacteria–viruses–rhizoflagellates–sponges.

C. bacteria–red algae–blue-green algae–rhizoflagellates–sponges.

D. bacteria–blue-green algae–green flagellates–rhizoflagellates–sponges.

E. bacteria–green flagellates–rhizoflagellates–sponges.

Answers and Explanations for the Practice Reading Comprehension Questions

1. **C.** Although the author does not express violent anger, the characterization of the treatment of the Indians as a *tragedy* and the pronouncement that the whites' behavior was *barbaric* certainly express strong disapproval.

2. **B.** Although justice was on the Indians' side (second paragraph), *the Indians were not equal to the firepower of the United States Army*. Each of the other choices contradicts information in the passage.

3. **C.** This is evidence that the whites killed buffalo for sport rather than for subsistence. The disappearance of the buffalo herd is not, of itself, evidence that the buffalo did not provide subsistence to the whites.

4. **D.** The point of comparison is that the Atlantic coast Indians were not fierce warriors like the plains Indians. Thus they did not pose any kind of violent threat.

5. **B.** Three of the four paragraphs of the passage are devoted to discussing the abuse of the plains Indians. The "weight" the author gives to this topic suggests its significance.

6. **A.** The author states that the government itself *tried to be fair* but that the *agents'* indifference or corruption failed the American Indians.

7. **C.** According to the final paragraph of the passage, the Indian agents were either too indifferent or corrupt to carry out the government's promises conscientiously. The army frequently ignored the Indian Bureau and failed to coordinate its policies with the civilians who were nominally in charge of Indian affairs. Choices **B** and **D** may be historically correct but cannot specifically be inferred from the passage.

8. **A.** Though the passage criticizes the railroads, it does not present them as overt enemies of the Indians, while the last paragraph cites the agents, the army, and the settlers.

9. **A.** Though **C** is a possible response, the best option here is **A.** The subject of the passage is the role of symbols in communication. Starting with that answer, choice **A** is better than **C** or the others.

10. **D.** An unconditioned stimulus is unprepared for and leads to an unconditioned response—in this case, no doubt, the holder's crying out and dropping the match.

11. **C.** The bell conditions the child's response, just as the buzzer conditions the eye's response in the example in the passage. That is, after many days of associating the bell with lunch, the child has been "taught" to feel hungry when the bell rings.

12. **B.** The passage suggests that complementary responses to common symbols are crucial in communication, even when there is no common language.

13. **C.** The discussion shows how perception by sight is determined by the availability of light and looks ahead to the conclusion that the imagination can work in darkness.

14. **C.** This answer might be arrived at by considering that the "hats" example is reasonable, relevant, pointed, and simply written; therefore, all choices except **C** are eliminated. But it may also be argued that the example does not describe a "real" situation.

15. **B.** This is the passage's final point, that one can think *yellow feather in blue hat* without seeing or having seen the items together.

16. **D.** The passage is most clearly relevant to linguistics (the science of language) and to psychology (the science dealing with the mind and mental processes).

17. **D.** Choices **A, B,** and **E** do not apply to science fiction as opposed to other fiction genres. Choice **C** may or may not be true. Since science fiction is concerned with the *relation between man and his technology,* it follows that as technology becomes more important, the fiction of technology would become more popular.

18. **D.** Paragraph two defines science fiction as postulating a change from known to unknown conditions.

19. **D.** The sentence beginning at line 38 explains why science fiction is called a subgenre of fiction.

20. C. Though short stories are a possible source, it is more probable that the longer novel is the source of science fiction films. The passage alludes to the scarcity of science fiction works in poetry or drama.

21. C. The first paragraph says science fiction is not *a major literary genre* but *well worth reading and studying.*

22. A. The theme is the controlling idea or meaning of a work of literature.

23. E. The final sentence presents a general comparison between *any other story or novel* and science fiction, emphasizing their similarities and thus suggesting that the subgenre of science fiction should be read as one reads fiction in general.

24. C. The first paragraph leads up to the central question—"What is science fiction?" All of the passage is an attempt to answer that question. Choices **A** and **D** are too specific; **B** is too general; and **E** does not fit the tone of the passage.

25. C. In lines 7–9, the passage says that in a semantic pair "the one (term) has no meaning without the other. We may define each by antonym with the other." In short, semantic pairs are pairs of direct opposites. Only **C** is not such a pair.

26. B. The first paragraph says, "subjects perceive or conceive objects in the process of knowing." The pair that may best be substituted in that is *knower* and *known.*

27. C. The passage uses "Drink to me only with thine eyes" to show that the poet is fundamentally concerned with sensations and emotions. The quotation is an example of the subjective. In fact, the author finishes the paragraph by saying, "This it is to be subjective."

28. A. Since the passage begins with the idea that the artist is subjective and the scientist objective, and the second paragraph deals with the subjectivity of the artist, you expect the third paragraph to be about the objectivity of the scientist.

29. A. The author tells us that scientists, whom he defines as *objective,* are "primarily concerned with the identity and continuity of the external object that stimulates (their) response." That is, to be objective one must believe that the world is a collection of stable objects, each of which always looks the same. **E** is a single example consistent with this assumption but is not itself broad enough to support the question of objectivity in general. **D** is also too broad to be the best answer. **C** is not an assumption allowed by the passage.

30. C. The author concludes by saying that "it is impossible even for the scientist to escape the essential subjectivity of his sensations, generalizations, and deductions." Since everything is subjective, since different people each see the same thing a bit differently, one is seeming to devalue this case by saying that "what you say you see is just in your head." *In your head* is not an unimportant place; according to the passage, it is the only place.

31. E. The third paragraph defines an *object* as the "external cause of a thing—a hypothesis," with its singularity or plurality indeterminable. This is a definition peculiar to this passage.

32. D. The first paragraph explains that a universal Adam would involve all of the particulars of his class in his actions.

33. C. According to Augustine, even a newborn would be guilty of the sin of Adam.

34. C. The sins of the will are those which are pleasant at the moment, such as eating. Sins of pride, envy, or wrath are sins of the intellect.

35. **B.** The second paragraph presents the notion of a good mind and evil body as Greek.

36. **B.** The terms *indicates* and *suggestion* imply that theories described are only theories and not universally accepted. The passage calls DNA "the common denominator of all living things."

37. **D.** *Evolution* is to *species* in the same way as *bush* is to *branches.* Just as the branches of a bush reach out every which way in varying lengths, the results of evolution (forms of life, species) have devolved in irregular "branches." This is the main point of the second paragraph.

38. **B.** Blue-green algae are the second step, emerging from bacteria.

39. **E.** The passage presents sponges as evolving from rhizoflagellates, which came from green flagellates, which came from bacteria.

Introduction to Sentence Correction

The Sentence Correction question type is composed of grammar-based questions and is very different from Reading Comprehension and Critical Reasoning.

Ability Tested

This section tests your knowledge of correct and effective English expression.

Basic Skills Necessary

Knowledge of the basic rules of grammar and usage will help in this section.

Directions

Some part of each sentence is underlined; sometimes the whole sentence is underlined. Five choices for rephrasing the underlined part follow each sentence; the first choice repeats the original, and the other four are different. If the first choice seems better than the alternatives, choose that answer; if not, choose one of the others.

For each sentence, consider the requirements of standard written English. Your choice should be a correct and effective expression, not awkward or ambiguous. Focus on grammar, word choice, sentence construction, and punctuation. If a choice changes the meaning of the original sentence, do not select it.

Analysis

Several alternatives to an underlined portion may be correct; you need to pick the *best* (most clear and exact) one.

Don't choose *any* alternative that changes the meaning of the sentence, no matter how clear or correct it is.

Suggested Approach with Samples

Pronouns

Look for pronoun errors first. Focus on words like he, him, she, her, we, us, they, them, who, whom, whoever, whomever, you, it, which, or that.

There are two common pronoun errors. The first is confusing a subject (*I, he, she, we, they*) and an object (*me, him, her, us, them*).

Samples

> **1.** <u>The Rotary Club applauded Tom and I</u> for our work helping the handicapped in town find secure jobs.
>
> **A.** The Rotary Club applauded Tom and I
>
> **B.** The Rotary Club applauded I and Tom
>
> **C.** Tom and me were applauded by the Rotary Club
>
> **D.** The Rotary Club applauded Tom and me
>
> **E.** Me and Tom were applauded by the Rotary Club

Choices **A** and **B** use a subject *(I)* where an object is needed *(me),* while choices **C** and **E** use an object *(me)* where a subject is needed. The answer is **D.**

> **2.** After extensive trials, the coach chose four swimmers to make up the relay <u>team, Joan, Judy, Alice, and me.</u>
>
> **A.** team, Joan, Judy, Alice, and me.
>
> **B.** team, Joan, Judy, Alice, and I.
>
> **C.** team, Joan and I, Alice and Judy.
>
> **D.** team, I, Joan, Judy, and Alice.
>
> **E.** team, and they are Joan, Judy, Alice and me.

The original version **A** is correct. The pronoun should be objective because the four names are in apposition to swimmers, the object of the verb *chose.* The subjective *I* in **B, C,** and **D** is incorrect. Choice **E** revises the sentence so that the subject of the second clause is *they*; the pronoun here should be the subjective *I,* not *me.*

> **The second common pronoun error is confusing singulars (***I, he, she***) and plurals (***we, they***).**

Samples

3. If either Mark or Jack is late again, <u>the bus will leave without them.</u>

   A. the bus will leave without them

   B. the bus will leave without him

   C. the bus will leave without their being on it

   D. they will miss the bus

   E. he will miss the bus

The problem here is the choice between the plural *them* and the singular *him.* Since the pronoun refers to either Mark or Jack, but not to both, the singular *him* in **B** is the right choice. The other choices either repeat the error or change the sentence meaning.

4. The director of the play, along with the costume designer, the set director, and the lighting technicians, <u>have made their recommendations</u> about the revision of the third act to the playwright.

   A. have made their recommendations

   B. has made their recommendations

   C. made their recommendations

   D. had made their recommendations

   E. has made his recommendations

The correct answer is **E.** The subject of the sentence is the singular *director.* The phrase beginning with *along with* is parenthetical and is not the subject of the verb or pronoun that follows. The singular verb form is correct in **B,** but the plural pronoun *their* is incorrect here and in all three other wrong answers.

Verbs

If the sentence contains no pronouns or if the pronouns are correct, focus on the verb.

There are two common verb errors. The first involves confusing singular and plural forms.

Samples

> **5.** The trunk containing <u>costumes, makeup, and props were left</u> at the stage entrance of the theater.
>
> **A.** costumes, makeup, and props were left
>
> **B.** costumes, makeup, and props were all left
>
> **C.** costumes, makeup, and props was left
>
> **D.** costumes, makeup, and props were to be left
>
> **E.** costumes, makeup, and props have been left

The correct answer is **C.** The verb in the underlined phrase is *were left.* Since the subject is singular *(trunk)* the verb must be singular—*was* instead of *were.* Don't assume that the subject immediately precedes the verb; in this case, the subject and verb are some distance apart.

> **6.** The film's silly plot, bad acting, and awkward camera work <u>has been the target of universally bad reviews.</u>
>
> **A.** has been the target of universally bad reviews.
>
> **B.** has been universally targeted by hostile reviewers.
>
> **C.** have been the target of universally bad reviews.
>
> **D.** is the target of universally bad reviews.
>
> **E.** has received universally bad reviews in the newspapers.

The compound subject of this sentence *(plot, acting, and camera work)* requires a plural verb. Only **C** uses the plural *(have)*; the other four versions have singular verbs.

The second common verb error is an error of tense (present, past, future).

Samples

> **7.** Tomorrow or the next day, <u>I went to New York.</u>
>
>   **A.**   I went to New York
>
>   **B.**   I have gone to New York
>
>   **C.**   I will go to New York
>
>   **D.**   I had gone to New York
>
>   **E.**   I did go to New York

The word *tomorrow* tells you that the action takes place in the future, so the correct answer must be **C,** the future tense of the verb—*will go.*

> **8.** Although he had spoken on television many times before, yesterday's interview <u>is the first time the governor has admitted</u> his interest in running for senator.
>
>   **A.**   is the first time the governor has admitted
>
>   **B.**   was the first time the governor admitted
>
>   **C.**   will be the first time the governor will admit
>
>   **D.**   had been the first time the governor had admitted
>
>   **E.**   shall be the first time the governor admitted

The description of the interview as *yesterday's* places the action in the past. Logically, the tense of the main verb must be past tense. The correct choice is **B,** which uses the past tense for both verbs in the underlined phrase.

Parallelism

Another common error is faulty parallelism. Look for a series of items separated by commas and make sure that each item has the same form.

Samples

> **9.** <u>To strive, to seek, to find, and not yielding</u> are the heroic goals of Ulysses in Tennyson's famous poem.
>
>   **A.**   To strive, to seek, to find, and not yielding
>
>   **B.**   To strive, to seek, finding and not yielding
>
>   **C.**   To strive, to seek, to find, and not to yield
>
>   **D.**   To strive, seeking, to find, and not yielding
>
>   **E.**   Striving, seeking, finding, and not to yield

Not yielding is incorrect; it should have the infinitive form *(to _____)* of the other items. Choice **C** is the best answer. Choices **A, B, D,** and **E** all have faulty parallelism, mixing infinitives (verbs with *to*) and gerunds (verbs with *-ing*).

---

10. Hard work and self-discipline often result <u>in not only a rise in one's salary but also your self-esteem.</u>

    A. in not only a rise in one's salary but also your self-esteem.

    B. not only in a rise in one's salary but also your self-esteem.

    C. not only in a rise in your salary but also your self-esteem.

    D. in a rise not only in one's salary but also in one's self-esteem.

    E. in a rise not only in one's salary but also in your self-esteem.

There are two parallelism problems here. Phrases such as *not only . . . but also* (correlatives) should be followed by phrases that are parallel in structure. And pronouns such as *one's* and *your* should not both be used in the same sentence. The correct version here is **D,** which follows *not only . . . but also* with parallel phrases (*in one's salary* and *in one's self-esteem*). It also uses the same pronoun (*one's*) in both phrases. All of the other versions have at least one, and sometimes two, parallelism errors.

Idioms

Sometimes a sentence contains an error in idiom; that is, it employs a word or phrase which is incorrect simply because it has not been established as standard usage. Such errors just don't "sound right."

Samples

---

11. The law prohibits passengers <u>to bring weapons in the plane.</u>

    A. to bring weapons in the plane.

    B. from bringing weapons in the plane.

    C. to bring weapons on the plane.

    D. from bringing weapons onto the plane.

    E. to bring weapons to the plane.

With the verb *prohibit,* the correct idiom is *from bringing* rather than *to bring*. The idiomatic preposition in this sentence is *onto* or *on* rather than *in* or *to*. The best choice is **D.**

> **12.** He lacks the ability <u>in running a large company and has no interest to expand</u> its market in Europe and Asia.
>
> A. in running a large company and has no interest to expand
>
> B. in running a large company and has no interest in expanding
>
> C. to run a large company and has no interest in expanding
>
> D. to run a large company and has no interest to expand
>
> E. in the running of a large company and has no interest in the expansion of

Two idioms are in question here. With the phrase *lacks the ability,* the better idiom is the infinitive *to run.* On the other hand, with the phrase *has no interest,* the preferred idiom is the preposition *in* and a gerund phrase—here, *expanding.* The correct answer is **C.**

Adjectives/Adverbs

Adjective or adverb misuse constitutes another type of error. One common type of problem is a matter of confusing when to use an adjective versus when to use an adverb.

Samples

> **13.** <u>The tired mechanic, happily to be finished with a hard day's work,</u> closed the hood over the newly tuned engine.
>
> A. The tired mechanic, happily to be finished with a hard day's work
>
> B. Happily, the tired mechanic being finished with a hard day's work
>
> C. Tired but happy with a hard day's work being done, the mechanic
>
> D. The tired mechanic, happy to be finished with a hard day's work
>
> E. With the pleasant fatigue of a job well done, the mechanic

Happily is used here to describe a person, the mechanic. The correct part of speech for describing a person or thing is an adjective, *happy.* Thus, **D** is the correct choice—grammatically correct, logical, economical, and clear without changing the intended meaning of the original sentence.

14. Though the game was in Foxboro, <u>most every fan in the stands was cheering loud</u> for the Jets.

    A. most every fan in the stands was cheering loud

    B. almost every fan in the stands was cheering loudly

    C. almost every fan in the stands was cheering loud

    D. most fans in the stand were cheering loud

    E. most every fan in the stand was cheering loudly

There are two adjective-adverb problems in this example. *Most* is an adjective, but here it modifies the adjective *every,* not the noun *fan.* The correct form should be the adverb *almost,* which can modify an adjective. *Loud* is another adjective, but here it modifies a verb *(was cheering).* The correct form is the adverb *loudly.* Only **B** gets both right.

Misplaced Modifiers

When a word or phrase is not placed close to the word it modifies, the error is called a *misplaced modifier.* If the word that should be modified is missing, the error is called a *dangling modifier.*

Samples

15. <u>Looking through the lens of a camera,</u> Mount Rushmore seemed much smaller and farther away than it had only seconds before.

    A. Looking through the lens of a camera

    B. With camera in hand

    C. Through the effects of the lens of a camera she looked through

    D. When she looked through the camera lens

    E. Against the camera

The sentence seems to say that Mount Rushmore is looking through the camera lens (dangling modifier). Choice **D** makes it clear that a person is looking through the lens and does so without the excessive wordiness of choice **C.**

16. Having cashed my refund check and deposited most of the money in my savings account, <u>a small sum was left to spend on new clothes.</u>

    A. a small sum was left to spend on new clothes.

    B. buying new clothes with the small sum left was possible.

    C. I had a small sum left with which to buy clothes.

    D. new clothes used up the small leftover sum

    E. the small leftover sum was spent on new clothes.

This is an example of dangling participles. The sentence begins with two participles (*having cashed* and *deposited*). These participles will dangle if the first clause is not followed by a reference to the human agent who did the cashing and depositing. Only **C** begins with a human subject—*I.*

Comparisons

A sentence may contain a comparison error. For example, sometimes a sentence may appear to compare two items that are not comparable. Also, comparative words are often misused.

Samples

> **17.** She wished that her career could be <u>as glamorous as the other women</u> but was not willing to work as hard as they had.
>
> **A.** as glamorous as the other women
>
> **B.** as glamorous as the other women's
>
> **C.** with the glamour of other women
>
> **D.** more glamorous than the careers of the other women
>
> **E.** glamorous

Here two very different incomparable things are being compared: Her career is compared to the other women. Choice **B,** the most clear, complete, and sensible construction, compares her career to the careers of other women.

> **18.** Like the better-known French fashion experts, <u>the clothes of the Italian fashion designer are copied all over the world.</u>
>
> **A.** the clothes of the Italian fashion designers are copied all over the world.
>
> **B.** copies of the clothes of Italian designers are made all over the world.
>
> **C.** Italian designers make clothes that are copied all over the world.
>
> **D.** the clothes copied all over the world are made by Italian designers.
>
> **E.** there are copies of the clothes of Italian designers all over the world.

The sentence begins with a comparison *(Like)* to French designers, so the subject of the clause that follows must be something comparable to the French designers. This subject cannot be clothes or copies. The correct choice is **C,** which begins with Italian designers.

Wordiness and Awkward Constructions

Watch for sentences that are awkward or wordy. You may need to choose between several versions of a sentence, none of which contains a specific grammar or usage error. One of the answers is simply stylistically better than the others; that is, it conveys the same meaning with superior precision, conciseness, and clarity. Verbosity (unnecessary wordiness) is an often-tested stylistic weakness.

Samples

19. <u>After the shipment of bananas had been unloaded, a tarantula's nest was discovered by the foreman</u> in the hold of the ship.

   A. After the shipment of bananas had been unloaded, a tarantula's nest was discovered by the foreman

   B. After unloading the shipment of bananas, a tarantula's nest was discovered by the foreman

   C. Having unloaded the shipment of bananas, a tarantula's nest was discovered by the foreman

   D. After the shipment of bananas had been unloaded, the foreman discovered a tarantula's nest

   E. After the shipment of bananas had been unloaded, the foreman discovers a tarantula's nest

Choices **B, C,** and **E** cannot be right—choices **B** and **C** because of their dangling gerund and dangling participle, choice **E** because of the improper verb tenses (a past perfect and a present). Both choices **A** and **D** are grammatical, but because it uses the passive voice, choice **A** is wordier than choice **D**. Given a choice like this, prefer the sentence in the active voice.

You cannot rewrite an active sentence using a passive verb without using at least two additional words. For example, consider:

I hit the ball. (four words, active)

The ball was hit by me. (six words, passive)

You should also note the ambiguity in choice **A,** because you are not sure if the foreman, the nest, or both are in the hold of the ship.

> **20.** Lured by the Florida sun, <u>Canadians by the thousands descend annually into St. Petersburg each year.</u>
>
> **A.** Canadians by the thousands descend annually into St. Petersburg each year.
>
> **B.** St. Petersburg receives thousands of Canadians each year.
>
> **C.** St. Petersburg annually receives thousands of Canadians.
>
> **D.** Canadians by the thousands descend on St. Petersburg each year.
>
> **E.** thousands of Canadians descend into St. Petersburg each year.

The best choice is **D.** Choice **A** is wordy (*annually* means *each year*) and misuses the idiom *descend on.* But choices **B** and **C** make *Lured* a dangling participle. The idiom *(descend into)* in choice **E** is wrong in this context.

Between an awkward sentence that is grammatically correct and a smoother sentence with a grammatical error, always choose the correct version. But when neither of the two sentences has an error, you must base your decision on style.

A Few Tips on Spotting Verbosity

Many phrases take two or more words to say what one word can say equally well. For example, the phrase *due to the fact that* takes five words to say what *because* says in one. A verbose sentence uses a phrase such as *his being of a generous nature* (six words) where a phrase such as *his generous nature* (three words) or *his generosity* (two words) can say the same thing. The following are examples of verbose phrases and formulas with a concise alternative.

Verbose	Concise
due to the fact that	because
owing to the fact that	because
inasmuch as	because
which was when	when
for the purpose of + gerund *i.e. for the purpose of eating*	to + verb *to eat*
in order to + verb *i.e. in order to fly*	to + verb *to fly*
so they can + verb *i.e. so they can appreciate*	to + verb *to appreciate*
not + negative adjective *i.e. not useless*	positive adjective *useful*
each and every	every

Verbose	Concise
he is a man who	he is
. . . is a . . . that *i.e. soccer is a game that*	is *soccer is*
the truth is that *i.e. the truth is that I am tired*	you can often omit altogether *I am tired*
the fact is that *i.e. the fact is that you were late*	you can often omit altogether *you were late*
it is *i.e. it is money that talks*	you can often omit altogether *money talks*
there are *i.e. there are some flowers that are poisonous*	you can often omit altogether *some flowers are poisonous*
in a situation where	where
in a condition where	where

Summary of Common Errors

Watch out for pronoun and verb errors, nonparallel constructions, misplaced words or phrases, and awkward or wordy sentences. Other possible errors that have not been explained above are fully explained in the answer sections following the practice questions and test.

A PATTERNED PLAN OF ATTACK
Sentence Correction

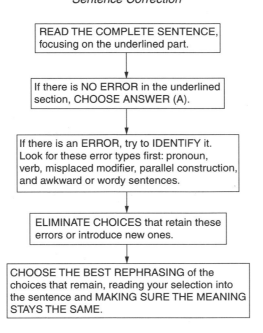

READ THE COMPLETE SENTENCE, focusing on the underlined part.

If there is NO ERROR in the underlined section, CHOOSE ANSWER (A).

If there is an ERROR, try to IDENTIFY it. Look for these error types first: pronoun, verb, misplaced modifier, parallel construction, and awkward or wordy sentences.

ELIMINATE CHOICES that retain these errors or introduce new ones.

CHOOSE THE BEST REPHRASING of the choices that remain, reading your selection into the sentence and MAKING SURE THE MEANING STAYS THE SAME.

Practice Sentence Correction Questions

Easy to Moderate

1. <u>Secretly determined to break up the drug dealer's ring, the undercover agent with the local pushers joined forces,</u> without their realizing his identity.

   A. Secretly determined to break up the drug dealer's ring, the undercover agent with the local pushers joined forces

   B. Secretly determined to break up the drug dealer's ring, the undercover agent joined forces with the local pushers

   C. The undercover agent secretly joined forces with local pushers in order to destroy their ring

   D. The undercover agent joined forces with the local pushers and secretly determined to destroy their ring

   E. Secretly determined to destroy the rings, the local pushers and the undercover agent joined forces

2. <u>In studying diabetes, many doctors have concluded</u> that early detection of the disease can permit control through diet.

   A. In studying diabetes, many doctors have concluded

   B. Many doctors, by studying diabetes, have concluded

   C. Many doctors studying diabetes have concluded

   D. Diabetes studies have led many doctors to conclude

   E. The conclusion of those doctors who have studied diabetes is

3. Although he is <u>liable to</u> make political enemies with the decision, the President will propose severe tax cuts that may both stimulate business and reduce the availability of home loans.

   A. liable to

   B. liable from

   C. able to

   D. of a mind to

   E. acknowledging his ability to

4. <u>To the behalf of many citizens who believe that some criminal statutes are unfair to the victims of crime,</u> legislators in California drafted a "Victim's Bill of Rights" law, which passed handily in the election.

   A. To the behalf of many citizens who believe that some criminal statutes are unfair to the victims of crime

   B. Listening for many citizens' belief that criminal statutes are unfair to the victims of crime

   C. With the belief of their citizens that the victims of crime are unfairly served by some criminal statutes

   D. On the behalf of many citizens who believe that some criminal statutes are unfair to the victims of crime

   E. To believe on the behalf of many citizens about criminal statutes that are unfair to crime victims

5. The recent increase in the prime interest rate has encouraged some economists and worried others, who recall all too vividly the skyrocketing rates and consequent economic stagnation of the late 1970s.

   A. The recent increase in the prime interest rate

   B. Increasing recently, the prime interest rate

   C. The recent rate of increase in prime interest

   D. The prime interest rate, recently increased,

   E. The recently increasing prime interest rate

6. Whatever he aspired to achieve, they were thwarted by his jealous older brothers, who controlled the stock in the family companies.

   A. Whatever he aspired to achieve, they

   B. Whatever he had any aspirations to, they

   C. Whatever aspirations he had

   D. Whatever be his aspirations, they

   E. Many of his aspirations and goals

7. Irregardless of the "new modernism" in literature, which produces novels that often read like the diaries of madmen, most readers still prefer a conventional plot and simple style.

   A. Irregardless of the "new modernism" in literature, which produces

   B. Irregardless of the "new modernism" in literature, which produced

   C. Regardless, the "new modernism" in literature, which produces

   D. Regardless of the "new modernism" in literature, which produces

   E. Regardless of the "new modernism" in literature, which produce

8. If Swift's *Gulliver's Travels* attracts less of a readership than he did in the eighteenth century, perhaps the reason is that modern readers do not know enough political history to appreciate the satire.

   A. attracts less of a readership than he did in the eighteenth century

   B. attracts less readers than the eighteenth century did

   C. attracts fewer readers than it did in the eighteenth century

   D. attracts fewer readers than he did in the eighteenth century

   E. attracts less reading than it did in the eighteenth century

9. <u>Proposing that inordinate government spending was causative of the high deficit, the president presented a budget</u> that maintained relatively high defense expenditures while it reduced funding for certain social programs which, the administration argued, were receiving sufficient support from the private sector.

 A. Proposing that inordinate government spending was causative of the high deficit, the president presented a budget

 B. Proposing that government spending causes deficits, the president presented a budget

 C. With a proposal that inordinate government spending was causative of the high deficit, the president presented a budget

 D. The president presented a budget proposal that inordinate government spending was causative of the high deficit

 E. Proposing that inordinate government spending caused the high deficit, the president presented a budget

Average

10. Although the advisory commission on Central America has completed <u>their report that address the political tensions in that area,</u> no easing of tensions has resulted.

 A. their report that address the political tensions in that area

 B. their report that addresses the political tensions in that area

 C. its report that address the political tensions for that area

 D. its report that addresses the political tensions with that area in mind

 E. its report that addresses the political tensions in that area

11. <u>To enjoy exploring marine life in general, and so that they could learn in particular about the ways in which certain sea animals possess "human" traits,</u> the university's school of oceanography offered supervised summer field trips for the elementary school children in the area.

 A. To enjoy exploring marine life in general, and so that they could learn in particular about the ways in which certain sea animals possess "human" traits

 B. To stress the enjoyment of marine life in general, and particularly the ways in which certain sea animals are "human"

 C. In order to teach young people about the "human" traits of certain sea animals, and to provide them an opportunity to enjoy marine exploration in general

 D. Because marine life in general shares certain "human" traits

 E. From general marine life to the specifically "human" possessions of sea animals

12. <u>To bring to an end the 1984 Olympics, the festivities were highlighted</u> by the arrival of an "alien" spaceship that hovered mysteriously over the Coliseum, to the amazement and delight of thousands of spectators.

   A. To bring to an end the 1984 Olympics, the festivities were highlighted

   B. The festivities to bring to an end the 1984 Olympics were highlighted

   C. With the festivities that ended the 1984 Olympics highlighted

   D. Festive highlights brought an end to the 1984 Olympics

   E. The festive conclusion of the 1984 Olympics was highlighted

13. Many of us bemoan our lack of foresight <u>by complaining that if we would have bought property twenty years ago, we could have taken advantage of the recent real estate boom.</u>

   A. by complaining that if we would have bought property twenty years ago, we could have taken advantage of the recent real estate boom

   B. , looking backward to a potential property purchase twenty years ago and wishing we had done so for present purposes

   C. : with real estate available so cheaply twenty years ago, the advantages of the recent boom would be ours for the asking

   D. , complaining that if we had bought property twenty years ago, we could have taken advantage of the recent real estate boom

   E. , the complaint being our lack of purchasing property twenty years ago and the consequent absence of profit in the recent real estate boom

14. Acting selfishly and impulsively, <u>the chairperson adapted the committee's recommendations to meet his own needs, without considering the negative affects of his changes.</u>

   A. the chairperson adapted the committee's recommendations to meet his own needs, without considering the negative affects of his changes

   B. without considering the negative effects of his changes, the chairperson adapted the committee's recommendations to meet his own needs

   C. the chairperson adapted the committee's recommendations to meet his own needs, without considering the negative effects of his changes

   D. necessarily, the chairperson adapted committee recommendations, despite negative effects

   E. negative effects notwithstanding, the chairperson adapted the recommendations of the committee

15. The more the union stubbornly refused to budge from its original demand for a 20% across-the-board salary increase, <u>the more the district administration reiterated its original proposal of a mere 1% raise.</u>

   A. the more the district administration reiterated its original proposal of a mere 1% raise

   B. the district administration's original proposal for a mere 1% raise was reiterated all the more

   C. proposing its original and mere 1% raise was the district administration's response, more and more

   D. the district administration reiterated its proposal of a mere 1% raise

   E. the more the district administration's original proposal of a mere 1% raise was reiterated

16. Homer's *Odyssey* is often dramatized as a series of hairbreadth escapes from terrible monsters and vengeful gods, <u>and while those episodes are exciting and important literary achievements,</u> they stand apart from the poem's extensive attention to domestic life, to domestic values, and to a hero whose most important achievement is the reestablishment of his home and family.

   A. and while those episodes are exciting and important literary achievements

   B. and although in fact these episodes are exciting, important achievements in literature

   C. and while an exciting and important literary achievement

   D. and those episodes are exciting and important literary achievements

   E. and with those episodes as exciting and important literary achievements

17. <u>Public enthusiasm that had been growing for airline travel, still in its infancy, when Amelia Earhart's plane disappeared in the 1930s, diminished for a while;</u> however, today fear of flying is rare.

   A. Public enthusiasm that had been growing for airline travel, still in its infancy, when Amelia Earhart's plane disappeared in the 1930s, diminished for a while

   B. Public enthusiasm that had been growing for airline travel, still in its infancy when Amelia Earhart's plane disappeared in the 1930s, diminished for a while

   C. Growing public enthusiasm for airline travel, still in its infancy, diminished after a while after Amelia Earhart's plane disappeared in the 1930s

   D. When Amelia Earhart's plane disappeared in the 1930s, growing public enthusiasm for airline travel, still in its infancy, diminished for a while

   E. After Amelia Earhart's plane disappeared in the 1930s, the enthusiasm that had been growing for airline travel in its infancy diminished for a while

18. Golding's most famous novel concerns little boys, <u>once a well-behaved and civilized group, whose</u> resort to murder and savagery during their brief time on a tropical island without adult supervision.

    A. once a well-behaved and civilized group, whose

    B. once well-behaved and civilized, who

    C. once a well-behaved and civilized herd, who

    D. once civilized and well-behaved, whose

    E. behaved and civilized, who

19. When reading some of the most rich and beautiful speeches in Shakespeare's *Romeo and Juliet,* <u>when one stresses the singsong cadence of iambic pentameter, the lines take on an almost simpleminded, childish quality.</u>

    A. when one stresses the singsong cadence of iambic pentameter, the lines take on an almost simpleminded, childish quality

    B. stressing the singsong cadence of iambic pentameter gives the lines an almost simpleminded, childish quality

    C. if one stresses the singsong cadence of iambic pentameter, it gives the lines an almost simpleminded, childish quality

    D. the simpleminded, childish quality of some lines results from the singsong cadence of iambic pentameter

    E. the singsong cadence of iambic pentameter, sounds almost simpleminded and childish

20. During the French Revolution, especially the Reign of Terror, <u>citizens whom the government suspected of treasonous tendencies were eventually put to death</u> by Monsieur Sanson, the infamous executioner who supervised the killing of hundreds at the guillotine.

    A. citizens whom the government suspected of treasonous tendencies were eventually put to death

    B. citizens of which the government had suspicions were eventually put to death

    C. suspicious citizens were eventually killed

    D. citizens who the government suspected of treason were eventually put to death

    E. the citizenry under suspicion were eventually put to death

21. During the last century, whaling voyages departed regularly from the New England states, <u>and because each voyage normally extends for years,</u> the hold was packed with supplies before a whaling ship set sail.

    A. and because each voyage normally extends for years

    B. and because each trip was long

    C. and because each voyage normally extended for years

    D. and while these were long trips

    E. and because the voyage had lasted for years

22. <u>As he looked out on an expanse that seemed empty of gods or goddesses,</u> Odysseus must certainly have felt abandoned by the rulers on Olympus.

   A. As he looked out on an expanse that seemed empty of gods or goddesses

   B. As he looked out on an empty expanse of gods and goddesses

   C. With no gods or goddesses as he looked out on the empty expanse

   D. Facing the empty expanse of gods and goddesses

   E. As he looked on an expanse that seemed empty of either a god or a goddess

Above Average to Difficult

23. <u>If the majority of your opponents have control, you may become defeated.</u>

   A. If the majority of your opponents have control, you may become defeated.

   B. If the majority of your opponents take control, you may lose.

   C. If the majority of your opponents assumes control, you may see defeat.

   D. If the majority of your opponents has control, you may lose.

   E. Most of you opponents will have control, and you may lose.

24. <u>Focusing across several generations,</u> Alex Haley wrote *Roots,* a novel explaining both his family history and the history of American bigotry.

   A. Focusing across several generations

   B. Centering around several generations

   C. Living through several generations

   D. With an eye on several generations

   E. Telling of several generations

25. In the early fourteenth century, almost 200 years before Columbus reached the West Indies, and 250 years before the Reformation, <u>Europe had been Catholic and the Church continued to influence virtually every phase of human life.</u>

   A. Europe had been Catholic and the Church continued to influence virtually every phase of human life

   B. the Catholic Church continued to influence every phase of human life

   C. the Europe that had been Catholic was still influenced in virtually every phase of human life by the Church

   D. Europe was Catholic and the Church influenced virtually every phase of human life

   E. every phase of human life bore traces of the European influence of the Catholic Church

26. <u>In the 1950s, toy stores sold thousands of play replicas of a gun popularized by the *Wyatt Earp* television series,</u> the "Buntline Special," a long-barreled six-gun named after the legendary Ned Buntline.

A. In the 1950s, toy stores sold thousands of play replicas of a gun popularized by the *Wyatt Earp* television series

B. Popularized by the 1950s *Wyatt Earp* television series, toy stores sold thousands of play replicas of a gun

C. In the 1950s, the *Wyatt Earp* television series popularized thousands of play replicas of a gun sold in toy stores

D. A play replica of a gun popularized by the *Wyatt Earp* television series, which sold thousands in toy stores in the 1950s

E. As toy stores sold thousands of the 1950s replicas of a gun popularized by the *Wyatt Earp* television series

27. During the literary renaissance of the 1920s, a large number of new writers—William Faulkner, Ernest Hemingway, John Dos Passos, and F. Scott Fitzgerald—sought to record the inner life of Americans and to scrutinize the American dream, <u>the dream that anyone can earn his own fortune and live happily ever after through hard work, which had become tarnished.</u>

A. the dream that anyone can earn his own fortune and live happily ever after through hard work, which had become tarnished

B. the tarnished dream that anyone can make his own fortune and live happily ever after through hard work

C. the tarnished dream that anyone can, through hard work, make his own fortune and live happily ever after

D. the dream that anyone can earn his own fortune and live happily ever after, though tarnished, through hard work

E. that making one's own fortune and living happily ever after, through hard work, had become tarnished

28. Much like Macbeth when he interprets the witches' prophecies all too literally, <u>the mysterious harpooner who Ahab takes aboard the *Pequod* has the captain accepting his strange prophecies without questioning their hidden meaning.</u>

A. the mysterious harpooner who Ahab takes aboard the *Pequod* has the captain accepting his strange prophecies without questioning their hidden meaning

B. the strange prophecies of the mysterious harpooner he has taken aboard the *Pequod* are accepted by Ahab without questioning their hidden meaning

C. the mysterious harpooner whom Ahab takes aboard the *Pequod* has the captain accepting his strange prophecies without questioning their hidden meaning

D. Ahab accepts the strange prophecy of the mysterious harpooner whom he has taken aboard the *Pequod*, without questioning their hidden meaning

E. Ahab accepts the strange prophecies of the mysterious harpooner he has taken aboard the *Pequod*, without questioning their hidden meaning

29. The weather in San Diego, California, is temperate for most of the year, and although the air is not so clean as it used to be, it has remained virtually smog free through recent years of rapid industrial growth, <u>unlike most urban areas in southern California.</u>

   A. unlike most urban areas in southern California

   B. unlike the air in most southern California urban areas

   C. unlike other southern California air

   D. unlike southern California urban areas

   E. in contrast to the smog condition elsewhere in urban southern California

30. Brokers who offer foreign cars on the "gray market," thus bypassing the car dealer by shipping directly from the manufacturer to the waiting customer at the dock, claim that their purpose is not to cheat dealerships out of a profit, but rather <u>to provide the consumer with the finest value for his or her dollar.</u>

   A. to provide the consumer with the finest value for his or her dollar

   B. the provision of the finest value for the dollar

   C. providing the finest values for consumer dollars

   D. that they have an obligation to give consumers value for their dollars

   E. to deliver value for the dollar

31. Two recent statements on the tenure of university professors offer conflicting points of view: <u>those that say that lifetime tenure ensures academic freedom and those that say that lifetime tenure encourages professional laziness and irresponsibility.</u>

   A. those that say that lifetime tenure ensures academic freedom and those that say that lifetime tenure encourages professional laziness and irresponsibility

   B. some declare that lifetime tenure ensures academic freedom, and others say that it encourages professional laziness and irresponsibility

   C. saying that lifetime tenure either ensures academic freedom or encourages irresponsible laziness

   D. one emphasizes the academic freedom that tenure ensures, and one stresses the professional laziness and irresponsibility it encourages

   E. advocacies of academic freedom and warnings about professional laziness and irresponsibility

32. <u>With an explosive capacity that can devastate life and property for a radius of hundreds of miles, proponents of peace from several Western bloc countries met to discuss the continuing manufacture and deployment of nuclear warheads.</u>

A. With an explosive capacity that can devastate life and property for a radius of hundreds of miles, proponents of peace from several Western bloc countries met to discuss the continuing manufacture and deployment of nuclear warheads.

B. Proponents of peace from several Western bloc countries with an explosive capacity that can devastate life and property for a radius of hundreds of miles met to discuss the continuing manufacture and deployment of nuclear warheads.

C. Meeting to discuss the continuing manufacture and deployment of nuclear warheads with an explosive capacity that can devastate life and property for a radius of hundreds of miles were several Western bloc countries.

D. Proponents of peace from several Western bloc countries met to discuss the continuing manufacture and deployment of nuclear warheads that can devastate life and property with an explosive capacity for a radius of hundreds of miles.

E. Proponents of peace from several Western bloc countries met to discuss the continuing manufacture and deployment of nuclear warheads with an explosive capacity that can devastate life and property for a radius of hundreds of miles.

33. Arms talks <u>from Geneva between China, the United States, Russia, and other nations may be even more effecting than many world leaders think they would be.</u>

A. from Geneva between China, the United States, Russia, and other nations may be even more effecting than many world leaders think they would be

B. in Geneva between China, the United States, Russia, and other nations may be even more effective than many world leaders suppose

C. in Geneva between China, the United States, Russia, and other nations may be even more affecting than many world leaders think they will be

D. in Geneva among China, the United States, Russia, and other nations may be even more effective than many world leaders expect

E. between China, the United States, Russia, and other nations in Geneva may be even more effective than many world leaders believe

34. <u>Acknowledging the volunteers' giving of a great deal of their time to canvass the neighborhood and collect donations from the neighbors, the chairman of the local United Way expressed his sincere gratitude.</u>

A. Acknowledging the volunteers' giving of a great deal of their time to canvass the neighborhood and collect donations from the neighbors, the chairman of the local United Way expressed his sincere gratitude.

B. Acknowledging the time spent by neighborhood volunteers to canvass and to collect neighborhood donations, the chairman of the local United Way expressed his sincere gratitude.

C. With sincere gratitude, the chairman of the local United Way expressed his acknowledgment of the neighborhood donations canvassed and collected on the volunteers' time.

D. The chairman of the local United Way offered sincere thanks to the volunteers who gave so much time to canvass the neighborhood to collect donations.

E. The chairman of the local United Way thanked the neighborhood volunteers, sincerely.

35. A diagonal line connecting two corners of a rectangle is also the hypotenuse of each of two right triangles contained within the rectangle, <u>which is longer than any of the sides.</u>

A. which is longer than any of the sides

B. and the line is longer than any of the sides

C. which is longer than the sides

D. that is longer than any of the sides

E. that is longer than any of the other sides

Answers and Explanations for the Practice Sentence Correction Questions

Easy to Moderate

1. **B.** Choice **B** corrects the poor structure of the original wording. Choices **C, D,** and **E** change the meaning of the original expression slightly—**C** and **D** suggesting that the ring belongs to the *pushers,* not to the *drug dealer,* and **E** implying that the *pushers* were determined to destroy the ring.

2. **C.** All choices are grammatically correct; however, choice **C** is the most direct expression of the original wording. Choices **D** and **E** change the meaning of the original, and choice **B** is awkward.

3. **A.** The original is better than any of the alternatives.

4. **D.** *To the behalf* is not idiomatic. Choice **D** corrects this error and does not make additional, unnecessary changes.

5. A. None of the alternatives is more direct and clear than the original underlined portion. Because the *increase* has encouraged some economists, not the *rate,* choices **B, C, D,** and **E** all change the meaning of the sentence.

6. C. Choice **C** best expresses the idea without changing the intent of the sentence as **E** does. The original and choices **B** and **D** are awkward.

7. D. *Irregardless* is nonstandard usage. Apart from this error, the original underlined portion is correct and clear. To make sense, choice **C** would require the preposition *of.* Choice **E** contains an agreement error.

8. C. *Fewer readers* is more economical than choice **A.** *Less* in choice **B** is incorrect when the noun (readers) can be numbered (for example: fewer gallons, less gasoline; fewer dollars, less money). Since the pronoun refers to the book, not to the author, *it,* not *he,* is correct. Choice **E** incorrectly uses the plural *attract—Gulliver's Travels* is the name of a book and is singular.

9. E. *Caused* is better than the wordy and pretentious phrase *was causative of* in choices **A, C,** and **D.** Choice **B** omits two adjectives and unnecessarily changes the tense in *causes.*

Average

10. E. Both *commission* and *report* are singular, so the singular pronoun *its* and the singular verb *addresses* must be used. The agreement is correct in choice **D,** but *with that area in mind* is needlessly wordy.

11. C. Along with having inconsistent verb tense and wordiness problems, the original sentence illustrates a long dangling modifier. The underlined portion seems to modify *the university's school of oceanography* and thereby seems to say that the *school* is enjoying *exploring marine life.* Only **C** offers an introductory phrase that is both correct and unambiguous. Choices **B** and **D,** although grammatically correct, significantly change the intended meaning of the original sentence.

12. E. This is the most direct, clear, and economical choice that retains the essential meaning of the original underlined portion. Compared to choice **E,** both **A** and **B** are wordy. Choice **C** is a sentence fragment, and **D** distorts the meaning.

13. D. The use of *would have* and *could have* as the main verbs here does not clearly indicate that buying property twenty years ago is a much earlier action; the verb *had* makes clear the distinction between distant past and recent past. Choice **D** supplies the appropriate verb and eliminates the unnecessary *by.*

14. C. The error in the original is a diction error. *Effects* (results) is preferable to *affects.* Choices **D** and **E** are economical but change the meaning of the original significantly.

15. A. The original underlined portion is the most clear and correct choice, resulting in a balanced sentence, with the structure of the second half (that is, the underlined portion) parallel to the structure of the first half: *the more* . . . subject . . . active verb. Choices **B, C,** and **D** omit *the more.* In choice **E,** the verb is passive.

16. A. The original underlined portion is the best choice. Choice **B** is wordy, **C** introduces an agreement error, **D** introduces a comma error, and **E,** by omitting *while,* changes the meaning.

17. **C.** The best choice here arranges the parts of the sentence in the most direct and clear way by keeping the modifiers as close as possible to the words they modify. In addition, choice **C** replaces *when* with a more appropriate and logical term, *after.*

18. **B.** Choice **B** is grammatically correct and economical. In choice **C,** *herd* introduces a meaning not in the original, while choice **E** omits details. Choices **A** and **D** are sentence fragments.

19. **B.** Choice **B** is the most economical and clear version of the original. Choices **A** and **C** are wordy, containing the unnecessary phrases *when one* and *if one.* Choices **D** and **E** omit the notion of stressing and so change the meaning.

20. **A.** The original underlined portion is the best choice. *Whom* is used correctly, as the object of *suspected.* Each of the other choices omits or changes this correct pronoun unnecessarily or changes the meaning of the original.

21. **C.** The original underlined portion contains a verb tense error. The verbs *extends* in choice **A** and *has lasted* in choice **E** are inconsistent with the past tense established through the rest of the sentence. Choice **C** supplies the simple past tense, *extended,* which agrees with the other verbs in the sentence. Choices **B** and **D,** while grammatically correct, substitute the vaguer *long* for the phrase *for years.*

22. **A.** The sentence refers to an expanse that is empty of gods, not an empty expanse of gods, so choices **B** and **D** are incorrect. Choice **E** is needlessly wordy, and **C** distorts the meaning.

Above Average to Difficult

23. **D.** *Majority* is a collective noun, which may take either a singular or plural verb, depending on whether the group as a whole or the individuals are emphasized. But *lose* is a clearer and more economical expression than *become defeated.* Choices **B, C,** and **E** change the meaning of the sentence.

24. **E.** *Focusing across* is idiomatically incorrect and also logically unsound (*focusing on* is better). The only choice that is both idiomatically correct and preserves the meaning of the original is **E.**

25. **D.** The verbs are the problem in the original underlined portion. The context supplied by the rest of the sentence suggests that the verbs should be simple past tense, both of them indicating what was true in the fourteenth century. As it stands, the underlined portion is internally contradictory. It states that Europe *had been* Catholic, implying that the region is no longer Catholic, but also states that Catholic influence *continued.* Choice **D** corrects this grammatical/logical problem while retaining the original intended meaning. Choices **B** and **E** are grammatically correct but omit information contained in the original sentence.

26. **A.** Although choice **A** is perhaps not the best choice one can imagine, it is decidedly the best choice of the five offered here. The phrase *"Buntline Special"* should be placed as close to *gun* as possible. In choice **B,** the opening phrase modifies *toy stores,* not *gun,* and the phrase *the 1950s* now modifies the *television series* instead of *sold.* Choice **C** also misplaces the phrase *in the 1950s.* Choices **D** and **E** are sentence fragments.

27. **C.** The original version is confusing because the clause *which had become tarnished* is awkwardly separated from *dream* and the prepositional phrase *through hard work* is awkwardly separated from the verb it modifies, *earn*. In choices **B, D,** and **E,** the prepositional phrase is misplaced.

28. **E.** The underlined portion must name Ahab immediately in order to clarify the comparison between Ahab and Macbeth. It is Ahab, not the *harpooner,* as in choices **A** or **C,** and not the *prophecies,* as in choice **B,** who is much like Macbeth. Choice **D** has the right structure but has an agreement error between *prophecy* and *their.*

29. **B.** The original underlined portion presents an illogical comparison, of *areas* to the topic of the first part of the sentence, *air.* Only choice **B** clarifies the air to air comparison without the inappropriate wordiness of choice **E.**

30. **A.** The original underlined portion is the best choice. It maintains parallel structure with *to provide.* Each of the other choices makes unnecessary changes in grammar and syntax that do not improve the original.

31. **D.** In the original underlined portion, *those* is incorrect. To express respectively two singular points of view, the noun or pronoun which refers to each must be singular; *those* is, of course, plural. Only choice **D** provides a clearly singular reference, *one,* for each viewpoint.

32. **E.** The introductory phrase in the original (preceding the comma) properly modifies *warheads*. Only choice **E** makes this necessary change while retaining the intended meaning of the original.

33. **D.** The original version contains several errors that must be corrected: the proposition *in* for *from,* the adjective *effective* for *effecting,* and the preposition *among* for *between.*

34. **D.** The original underlined sentence as well as choices **B** and **C** are unnecessarily wordy. Choice **D** is an efficient, direct, and clear expression that retains the meaning of the original. Choice **E** leaves out essential information from the original.

35. **B.** Though choice **B** requires more words, it is the only version that avoids the ambiguous pronouns—*which* in choices **A** and **C** and *that* in choices **D** and **E**—which seem at first to refer to *rectangle.*

Introduction to Critical Reasoning

The Critical Reasoning questions are similar to Reading Comprehension questions, but the passages are shorter and the questions are reasoning-oriented. There is usually only one question per short passage.

Ability Tested

These questions test your ability to read and understand the logic presented in brief passages or conversations.

Basic Skills Necessary

Candidates who read critically and understand simple logic and reasoning do well in this section. The ability to isolate the key issue and to identify irrelevant issues is important.

Directions

As you read the brief passage, follow the line of reasoning using only common-sense standards of logic. No knowledge of formal logic is required. Then you must choose the best answer, realizing that several choices may be possible, but only one will be best.

Analysis

To score well in this section:

- Rely on common sense. No special expertise is necessary.

- Use only what is presented or implied by the passage. Do not make leaps in logic to arrive at an answer choice. Don't read anything into the passage that isn't there.

- Choose the *best* answer choice. The test makers strongly imply that there may be more than one good answer.

Suggested Approach with Samples

Preread the question following the passage.

In most instances, one question follows each brief passage. For these one-question passages, it may be time-effective to read the question before reading the passage. Many GMAT candidates have found that prereading the question eliminates having to read the passage a second time while searching for the answer, thus saving valuable minutes. Knowing what the question is before reading the passage enables you to focus on those elements of the passage essential to the question.

If you decide to preread the question, *do not* preread the answer choices. Four of the five answer choices are incorrect, so scanning them exposes you to irrelevant and/or inconsistent information. Prereading the answer choices is a waste of time and energy. Practice can help you determine when prereading the question is effective for you.

Sample

Try reading the *question* about the following passage first; then read the passage:

1. That seniors in the inner cities have inadequate health care available to them is intolerable. The medical facilities in the urban ghetto rarely contain basic medical supplies, and the technology in these hospitals is reflective of the 1960s, if that. Seniors living in the affluent suburbs, however, have available to them state-of-the-art technology and the latest in medical advances, drugs, and procedures.

   Which of the following best expresses the primary point of the passage?

   A. Inner-city and suburban seniors should be cared for in hospitals equidistant from both.

   B. Inner-city seniors should be transported to suburban hospitals.

   C. Doctors should treat inner-city and suburban seniors equally.

   D. Better medical care and facilities should be provided for inner-city seniors.

   E. Inner-city seniors should have the same health care as that available to suburban seniors.

Prereading the question helps you to read the passage with a focus; that is, what is the author's primary point? The main point will be the overall thrust of the entire passage.

The major issue here is health care, and the author's point is that inner-city seniors should have health care better than that available to them now. The heavily charged word *intolerable* in the first sentence indicates that the author feels strongly that inadequate health care for inner-city seniors is not sufficient. Better care should be provided. Choice **D** is the best answer.

Notice that while a comparison is made to suburban seniors having superior health care, no direct argument is made that inner-city seniors should have the *same* health care as suburban seniors. The superior, *state-of-the-art* quality of suburban health care is presented in order to contrast with that of inner-city health care, and the contrast simply shows how abysmal inner-city health care is in comparison. But nothing in the passage directly indicates that health care for inner-city seniors should necessarily be equivalent with that provided suburban seniors. Inferring this would be beyond the scope of the passage; choice **E** as the author's primary point is incorrect.

Choices **A** and **B** are incorrect because the passage never raises the issues of hospital relocation and transportation. And choice **C** not only raises the problematic issue of "equal" treatment (which, as stated previously, is not directly indicated in the passage) but also alters the focus simply to doctors, which in the context of a passage noting medical facilities, technology, supplies, and so on, is far too narrow.

Read and analyze all the choices.

As you work through the Critical Reasoning questions, make sure that you assess *all* the choices, eliminating those that are off-topic, irrelevant, inconsistent, or beyond the scope of the passage, and retaining and considering those that you think apply. Keep in mind that several choices may appear to be correct. Choose the one that answers the question *best,* the one most directly relevant to the passage.

Know the Critical Reasoning question prototypes.

Most of the Critical Reasoning questions fall into a small number of categories, or prototypes. These prototypes are scrambled throughout the verbal section and delivered in different ways. Knowing and anticipating these prototype questions and what they require in terms of an answer can be of great help, especially when a question appears long and confusing. Once you identify the prototype, you can spend the bulk of your time understanding the passage and the answer choices.

Prototype 1: Main Idea

The test may ask you to identify the main idea of a passage, and it may do this in a number of ways. As you can see in the health care passage, the main idea can be expressed as "the primary point of the passage" or "the author's primary point." Most of the time, the main idea is not directly stated in the passage; you have to derive it. Be careful to derive only what is most directly indicated by the passage. A jump of logic may take you beyond the scope of the passage (for example, in the previous passage, jumping from "providing better health care" to "providing health care equal to suburban care") and lead you to an incorrect choice.

Some (but not all) other ways that the main idea prototype can be asked are

- Which of the following best expresses the point the author is attempting to make?

- The author's argument is best expressed as . . .

- Which of the following statements best expresses the author's central point in the passage above?

- In the passage above, the author argues that . . .

Sample

Following is an example of a question that follows this prototype.

---

2. Whatever else might be said about American elections, they are quite unlike those in totalitarian countries in that Americans make choices. And one choice they can make in this free country is to stay home.

What is the author's point in the above passage?

A. Americans who do decide to vote make more choices than those who do not.

B. American elections embody many negative aspects, most of which are not embodied by elections in totalitarian countries.

C. Choosing not to vote is the prerogative of a free citizen.

D. All citizens vote in every election in totalitarian countries.

E. Most American voters are not well informed enough to vote wisely.

When considering the multiple choices, immediately eliminate those items which are (1) irrelevant to the question and/or the major issue of the passage and (2) not at all addressed by the passage. Consider the passage above. The author's point is necessarily connected with the major issues of the passage—in this case, free choice. The author stresses the free choice *not to vote,* by way of making the point. You may eliminate all choices which do not address the free choice not to vote: **A** is irrelevant because it addresses the number of choices rather than the freedom of choice, and **B** raises issues scarcely addressed in the passage. **D** doesn't address the issue of choosing not to vote; although it notes that all citizens in totalitarian countries must vote, it neglects the main point—that Americans don't have to. **E** is irrelevant to the issue of free choice, stressing voter information instead. The best choice is **C,** which addresses the major issue, free choice, and also the author's specific point, the free choice not to vote.

Prototype 2: Inference

The dictionary defines *inference* as the act or process of deriving logical conclusions from a line of reasoning. For example, you can infer from the statement "only a minority of children under the age of six have visited a dentist" that a "majority of children under the age of six have not visited a dentist." This type of Critical Reasoning question asks you to determine an inference or implication in a passage.

The distinction between the meanings of "infer" and "imply" is not very important in this section. The words differ in meaning in the same way as "push" and "pull." A statement implies ("pushes out to you"); you infer ("pull from"). This distinction is not the operant element in this section; rather, you should be aware that "infers" or "implies" means the next logical step in an argument.

Other ways this prototype may be expressed are

- Which of the following can be inferred from the passage?
- The author of the passage implies that . . .
- Which inference can be most reliably drawn from the passage?
- What can be validly inferred from the facts and premises expressed in the passage?

Sample

3. We doubt that the latest government report will scare Americans away from ham, bacon, sausages, hot dogs, bologna, and salami or that it will empty out the bars or cause a run on natural food supplies. If a diet were to be mandated from Washington, Americans probably would order the exact opposite course. Therefore, the diet that does make sense is to eat a balanced and varied diet composed of foods from all food groups and containing a reasonable caloric intake.

Which of the following is (are) specifically implied by the passage?

   I. Vitamins are necessary to combat disease.

  II. A recent report warned of the risks of meat and alcoholic beverages.

 III. Unorthodox suggestions for a more nutritional diet were recently made by the government.

  A. I only

  B. II only

  C. III only

  D. I and II only

  E. II and III only

Because the author doubts that Americans will stop eating meats or visiting bars, one must conclude that the author is referring to the latest government report warning of the risks of meat and alcoholic beverages, Statement II. Statement I concerning vitamins may be true but is not specifically implied other than in a very general sense (nutrition). Statement III is not true: The passage does not suggest that the government report made *unorthodox* suggestions. The correct answer is **B.**

Prototype 3: Assumption

An assumption is an *unstated* notion on which a statement rests. For example, "I don't like people who continually interrupt me; therefore, you may conclude that I don't like Jack." For this argument to be logically valid, it must be assumed that Jack continually interrupts the author. In this type of question, you are asked to determine what assumption lies behind the author's argument.

Other ways this prototype may be expressed are

- Which of the following underlies the passage above?

- The author assumes that . . .

- The argument above logically depends on which of the following assumptions?

- What is the presupposition of the passage above?

- Necessary to the reasoning above is the assumption that . . .

Sample

> **4.** In his first message to Congress, Harry Truman said, "The responsibility of the United States is to serve and not dominate the world."
>
> Which of the following is one basic assumption underlying Truman's statement?
>
> **A.** The United States is capable of dominating the world.
>
> **B.** The United States chooses to serve rather than dominate the world.
>
> **C.** World domination is a virtue.
>
> **D.** One must be decisive when facing a legislative body for the first time.
>
> **E.** The United States, preceding Truman's administration, had been irresponsible.

Truman's statement is not warranted unless one assumes the United States' capability to dominate the world, as in choice **A;** that assumed capability makes the choice between serving and dominating possible and is thus a basic assumption.

Prototype 4: Support/Weaken

This question type asks for the answer choice that would support or weaken the passage.

Samples

---

5. Research comparing children of cigarette-smoking parents in Virginia with children of nonsmoking parents in West Virginia found that children of smoking parents in Virginia have lower test scores than do children of nonsmokers in West Virginia. Therefore, secondhand cigarette smoke is a cause of the lower test scores.

Which of the following, if true, would weaken the conclusion above?

A. Children in Virginia have lower test scores than children in West Virginia, regardless of whether their parents smoke or not.

B. More people smoke in Virginia than in West Virginia.

C. Some children of nonsmoking parents in South Dakota have good test scores.

D. Nonsmoking parents in Virginia have more children, on average, than those in most other states.

E. Research has shown that smoking is not only unhealthy for the smoker, but for others in the nearby vicinity.

The correct answer would be "Children in Virginia have lower test scores than children in West Virginia, regardless of whether their parents smoke or not." Notice that if children in Virginia have lower test scores than children in West Virginia, regardless of whether their parents smoke or not, then the cigarette-smoking parents cannot logically be claimed to be a cause of the lower test scores. This choice would weaken the conclusion. However, the question could have been

---

6. Which of the following, if true, would strengthen the logic of the argument?

A. A recent study indicates that, in general, children in any particular state tend to have similar scores to children in any other state.

B. Parents in any particular state have different test scores than parents in another state.

C. Test scores, in general, are limited in their ability to measure content areas.

D. Children of nonsmoking parents are healthier than children of smoking parents.

E. Some children of smoking parents in Iowa have good test scores.

A correct answer would be "A recent study indicates that, in general, children in any particular state tend to have similar test scores to children in any other state." Notice that this choice would strengthen the logic of the passage. If children in general have similar test scores state to state, then a subpopulation of children from smoking parents having lower test scores than a subpopulation of children from nonsmoking parents strengthens the conclusion that the smoking parents may have been the cause of the difference in scores.

Sometimes the question asks for what would be "relevant" to the reasoning. The choice that would strengthen or weaken the logic would be the relevant choice.

Notice that this question type may contain the words *if true*. That means accept all of the choices as being true: Do not challenge their reasonableness or the possibility of their occurring. Accept all the choices as being true and from there decide which would strengthen or weaken the argument, whatever the question requires.

Other ways this question type may be expressed are

- Which of the following, if true, would support the argument?

- Which of the following, if true, would undermine the conclusion?

- Which of the following, if true, would challenge the logic of the reasoning of the passage?

- Which of the following would confirm the author's conclusion?

---

7. Experience shows that for every burglar shot by a homeowner there are many more fatal accidents involving small children, family slayings that could have been avoided but for the handy presence of a gun, and thefts of handguns by the criminals they are intended to protect against.

Which of the following facts, if true, would most seriously weaken the above contention?

A. Criminals tend to sell the handguns they steal during the commission of a burglary.

B. Burglars are also capable of causing fatal accidents.

C. Every burglar shot by a homeowner is stopped from committing scores of further burglaries and injuring scores of other citizens.

D. The number of burglars shot by homeowners is larger than the number of burglars shot by renters.

E. Not all fatal accidents involve guns.

Choice **C** most directly addresses the argument of the passage. The passage argues that for every burglar shot, there are scores of slayings of the innocent; **C** argues that for every burglar shot, there are scores of prevented burglaries.

Prototype 5: Conclusion

This prototype question asks for the conclusion that has not yet been stated in the passage.

Samples

8. The county legislature has finally, after ten years of legal challenges, passed an antipollution ordinance. From a reading of the language, the legislation promises to be one of the most effective bills in the history of the state.

   Which of the following can be deduced from the passage?

   A. The pollution problem will be eliminated in the county.

   B. The pollution problem will be reduced in the county.

   C. Pollution is not now a problem in the county.

   D. Pollution will be reduced in the state.

   E. To reduce pollution, the legislation must now be enforced.

When you are selecting a conclusion for a passage, do not merely choose what may be possible. Usually several of the choices are possible. You need to select the one choice that may necessarily be concluded. So, in the above example, notice that while **A** and **B** are possible, they don't necessarily have to occur; the ordinance, after all, may not be effective despite its tough language. Choices **C** and **D** are even more remote. But of the five choices, **E** is the safest conclusion that can be drawn. When seeking a conclusion, choose the "safest" of the five choices.

Other ways this question type may be presented are

- If the passage is true, then which of the following must necessarily be true?

- Which of the following is the best deduction based on the passage?

- If the passage is true, which of the following must logically follow?

- From the passage, which of the following can reasonably be deduced?

- Based on the passage, the author would conclude . . .

9. Which of the following is the most logical completion of the passage below?

In the 1940s, the introduction of the 33 rpm long-playing vinyl record completely changed the way we listen to music. The breakable and three-minute 78 rpm record soon disappeared from the marketplace. In our day, the compact disk, superior in quality and convenience, has replaced the vinyl long-playing record and will . . .

A. increase the size of the record-buying public.

B. increase the profits of the record industry.

C. drive the 78 rpm record from the second-hand market.

D. make the manufacture of phonographs that play 33 rpm records unnecessary.

E. encourage the growth of computer-generated music.

The passage compares the obsolescence of the 78 rpm record when the 33 rpm was introduced with the present-day situation in which the compact disk has replaced the 33 rpm. The passage offers no information on the potential sales of the new disks and tells us nothing of their effect on 78 rpm records or their relation to computer-generated music. If 33 rpm records have become obsolete, it follows that manufacturers will not make the machines to play them, so the answer is **D.**

Prototype 6: Technique

This prototype question asks for the technique of reasoning used in the passage. For example, the passage may use a generalization to prove a specific point, or vice versa. Or it may use an analogy (a comparison) to further an argument. It may present a conclusion without adequately supporting it, or it may contradict its original premise within the passage. As you can see, a line of reasoning may be structured—or may be faulty—in many ways. Be aware that it usually does not matter whether you agree or disagree with the logic presented in the passage because in this case you are not being asked to determine the passage's validity. (That's another question type.) Rather, you need to identify in structural terms how the author has set up the argument.

This prototype may be expressed in many ways, including

- The author makes her point primarily by . . .
- The author of the passage uses which of the following methods of persuasion?
- In the passage above, the author does which of the following?
- The author is using what line of reasoning to make the point?

Sample

> **10.** Tom's writing is always straightforward and honest. After all, whenever he writes a critique, he includes a special note that forewarns us that he will not mince words or make any untruthful statements. Therefore, his prose is direct and always tells the truth.
>
> The statement above uses which of the following to support the argument?
>
> A. Generalization
>
> B. Circular reasoning
>
> C. Specific examples
>
> D. Deductive reasoning
>
> E. Formal logic

The statement supports itself by restating its assumption in a slightly different way. This is circular reasoning, choice **B.**

Prototype 7: Error

This prototype asks you to find a logical mistake in the reasoning. As you read the passage, look for an inconsistency or flaw in logic. Typically the error is so striking that, even if you are not looking for it, it will cause you to stop in consternation, realizing that the logic of the passage has somehow broken. Prereading the question is effective for this prototype. If you know you're looking for an error, as soon as you reach it, instead of wondering why you're having trouble with the reasoning, you realize that you have just discovered the flaw.

Ways that this prototype may be presented are

- The conclusion above is unsound because the author . . .
- Which of the following inconsistencies seriously undermines the author's argument?
- The reasoning in the passage above is flawed because . . .
- Which of the following is an inherent error in logic in the passage above?

Sample

> **11.** *Speaker:* One need not look very far to find abundant examples of incivility and brutality in the most genteel corners of American society.
>
> *Questioner:* Then why don't we step up law enforcement in the slums of our cities?
>
> The question reveals which of the following misunderstandings?
>
> **A.** the misunderstanding that incivility and brutality have become more abundant
>
> **B.** the misunderstanding that law enforcement is related to the problems of incivility and brutality
>
> **C.** the misunderstanding of the speaker's position relative to incivility and brutality
>
> **D.** misunderstanding of the meaning of the word "genteel"
>
> **E.** misunderstanding of the meaning of the words "incivility" and "brutality"

The questioner understands the speaker to be referring to a problem restricted to the slums and so does not understand that *genteel* refers to upper-class situations. The answer is **D.**

Prototype 8: Parallel

This kind of question does not ask you to identify how the author structures the line of reasoning or to identify an error in reasoning, but to "parallel" whatever line of reasoning is presented. That is to say, you need to select the answer choice that uses either the same method of reasoning or the same type of error as the passage. Here again, whether the reasoning is faulty is not the important issue; paralleling the specific reasoning or error in the passage is your concern.

Samples

---

12. Since all dogs are animals, and cats are animals, then all cats are dogs.

Which of the following parallels the reasoning in the passage above?

A. All men are human beings, and children are human beings. Therefore all men are children.

B. All children are human beings, and some men are children. Therefore all men are human beings.

C. Some men are heavy, and some men are tall. Therefore all tall men are heavy.

D. Some animals are dogs, and some animals are cats. Therefore all dogs and cats are animals.

E. All cats are animals, and some animals are dogs. Therefore some animals could be cats or dogs.

The correct answer is **A,** "All men are human beings, and children are human beings. Therefore all men are children." Notice how this choice is faulty in the same structural way as the original passage.

Other ways this prototype may be expressed are

- Which of the following contains a logical flaw similar to the logical flaw in the passage above?

- The argument above exhibits the same principles of inference as which of the following arguments?

- Which of the following is logically most similar to the argument above?

- Which of the following supports its conclusion in the same way as the passage above?

13. Because cigarette smokers usually have a bad cough and Butch has a bad cough, it follows that Butch is probably a cigarette smoker.

Which of the following most closely parallels the reasoning used in the argument above?

A. Because nonsmokers don't get emphysema and Bud doesn't have emphysema, it follows that Bud is probably not a smoker.

B. Because weightlifters usually have large muscles and Bill is a weightlifter, it follows that Bill has large muscles.

C. Because diamonds usually have little color and this gem has little color, it follows that this gem is probably a diamond.

D. Because people with short hair usually get more haircuts and Al has short hair, it follows that Al recently got a haircut.

E. Because coughing spreads germs and Sam is coughing, Sam is spreading germs.

The direct connection between cigarette smoking and coughing made in the passage is not an exclusive connection that would warrant the conclusion that because Butch has a bad cough, he's probably a cigarette smoker. Butch could have a cold. In the same way, just because diamonds have little color, you cannot conclude that a gem with little color probably is a diamond (it could be clear glass). There is a presumption of exclusivity in both instances. Choice **C** is a stronger answer than **A** because the form of the argument is precisely the same in **C** and the original. Also, **A** is an absolute *(don't)*, and **C** uses the word *usually* as does the original.

There may be several other types of Critical Reasoning question types. The inclusion here of only eight does not mean that these are the only question types appearing in the GMAT. However, your understanding and anticipation of these eight should help you more quickly identify what is being asked and therefore allow you to spend the bulk of your time reading and analyzing the passage and the answer choices.

A PATTERNED PLAN OF ATTACK
Critical Reasoning

PRE-READ THE QUESTION.

Read the passage FOCUSING ON THE MAJOR ISSUE and/or tone of the passage.

ELIMINATE WRONG answer choices.

ELIMINATE ANSWER CHOICES THAT ARE IRRELEVANT OR NOT ADDRESSED in the passage.

CHOOSE THE BEST of the answer choices.

Practice Critical Reasoning Questions

Easy to Moderate

Read the following passage and answer Question 1.

Famous painter James Whistler said, "Industry in art is a necessity—not a virtue—and any evidence of the same, in the production, is a blemish, not a quality."

1. Whistler is arguing that

   A. of necessity, art becomes industrialized.

   B. the qualities of art are its virtues.

   C. blemished paintings are the work of overindustrious artists.

   D. the product reflects the means of production.

   E. the artist must work hard, but the art should look easy.

Read the following passage and answer Question 2.

Deliberations of our governing bodies are held in public in order to allow public scrutiny of each body's actions and take to task those actions that citizens feel are not, for whatever reason, in their best interest.

2. With which of the following statements would the author of the above passage probably agree?

   A. Deliberations of our governing bodies should be held in public.

   B. Public scrutiny usually results in the criticism of our governing bodies.

   C. The best interests of the public usually do not coincide with the motives of our governing bodies.

   D. No government decisions ought to be kept from the public.

   E. Citizens in other countries are not cared for by the government.

Read the following passage and answer Questions 3–4.

Recent studies indicate that more violent crimes are committed during hot weather than during cold weather. Thus, if we could control the weather, the violent crime rate would drop.

3. The argument above makes which of the following assumptions?

   I. The relationship between weather conditions and crime rate is merely coincidental.

   II. The relationship between weather conditions and crime rate is causal.

   III. The relationship between weather conditions and crime rate is controllable.

   A. I only

   B. II only

   C. I and II only

   D. II and III only

   E. I, II, and III

4. The argument would be strengthened if it pointed out that

   A. the annual crime statistics for New York are higher than those for Los Angeles.

   B. in laboratory tests, increased heat alone accounted for increased aggressive behavior between members of the test group.

   C. poor socioeconomic conditions, more uncomfortable in hot weather than in cold, are the direct causes of increased crime.

   D. weather control will be possible in the near future.

   E. more people leave their doors and windows open during hot weather.

Read the following passage and answer Question 5.

By appropriating bailout money for the depressed housing industry, Congress is opening the door to a flood of special relief programs for other recession-affected businesses.

5. The author's attitude toward Congress's action is probably

   A. neutral

   B. disapproving

   C. confused

   D. supportive

   E. irate

Read the following passage and answer Question 6.

The value of a close examination of the circumstances of an aircraft accident lies not only in fixing blame but in learning lessons.

6. The above statement fits most logically into which of the following types of passages?

   A. a survey of the "scapegoat phenomenon" in modern society

   B. an argument in favor of including specific details in any academic essay

   C. an argument against the usefulness of the National Transportation Safety Board

   D. a brief history of aeronautics

   E. a description of the causes of a particular aircraft accident

Read the following passage and answer Question 7.

The department store owned by my competitor sells green necklaces that glow in the dark. Only those customers of mine wearing those necklaces must be giving business to the competition.

7. The author foolishly assumes that

    A. the customers might find the necklaces attractive.

    B. customers are not buying other products from the competition.

    C. customers will wear the necklaces in daylight.

    D. a department store should not sell necklaces.

    E. the competition is outselling the author.

Read the following passage and answer Question 8.

Marketing literature for a computer program called "LingoLango" cites a study in which students who used LingoLango software scored 15 percent higher in school than students who didn't use its software. Therefore, the software company asserts that using "LingoLango" will increase a student's school grades by 15 percent.

8. Which of the following statements, if true, would most seriously weaken the company's claim?

    A. "LingoLango" teaches students skills that may also help them perform better on standardized tests.

    B. Students who didn't use "LingoLango" benefited from private tutoring.

    C. Students who used "LingoLango" and then did poorly in school were more likely to report their school grades inaccurately.

    D. "LingoLango" was listed as the "Cadillac of academic preparation software" by an independent testing consultant.

    E. An equal number of male and female students used the software.

Average

Read the following passage and answer Question 9.

Without sign ordinances, everyone with the price of a can of spray paint can suddenly decide to publicly create their own personal Picassos, and soon the entire town would start to look like something out of *Alice in Wonderland*. Therefore, we need sign ordinances.

9. The author makes which of the following basic assumptions?

    I. Spray paint is used for many signs.

    II. The entire town looking like *Alice in Wonderland* is undesirable.

    III. Sign ordinances are effective.

    A. I only

    B. II only

    C. III only

    D. I and III only

    E. I, II, and III

Read the following passage and answer Questions 10–11.

In most economies, the government plays a role in the market system. Governments enforce the "rules of the game," impose taxes, and may control prices through price ceilings or price supports. These actions necessarily may create shortages or surpluses. In most developed and interdependent economies, the necessity of the government's playing some role in the economy is disputed.

10. The final sentence in the passage suggests that

    A. interdependence goes hand in hand with development.

    B. there are underdeveloped countries whose attitude toward government control may be hostile.

    C. disputes over government control usually come from an illiterate populace.

    D. price supports are necessary.

    E. economic success is a sophisticated achievement.

11. The author of the passage would probably agree that

    A. economic surpluses are always good.

    B. market shortages are a necessary evil.

    C. higher prices strengthen the economy.

    D. price ceilings add to the shortages.

    E. surpluses are not usually created intentionally.

Read the following passage and answer Questions 12–13.

The new vehicle inspection program is needed to protect the quality of the state's air, for us and for our children. Auto exhausts are a leading contributor to coughing, wheezing, choking, and pollution. The state's long-term interests in the health of its citizens and in this area as a place to live, work, and conduct business depend on clean air.

12. Which of the following, if true, would most seriously weaken the argument above?

    A. Since smog devices were made mandatory automotive equipment by the existing inspection program three years ago, pollution has decreased dramatically and continues to decrease.

    B. Pollution problems are increasing in other states as well as in this one.

    C. Sometimes coughing, wheezing, and choking are caused by phenomena other than pollution.

    D. Vehicle inspectors are not always careful.

    E. The state should not impose its interests upon the citizenry but should instead allow public health to be regulated by private enterprise.

13. Which of the following is an unstated assumption made by the author?

A. Working and conducting business may be different activities.

B. The state has been interested in the health of its citizens even before this inspection program was proposed.

C. Exhaust emissions contribute to pollution.

D. The new inspection program will be effective.

E. Our ancestors did not suffer from air pollution.

Read the following passage and answer Questions 14–17.

The older we get, the less sleep we should desire. This is because our advanced knowledge and capabilities are most enjoyable when used; therefore, "mindless" sleep becomes a waste of time.

14. Which of the following distinctions is NOT expressed or implied by the author?

A. between sleep and wakefulness

B. between youth and maturity

C. between productivity and waste

D. between a desire and a requirement

E. between more sleep and less sleep

15. The author of this statement assumes that

A. less sleep is not desirable.

B. sleep advances knowledge and capabilities.

C. mindlessness coincides with wakefulness.

D. knowledge and capabilities naturally improve with age.

E. sleep is only for the young.

16. This author's statement might be strengthened if he or she pointed out that

A. advanced knowledge is often manifested in creative dreams.

B. the mind is quite active during sleep.

C. few empirical studies have concluded that sleep is an intellectual stimulant.

D. advanced capabilities are not necessarily mind-associated.

E. dreams teach us how to use waking experiences more intelligently.

17. The author's statement might be weakened by pointing out that

A. eight hours of sleep is a cultural, not a physical, requirement.

B. the most capable people rarely sleep.

C. rest is a positive contribution to knowledge and capability.

D. young children enjoy themselves less than knowledgeable adults.

E. people rarely waste time during their waking hours.

Read the following passage and answer Questions 18–19.

It is evident that the methods of science have been highly successful. Psychologist B.F. Skinner believes that the methods of science should be applied to the field of human affairs. We are all controlled by the world, part of which is constructed by humans. Is this control to occur by accident, by tyrants, or by ourselves? A scientific society should reject accidental manipulation. He asserts that a specific plan is needed to promote fully the development of human beings and society. We cannot make wise decisions if we continue to pretend that we are not controlled.

As Skinner points out, the possibility of behavioral control is offensive to many people. We have traditionally regarded humans as free agents whose behavior occurs by virtue of spontaneous inner changes. We are reluctant to abandon the internal "will," which makes prediction and control of behavior impossible.

18. According to the passage, Skinner would probably agree with each of the following statements EXCEPT:

   A. Rats and pigeons are appropriate animals for behavioristic study.

   B. These behaviors we normally exhibit are not the only ones we are capable of.

   C. The concept of behavioral control has popular appeal.

   D. Inner causes of behavior are more difficult to observe than outer ones.

   E. Positive reinforcement will affect learning in school.

19. The author implies that Skinner feels that the scientific procedure he advocates might be effective as

   A. a means of enhancing our future.

   B. an explanation of the causes of dictatorships.

   C. a means for replacing teachers with computers.

   D. a way of identifying characteristics common to rats, pigeons, and humans.

   E. a way to understand the human mind.

Above Average to Difficult

Read the following passage and answer Questions 20–21.

Votes on June 8 approved a $495 million bond issue for a state prison construction that is an obvious priority. Now the legislature has voted to put five more general obligation bond issues on the November ballot, adding another $1.5 billion to the state's long-term debt. Those on the November menu include $500 million for building and remodeling public schools, $450 million to extend the veterans home loan program, $200 million to subsidize low-interest mortgages for first-time home buyers, $85 million to acquire land for environmental protection, and $280 million to help counties expand or remodel their jails.

20. Which of the following statements is a point to which the author is most probably leading?

    A. Two of these bond issues are certainly more important than the others.

    B. We must face the obvious conclusion that prison construction is much less important than the improvement of public education and social programs for lawful citizens.

    C. The cost of these bond issues is, on the face of it, negligible.

    D. The voters cannot be expected to help make financial decisions for the state because most voters are suffering from their own severe financial problems.

    E. These five bond proposals are quite enough, and between now and November, voters will have to study them carefully to make sure that five is not too many.

21. Which of the following facts would most strongly weaken an argument for approval of the five new bond issues?

    A. Environmental protection is not an overriding concern of the constituency.

    B. The state's long-term debt cannot lawfully exceed $1.5 billion.

    C. Improvements in education, the environment, criminal prosecution, and the real estate market are favored by the voters.

    D. Similar bond proposals in other states have not been successful.

    E. Two bills related to the housing of criminals are quite enough.

Read the following passage and answer Question 22.

The state's empty $4 million governor's mansion on the banks of the Capitol River may be sort of a suburban Taj Mahal, as the governor once said. But why shouldn't the state unload it?

22. Which of the following is one of the author's basic assumptions?

    A. The governor's mansion is out of place in the suburbs.

    B. The reader is aware of the state's intention to "unload" the governor's mansion.

    C. No one has yet lived in the governor's mansion.

    D. The state is trying to sell the governor's mansion.

    E. The governor was correct.

Read the following passage and answer Question 23.

In 1994, when implementing an employee evaluation program, Acme Company's gross income reached an all-time high; however, after dropping the program during 1995, Acme's income dropped by 50 percent. Therefore, it's clear that Acme's employees perform better when being evaluated.

23. Which of the following statements, if true, would most seriously weaken the conclusion above?

    A. Acme employees received executive performance evaluations in 1994.

    B. the economy in 1995 was different from the economy in 1994.

    C. Acme employees worked harder when they knew they would be evaluated.

D. The employee evaluation program served to increase the company moral during 1994.

E. Acme retained leadership in the industry, despite falling sales.

Read the following passage and answer Question 24.

One form of paper recycling draws from post-consumer waste products. This means that the paper is produced from paper products that were once used in homes or industry. However, another kind of paper can also be called "recycled." This paper is produced from byproducts in the paper-making process itself, which means the paper has never been used by a consumer. Although the former method is more environmentally sound, the latter produces a paper with higher aesthetic quality.

24. If the passage above is true, then it is also true that people who buy the best-looking recycled paper are

   A. buying paper that was once used in homes and industry.

   B. inspecting the byproducts of the paper-making process.

   C. insisting on a bleached paper made from post-consumer waste.

   D. purchasing paper that does not come from the most environmentally sound process.

   E. reducing the amount of paper they use.

Read the following passage and answer Question 25.

The *Financial Times Magazine* devoted two pages to the stock market crash of 1929; however, the same magazine covered 1985's Black Monday with 25 pages.

25. The best explanation for this difference is that

   A. the crash of 1929 was viewed as more important than Black Monday.

   B. the *Financial Times Magazine* regretted their underreporting of the 1929 crash and did not wish to make the same mistake.

   C. the implications of the 1929 crash were more immediately apparent.

   D. the size of the magazine had increased so editors could devote more space to the 1985 story.

   E. the press in 1929 devoted more time to covering stories about successes instead of failures.

Answers and Explanations for the Practice Critical Reasoning Questions

Easy to Moderate

1. **E.** Whistler is saying that constant effort (industry) is necessary but that the artwork (production) should not evidence that effort.

2. **A.** By describing in very positive terms the effects of public deliberations, the author suggests the opinion that such deliberations *should* be public.

3. **B.** The only correct choice is II; it is argued that hot weather *causes* crime. This is not mere coincidence, and the statement does not say that we *can* control the weather.

4. **B.** The argument posits an exclusive relationship between hot weather and crime. **A, C,** and **E** contradict such an exclusive relationship. **D** is irrelevant to the relationship, but **B** provides evidence supporting and strengthening the heat/crime relationship.

5. **B.** By describing the special relief programs as a *flood,* the author gives the programs a negative connotation and suggests disapproval.

6. **E.** This choice is related most fully to the subject matter of the original statement.

7. **B.** The author does not realize that customers not wearing green necklaces may have bought other items from the competition.

8. **C.** This question asks you to select the answer choice that would weaken the claim that purchasing "LingoLango" improves a person's school grades. The best strategy is to read through the choices and eliminate those that are irrelevant or that strengthen (rather than weaken) the argument. After you do this, you are left with choice **C:** Students who purchased the software and then scored poorly were more likely to report inaccurately their scores. They may likely have reported their grades higher than what they actually were. If so, the results of the study are suspect, and "LingoLango" may not be as helpful as claimed.

Average

9. **E.** All of the statements are assumptions of the author essential to the argument. The author assumes spray paint to be the medium that graffiti painters use and implicitly abhors the possibility of a town looking like *Alice in Wonderland.* In addition, his or her desire for sign ordinances assumes that they work and are effective in deterring spray painting.

10. **B.** The last sentence says that *developed* or *interdependent* economies acquiesce to the idea that government must control the economy to some extent. This leaves underdeveloped countries unspoken for and raises the possibility they might *not* acquiesce to government control.

11. **B.** The paragraph states that government action "may create shortages or surpluses."

12. **A.** The argument for further supervision of vehicle use is most weakened by the statement that present safeguards are already doing the job. **C** and **D** slightly weaken the argument but do not address the overall position of the author.

13. D. In order to argue for a new inspection program, the author must assume that that particular program, if enacted, will be effective. **C**, the only other choice related to the points of the argument, expresses stated information rather than an unstated assumption.

14. D. The author does not address the distinction between how much sleep we desire and how much our bodies require. Each of the other distinctions is addressed in the passage.

15. D. In the passage, becoming older corresponds with *advanced knowledge and capabilities.* Choices **A, B,** and **C** should be eliminated because each is contradicted by the assumptions of the passage. (The passage suggests that *more* sleep is undesirable, knowledge and capabilities are connected with *wakefulness,* and mindlessness is connected with *sleep.*) Choice **E** is a generalization not at all concerned with amount of sleep and therefore not relevant to the passage.

16. C. Choices **A, B,** and **E** present information that supports the value of sleep, and **D** dissociates advanced capabilities from the mind, thus damaging the author's mind/mindlessness distinction.

17. C. Only choice **C** asserts the positive value of sleep and thus weakens the author's stance in favor of decreased sleep.

18. C. In the second paragraph, we read of his recognition that behaviorism is offensive to many people—that it does *not* have popular appeal.

19. A. The passage discusses the possible application of Skinner's theory to the field of human affairs and in promoting the development of humankind.

Above Average to Difficult

20. E. By listing high costs, the author is probably leading to the conclusion that the state's debt is being strained, a conclusion expressed in **E. C** contradicts the author's emphasis on high costs. **A, B,** and **D** are neither expressed nor implied by the passage; their choice would rely on extraneous assumptions.

21. B. This fact indicates that the passage of all the bond measures, which would take the debt over $1.5 billion, is illegal.

22. B. The author's final question necessarily rests on the assumption that the reader is aware of the state's intention; the author omits information expressing or explaining this intention.

23. B. Your task here is to find a statement that weakens the conclusion in the passage: The evaluation program boosted productivity. There are lots of possible weak points in this claim, but the only one listed in the choices is choice **B**—that the economy was different. If the economy was different for those two years, you cannot confidently say the evaluation program was the cause of increased income in 1994. If the economy was lousy in 1995, the income plausibly would still be bad, even if an evaluation program were in place. Therefore, choice **B** seriously weakens the conclusion in the passage.

24. **D.** This question requires you to read through the information on recycled paper and then draw a conclusion based on that information. The question here is if people insist on the best-looking recycled paper, then which paper have they purchased? The passage states that post-consumer waste paper is not the best-looking. So these people won't buy this kind of paper; instead, they will buy paper made from byproducts. To find the right choice, you also have to remember that using post-consumer waste is the most environmentally sound process. Once you put these facts together (the best-looking paper does not come from the most environmentally sound process), you have your answer, choice **D.**

25. **D.** Your job in this question is to find the most reasonable explanation for the huge difference in coverage for the two financial disasters. The secret here is simply to read through the choices and ask yourself: Does this make sense, and how reasonable is this explanation? After doing this for each choice, you should find that, although not perfect, choice **D** is the best choice: The magazine had grown in size and could therefore cover the 1985 crash with more pages.

PART III

FULL-LENGTH GMAT CAT PRACTICE TEST

ANALYTICAL WRITING ASSESSMENT

TIME: 60 Minutes

2 Questions

General Directions: In this section, you will have a total time of 60 minutes to plan and write two essays, one for each topic given. The specific time allotted for each essay is 30 minutes.

Analysis of an Issue

TIME: 30 Minutes

Directions: This section will require you to analyze and explain your views on the issue given. Consider many points of view as you develop your own position on the issue. There is no right or wrong answer to the question.

Read the statement and directions carefully. Make any notes or do any prewriting on your scratch paper. Then type your response into the computer.

> "Regardless of what business you're in, the better your computer skills, the better your chances of success."

Do you agree with this statement? Using reasons and/or examples from your work experience or from your observations, explain your position.

Analysis of an Argument

TIME: 30 Minutes

Directions: This section will require you to critique the argument given. Questioning underlying assumptions, finding alternative explanations or counterexamples, and delineating evidence to strengthen or weaken an argument are some possible approaches.

Read the argument and directions carefully. Make any notes or do any prewriting on your scratch paper. Then type your response into the computer.

The following advertisement appeared in newspapers throughout New York and New Jersey:

"Try Frostie Lo Calorie Ice Cream to lose weight fast! Seven of ten doctors surveyed recommend Frostie Lo Calorie Ice Cream. You can lose weight and still enjoy your favorite dessert in six delicious lo-calorie flavors."

Write a critique of the argument. You should consider what doubtful assumptions underlie the reasoning, what other explanations might apply and weaken the conclusions, and/or what other evidence would strengthen or weaken the argument. Do NOT write an essay on your views of the issue.

QUANTITATIVE SECTION

TIME: 75 Minutes

37 Questions

General Directions: Your score on the quantitative section will be based on how well you do on the questions presented and also on the number of questions you answer. You should try to pace yourself so that you have sufficient time to consider every question. If possible, answer all 37 questions in this section. Guess if you need to. Select the best answer choice for each question.

Note: Because you are checking answers as you go on this simulation, you should add about 5 to 10 minutes to your testing time.

Problem Solving Directions: Solve each problem in this section by using the information given and your own mathematical calculations. Then select the correct answer of the five choices given. Use the scratch paper given for any necessary calculations.

Note: Some problems may be accompanied by figures or diagrams. These figures are drawn as accurately as possible except when it is stated in a specific problem that the figure is not drawn to scale. The figure is meant to provide information useful in solving the problem or problems. Unless otherwise stated or indicated, all figures lie in a plane. All numbers used are real numbers.

Data Sufficiency Directions: Each of the problems below consists of a question and two statements, labeled (1) and (2), in which certain data are given. You must decide whether the data given in the statements are *sufficient* to answer the question. Using the data given in the statements plus your knowledge of mathematics and everyday facts (such as the number of days in July or the meaning of *counterclockwise*), you are to choose oval

- **A.** if statement (1) ALONE is sufficient, but statement (2) alone is not sufficient to answer the question asked;

- **B.** if statement (2) ALONE is sufficient, but statement (1) alone is not sufficient to answer the question asked;

- **C.** if both statements (1) and (2) TOGETHER are sufficient to answer the question asked, but NEITHER statement ALONE is sufficient;

- **D.** if EACH statement ALONE is sufficient to answer the question asked;

- **E.** if statements (1) and (2) TOGETHER are NOT sufficient to answer the question asked, and additional data specific to the problem are needed.

GO ON TO THE NEXT PAGE

1-3. A sporting goods store sold 64 Frisbees in one week, some for $3 and the rest for $4 each. If receipts from Frisbee sales for the week totaled $204, what is the fewest number of $4 Frisbees that could have been sold?

    A. 24

    B. 12

    C. 8

    D. 4

    E. 2

ANSWERS: 1-3 **B.**

If you answered 1-3 **incorrectly, go to 2-2**.
If you answered 1-3 **correctly, go to 2-4**.

2-2. If $2/x = 4$ and if $2/y = 8$, then $x - y =$

    A. $1/8$

    B. $1/4$

    C. $3/4$

    D. 4

    E. 24

2-4. A bus leaves Burbank at 9:00 a.m. traveling east at 50 miles per hour. At 1:00 p.m. a plane leaves Burbank traveling east at 300 miles per hour. At what time will the plane overtake the bus?

    A. 12:45 p.m.

    B. 1:10 p.m.

    C. 1:40 p.m.

    D. 1:48 p.m.

    E. 1:55 p.m.

ANSWERS: 2-2 **B**, 2-4 **D.**

If you answered 2-2 **incorrectly, go to 3-1**.
If you answered 2-2 **correctly, go to 3-3**.

If you answered 2-4 **incorrectly, go to 3-3**.
If you answered 2-4 **correctly, go to 3-5**.

3-1. An astronaut weighing 207 pounds on Earth would weigh 182 pounds on Venus. The weight of the astronaut on Venus would be approximately what percent of the astronaut's weight on Earth?

    A. 50%

    B. 60%

    C. 70%

    D. 80%

    E. 90%

3-3. If the ratio of the side of cube A to the side of cube B is 2:1, then which of the following is the ratio of the surface areas?

    A. 1:2

    B. 2:1

    C. 3:1

    D. 4:1

    E. 8:1

3-5. Three business people wish to invest in a new company. Each person is willing to pay one third of the total investment. After careful calculations, they realize that each of them would pay $7,200 less if they could find two more equal investors. How much is the total investment in the new business?

   A. $64,000

   B. $54,000

   C. $21,000

   D. $ 5,400

   E. $ 3,600

ANSWERS: 3-1 **E**, 3-3 **D**, 3-5 **B**.

If you answered 3-1 **incorrectly**, go to **4-1**.
If you answered 3-1 **correctly**, go to **4-2**.

If you answered 3-3 **incorrectly**, go to **4-2**.
If you answered 3-3 **correctly**, go to **4-4**.

If you answered 3-5 **incorrectly**, go to **4-4**.
If you answered 3-5 **correctly**, go to **4-5**.

4-1. The closest approximation of $(69.28 \times 0.004)/0.03$ is

   A. 0.092

   B. 0.92

   C. 9.2

   D. 92

   E. 920

4-2. What is the largest integer if the sum of three consecutive even integers is 318?

   A. 100

   B. 104

   C. 106

   D. 108

   E. 111

4-4. A woman invested $1,000, part at 5% and the rest at 6%. Her total investment with interest at the end of the year was $1,053. How much did she invest at 5%?

   A. $500

   B. $600

   C. $700

   D. $900

   E. $950

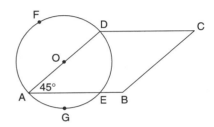

4-5. In the rhombus, $BC = 6$, $AE \cong 4$, and angle $DAE = 45°$. AD is the diameter of the circle. If a man started at C and followed around the outer edge of this figure to D, F, A, G, E, B, and back to C, approximately how far did he travel?

   A. $14 + \dfrac{27}{4}\pi$

   B. $14 + 6\pi$

   C. $12 + 6\pi$

   D. $14 + \dfrac{9}{2}\pi$

   E. $12 + \dfrac{9}{2}\pi$

ANSWERS: 4-1 **C**, 4-2 **D**, 4-4 **C**, 4-5 **D**.

If you answered 4-1 **incorrectly**, go to **5-1**.
If you answered 4-1 **correctly**, go to **5-2**.

If you answered 4-2 **incorrectly**, go to **5-1**.
If you answered 4-2 **correctly**, go to **5-3**.

If you answered 4-4 **incorrectly**, go to **5-3**.
If you answered 4-4 **correctly**, go to **5-5**.

If you answered 4-5 **incorrectly**, go to **5-4**.
If you answered 4-5 **correctly**, go to **5-5**.

GO ON TO THE NEXT PAGE

5-1. Three consecutive traffic signals each show either red or green. How many different arrangements of the three signals are possible? (Note: "Red-red-green" is different from "green-red-red.")

A. 10
B. 9
C. 8
D. 7
E. 6

5-2. There are 36 students in a certain geometry class. If two thirds of the students are boys and three fourths of the boys are under six feet tall, how many boys in the class are under six feet tall?

A. 6
B. 12
C. 18
D. 24
E. 27

5-3. How may different three-person committees can be formed from six people?

A. 2
B. 18
C. 20
D. 36
E. 108

5-4. A woman has three blouses of different colors, three skirts of different colors, and two different pairs of shoes. She refuses to wear her pink blouse with her green skirt. How many different blouse-skirt-shoe combinations could she wear?

A. 8
B. 12
C. 16
D. 17
E. 18

5-5. A drawer contains red socks, black socks, and white socks. What is the least number of socks that must randomly be taken out of the drawer to be sure of having four pairs of socks? (A pair is two socks of the same color.)

A. 8
B. 10
C. 12
D. 14
E. 16

ANSWERS: 5-1 **C**, 5-2 **C**, 5-3 **C**, 5-4 **C**, 5-5 **B**.

If you answered 5-1 **incorrectly**, go to 6-1.
If you answered 5-1 **correctly**, go to 6-2.

If you answered 5-2 **incorrectly**, go to 6-1.
If you answered 5-2 **correctly**, go to 6-3.

If you answered 5-3 **incorrectly**, go to 6-2.
If you answered 5-3 **correctly**, go to 6-4.

If you answered 5-4 **incorrectly**, go to 6-3.
If you answered 5-4 **correctly**, go to 6-5.

If you answered 5-5 **incorrectly**, go to 6-4.
If you answered 5-5 **correctly**, go to 6-5.

6-1. How much precipitation does Springfield need this month to attain its long-term average of 35 inches per year?

(1) Over the last 11 months, the city has averaged 3 inches of precipitation per month.

(2) Springfield has accumulated 94.3% of its mean annual precipitation during the last 11 months.

A. Statement (1) ALONE is sufficient, but (2) alone is not sufficient.

B. Statement (2) ALONE is sufficient, but statement (1) alone is not sufficient.

C. BOTH statements (1) and (2) TOGETHER are sufficient, but NEITHER statement ALONE is sufficient.

D. EACH statement ALONE is sufficient.

E. Statements (1) and (2) TOGETHER are NOT sufficient.

6-2. Is a tick longer in duration than a tock?

(1) There are 48 tocks each day.

(2) A tick is longer than a minute.

A. Statement (1) ALONE is sufficient, but statement (2) alone is not sufficient.

B. Statement (2) ALONE is sufficient, but statement (1) alone is not sufficient.

C. BOTH statements (1) and (2) TOGETHER are sufficient, but NEITHER statement ALONE is sufficient.

D. EACH statement ALONE is sufficient.

E. Statements (1) and (2) TOGETHER are NOT sufficient.

6-3. Three spies—Ex, Why, and Zee—together know 19 different secrets. There is no overlap of information. How many secrets does Why know?

(1) Ex knows one more than Why and twice as many as Zee.

(2) Why knows three more secrets than Zee.

A. Statement (1) ALONE is sufficient, but statement (2) alone is not sufficient.

B. Statement (2) ALONE is sufficient, but statement (1) alone is not sufficient.

C. BOTH statements (1) and (2) TOGETHER are sufficient, but NEITHER statement ALONE is sufficient.

D. EACH statement ALONE is sufficient.

E. Statements (1) and (2) TOGETHER are NOT sufficient.

6-4. A school play requires 24 actors to be cast among boys, girls, and adults. If no actors may take two roles, how many adult actors are needed?

(1) The ratio of boys needed to girls is 2 to 1.

(2) The ratio of children needed to adults is 3 to 1.

A. Statement (1) ALONE is sufficient, but statement (2) alone is not sufficient.

B. Statement (2) ALONE is sufficient, but statement (1) alone is not sufficient.

GO ON TO THE NEXT PAGE

C. BOTH statements (1) and (2) TOGETHER are sufficient, but NEITHER statement ALONE is sufficient.

D. EACH statement ALONE is sufficient.

E. Statements (1) and (2) TOGETHER are NOT sufficient.

6-5. During 1996, 17,500 patients were admitted to Warehall Hospital, and exactly one sixth of these patients were discharged within one day. Of those patients discharged within one hour, one fourth were seen by only one doctor. How many patients during 1996 were seen by only one doctor?

(1) Of the total number of patients admitted to Warehall Hospital in 1996, one ninth were discharged within one hour.

(2) Exactly 11,050 patients were discharged within one hour.

A. Statement (1) ALONE is sufficient, but statement (2) alone is not sufficient.

B. Statement (2) ALONE is sufficient, but statement (1) alone is not sufficient.

C. BOTH statements (1) and (2) TOGETHER are sufficient, but NEITHER statement ALONE is sufficient.

D. EACH statement ALONE is sufficient.

E. Statements (1) and (2) TOGETHER are NOT sufficient.

ANSWERS: 6-1 D, 6-2 **E**, 6-3 **A**, 6-4 **B**, 6-5 **E**.

If you answered 6-1 **incorrectly, go to 7-1.**
If you answered 6-1 **correctly, go to 7-2.**

If you answered 6-2 **incorrectly, go to 7-1.**
If you answered 6-2 **correctly, go to 7-3.**

If you answered 6-3 **incorrectly, go to 7-2.**
If you answered 6-3 **correctly, go to 7-4.**

If you answered 6-4 **incorrectly, go to 7-3.**
If you answered 6-4 **correctly, go to 7-5.**

If you answered 6-5 **incorrectly, go to 7-4.**
If you answered 6-5 **correctly, go to 7-5.**

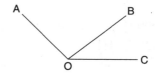

7-1. How many degrees is angle *AOB*?

(1) Angle $BOC = 35°$.

(2) $\overline{AO}$ is perpendicular to $\overline{OB}$.

A. Statement (1) ALONE is sufficient, but statement (2) alone is not sufficient.

B. Statement (2) ALONE is sufficient, but statement (1) alone is not sufficient.

C. BOTH statements (1) and (2) TOGETHER are sufficient, but NEITHER statement ALONE is sufficient.

D. EACH statement ALONE is sufficient.

E. Statements (1) and (2) TOGETHER are NOT sufficient.

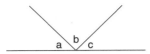

7-2. How many degrees is angle c?

(1) b is a right angle.

(2) $a + b = 131°$

A. Statement (1) ALONE is sufficient, but statement (2) alone is not sufficient.

B. Statement (2) ALONE is sufficient, but statement (1) alone is not sufficient.

C. BOTH statements (1) and (2) TOGETHER are sufficient, but NEITHER statement ALONE is sufficient.

D. EACH statement ALONE is sufficient.

E. Statements (1) and (2) TOGETHER are NOT sufficient.

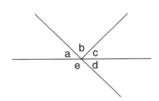

7-3. How many degrees is angle e?

(1) $a + d = 82°$

(2) $b + d = 111°$

A. Statement (1) ALONE is sufficient, but statement (2) alone is not sufficient.

B. Statement (2) ALONE is sufficient, but statement (1) alone is not sufficient.

C. BOTH statements (1) and (2) TOGETHER are sufficient, but NEITHER statement ALONE is sufficient.

D. EACH statement ALONE is sufficient.

E. Statements (1) and (2) TOGETHER are NOT sufficient.

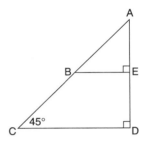

7-4. What is the ratio of the area of quadrilateral *BCDE* to the area of triangle *ABE*?

(1) $BC = ½AC$

(2) Angle *CBE* = 135°

A. Statement (1) ALONE is sufficient, but statement (2) alone is not sufficient.

B. Statement (2) ALONE is sufficient, but statement (1) alone is not sufficient.

C. BOTH statements (1) and (2) TOGETHER are sufficient, but NEITHER statement ALONE is sufficient.

D. EACH statement ALONE is sufficient.

E. Statements (1) and (2) TOGETHER are NOT sufficient.

GO ON TO THE NEXT PAGE

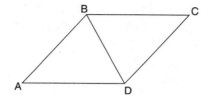

7-5. In rhombus *ABCD*, what is angle *BCD?*

(1) $BC = BD$

(2) Angle $BDA = 60°$

A. Statement (1) ALONE is sufficient, but statement (2) alone is not sufficient.

B. Statement (2) ALONE is sufficient, but statement (1) alone is not sufficient.

C. BOTH statements (1) and (2) TOGETHER are sufficient, but NEITHER statement ALONE is sufficient.

D. EACH statement ALONE is sufficient.

E. Statements (1) and (2) TOGETHER are NOT sufficient.

ANSWERS: 7-1 **B**, 7-2 **B**, 7-3 **A**, 7-4 **A**, 7-5 **D**.

If you answered 7-1 **incorrectly, go to 8-1.**
If you answered 7-1 **correctly, go to 8-2.**

If you answered 7-2 **incorrectly, go to 8-1.**
If you answered 7-2 **correctly, go to 8-3.**

If you answered 7-3 **incorrectly, go to 8-2.**
If you answered 7-3 **correctly, go to 8-4.**

If you answered 7-4 **incorrectly, go to 8-3.**
If you answered 7-4 **correctly, go to 8-5.**

If you answered 7-5 **incorrectly, go to 8-4.**
If you answered 7-5 **correctly, go to 8-5.**

8-1. What are the individual prices of three cameras?

(1) The three cameras have an average price of $172.

(2) Two are the same price and sell for $332 together.

A. Statement (1) ALONE is sufficient, but statement (2) alone is not sufficient.

B. Statement (2) ALONE is sufficient, but statement (1) alone is not sufficient.

C. BOTH statements (1) and (2) TOGETHER are sufficient, but NEITHER statement ALONE is sufficient.

D. EACH statement ALONE is sufficient.

E. Statements (1) and (2) TOGETHER are NOT sufficient.

8-2. What is the average of ten numbers?

(1) Nine of the numbers sum to 45.

(2) One of the numbers is 15.

A. Statement (1) ALONE is sufficient, but statement (2) alone is not sufficient.

B. Statement (2) ALONE is sufficient, but statement (1) alone is not sufficient.

C. BOTH statements (1) and (2) TOGETHER are sufficient, but NEITHER statement ALONE is sufficient.

D. EACH statement ALONE is sufficient.

E. Statements (1) and (2) TOGETHER are NOT sufficient.

8-3. What is the sum of five numbers?

  (1) The average of the numbers is zero

  (2) Only one of the numbers is positive.

  A. Statement (1) ALONE is sufficient, but statement (2) alone is not sufficient.

  B. Statement (2) ALONE is sufficient, but statement (1) alone is not sufficient.

  C. BOTH statements (1) and (2) TOGETHER are sufficient, but NEITHER statement ALONE is sufficient.

  D. EACH statement ALONE is sufficient.

  E. Statements (1) and (2) TOGETHER are NOT sufficient.

8-4. Is the product $xy > 27$?

  (1) $2 < x < 5$

  (2) $6 > y$

  A. Statement (1) ALONE is sufficient, but statement (2) alone is not sufficient.

  B. Statement (2) ALONE is sufficient, but statement (1) alone is not sufficient.

  C. BOTH statements (1) and (2) TOGETHER are sufficient, but NEITHER statement ALONE is sufficient.

  D. EACH statement ALONE is sufficient.

  E. Statements (1) and (2) TOGETHER are NOT sufficient.

8-5. Is $x < 2$?

  (1) $x > x^2$

  (2) $1/x > 3$

  A. Statement (1) ALONE is sufficient, but statement (2) alone is not sufficient.

  B. Statement (2) ALONE is sufficient, but statement (1) alone is not sufficient.

  C. BOTH statements (1) and (2) TOGETHER are sufficient, but NEITHER statement ALONE is sufficient.

  D. EACH statement ALONE is sufficient.

  E. Statements (1) and (2) TOGETHER are NOT sufficient.

ANSWERS: 8-1 **C**, 8-2 **E**, 8-3 **A**, 8-4 **E**, 8-5 **D**.

If you answered 8-1 **incorrectly**, go to **9-1**.
If you answered 8-1 **correctly**, go to **9-2**.

If you answered 8-2 **incorrectly**, go to **9-1**.
If you answered 8-2 **correctly**, go to **9-3**.

If you answered 8-3 **incorrectly**, go to **9-2**.
If you answered 8-3 **correctly**, go to **9-4**.

If you answered 8-4 **incorrectly**, go to **9-3**.
If you answered 8-4 **correctly**, go to **9-5**.

If you answered 8-5 **incorrectly**, go to **9-4**.
If you answered 8-5 **correctly**, go to **9-5**.

GO ON TO THE NEXT PAGE

9-1. What is Toni's typing speed in words per minute?

(1) She completed a report of 3,150 words in one hour.

(2) The report had 7 pages, each averaging 450 words.

A. Statement (1) ALONE is sufficient, but statement (2) alone is not sufficient.

B. Statement (2) ALONE is sufficient, but statement (1) alone is not sufficient.

C. BOTH statements (1) and (2) TOGETHER are sufficient, but NEITHER statement ALONE is sufficient.

D. EACH statement ALONE is sufficient.

E. Statements (1) and (2) TOGETHER are NOT sufficient.

9-2. How long would it take Joan to count the books in a small library?

(1) She counts twice as fast as Emily.

(2) Working together, Joan and Emily count the books in 26 hours.

A. Statement (1) ALONE is sufficient, but statement (2) alone is not sufficient.

B. Statement (2) ALONE is sufficient, but statement (1) alone is not sufficient.

C. BOTH statements (1) and (2) TOGETHER are sufficient, but NEITHER statement ALONE is sufficient.

D. EACH statement ALONE is sufficient.

E. Statements (1) and (2) TOGETHER are NOT sufficient.

9-3. How long would it take Sue to paint the room?

(1) Working with Bob, the project would last 2 hours.

(2) Bob could accomplish the painting alone in 3 1/4 hours.

A. Statement (1) ALONE is sufficient, but statement (2) alone is not sufficient.

B. Statement (2) ALONE is sufficient, but statement (1) alone is not sufficient.

C. BOTH statements (1) and (2) TOGETHER are sufficient, but NEITHER statement ALONE is sufficient.

D. EACH statement ALONE is sufficient.

E. Statements (1) and (2) TOGETHER are NOT sufficient.

9-4. Beverage cans are manufactured of steel or aluminum. From the following graphs, what was the approximate percentage change in number of beverage cans manufactured from 1990 to 1995?

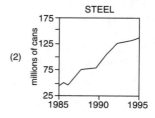

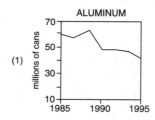

A. Statement (1) ALONE is sufficient, but statement (2) alone is not sufficient.

B. Statement (2) ALONE is sufficient, but statement (1) alone is not sufficient.

C. BOTH statements (1) and (2) TOGETHER are sufficient, but NEITHER statement ALONE is sufficient.

D. EACH statement ALONE is sufficient.

E. Statements (1) and (2) TOGETHER are NOT sufficient.

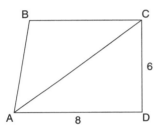

9-5. In the trapezoid *ABCD*, what is the area of triangle *ABC*?

(1) $AC = 10$

(2) $BC = 7$

A. Statement (1) ALONE is sufficient, but statement (2) alone is not sufficient.

B. Statement (2) ALONE is sufficient, but statement (1) alone is not sufficient.

C. BOTH statements (1) and (2) TOGETHER are sufficient, but NEITHER statement ALONE is sufficient.

D. EACH statement ALONE is sufficient.

E. Statements (1) and (2) TOGETHER are NOT sufficient.

ANSWERS: 9-1 **A**, 9-2 **C**, 9-3 **C**, 9-4 **C**, 9-5 **C**.

If you answered 9-1 **incorrectly, go to 10-1.**
If you answered 9-1 **correctly, go to 10-2.**

If you answered 9-2 **incorrectly, go to 10-1.**
If you answered 9-2 **correctly, go to 10-3.**

If you answered 9-3 **incorrectly, go to 10-2.**
If you answered 9-3 **correctly, go to 10-4.**

If you answered 9-4 **incorrectly, go to 10-3.**
If you answered 9-4 **correctly, go to 10-5.**

If you answered 9-5 **incorrectly, go to 10-4.**
If you answered 9-5 **correctly, go to 10-5.**

10-1. A small college reduced its faculty by approximately 13 percent to 195 professors. What was the original number of faculty members?

A. 182

B. 208

C. 224

D. 254

E. 302

10-2. If 15 students in a class average 80% on an English exam and 10 students average 90% on the same exam, what is the average in percent for all 25 students?

A. 83%

B. 83½%

C. 84%

D. 85%

E. 86⅔%

GO ON TO THE NEXT PAGE

10-3. The average of 9 numbers is 7 and the average of 7 other numbers is 9. What is the average of all 16 numbers?

  A. 9

  B. 8

  C. 7⅞

  D. 7½

  E. 7¼

10-4. If 20% of a class averages 80% on a test, 50% of the class averages 60% on the test, and the remainder of the class averages 40% on the test, what is the overall class average?

  A. 80%

  B. 74%

  C. 58%

  D. 56%

  E. 50%

10-5. Thirty percent of the women in a college class are science majors, and the non-science majors make up 80% of the class. What percentage of the men are science majors if 40% of the class are men?

  A. 2%

  B. 5%

  C. 28%

  D. 30%

  E. 45%

ANSWERS: 10-1 **C**, 10-2 **C**, 10-3 **C**, 10-4 **C**, 10-5 **B**.

If you answered 10-1 **incorrectly, go to 11-1**.
If you answered 10-1 **correctly, go to 11-2**.

If you answered 10-2 **incorrectly, go to 11-1**.
If you answered 10-2 **correctly, go to 11-3**.

If you answered 10-3 **incorrectly, go to 11-2**.
If you answered 10-3 **correctly, go to 11-4**.

If you answered 10-4 **incorrectly, go to 11-3**.
If you answered 10-4 **correctly, go to 11-5**.

If you answered 10-5 **incorrectly, go to 11-4**.
If you answered 10-5 **correctly, go to 11-5**.

11-1. If it takes a machine ⅔ minute to produce one item, how many items will it produce in 2 hours?

  A. ⅓

  B. ⁴⁄₃

  C. 80

  D. 120

  E. 180

11-2. The large square above consists of squares and isosceles right triangles. If the large square has side 4 cm, then the area of the shaded portion in square cm is

  A. 2

  B. 4

  C. 6

  D. 8

  E. 12

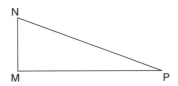

11-3. On $\triangle MNP$, $MN \perp MP$, $MP = 24$, and $NP = 26$. What is the area of $\triangle MNP$ in square units?

A. 312

B. 240

C. 120

D. 60

E. 30

11-4. Manny rides a bicycle 6 miles east, 5 miles north, 18 miles west, and 14 miles south, at a rate of 10 miles per hour. If Irv leaves at the same time and from the same place and walks directly to Manny's final destination at a rate of 5 miles per hour, he will arrive

A. at the same time as Manny

B. more than one hour before Manny

C. more than one hour after Manny

D. less than one hour before Manny

E. less than one hour after Manny

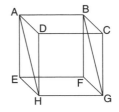

11-5. In the cube above, *AH* and *BG* are diagonals and the surface area of side *ABFE* is 16. What is the area of rectangle *ABGH?*

A. $4\sqrt{2}$

B. $16\sqrt{2}$

C. $16 + \sqrt{2}$

D. 16

E. $15\sqrt{3}$

ANSWERS: 11-1 **E,** 11-2 **D,** 11-3 **C,** 11-4 **B,** 11-5 **B.**

If you answered 11-1 **incorrectly, go to 12-1.**
If you answered 11-1 **correctly, go to 12-2.**

If you answered 11-2 **incorrectly, go to 12-1.**
If you answered 11-2 **correctly, go to 12-3.**

If you answered 11-3 **incorrectly, go to 12-2.**
If you answered 11-3 **correctly, go to 12-4.**

If you answered 11-4 **incorrectly, go to 12-3.**
If you answered 11-4 **correctly, go to 12-5.**

If you answered 11-5 **incorrectly, go to 12-4.**
If you answered 11-5 **correctly, go to 12-5.**

12-1. What number times $(1/3)^2$ will give the value of 3^3?

A. 3

B. 9

C. 27

D. 108

E. 243

GO ON TO THE NEXT PAGE

12-2. If $x = \dfrac{1+y}{y}$, then $y =$

    A. $\dfrac{1}{x-1}$

    B. $\dfrac{1}{x+1}$

    C. $\dfrac{1+x}{x}$

    D. $\dfrac{1-x}{x}$

    E. x

12-3. Which of the five choices is equivalent to the expression $\dfrac{x-4}{2x^2-10x+8}$?

    A. $\dfrac{1}{2x^2-9x}$

    B. $\dfrac{1}{2x^2-9x+4}$

    C. $\dfrac{1}{2x+4}$

    D. $\dfrac{1}{2x}$

    E. $\dfrac{1}{2x-2}$

12-4. If $\dfrac{x^2+5x+6}{x^2-4} = \dfrac{3}{2}$, then the value of x is

    A. -12

    B. $-2\frac{2}{5}$

    C. -2

    D. 2

    E. 12

12-5. If one root of the equation $x^2 - 5x + m = 0$ is 10, what is the value of $m + 3$?

    A. 50

    B. 10

    C. -5

    D. -47

    E. -50

ANSWERS: 12-1 **E**, 12-2 **A**, 12-3 **E**, 12-4 **E**, 12-5 **D**.

If you answered 12-1 **incorrectly**, go to **13-1**.
If you answered 12-1 **correctly**, go to **13-2**.

If you answered 12-2 **incorrectly**, go to **13-1**.
If you answered 12-2 **correctly**, go to **13-3**.

If you answered 12-3 **incorrectly**, go to **13-2**.
If you answered 12-3 **correctly**, go to **13-4**.

If you answered 12-4 **incorrectly**, go to **13-3**.
If you answered 12-4 **correctly**, go to **13-5**.

If you answered 12-5 **incorrectly**, go to **13-4**.
If you answered 12-5 **correctly**, go to **13-5**.

13-1. The purchase price of an article is $48. In order to include 15% of cost for overhead and to provide $12 of net profit, the markup should be

    A. 15%

    B. 25%

    C. 35%

    D. 40%

    E. 45%

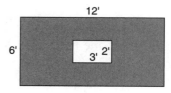

13-2. How many 2-inch by 3-inch rectangular tiles are required to tile this shaded region?

    A. Less than 10

    B. 10—100

    C. 101—1,000

    D. 1,001—1,500

    E. 1,500+

	60	
70	y	
80	x	
80		

13-3. The horizontal length of each rectangle is marked within. What is the total horizontal length of $x + y$?

A. 40

B. 50

C. 80

D. 90

E. It cannot be determined from the information given.

13-4. If the diameter of circle R is 30% of the diameter of circle S, the area of circle R is what percent of the area of circle S?

A. 9%

B. 15%

C. 30%

D. 60%

E. 90%

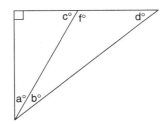

13-5. In the right triangle, $c = 2a$ and $d > 2b$; therefore, which of the following must be true?

A. $c > b + d$

B. Angle a is greater than angle b.

C. Angle a equals angle b.

D. Angle b is greater than angle a.

E. Angle d equals twice angle a.

ANSWERS: 13-1 **D**, 13-2 **E**, 13-3 **E**, 13-4 **A**, 13-5 **B**.

If you answered 13-1 **incorrectly**, go to **14-1**.
If you answered 13-1 **correctly**, go to **14-2**.

If you answered 13-2 **incorrectly**, go to **14-1**.
If you answered 13-2 **correctly**, go to **14-3**.

If you answered 13-3 **incorrectly**, go to **14-2**.
If you answered 13-3 **correctly**, go to **14-4**.

If you answered 13-4 **incorrectly**, go to **14-3**.
If you answered 13-4 **correctly**, go to **14-5**.

If you answered 13-5 **incorrectly**, go to **14-4**.
If you answered 13-5 **correctly**, go to **14-5**.

14-1. How much gross profit did White Store make during its Great Refrigerator Sale?

(1) The store sold 112 refrigerators for $33,060.

(2) The refrigerators cost White an average of $186.

A. Statement (1) ALONE is sufficient, but statement (2) alone is not sufficient.

B. Statement (2) ALONE is sufficient, but statement (1) alone is not sufficient.

C. BOTH statements (1) and (2) TOGETHER are sufficient, but NEITHER statement ALONE is sufficient.

D. EACH statement ALONE is sufficient.

E. Statements (1) and (2) TOGETHER are NOT sufficient.

GO ON TO THE NEXT PAGE

14-2. How much principal and interest are still owed on a home originally sold for $179,000?

(1) The interest rate when the home was purchased was 9%.

(2) The owner has yet to make 84 payments of $1,124 each.

A. Statement (1) ALONE is sufficient, but statement (2) alone is not sufficient.

B. Statement (2) ALONE is sufficient, but statement (1) alone is not sufficient.

C. BOTH statements (1) and (2) TOGETHER are sufficient, but NEITHER statement ALONE is sufficient.

D. EACH statement ALONE is sufficient.

E. Statements (1) and (2) TOGETHER are NOT sufficient.

14-3. A savings account earned 1% interest compounded each month, credited on the last day of the month. On December 8 there was $1,115.67 in the account. During which month did the account first exceed $1,100?

(1) $1,000 was deposited on the previous December 31.

(2) There were no deposits or withdrawals this year.

A. Statement (1) ALONE is sufficient, but statement (2) alone is not sufficient.

B. Statement (2) ALONE is sufficient, but statement (1) alone is not sufficient.

C. BOTH statements (1) and (2) TOGETHER are sufficient, but NEITHER statement ALONE is sufficient.

D. EACH statement ALONE is sufficient.

E. Statements (1) and (2) TOGETHER are NOT sufficient.

14-4. So far this year, Mr. and Mrs. Dufaa have paid what percent of their annual home expenses?

(1) So far the Dufaas have paid ½ of their annual electricity bill, ½ of their annual gas bill, ¼ of their annual water bill, and ¾ of their annual trash bill.

(2) The Dufaas' annual home expenses include four items: electricity, gas, water, and trash removal.

A. Statement (1) ALONE is sufficient, but statement (2) alone is not sufficient.

B. Statement (2) ALONE is sufficient, but statement (1) alone is not sufficient.

C. BOTH statements (1) and (2) TOGETHER are sufficient, but NEITHER statement ALONE is sufficient.

D. EACH statement ALONE is sufficient.

E. Statements (1) and (2) TOGETHER are NOT sufficient.

14-5. How many people are employed at a certain manufacturing plant with an annual payroll of $2,342,000?

    (1) Three-fourths of the employees are clerical, at an average salary of $16,020.

    (2) With 8% more employees, the payroll would equal $2,548,000.

  A. Statement (1) ALONE is sufficient, but statement (2) alone is not sufficient.

  B. Statement (2) ALONE is sufficient, but statement (1) alone is not sufficient.

  C. BOTH statements (1) and (2) TOGETHER are sufficient, but NEITHER statement ALONE is sufficient.

  D. EACH statement ALONE is sufficient.

  E. Statements (1) and (2) TOGETHER are NOT sufficient.

ANSWERS: 14-1 **C**, 14-2 **B**, 14-3 **B**, 14-4 **E**, 14-5 **E**.

If you answered 14-1 **incorrectly, go to 15-1.**
If you answered 14-1 **correctly, go to 15-2.**

If you answered 14-2 **incorrectly, go to 15-1.**
If you answered 14-2 **correctly, go to 15-3.**

If you answered 14-3 **incorrectly, go to 15-2.**
If you answered 14-3 **correctly, go to 15-4.**

If you answered 14-4 **incorrectly, go to 15-3.**
If you answered 14-4 **correctly, go to 15-5.**

If you answered 14-5 **incorrectly, go to 15-4.**
If you answered 14-5 **correctly, go to 15-5.**

15-1. Is the number N an integer?

    (1) The factors of N are 3, 5, and 7.

    (2) N cannot be divided evenly by 2.

  A. Statement (1) ALONE is sufficient, but statement (2) alone is not sufficient.

  B. Statement (2) ALONE is sufficient, but statement (1) alone is not sufficient.

  C. BOTH statements (1) and (2) TOGETHER are sufficient, but NEITHER statement ALONE is sufficient.

  D. EACH statement ALONE is sufficient.

  E. Statements (1) and (2) TOGETHER are NOT sufficient.

15-2. Which is greater, cf or fg?

    (1) $c > g$

    (2) $f^2 = cg$

  A. Statement (1) ALONE is sufficient, but statement (2) alone is not sufficient.

  B. Statement (2) ALONE is sufficient, but statement (1) alone is not sufficient.

  C. BOTH statements (1) and (2) TOGETHER are sufficient, but NEITHER statement ALONE is sufficient.

  D. EACH statement ALONE is sufficient.

  E. Statements (1) and (2) TOGETHER are NOT sufficient.

GO ON TO THE NEXT PAGE

15-3. Given that $x = y + z$, where the three values are different positive integers, is x a prime number?

    (1) y and z are odd.

    (2) $z = 3y$

    A. Statement (1) ALONE is sufficient, but statement (2) alone is not sufficient.

    B. Statement (2) ALONE is sufficient, but statement (1) alone is not sufficient.

    C. BOTH statements (1) and (2) TOGETHER are sufficient, but NEITHER statement ALONE is sufficient.

    D. EACH statement ALONE is sufficient.

    E. Statements (1) and (2) TOGETHER are NOT sufficient.

15-4. Given $2m^2 + n^2 = 27$, what is the value of m?

    (1) n is positive.

    (2) $m = n$

    A. Statement (1) ALONE is sufficient, but statement (2) alone is not sufficient.

    B. Statement (2) ALONE is sufficient, but statement (1) alone is not sufficient.

    C. BOTH statements (1) and (2) TOGETHER are sufficient, but NEITHER statement ALONE is sufficient.

    D. EACH statement ALONE is sufficient.

    E. Statements (1) and (2) TOGETHER are NOT sufficient.

15-5. Given that $m = n + 2$, what is the value of $m^2 - 4m + 4$?

    (1) $n = 20$

    (2) $n^2 = 400$

    A. Statement (1) ALONE is sufficient, but statement (2) alone is not sufficient.

    B. Statement (2) ALONE is sufficient, but statement (1) alone is not sufficient.

    C. BOTH statements (1) and (2) TOGETHER are sufficient, but NEITHER statement ALONE is sufficient.

    D. EACH statement ALONE is sufficient.

    E. Statements (1) and (2) TOGETHER are NOT sufficient.

ANSWERS: 15-1 A, 15-2 E, 15-3 D, 15-4 C, 15-5 D.

If you answered 15-1 **incorrectly, go to 16-1.**
If you answered 15-1 **correctly, go to 16-2.**

If you answered 15-2 **incorrectly, go to 16-1.**
If you answered 15-2 **correctly, go to 16-3.**

If you answered 15-3 **incorrectly, go to 16-2.**
If you answered 15-3 **correctly, go to 16-4.**

If you answered 15-4 **incorrectly, go to 16-3.**
If you answered 15-4 **correctly, go to 16-5.**

If you answered 15-5 **incorrectly, go to 16-4.**
If you answered 15-5 **correctly, go to 16-5.**

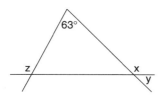

16-1. How many degrees is angle *x*?

(1) $y = 47°$

(2) $z = 110°$

A. Statement (1) ALONE is sufficient, but statement (2) alone is not sufficient.

B. Statement (2) ALONE is sufficient, but statement (1) alone is not sufficient.

C. BOTH statements (1) and (2) TOGETHER are sufficient, but NEITHER statement ALONE is sufficient.

D. EACH statement ALONE is sufficient.

E. Statements (1) and (2) TOGETHER are NOT sufficient.

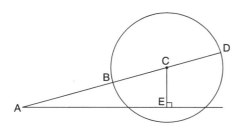

16-2. In the circle with center *C* above, what is the area of right triangle *ACE*?

(1) *AE* equals 16 inches.

(2) *BD* equals 12 inches.

A. Statement (1) ALONE is sufficient, but statement (2) alone is not sufficient.

B. Statement (2) ALONE is sufficient, but statement (1) alone is not sufficient.

C. BOTH statements (1) and (2) TOGETHER are sufficient, but NEITHER statement ALONE is sufficient.

D. EACH statement ALONE is sufficient.

E. Statements (1) and (2) TOGETHER are NOT sufficient.

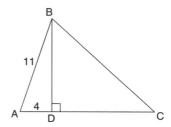

16-3. Given *BD* perpendicular to *AC*, what is the area of triangle *BCD*?

(1) Angle *BAD* = 69°

(2) *BD* = *CD*

A. Statement (1) ALONE is sufficient, but statement (2) alone is not sufficient.

B. Statement (2) ALONE is sufficient, but statement (1) alone is not sufficient.

C. BOTH statements (1) and (2) TOGETHER are sufficient, but NEITHER statement ALONE is sufficient.

D. EACH statement ALONE is sufficient.

E. Statements (1) and (2) TOGETHER are NOT sufficient.

GO ON TO THE NEXT PAGE

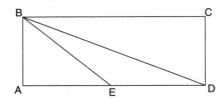

16-4. In the figure above, *ABCD* is a rectangle and *E* is the midpoint of one side. What is the area of triangle *BCD*?

(1) *BE* = 5 inches

(2) *CD* = 3 inches

A. Statement (1) ALONE is sufficient, but statement (2) alone is not sufficient.

B. Statement (2) ALONE is sufficient, but statement (1) alone is not sufficient.

C. BOTH statements (1) and (2) TOGETHER are sufficient, but NEITHER statement ALONE is sufficient.

D. EACH statement ALONE is sufficient.

E. Statements (1) and (2) TOGETHER are NOT sufficient.

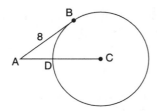

16-5. Given that *AB* is tangent to the circle with center *C*, what is the length of the circle's radius?

(1) *AD* = 4

(2) *AC* = 10

A. Statement (1) ALONE is sufficient, but statement (2) alone is not sufficient.

B. Statement (2) ALONE is sufficient, but statement (1) alone is not sufficient.

C. BOTH statements (1) and (2) TOGETHER are sufficient, but NEITHER statement ALONE is sufficient.

D. EACH statement ALONE is sufficient.

E. Statements (1) and (2) TOGETHER are NOT sufficient.

ANSWERS: 16-1 **D**, 16-2 **E**, 16-3 **B**, 16-4 **C**, 16-5 **D**.

If you answered 16-1 **incorrectly, go to 17-1.**
If you answered 16-1 **correctly, go to 17-2.**

If you answered 16-2 **incorrectly, go to 17-1.**
If you answered 16-2 **correctly, go to 17-3.**

If you answered 16-3 **incorrectly, go to 17-2.**
If you answered 16-3 **correctly, go to 17-4.**

If you answered 16-4 **incorrectly, go to 17-3.**
If you answered 16-4 **correctly, go to 17-5.**

If you answered 16-5 **incorrectly, go to 17-4.**
If you answered 16-5 **correctly, go to 17-5.**

17-1. The first five numbers in a regular sequence are 4, 10, 22, 46, and 94. What is the next number in the sequence?

A. 142

B. 154

C. 176

D. 182

E. 190

17-2. $2,000 is deposited in a savings account that pays 6% annual interest compounded semiannually. To the nearest dollar, how much is in the account at the end of the year?

A. $2,060

B. $2,120

C. $2,122

D. $2,247

E. $2,258

17-3. How much tea worth $0.93 per pound must be mixed with tea worth $0.75 per pound to produce 10 pounds worth $0.85 per pound?

A. $2\frac{2}{9}$

B. $3\frac{1}{2}$

C. $4\frac{4}{9}$

D. $5\frac{5}{9}$

E. $9\frac{1}{2}$

17-4. In a class of 200 students, 120 study Spanish and 100 study French. If a student must study at least one of these two languages, what percent of the students study French but NOT Spanish?

A. 80%

B. 40%

C. 30%

D. 20%

E. 10%

17-5. Which of the following CANNOT be weighed using a balance scale and these unit weights: 1, 4, 7, and 10?

A. 13

B. 15

C. 17

D. 19

E. 21

ANSWERS: 17-1 **E**, 17-2 **C**, 17-3 **D**, 17-4 **B**, 17-5 **D**.

If you answered 17-1 **incorrectly, go to 18-1.**
If you answered 17-1 **correctly, go to 18-2.**

If you answered 17-2 **incorrectly, go to 18-1.**
If you answered 17-2 **correctly, go to 18-3.**

If you answered 17-3 **incorrectly, go to 18-2.**
If you answered 17-3 **correctly, go to 18-4.**

If you answered 17-4 **incorrectly, go to 18-3.**
If you answered 17-4 **correctly, go to 18-5.**

If you answered 17-5 **incorrectly, go to 18-4.**
If you answered 17-5 **correctly, go to 18-5.**

18-1. A $74.95 lawn chair was sold for $59.95 at a special sale. By approximately what percent was the price decreased?

A. 15%

B. 20%

C. 25%

D. 60%

E. 80%

GO ON TO THE NEXT PAGE

18-2. Mr. Smitherly leaves Cedar Rapids at 8 a.m. and drives north on the highway at an average speed of 50 miles per hour. Mr. Dinkle leaves Cedar Rapids at 8:30 a.m. and drives north on the same highway at an average speed of 60 miles per hour. Mr. Dinkle will

   A. overtake Mr. Smitherly at 9:30 a.m.

   B. overtake Mr. Smitherly at 10:30 a.m.

   C. overtake Mr. Smitherly at 11:00 a.m.

   D. be 30 miles behind at 8:35 a.m.

   E. never overtake Mr. Smitherly

18-3. On a trip covering 360 miles, a bicyclist travels the first 150 miles at 30 mile per hour and the remainder of the distance at 35 miles per hour. What is the average speed, in miles per hour, for the entire trip?

   A. 28

   B. $32\frac{1}{2}$

   C. $32\frac{8}{11}$

   D. $46\frac{4}{11}$

   E. 65

18-4. A man walks from *B* to *C*, a distance of *x* miles, at 8 miles per hour and returns at 12 miles per hour. What is his average speed?

   A. 10 mph

   B. 9.6 mph

   C. 8.8 mph

   D. 8.4 mph

   E. 4 mph

18-5. The current in a river is 4 mph. A boat can travel 20 mph in still water. How far up the river can the boat travel if the round trip is to take 10 hours?

   A. 69 miles

   B. 88 miles

   C. 96 miles

   D. 100 miles

   E. 112 miles

ANSWERS: 18-1 **B**, 18-2 **C**, 18-3 **C**, 18-4 **B**, 18-5 **C**.

If you answered 18-1 **incorrectly**, go to 19-1.
If you answered 18-1 **correctly**, go to 19-2.

If you answered 18-2 **incorrectly**, go to 19-1.
If you answered 18-2 **correctly**, go to 19-3.

If you answered 18-3 **incorrectly**, go to 19-2.
If you answered 18-3 **correctly**, go to 19-4.

If you answered 18-4 **incorrectly**, go to 19-3.
If you answered 18-4 **correctly**, go to 19-5.

If you answered 18-5 **incorrectly**, go to 19-4.
If you answered 18-5 **correctly**, go to 19-5.

19-1. If the radius of a circle is decreased 20%, what happens to the area?

   A. 10% decrease

   B. 20% decrease

   C. 36% decrease

   D. 40% decrease

   E. 50% decrease

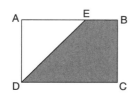

19-2. What is the area of the shaded portion of this rectangle, given that $AD = 6$, $CD = 8$, and $AE = x$?

   A. $48 - 3x$

   B. $48 + 3x$

   C. $3x + 16$

   D. $24 - 3x$

   E. $24 + 3x$

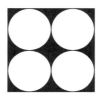

19-3. In the figure above, four equal circles are drawn within a square whose perimeter is 32. What is the area of the shaded region?

   A. $32 - 16\pi$

   B. $64 - 16\pi$

   C. $64 - 32\pi$

   D. $32\pi - 32$

   E. $64\pi - 64$

19-4. In the figure above, the centers of four equal circles lie along the diameter of the large circle. If the circumference of the large circle is 64π, what is the area of the shaded region?

   A. 16π

   B. 32π

   C. 64π

   D. 128π

   E. 256π

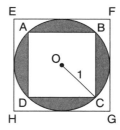

19-5. Square *ABCD* is inscribed in circle *0*, which is inscribed in larger square *EFGH*, as shown in the diagram above. If the radius of circle *0* is 1, then the shaded area is approximately what percent of the area of square *EFGH*?

   A.   3%

   B.   4%

   C.   25%

   D.   50%

   E.   75%

GO ON TO THE NEXT PAGE

ANSWERS: 19-1 **C**, 19-2 **A**, 19-3 **B**, 19-4 **E**, 19-5 **C**.

If you answered 19-1 **incorrectly**, go to **20-1**.
If you answered 19-1 **correctly**, go to **20-2**.

If you answered 19-2 **incorrectly**, go to **20-1**.
If you answered 19-2 **correctly**, go to **20-3**.

If you answered 19-3 **incorrectly**, go to **20-2**.
If you answered 19-3 **correctly**, go to **20-4**.

If you answered 19-4 **incorrectly**, go to **20-3**.
If you answered 19-4 **correctly**, go to **20-5**.

If you answered 19-5 **incorrectly**, go to **20-4**.
If you answered 19-5 **correctly**, go to **20-5**.

20-1. ¼ of ⅗ is what percent of ¾?

    A. 15%

    B. 20%

    C. 33⅓%

    D. 75%

    E. 80%

20-2. A sales representative receives a salary of $150 per week and earns a commission of 15% on all sales she makes. How many dollars' worth of sales does she need to make in order to bring her total weekly income to $600?

    A. $3,000

    B. $3,150

    C. $4,000

    D. $4,150

    E. $5,000

20-3. A couple who own an appliance store discover that if they advertise a sales discount of 10% on every item in the store, at the end of one month the number of total items sold increases 20%. Their gross income from sales for one month increases by what percent?

    A. 2%

    B. 4%

    C. 5%

    D. 8%

    E. 12%

20-4. A furniture store owner decided to drop the price of her recliners by 20% to spur business. By the end of the week she had sold 50% more recliners. What is the percentage increase of the gross?

    A. 10%

    B. 15%

    C. 20%

    D. 25%

    E. 50%

20-5. The product of x and y is a constant. If the value of x is increased by 50%, by what percentage must the value of y be decreased?

    A. 50%

    B. 40%

    C. 33⅓%

    D. 25%

    E. 12½%

21-1. Assuming that neither m nor n is zero, is the product m^2n positive?

(1) $m > 0$

(2) $n > 0$

A. Statement (1) ALONE is sufficient, but statement (2) alone is not sufficient.

B. Statement (2) ALONE is sufficient, but statement (1) alone is not sufficient.

C. BOTH statements (1) and (2) TOGETHER are sufficient, but NEITHER statement ALONE is sufficient.

D. EACH statement ALONE is sufficient.

E. Statements (1) and (2) TOGETHER are NOT sufficient.

21-2. Is m, which does not equal zero, a positive number?

(1) $m = m^2$

(2) $m^2 = m^3$

A. Statement (1) ALONE is sufficient, but statement (2) alone is not sufficient.

B. Statement (2) ALONE is sufficient, but statement (1) alone is not sufficient.

C. BOTH statements (1) and (2) TOGETHER are sufficient, but NEITHER statement ALONE is sufficient.

D. EACH statement ALONE is sufficient.

E. Statements (1) and (2) TOGETHER are NOT sufficient.

21-3. What is the value of $x + y + z$?

(1) $y + z = 2x$

(2) $\frac{1}{x} + \frac{1}{y} + \frac{1}{z} = \frac{4}{9}$

A. Statement (1) ALONE is sufficient, but statement (2) alone is not sufficient.

B. Statement (2) ALONE is sufficient, but statement (1) alone is not sufficient.

C. BOTH statements (1) and (2) TOGETHER are sufficient, but NEITHER statement ALONE is sufficient.

D. EACH statement ALONE is sufficient.

E. Statements (1) and (2) TOGETHER are NOT sufficient.

GO ON TO THE NEXT PAGE

281

21-4. If $x < y$, is $(x - y) < yz$?

   (1) $y < 0$

   (2) $z < 0$

   A.   Statement (1) ALONE is sufficient, but statement (2) alone is not sufficient.

   B.   Statement (2) ALONE is sufficient, but statement (1) alone is not sufficient.

   C.   BOTH statements (1) and (2) TOGETHER are sufficient, but NEITHER statement ALONE is sufficient.

   D.   EACH statement ALONE is sufficient.

   E.   Statements (1) and (2) TOGETHER are NOT sufficient.

21-5. Given three different integers, does the exponential quantity $(a - b)^c$ exceed zero?

   (1) $b < a$

   (2) $c = 2a$

   A.   Statement (1) ALONE is sufficient, but statement (2) alone is not sufficient.

   B.   Statement (2) ALONE is sufficient, but statement (1) alone is not sufficient.

   C.   BOTH statements (1) and (2) TOGETHER are sufficient, but NEITHER statement ALONE is sufficient.

   D.   EACH statement ALONE is sufficient.

   E.   Statements (1) and (2) TOGETHER are NOT sufficient.

ANSWERS: 21-1 B, 21-2 D, 21-3 E, 21-4 C, 21-5 D.

If you answered 21-1 **incorrectly, go to 22-1.**
If you answered 21-1 **correctly, go to 22-2.**

If you answered 21-2 **incorrectly, go to 22-1.**
If you answered 21-2 **correctly, go to 22-3.**

If you answered 21-3 **incorrectly, go to 22-2.**
If you answered 21-3 **correctly, go to 22-4.**

If you answered 21-4 **incorrectly, go to 22-3.**
If you answered 21-4 **correctly, go to 22-5.**

If you answered 21-5 **incorrectly, go to 22-4.**
If you answered 21-5 **correctly, go to 22-5.**

22-1. What is the volume of a cylindrical can?

   (1)   The radius of the can is 3 inches.

   (2)   The area of the bottom is 9π square inches.

   A.   Statement (1) ALONE is sufficient, but statement (2) alone is not sufficient.

   B.   Statement (2) ALONE is sufficient, but statement (1) alone is not sufficient.

   C.   BOTH statements (1) and (2) TOGETHER are sufficient, but NEITHER statement ALONE is sufficient.

   D.   EACH statement ALONE is sufficient.

   E.   Statements (1) and (2) TOGETHER are NOT sufficient.

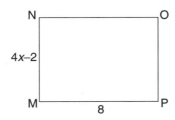

22-2. What is the width of *MN* of rectangle *MNOP*?

(1) $OP = x + 4$

(2) The area is 48

A. Statement (1) ALONE is sufficient, but statement (2) alone is not sufficient.

B. Statement (2) ALONE is sufficient, but statement (1) alone is not sufficient.

C. BOTH statements (1) and (2) TOGETHER are sufficient, but NEITHER statement ALONE is sufficient.

D. EACH statement ALONE is sufficient.

E. Statements (1) and (2) TOGETHER are NOT sufficient.

22-3. What is the area of a rectangular field?

(1) The diagonal is twice the width.

(2) The length is 173 feet.

A. Statement (1) ALONE is sufficient, but statement (2) alone is not sufficient.

B. Statement (2) ALONE is sufficient, but statement (1) alone is not sufficient.

C. BOTH statements (1) and (2) TOGETHER are sufficient, but NEITHER statement ALONE is sufficient.

D. EACH statement ALONE is sufficient.

E. Statements (1) and (2) TOGETHER are NOT sufficient.

22-4. A farmer wants to fence in a rectangular lot of 3,000 square feet in which to raise pigs. Should the farmer employ configuration *X* or configuration *Y* in order to minimize the cost of fencing?

(1) Lot *X* would be 75 feet long, and lot *Y* would be 50 feet wide.

(2) Lot *X* would be 87½ percent longer than wide, and lot Y would be 20 percent longer than wide.

A. Statement (1) ALONE is sufficient, but statement (2) alone is not sufficient.

B. Statement (2) ALONE is sufficient, but statement (1) alone is not sufficient.

C. BOTH statements (1) and (2) TOGETHER are sufficient, but NEITHER statement ALONE is sufficient.

D. EACH statement ALONE is sufficient.

E. Statements (1) and (2) TOGETHER are NOT sufficient.

GO ON TO THE NEXT PAGE

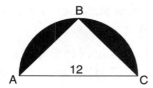

22-5. What is the area of the shaded portion of the half-circle?

(1) B is the midpoint of $\overset{\frown}{AC}$.

(2)   Angle ABC is a right angle.

A.   Statement (1) ALONE is sufficient, but statement (2) alone is not sufficient.

B.   Statement (2) ALONE is sufficient, but statement (1) alone is not sufficient.

C.   BOTH statements (1) and (2) TOGETHER are sufficient, but NEITHER statement ALONE is sufficient.

D.   EACH statement ALONE is sufficient.

E.   Statements (1) and (2) TOGETHER are NOT sufficient.

Answers: 22-1 **E**, 22-2 **D**, 22-3 **C**, 22-4 **D**, 22-5 **A**.

If you answered 22-1 **incorrectly, go to 23-1.**
If you answered 22-1 **correctly, go to 23-2.**

If you answered 22-2 **incorrectly, go to 23-1.**
If you answered 22-2 **correctly, go to 23-3.**

If you answered 22-3 **incorrectly, go to 23-2.**
If you answered 22-3 **correctly, go to 23-4.**

If you answered 22-4 **incorrectly, go to 23-3.**
If you answered 22-4 **correctly, go to 23-5.**

If you answered 22-5 **incorrectly, go to 23-4.**
If you answered 22-5 **correctly, go to 23-5.**

23-1. What is the value of p?

(1) $2p + 3r = 11$

(2) $p - r = 5$

A.   Statement (1) ALONE is sufficient, but statement (2) alone is not sufficient.

B.   Statement (2) ALONE is sufficient, but statement (1) alone is not sufficient.

C.   BOTH statements (1) and (2) TOGETHER are sufficient, but NEITHER statement ALONE is sufficient.

D.   EACH statement ALONE is sufficient.

E.   Statements (1) and (2) TOGETHER are NOT sufficient.

23-2. What is the value of $\dfrac{14m^4}{s^6}$?

(1) $m^2 = 3s^3$

(2) $s^6 = 64$

A.   Statement (1) ALONE is sufficient, but statement (2) alone is not sufficient.

B.   Statement (2) ALONE is sufficient, but statement (1) alone is not sufficient.

C.   BOTH statements (1) and (2) TOGETHER are sufficient, but NEITHER statement ALONE is sufficient.

D.   EACH statement ALONE is sufficient.

E.   Statements (1) and (2) TOGETHER are NOT sufficient.

23-3. In the expression $3x - 2y < z$, is y positive?

(1) $x = 3$

(2) $z = 17$

A. Statement (1) ALONE is sufficient, but statement (2) alone is not sufficient.

B. Statement (2) ALONE is sufficient, but statement (1) alone is not sufficient.

C. BOTH statements (1) and (2) TOGETHER are sufficient, but NEITHER statement ALONE is sufficient.

D. EACH statement ALONE is sufficient.

E. Statements (1) and (2) TOGETHER are NOT sufficient.

23-4. Is the product cd positive?

(1) $3c = -8d^3$

(2) $d > c + 4$

A. Statement (1) ALONE is sufficient, but statement (2) alone is not sufficient.

B. Statement (2) ALONE is sufficient, but statement (1) alone is not sufficient.

C. BOTH statements (1) and (2) TOGETHER are sufficient, but NEITHER statement ALONE is sufficient.

D. EACH statement ALONE is sufficient.

E. Statements (1) and (2) TOGETHER are NOT sufficient.

23-5. What is the value of $x^3 - 2x^2 + 7$?

(1) $3x^3 - x = 2$

(2) $x^5 = 1$

A. Statement (1) ALONE is sufficient, but statement (2) alone is not sufficient.

B. Statement (2) ALONE is sufficient, but statement (1) alone is not sufficient.

C. BOTH statements (1) and (2) TOGETHER are sufficient, but NEITHER statement ALONE is sufficient.

D. EACH statement ALONE is sufficient.

E. Statements (1) and (2) TOGETHER are NOT sufficient.

ANSWERS: 23-1 **C**, 23-2 **A**, 23-3 **E**, 23-4 **A**, 23-5 **B**.

If you answered 23-1 **incorrectly, go to 24–1.**
If you answered 23-1 **correctly, go to 24–2.**

If you answered 23-2 **incorrectly, go to 24–1.**
If you answered 23-2 **correctly, go to 24–3.**

If you answered 23-3 **incorrectly, go to 24–2.**
If you answered 23-3 **correctly, go to 24–4.**

If you answered 23-4 **incorrectly, go to 24–3.**
If you answered 23-4 **correctly, go to 24–5.**

If you answered 23-5 **incorrectly, go to 24–4.**
If you answered 23-5 **correctly, go to 24–5.**

GO ON TO THE NEXT PAGE

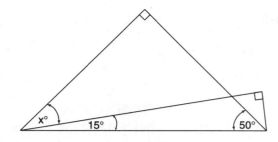

24-1. In the figure above, $x =$

A. 15

B. 25

C. 35

D. 45

E. 55

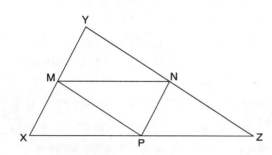

24-2. In $\triangle XYZ$, points M, N, and P are midpoints. If $XY = 10$, $YZ = 15$, and $XZ = 17$, what is the perimeter of $\triangle MNP$?

A. $10\frac{2}{3}$

B. 14

C. 16

D. 21

E. 26

24-3. In a circle, a 10-inch chord is drawn at a distance of 12 inches from the center. What is the radius of the circle?

A. $2\sqrt{61}$ inches

B. 26 inches

C. $5\sqrt{3}$ inches

D. 13 inches

E. $2\sqrt{11}$ inches

24-4. In a triangle, the ratio of two angles is 5:2, and the third angle is equal to the difference between the other two. What is the number of degrees in the smallest angle?

A. 18

B. $25\frac{2}{7}$

C. $25\frac{5}{7}$

D. 36

E. 54

24-5. If a 32-inch chord is drawn in a circle of radius 20 inches, how far is the chord from the center of the circle?

A. 4 inches

B. 6 inches

C. 8 inches

D. 10 inches

E. 12 inches

Answers: 24-1 **B**, 24-2 **D**, 24-3 **D**, 24-4 **D**, 24-5 **E**.

If you answered 24-1 **incorrectly, go to 25-1.**
If you answered 24-1 **correctly, go to 25-2.**

If you answered 24-2 **incorrectly, go to 25-1.**
If you answered 24-2 **correctly, go to 25-3.**

If you answered 24-3 **incorrectly, go to 25-2.**
If you answered 24-3 **correctly, go to 25-4.**

If you answered 24-4 **incorrectly, go to 25-3.**
If you answered 24-4 **correctly, go to 25-5.**

If you answered 24-5 **incorrectly, go to 25-4.**
If you answered 24-5 **correctly, go to 25-5.**

25-1. N is a positive integer. When $N+1$ is divided by 5, the remainder is 4. What is the remainder when N is divided by 5?

    A. 6

    B. 5

    C. 4

    D. 3

    E. 2

25-2. How many two-digit numbers are there whose remainder when divided by 10 is 1, and whose remainder when divided by 6 is 5?

    A. 3

    B. 4

    C. 5

    D. 6

    E. 7

25-3. The denominator of a fraction is 5 greater than the numerator. If the numerator and the denominator are increased by 2, the resulting fraction is equal to $7/12$. What is the value of the original fraction?

    A. $5/12$

    B. $1/2$

    C. $9/14$

    D. $2/3$

    E. $12/17$

25-4. If the numerator of a fraction is tripled, and the denominator of a fraction is doubled, the resulting fraction will reflect an increase of what percent?

    A. $16\frac{1}{6}\%$

    B. 25%

    C. $33\frac{1}{3}\%$

    D. 50%

    E. $66\frac{2}{3}\%$

25-5. If @ is a binary operation defined as the difference between an integer n and the product of n and 5, then what is the largest positive integer n such that the outcome of the binary operation @ of n is less than 10?

    A. 1

    B. 2

    C. 3

    D. 4

    E. 5

ANSWERS: 25-1 **D**, 25-2 **A**, 25-3 **B**, 25-4 **D**, 25-5 **B**.

If you answered 25-1 **incorrectly, go to 26-1.**
If you answered 25-1 **correctly, go to 26-2.**

If you answered 25-2 **incorrectly, go to 26-1.**
If you answered 25-2 **correctly, go to 26-3.**

If you answered 25-3 **incorrectly, go to 26-2.**
If you answered 25-3 **correctly, go to 26-4.**

If you answered 25-4 **incorrectly, go to 26-3.**
If you answered 25-4 **correctly, go to 26-5.**

If you answered 25-5 **incorrectly, go to 26-4.**
If you answered 25-5 **correctly, go to 26-5.**

26-1. A bookseller sells his books at a 20% markup in price. If he sells a book for $12.00, how much did he pay for it?

    A. $14.40

    B. $14.00

    C. $10.00

    D. $9.60

    E. $5.00

GO ON TO THE NEXT PAGE

Houses Sold in One Year

Age	Number
1–2	1,200
3–4	1,570
5–6	1,630
7–8	1,440
9–10	1,520

26-2. According to the chart, how many more houses from 5 to 10 years old were sold than those 4 to 8 years old?

    A.   2,455

    B.   1,570

    C.   150

    D.   130

    E.   It cannot be determined from the information given.

Products	1986	1988	1990	1992	1994	1996
A	$4.20	$4.60	$5.00	$5.40	$5.80	$6.20
B	$6.30	$6.45	$6.60	$6.75	$6.90	$7.05

26-3. The chart above shows the prices of products A and B from 1986 to 1996. Using the chart, in what year will product A cost 40 cents more than product B?

    A.   2000

    B.   2002

    C.   2003

    D.   2004

    E.   2006

Toys	Cost of Manufacture	Profit per Toy
A	$2.5796	$2.4431
B	$2.5768	$2.4312

26-4. According to the chart above, how many of each toy would have to be manufactured so that the total price of toy A exceeds the total price of toy B by $147.00?

    A.   100

    B.   1,000

    C.   10,000

    D.   100,000

    E.   1,000,000

Station-to-Station and Credit Card	Person-to-Person	Each Additional Minute		
		8:00 A.M. to 5:00 P.M. Mon.–Fri.	5:00 P.M. to 11:00 P.M. Mon.–Sat.	11:00 P.M. to 8:00 A.M. Sun.–Fri.
first three minutes	first three minutes			
$2.75	$4.35	$0.46	$0.30	$0.19

26-5. Listed above are the rates for operator-assisted telephone calls from San Diego to New York City. On a Friday at 4:17 p.m., Mr. Talbot made a person-to-person phone call from San Diego to New York City. When he received his monthly phone bill, Mr. Talbot noted that this call cost $14.09. To the nearest minute, how long did this call last?

    A.   23

    B.   24

    C.   25

    D.   26

    E.   27

27-1. How many rectangular tiles are required for the kitchen floor?

(1) Each tile is 48 square inches.

(2) The kitchen measures 10 feet by 7 feet.

A. Statement (1) ALONE is sufficient, but statement (2) alone is not sufficient.

B. Statement (2) ALONE is sufficient, but statement (1) alone is not sufficient.

C. BOTH statements (1) and (2) TOGETHER are sufficient, but NEITHER statement ALONE is sufficient.

D. EACH statement ALONE is sufficient.

E. Statements (1) and (2) TOGETHER are NOT sufficient.

27-2. How much wallpaper is needed to cover the two largest walls of a narrow room that is 9 feet high?

(1) The room is 10 feet wide.

(2) The room is 24 feet long.

A. Statement (1) ALONE is sufficient, but statement (2) alone is not sufficient.

B. Statement (2) ALONE is sufficient, but statement (1) alone is not sufficient.

C. BOTH statements (1) and (2) TOGETHER are sufficient, but NEITHER statement ALONE is sufficient.

D. EACH statement ALONE is sufficient.

E. Statements (1) and (2) TOGETHER are NOT sufficient.

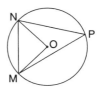

27-3. Within the circle with center *O*, how many degrees is angle *MNO*?

(1) Angle *ONP* = 31°

(2) Angle *NPM* = 48°

A. Statement (1) ALONE is sufficient, but statement (2) alone is not sufficient.

B. Statement (2) ALONE is sufficient, but statement (1) alone is not sufficient.

C. BOTH statements (1) and (2) TOGETHER are sufficient, but NEITHER statement ALONE is sufficient.

D. EACH statement ALONE is sufficient.

E. Statements (1) and (2) TOGETHER are NOT sufficient.

GO ON TO THE NEXT PAGE

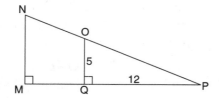

27-4. How long is *MN*?

(1) $ON = 6\frac{1}{2}$

(2) $MQ = 6$

A. Statement (1) ALONE is sufficient, but statement (2) alone is not sufficient.

B. Statement (2) ALONE is sufficient, but statement (1) alone is not sufficient.

C. BOTH statements (1) and (2) TOGETHER are sufficient, but NEITHER statement ALONE is sufficient.

D. EACH statement ALONE is sufficient.

E. Statements (1) and (2) TOGETHER are NOT sufficient.

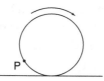

27-5. What is the diameter of the wheel above?

(1)   The wheel has rolled 36 feet.

(2)   Point P has touched the ground 5 times.

A. Statement (1) ALONE is sufficient, but statement (2) alone is not sufficient.

B. Statement (2) ALONE is sufficient, but statement (1) alone is not sufficient.

C. BOTH statements (1) and (2) TOGETHER are sufficient, but NEITHER statement ALONE is sufficient.

D. EACH statement ALONE is sufficient.

E. Statements (1) and (2) TOGETHER are NOT sufficient.

ANSWERS: 27-1 C, 27-2 B, 27-3 B, 27-4 D, 27-5 E.

If you answered 27-1 **incorrectly**, go to **28-1.**
If you answered 27-1 **correctly**, go to **28-2.**

If you answered 27-2 **incorrectly**, go to **28-1.**
If you answered 27-2 **correctly**, go to **28-3.**

If you answered 27-3 **incorrectly**, go to **28-2.**
If you answered 27-3 **correctly**, go to **28-4.**

If you answered 27-4 **incorrectly**, go to **28-3.**
If you answered 27-4 **correctly**, go to **28-5.**

If you answered 27-5 **incorrectly**, go to **28-4.**
If you answered 27-5 **correctly**, go to **28-5.**

28-1. A man's suit was discounted to $140. What was its list price?

(1)   There would be a $10 fee for alterations.

(2)   The sale was at "30% off."

A. Statement (1) ALONE is sufficient, but statement (2) alone is not sufficient.

B. Statement (2) ALONE is sufficient, but statement (1) alone is not sufficient.

C. BOTH statements (1) and (2) TOGETHER are sufficient, but NEITHER statement ALONE is sufficient.

D. EACH statement ALONE is sufficient.

E. Statements (1) and (2) TOGETHER are NOT sufficient.

28-2. What is the value of m?

   (1) $4m - 5 = 7$

   (2) $m^2 + 9 = 6m$

  A.   Statement (1) ALONE is sufficient, but statement (2) alone is not sufficient.

  B.   Statement (2) ALONE is sufficient, but statement (1) alone is not sufficient.

  C.   BOTH statements (1) and (2) TOGETHER are sufficient, but NEITHER statement ALONE is sufficient.

  D.   EACH statement ALONE is sufficient.

  E.   Statements (1) and (2) TOGETHER are NOT sufficient.

28-3. Does $x = y$?

   (1) $4x - 2y = 80$

   (2) $x = \dfrac{40 + y}{2}$

  A.   Statement (1) ALONE is sufficient, but statement (2) alone is not sufficient.

  B.   Statement (2) ALONE is sufficient, but statement (1) alone is not sufficient.

  C.   BOTH statements (1) and (2) TOGETHER are sufficient, but NEITHER statement ALONE is sufficient.

  D.   EACH statement ALONE is sufficient.

  E.   Statements (1) and (2) TOGETHER are NOT sufficient.

28-4. If a is to b as b is to c, is c positive?

   (1) $c = 2a$

   (2) $b^2 = 32$

  A.   Statement (1) ALONE is sufficient, but statement (2) alone is not sufficient.

  B.   Statement (2) ALONE is sufficient, but statement (1) alone is not sufficient.

  C.   BOTH statements (1) and (2) TOGETHER are sufficient, but NEITHER statement ALONE is sufficient.

  D.   EACH statement ALONE is sufficient.

  E.   Statements (1) and (2) TOGETHER are NOT sufficient.

28-5. The positive integer C is a perfect cube; what is its value?

   (1) $30 < C < 100$

   (2) C is an even number.

  A.   Statement (1) ALONE is sufficient, but statement (2) alone is not sufficient.

  B.   Statement (2) ALONE is sufficient, but statement (1) alone is not sufficient.

  C.   BOTH statements (1) and (2) TOGETHER are sufficient, but NEITHER statement ALONE is sufficient.

  D.   EACH statement ALONE is sufficient.

  E.   Statements (1) and (2) TOGETHER are NOT sufficient.

GO ON TO THE NEXT PAGE

ANSWERS: 28-1 **B**, 28-2 **D**, 28-3 **E**, 28-4 **E**, 28-5 **A**.

If you answered 28-1 **incorrectly, go to 29-1.**
If you answered 28-1 **correctly, go to 29-2.**

If you answered 28-2 **incorrectly, go to 29-1.**
If you answered 28-2 **correctly, go to 29-3.**

If you answered 28-3 **incorrectly, go to 29-2.**
If you answered 28-3 **correctly, go to 29-4.**

If you answered 28-4 **incorrectly, go to 29-3.**
If you answered 28-4 **correctly, go to 29-5.**

If you answered 28-5 **incorrectly, go to 29-4.**
If you answered 28-5 **correctly, go to 29-5.**

29-1. What is the volume of a certain box?

(1) One side of the box has an area of 16 square inches.

(2) The box is cubical.

A. Statement (1) ALONE is sufficient, but statement (2) alone is not sufficient.

B. Statement (2) ALONE is sufficient, but statement (1) alone is not sufficient.

C. BOTH statements (1) and (2) TOGETHER are sufficient, but NEITHER statement ALONE is sufficient.

D. EACH statement ALONE is sufficient.

E. Statements (1) and (2) TOGETHER are NOT sufficient.

29-2. Where is the center of a circle on the *xy* plane?

(1) The circle passes through both the origin and (0,7).

(2) The diameter equals 10.

A. Statement (1) ALONE is sufficient, but statement (2) alone is not sufficient.

B. Statement (2) ALONE is sufficient, but statement (1) alone is not sufficient.

C. BOTH statements (1) and (2) TOGETHER are sufficient, but NEITHER statement ALONE is sufficient.

D. EACH statement ALONE is sufficient.

E. Statements (1) and (2) TOGETHER are NOT sufficient.

29-3. What is the orientation of a line in the *xy* plane?

(1) The line passes through the point (5, a).

(2) $a = -3$

A. Statement (1) ALONE is sufficient, but statement (2) alone is not sufficient.

B. Statement (2) ALONE is sufficient, but statement (1) alone is not sufficient.

C. BOTH statements (1) and (2) TOGETHER are sufficient, but NEITHER statement ALONE is sufficient.

D. EACH statement ALONE is sufficient.

E. Statements (1) and (2) TOGETHER are NOT sufficient.

29-4. Is the diagonal of square Q a rational number?

(1) The area equals the side multiplied by itself.

(2) The side equals $\sqrt{8}$.

A. Statement (1) ALONE is sufficient, but statement (2) alone is not sufficient.

B. Statement (2) ALONE is sufficient, but statement (1) alone is not sufficient.

C. BOTH statements (1) and (2) TOGETHER are sufficient, but NEITHER statement ALONE is sufficient.

D. EACH statement ALONE is sufficient.

E. Statements (1) and (2) TOGETHER are NOT sufficient.

29-5. The centers of the three circles lie on one line (the circles intersect as shown). What is the area of the shaded part of the figure?

(1) Each of the small circles has a diameter of 5.

(2) The large circle has a radius of 5.

A. Statement (1) ALONE is sufficient, but statement (2) alone is not sufficient.

B. Statement (2) ALONE is sufficient, but statement (1) alone is not sufficient.

C. BOTH statements (1) and (2) TOGETHER are sufficient, but NEITHER statement ALONE is sufficient.

D. EACH statement ALONE is sufficient.

E. Statements (1) and (2) TOGETHER are NOT sufficient.

ANSWERS: 29-1 **C**, 29-2 **E**, 29-3 **E**, 29-4 **B**, 29-5 **A**.

If you answered 29-1 **incorrectly, go to 30-1.**
If you answered 29-1 **correctly, go to 30-2.**

If you answered 29-2 **incorrectly, go to 30-1.**
If you answered 29-2 **correctly, go to 30-3.**

If you answered 29-3 **incorrectly, go to 30-2.**
If you answered 29-3 **correctly, go to 30-4.**

If you answered 29-4 **incorrectly, go to 30-3.**
If you answered 29-4 **correctly, go to 30-5.**

If you answered 29-5 **incorrectly, go to 30-4.**
If you answered 29-5 **correctly, go to 30-5.**

30-1. $\dfrac{\dfrac{7}{10} \times 14 \times 5 \times \dfrac{1}{28}}{\dfrac{10}{17} \times \dfrac{3}{5} \times \dfrac{1}{6} \times 17} =$

A. $\dfrac{4}{7}$

B. 1

C. $\dfrac{7}{4}$

D. 2

E. $\dfrac{17}{4}$

GO ON TO THE NEXT PAGE

30-2. Mary spent $\frac{2}{5}$ of her money on new clothes and then deposited $\frac{1}{2}$ of what remained into her savings account. If she then had $21 left, how much did she have at the start?

    A. $30

    B. $35

    C. $70

    D. $105

    E. $210

30-3. Five A's and two B's exactly balance six B's and five C's. One A and four C's exactly balance two A's and four B's. What is the weight of A in terms of C?

    A. $\frac{3}{2}C$

    B. $\frac{6}{5}C$

    C. $\frac{5}{6}C$

    D. $\frac{2}{3}C$

    E. $\frac{1}{2}C$

30-4. Felix earned 30% more per month than Oscar. If Felix's salary is decreased 10% and Oscar's salary is increased by 10%, then Felix would be earning what percent more than Oscar?

    A. 10%

    B. 9.09%

    C. 7%

    D. 6.36%

    E. It cannot be determined from the information given.

30-5. In 1995, the Johnsons spent $800 on the family's water bills. Anticipating that water rates would increase in 1996 by 50%, the Johnsons cut back their water usage. By how much must the Johnsons have reduced their 1996 water usage to pay exactly the same amount in 1996 as they paid in 1995?

    A. $33\frac{1}{3}$%

    B. 40%

    C. 50%

    D. $66\frac{2}{3}$%

    E. 100%

ANSWERS: 30-1 C, 30-2 C, 30-3 A, 30-4 D, 30-5 A.

If you answered 30-1 **incorrectly**, go to **31-1**.
If you answered 30-1 **correctly**, go to **31-2**.

If you answered 30-2 **incorrectly**, go to **31-1**.
If you answered 30-2 **correctly**, go to **31-3**.

If you answered 30-3 **incorrectly**, go to **31-2**.
If you answered 30-3 **correctly**, go to **31-4**.

If you answered 30-4 **incorrectly**, go to **31-3**.
If you answered 30-4 **correctly**, go to **31-5**.

If you answered 30-5 **incorrectly**, go to **31-4**.
If you answered 30-5 **correctly**, go to **31-5**.

31-1. Given positive integer y, which of the following CANNOT be evenly divisible by y?

    A. $y + 1$

    B. $y + 2$

    C. $2y + 1$

    D. $y - 1$

    E. $y + \frac{1}{2}$

31-2. How many positive two-digit numbers, *ab*, are possible such that *ab* is divisible by 8 and the sum of *a* and *b* is divisible by 8?

    A. 0

    B. 1

    C. 2

    D. 3

    E. 4

31-3. Given the two equations $3r + s = 17$ and $r + 2s = 9$, by how much does r exceed s?

    A. 3

    B. 4

    C. 5

    D. 6

    E. 7

31-4. $6x - 12 = 6y$

    $5y + 5x = 15$

Which of the following is the number of solutions to the system of equations shown above?

    A. More than three

    B. Exactly three

    C. Exactly two

    D. Exactly one

    E. None

31-5. If $x^2 + y^2 = 14$ and $xy + 3$, then $(x - y)^2 =$

    A. 8

    B. 11

    C. 14

    D. 17

    E. 20

ANSWERS: 31-1 E, 31-2 C, 31-3 A, 31-4 E, 31-5 A.

If you answered 31-1 **incorrectly, go to 32-1.**
If you answered 31-1 **correctly, go to 32-2.**

If you answered 31-2 **incorrectly, go to 32-1.**
If you answered 31-2 **correctly, go to 32-3.**

If you answered 31-3 **incorrectly, go to 32-2.**
If you answered 31-3 **correctly, go to 32-4.**

If you answered 31-4 **incorrectly, go to 32-3.**
If you answered 31-4 **correctly, go to 32-5.**

If you answered 31-5 **incorrectly, go to 32-4.**
If you answered 31-5 **correctly, go to 32-5.**

32-1. Simplify: $2 + \cfrac{1}{2 + \cfrac{1}{2 + \frac{1}{2}}}$

    A. $^{29}/_{12}$

    B. $^{12}/_{5}$

    C. $^{70}/_{29}$

    D. $^{19}/_{8}$

    E. $^{12}/_{29}$

32-2. During one season, a tennis team won 21 matches and lost 30% of their matches. What was the number of matches that the team lost?

    A. 70

    B. 30

    C. 9

    D. 7

    E. 5

GO ON TO THE NEXT PAGE

32-3. Three factories of Conglomerate Corporation are capable of manufacturing hubcaps. Two of the factories can each produce 100,000 hubcaps in 15 days. The third factory can produce hubcaps 30% faster. Approximately how many days would it take to produce a million hubcaps with all three factories working simultaneously?

    A.   38

    B.   42

    C.   46

    D.   50

    E.   54

32-4. Dan can do a job alone in 15 hours. Fred, working alone, can do the same job in just 10 hours. If Dan works alone for 9 hours and then stops, how many hours will it take Fred, working alone, to complete the job?

    A.   4

    B.   5

    C.   6

    D.   12

    E.   12.5

32-5. Machine A can do a certain job in 8 hours. Machine B can do the same job in 10 hours. Machine C can do the same job in 12 hours. All three machines start the job at 9:00 a.m. Machine A breaks down at 11:00 a.m., and the other two machines finish the job. Approximately what time will the job be finished?

    A.   Noon

    B.   12:30 p.m.

    C.   1:00 p.m.

    D.   1:30 p.m.

    E.   2:00 p.m.

ANSWERS: 32-1 **A**, 32-2 **C**, 32-3 **C**, 32-4 **A**, 32-5 **C**.

If you answered 32-1 **incorrectly, go to 33-1.**
If you answered 32-1 **correctly, go to 33-2.**

If you answered 32-2 **incorrectly, go to 33-1.**
If you answered 32-2 **correctly, go to 33-3.**

If you answered 32-3 **incorrectly, go to 33-2.**
If you answered 32-3 **correctly, go to 33-4.**

If you answered 32-4 **incorrectly, go to 33-3.**
If you answered 32-4 **correctly, go to 33-5.**

If you answered 32-5 **incorrectly, go to 33-4.**
If you answered 32-5 **correctly, go to 33-5.**

33-1. What is the range of a sports car on one tank of gasoline?

    (1)   The tank holds 50 liters.

    (2)   It consumers 8 liters of gasoline each 100 kilometers.

    A.   Statement (1) ALONE is sufficient, but statement (2) alone is not sufficient.

    B.   Statement (2) ALONE is sufficient, but statement (1) alone is not sufficient.

    C.   BOTH statements (1) and (2) TOGETHER are sufficient, but NEITHER statement ALONE is sufficient.

    D.   EACH statement ALONE is sufficient.

    E.   Statements (1) and (2) TOGETHER are NOT sufficient.

33-2. Five persons sat next to each other around a circular table to play cards. Did Grace sit next to Bill?

    (1)   Dora sat next to Ethyl and Carl.

    (2)   Grace sat next to Carl.

A. Statement (1) ALONE is sufficient, but statement (2) alone is not sufficient.

B. Statement (2) ALONE is sufficient, but statement (1) alone is not sufficient.

C. BOTH statements (1) and (2) TOGETHER are sufficient, but NEITHER statement ALONE is sufficient.

D. EACH statement ALONE is sufficient.

E. Statements (1) and (2) TOGETHER are NOT sufficient.

33-3. An ice-cream stand sells two sizes of cones, Generous and Colossal. How many Colossal cones were sold one day?

(1) The total sales were $209.15.

(2) Generous cones sold for 75 cents, and Colossal cones sold for $1.25.

A. Statement (1) ALONE is sufficient, but statement (2) alone is not sufficient.

B. Statement (2) ALONE is sufficient, but statement (1) alone is not sufficient.

C. BOTH statements (1) and (2) TOGETHER are sufficient, but NEITHER statement ALONE is sufficient.

D. EACH statement ALONE is sufficient.

E. Statements (1) and (2) TOGETHER are NOT sufficient.

33-4. If gasoline costs $1.09 per gallon and alcohol costs $1.81, what fraction of each would be used to make Gasohol 99?

(1) The mixture is predominantly gasoline.

(2) A gallon of Gasohol 99 costs $1.22.

A. Statement (1) ALONE is sufficient, but statement (2) alone is not sufficient.

B. Statement (2) ALONE is sufficient, but statement (1) alone is not sufficient.

C. BOTH statements (1) and (2) TOGETHER are sufficient, but NEITHER statement ALONE is sufficient.

D. EACH statement ALONE is sufficient.

E. Statements (1) and (2) TOGETHER are NOT sufficient.

33-5. Each of 200 electrical switches controls a separate light bulb. How many of the switches are in the off position?

(1) Forty percent of the bulbs are glowing.

(2) Five percent of the bulbs are burnt out.

A. Statement (1) ALONE is sufficient, but statement (2) alone is not sufficient.

B. Statement (2) ALONE is sufficient, but statement (1) alone is not sufficient.

GO ON TO THE NEXT PAGE

C. BOTH statements (1) and (2) TOGETHER are sufficient, but NEITHER statement ALONE is sufficient.

D. EACH statement ALONE is sufficient.

E. Statements (1) and (2) TOGETHER are NOT sufficient.

Answers: 33-1 **C**, 33-2 **A**, 33-3 **E**, 33-4 **B**, 33-5 **E**.

If you answered 33-1 **incorrectly, go to 34-1.**
If you answered 33-1 **correctly, go to 34-2.**

If you answered 33-2 **incorrectly, go to 34-1.**
If you answered 33-2 **correctly, go to 34-3.**

If you answered 33-3 **incorrectly, go to 34-2.**
If you answered 33-3 **correctly, go to 34-4.**

If you answered 33-4 **incorrectly, go to 34-3.**
If you answered 33-4 **correctly, go to 34-5.**

If you answered 33-5 **incorrectly, go to 34-4.**
If you answered 33-5 **correctly, go to 34-5.**

34-1. How many black shoes were sold by Shepard's Shoe Emporium?

(1) Three-quarters of the shoes sold were brown.

(2) The Emporium sold 1,284 left shoes.

A. Statement (1) ALONE is sufficient, but statement (2) alone is not sufficient.

B. Statement (2) ALONE is sufficient, but statement (1) alone is not sufficient.

C. BOTH statements (1) and (2) TOGETHER are sufficient, but NEITHER statement ALONE is sufficient.

D. EACH statement ALONE is sufficient.

E. Statements (1) and (2) TOGETHER are NOT sufficient.

34-2. How much ethylene glycol antifreeze must be mixed with water to fill a car radiator?

(1) The radiator has a capacity of 3 gallons.

(2) The solution must be 40% water.

A. Statement (1) ALONE is sufficient, but statement (2) alone is not sufficient.

B. Statement (2) ALONE is sufficient, but statement (1) alone is not sufficient.

C. BOTH statements (1) and (2) TOGETHER are sufficient, but NEITHER statement ALONE is sufficient.

D. EACH statement ALONE is sufficient.

E. Statements (1) and (2) TOGETHER are NOT sufficient.

34-3. What is Mary's age?

(1) In two years, Mary will be twice as old as Beth is now.

(2) Susan's age is the average of Mary's and Beth's ages.

A. Statement (1) ALONE is sufficient, but statement (2) alone is not sufficient.

B. Statement (2) ALONE is sufficient, but statement (1) alone is not sufficient.

C. BOTH statements (1) and (2) TOGETHER are sufficient, but NEITHER statement ALONE is sufficient.

D. EACH statement ALONE is sufficient.

E. Statements (1) and (2) TOGETHER are NOT sufficient.

34-4. How many years old is Anne?

(1) Next year, Anne will be half as old as her mother.

(2) In five years, Anne will be twice as old as a decade ago.

A. Statement (1) ALONE is sufficient, but statement (2) alone is not sufficient.

B. Statement (2) ALONE is sufficient, but statement (1) alone is not sufficient.

C. BOTH statements (1) and (2) TOGETHER are sufficient, but NEITHER statement ALONE is sufficient.

D. EACH statement ALONE is sufficient.

E. Statements (1) and (2) TOGETHER are NOT sufficient.

34-5. One number is five more than half a second number, which is evenly divisible by a third number. What is the second number?

(1) The first number is one less than the second.

(2) The third number is two less than half the second.

A. Statement (1) ALONE is sufficient, but statement (2) alone is not sufficient.

B. Statement (2) ALONE is sufficient, but statement (1) alone is not sufficient.

C. BOTH statements (1) and (2) TOGETHER are sufficient, but NEITHER statement ALONE is sufficient.

D. EACH statement ALONE is sufficient.

E. Statements (1) and (2) TOGETHER are NOT sufficient.

Answers: 34-1 **E**, 34-2 **C**, 34-3 **E**, 34-4 **B**, 34-5 **A**.

If you answered 34-1 **incorrectly**, go to 35-1.
If you answered 34-1 **correctly**, go to 35-2.

If you answered 34-2 **incorrectly**, go to 35-1.
If you answered 34-2 **correctly**, go to 35-3.

If you answered 34-3 **incorrectly**, go to 35-2.
If you answered 34-3 **correctly**, go to 35-4.

If you answered 34-4 **incorrectly**, go to 35-3.
If you answered 34-4 **correctly**, go to 35-5.

If you answered 34-5 **incorrectly**, go to 35-4.
If you answered 34-5 **correctly**, go to 35-5.

35-1. If paint costs $3.20 per quart, and a quart covers 20 square feet, how much will it cost to paint the outside of a cube 10 feet on each edge?

A. $ 1.60
B. $ 16.00
C. $ 96.00
D. $108.00
E. $196.00

GO ON TO THE NEXT PAGE

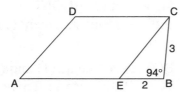

35-2. The area of parallelogram *AECD*

    A. is greater than 24 square units

    B. is less than 24 square units

    C. is equal to 24 square units

    D. is equal to 40 square units

    E. is equal to 60 square units

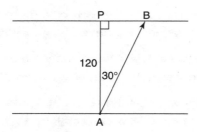

35-3. A boat leaves point *A* heading directly across the river to point *P*, 120 yards away. A swift current immediately changes the boat's direction, causing it to land instead at point *B*. How many yards is point *B* from the intended destination, *P*?

    A. 40

    B. 45

    C. 60

    D. $40\sqrt{3}$

    E. $60\sqrt{3}$

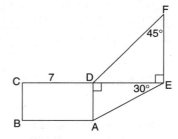

35-4. In the figure above, rectangle *ABCD* has perimeter 22; the length of *DC* is 7. What is the area of △*DEF*?

    A. 12

    B. $8\sqrt{3}$

    C. 24

    D. 32

    E. 64

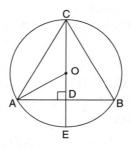

35-5. Equilateral triangle *ABC* is inscribed in a circle with center *O*, as shown. If the radius of the circle is 2, what is the area of triangle *ABC*?

    A. 3

    B. $2\sqrt{3}$

    C. $3\sqrt{2}$

    D. $3\sqrt{3}$

    E. $4\sqrt{2}$

ANSWERS: 35-1 C, 35-2 B, 35-3 D, 35-4 C, 35-5 D.

If you answered 35-1 **incorrectly, go to 36-1.**
If you answered 35-1 **correctly, go to 36-2.**

If you answered 35-2 **incorrectly, go to 36-1.**
If you answered 35-2 **correctly, go to 36-3.**

If you answered 35-3 **incorrectly, go to 36-2.**
If you answered 35-3 **correctly, go to 36-4.**

If you answered 35-4 **incorrectly, go to 36-3.**
If you answered 35-4 **correctly, go to 36-5.**

If you answered 35-5 **incorrectly, go to 36-4.**
If you answered 35-5 **correctly, go to 36-5.**

36-1. Gasoline varies in cost from $0.96 to $1.12 per gallon. If a car's mileage varies from 16 to 24 miles per gallon, what is the difference between the most and least that the gasoline for a 48-mile trip will cost?

A. $ 5.12
B. $ 7.04
C. $11.52
D. $14.40
E. $52.80

36-2. A ferry can transport 78 tons of vehicles. Automobiles range in weight from 1,800 to 3,200 pounds. What is the greatest number of automobiles that can be loaded onto the ferry?

A. 23
B. 41
C. 48
D. 62
E. 86

36-3. Two quarts containing $2/3$ water and $1/3$ formula are mixed with three quarts containing $3/8$ water and $5/8$ formula. Approximately what percent of the combined five-quart mixture is water?

A. 40%
B. 45%
C. 50%
D. 55%
E. 60%

36-4. How much water must be added to 10 gallons of 10% brine solution to decrease the concentration to 7%?

A. 0—1.5 gal
B. 1.5—3 gal
C. 3—4.5 gal
D. 4.5—6 gal
E. 6+ gal

36-5. An incredible punch is composed of buttermilk, orange juice, and brandy. How many pints of orange juice are required to make 7½ gallons of punch containing twice as much buttermilk as orange juice and three times as much orange juice as brandy?

A. 16
B. 18
C. 20
D. 22
E. 24

GO ON TO THE NEXT PAGE

Answers: 36-1 **D**, 36-2 **E**, 36-3 **C**, 36-4 **C**, 36-5 **B**.

If you answered 36-1 **incorrectly, go to 37-1**.
If you answered 36-1 **correctly, go to 37-2**.

If you answered 36-2 **incorrectly, go to 37-1**.
If you answered 36-2 **correctly, go to 37-3**.

If you answered 36-3 **incorrectly, go to 37-2**.
If you answered 36-3 **correctly, go to 37-4**.

If you answered 36-4 **incorrectly, go to 37-3**.
If you answered 36-4 **correctly, go to 37-5**.

If you answered 36-5 **incorrectly, go to 37-4**.
If you answered 36-5 **correctly, go to 37-5**.

37-1. If $(x + 1)$ times $(2x + 1)$ is an odd integer, then x must be

   A. an odd integer

   B. an even integer

   C. a prime number

   D. a composite number

   E. a negative integer

37-2. If x is a positive even number, then each of the following is odd EXCEPT

   A. $(x + 3)(x + 5)$

   B. $x^2 + 5$

   C. $x^2 + 6x + 9$

   D. $3x^2 + 4$

   E. $5(x + 3)$

37-3. A corporation triples its annual bonus to 50 of its employees. What percent of the employees' new bonus is the increase?

   A. 50%

   B. 66⅔%

   C. 100%

   D. 200%

   E. 300%

37-4. To rent an office, each member of a club must pay n dollars. If two more members join the club, the per-member payment would be reduced by two dollars. Which of the following could be the number of members currently in the club?

   I. 16

   II. 17

   III. 18

   A. I only

   B. II only

   C. I and III only

   D. II and III only

   E. I, II, and III

37-5. Grace has enough money to buy 45 bricks. If the bricks each cost 10 cents less, Grace could buy 5 more bricks. How much money does Grace have to spend on bricks?

   A. $100

   B. $50

   C. $45

   D. $40

   E. $30

ANSWERS: 37-1 **B**, 37-2 **D**, 37-3 **B**, 37-4 **E**, 37-5 **C**.

IF YOU FINISH BEFORE TIME IS CALLED, CHECK YOUR WORK ON THIS SECTION ONLY. DO NOT WORK ON ANY OTHER SECTION IN THE TEST.

TIME: 75 Minutes

41 Questions

General Directions: Your score on the verbal section will be based on how well you do on the questions presented and also on the number of questions you answer. You should try to pace yourself so that you have sufficient time to consider every question. If possible, answer all 41 questions in this section. Guess if you need to. Select the best answer choice for each question.

Note: Because you are checking answers as you go, you should add about 5 to 10 minutes to your testing time.

Reading Comprehension Directions: A passage is followed by questions based on its content. After reading the passage, choose the best answer to each question. Answer all questions about the passage on the basis of what is *stated* or *implied* in the passage. You may refer back to the passage.

Sentence Correction Directions: Some part of each sentence is underlined; sometimes the whole sentence is underlined. Five choices for rephrasing the underlined part follow each sentence; the first choice repeats the original, and the other four are different. If the first choice seems better than the alternatives, choose that answer; if not, choose one of the others.

For each sentence, consider the requirements of standard written English. Your choice should be a correct and effective expression, not awkward or ambiguous. Focus on grammar, word choice, sentence construction, and punctuation. If a choice changes the meaning of the original sentence, do not select it.

Critical Reasoning Directions: As you read the brief passage, follow the line of reasoning using only commonsense standards of logic. No knowledge of formal logic is required. Then choose the best answer, realizing that several choices may be possible, but only one is best.

Read the passage and answer Questions 1–4.

When the new discipline of social psychology was born at the beginning of this century, its first experiments were essentially adaptations of the suggestion
(5) demonstration. The subjects, usually college students, were asked to give their opinions or preferences concerning various matters; some time later they were again asked to state their choices,
(10) but now they were also informed of the opinions held by authorities or large groups of their peers on the same matters. (Often the alleged consensus was fictitious.) Most of these studies had
(15) substantially the same result: Confronted with opinions contrary to their own, many subjects apparently shifted their judgments in the direction of the view of the majorities or the ex-
(20) perts. Other studies reported that people's evaluations of the merit of a

GO ON TO THE NEXT PAGE

literary passage could be raised or low-ered by ascribing the passage to differ-ent authors. Apparently the sheer weight
(25) of numbers or authority sufficed to change opinions, even when no argu-ments for the opinions themselves were provided.

Now the very ease of success in these
(30) experiments arouses suspicion. Did the subjects actually change their opinions, or were the experimental victories scored only on paper? On grounds of common sense, one must question
(35) whether opinions are generally as watery as these studies indicate. There is some reason to wonder whether it was not the investigators who, in their enthusiasm for a theory, were suggestible, and
(40) whether the ostensibly gullible subjects were not providing answers which they thought good subjects were expected to give.

The investigations were guided by the
(45) underlying assumptions that people sub-mit uncritically and painlessly to exter-nal manipulation by suggestion or prestige, and that any given idea or value can be "sold" or "unsold" without
(50) reference to its merits. We should be skeptical, however, of the supposition that the power of social pressure neces-sarily implies uncritical submission to it; independence and the capacity to rise
(55) above group passion are also open to human beings. Further, one may ques-tion on psychological grounds whether it is possible to change a person's judg-ment of a situation or an object without
(60) first changing his or her knowledge or assumptions about it.

1. The first experiments in social psychology appeared to demonstrate all of the following EXCEPT that

A. many people will agree with what they believe to be the opinion held by the majority of their peers.

B. many people will agree with what they believe to be the opinion of experts.

C. many people change their opinions given good arguments for doing so.

D. an individual's evaluation of a literary work can be altered by ascribing the work to a different writer.

E. college students' opinions can be changed.

2. The author implies that persons who altered their opinion on a controversial topic have most likely done so because they

A. have been influenced by overt social pressures.

B. have been influenced by covert external manipulation.

C. have learned more about the topic.

D. have learned how experts judge the topic.

E. are incapable of independent thought.

3. The main point of the passage is to

A. question some assumptions about the influence of social pressures.

B. show that a judgment of a situation cannot change without a change in the knowledge of the situation.

C. demonstrate the gullibility of psychological investigators and their subjects.

D. question the notion that any idea can be "sold" or "unsold."

E. support investigation into ideas of propaganda.

4. With which of the following ideas would the author be most likely to agree?

A. Human beings can be programmed like machines.

B. Women are more likely to agree with men than with other women.

C. Women are more likely to agree with other women than with men.

D. Like women, men are capable of independent thought.

E. Like men, women submit uncritically to external manipulation.

ANSWERS: 1 C, 2 C, 3 A, 4 D.

If you answered **none** of the four reading questions **correctly, go to 5-1.**

If you answered **one** of the four reading questions **correctly, go to 5-2.**

If you answered **two** of the four reading questions **correctly, go to 5-3.**

If you answered **three** of the four reading questions **correctly, go to 5-4.**

If you answered **all four** reading questions **correctly, go to 5-5.**

5-1. As the rising toll of victims at Chernobyl made clear, <u>neither the scientists nor the ecologists knows</u> how to deal with the lethal effects of nuclear power plant accidents.

A. neither the scientists nor the ecologists knows

B. neither the scientists nor the ecologists know

C. neither the scientists or the ecologists know

D. neither the scientists together with the ecologists knows

E. not the scientist or the ecologists know

5-2. As the shrill, piercing sound of the sirens <u>approached, several of my neighbors' dogs start</u> to howl, waking up every household in the neighborhood.

A. approached, several of my neighbors' dogs start

B. approached, several of my neighbors' dogs started

C. approach, several of my neighbors' dogs starts

D. approach, several of my neighbors' dogs start

E. approach, several dogs of my neighbor started

GO ON TO THE NEXT PAGE

5-3. <u>That she neglected the children, the house remained dirty and cluttered, and poor personal hygiene were reasons for firing the housekeeper.</u>

A. That she neglected the children, that the house remained dirty and cluttered, and poor personal hygiene were reasons for firing the housekeeper.

B. That she neglected the children, house dirt and clutter, and poor personal hygiene were reasons for firing the housekeeper.

C. That she neglected the children, dirty and cluttered house, and not good personal hygiene were reasons for firing the housekeeper.

D. Neglect of the children, poor housecleaning, and that she had poor personal hygiene were reasons for firing the housekeeper.

E. The housekeeper's neglect of the children, poor housecleaning, and lack of good personal hygiene were reasons for her firing.

5-4. After reconsidering my original judgments, I feel obliged to reread <u>the book I maligned and which initially seemed so inconsequential.</u>

A. the book I maligned and which initially seemed so inconsequential

B. the book in which I maligned what first seemed so inconsequential

C. the maligned book which I initially deemed inconsequential

D. the book I malign initially and inconsequentially

E. the book I will malign because of its initial inconsequentiality

5-5. After battling hypertension for years, Marvin Murphy was relieved by the results of <u>his doctor's annual physical examination, which</u> indicated his blood pressure was normal.

A. his doctor's annual physical examination, which

B. his annual physical examination by which it was

C. his annual physical examination, which

D. an annual physical examination by his doctor, which

E. his doctor's annual physical examination that

ANSWERS: 5-1 B, 5-2 B, 5-3 E, 5-4 A, 5-5 D.

If you answered 5-1 **incorrectly, go to 6-1.**
If you answered 5-1 **correctly, go to 6-2.**

If you answered 5-2 **incorrectly, go to 6-1.**
If you answered 5-2 **correctly, go to 6-3.**

If you answered 5-3 **incorrectly, go to 6-2.**
If you answered 5-3 **correctly, go to 6-4.**

If you answered 5-4 **incorrectly, go to 6-3.**
If you answered 5-4 **correctly, go to 6-5.**

If you answered 5-5 **incorrectly, go to 6-4.**
If you answered 5-5 **correctly, go to 6-5.**

6-1. Because they refuse to follow the conventional dress code, neither Barbara nor her friends <u>is invited to pledge the local sorority.</u>

A. is invited to pledge the local sorority

B. are invited to pledge the local sorority

C. is pledging the local sorority

D. are pledging the local sorority

E. will pledge

6-2. <u>The governor understood that if she did not sign the new budget quick, the state</u> might begin the new fiscal year not only with a significant deficit but also with no budgetary guidelines for lessening that deficit.

   A. The governor understood that if she did not sign the new budget quick, the state

   B. Not signing the new state budget quickly, the governor knew that the state

   C. Without a quick signing, the governor new that as far as the budget was concerned, the state

   D. The governor understood that if she did not sign the new budget quickly, the state

   E. The governor understood that if she did not sign the budget and sign it quickly, that the effects of that action might cause the state to

6-3. <u>If all the local candidates would have participated in the debate</u>, the voters would have a better understanding of the contending points of view.

   A. If all the local candidates would have participated in the debate

   B. If all the candidates had engaged in local debate

   C. If all the local candidates had participated in the debate

   D. Debating as they should have

   E. After a debate

6-4. The statement <u>that the consequences of smoking marijuana are no greater than drinking alcohol</u> is an argument often given for legalizing the use of marijuana.

   A. that the consequences of smoking marijuana are no greater than drinking alcohol

   B. that the consequences of marijuana are no greater than the consequences of alcohol

   C. that the consequences of drinking alcohol are as great as the consequences of smoking marijuana

   D. that the consequences of smoking marijuana are no greater than those of drinking alcohol

   E. that the consequences of smoking marijuana are as great as drinking alcohol are great

6-5. The vice president of the local bank spoke <u>for a half an hour and told his colleague that he, his colleague, must consider finding a new job</u>, or accept a reduction in salary.

   A. for a half an hour and told his colleague that he, his colleague, must consider finding a new job

   B. for a half hour and told his colleague that he must consider to find a new job

   C. for half an hour and told his colleague that the colleague must get employed by a new bank

   D. for half an hour telling his colleague that he must find a new job

   E. for a half hour and told his colleague to consider finding a new job

GO ON TO THE NEXT PAGE

307

ANSWERS: 6-1 **B**, 6-2 **D**, 6-3 **C**, 6-4 **D**, 6-5 **E**.

If you answered 6-1 **incorrectly, go to 7-1.**
If you answered 6-1 **correctly, go to 7-2.**

If you answered 6-2 **incorrectly, go to 7-1.**
If you answered 6-2 **correctly, go to 7-3.**

If you answered 6-3 **incorrectly, go to 7-2.**
If you answered 6-3 **correctly, go to 7-4.**

If you answered 6-4 **incorrectly, go to 7-3.**
If you answered 6-4 **correctly, go to 7-5.**

If you answered 6-5 **incorrectly, go to 7-4.**
If you answered 6-5 **correctly, go to 7-5.**

7-1. According to legend, while working as an engineer, a train collided with Casey Jones and killed him, but he remains with us as a part of a rich American folk history of songs and legends.

- **A.** According to legend, while working as an engineer, a train collided with Casey Jones and killed him

- **B.** The legendary engineer Casey Jones experienced a collision with another train on the job that killed him

- **C.** Engineer Casey Jones was killed when his train collided with another

- **D.** Driving an engine, another train killed Casey Jones

- **E.** An engineer's work brought Casey Jones to his death when he was hit by a train while working

7-2. Among the members of the legal profession there are many who try to keep their clients out of court and save their clients' money.

- **A.** many who try to keep their clients out of court

- **B.** ones who try to keep their clients out of court

- **C.** they who try to keep their clients out of court

- **D.** many of whom try to keep their clients out of court

- **E.** a few who try to keep their clients out of court

7-3. Understanding the droning lecturer with comprehension required the intense concentration of the class members present in the lecture hall, all of whom were students.

- **A.** Understanding the droning lecturer with comprehension required the intense concentration of the class members present in the lecture hall, all of whom were students.

- **B.** Comprehending the droning lecturer with the intense concentration of the class members present.

- **C.** To understand the droning lecturer, the students had to concentrate intensely.

- **D.** As the lecturer droned on, the students found themselves required to concentrate in order to understand.

- **E.** The students listening to the lecturer, who was droning, increased their comprehension by concentrating.

7-4. <u>Clarity and brilliance, in addition to enjoying the beauty: These are the qualities of a beautiful diamond and along with it a beautiful painting</u>.

  A. Clarity and brilliance, in addition to enjoying the beauty: These are the qualities of a beautiful diamond and along with it a beautiful painting.

  B. Clarity, brilliance, and beauty: These are the qualities of a beautiful diamond as well as a beautiful painting.

  C. To be clear, brilliant and beautiful is to be either a beautiful diamond or a beautiful painting.

  D. Diamonds and paintings give out clarity, brilliance, and beauty.

  E. Where there are clarity and brilliance and beauty there are the qualities of not only a beautiful diamond but also a beautiful painting.

7-5. With the advent of sound, many stars of silent films found themselves unable to adapt to the "talkies" <u>because their speaking voices were either unattractive or their acting consisted of only exaggerated pantomime</u>.

  A. because their speaking voices were either unattractive or their acting consisted of only exaggerated pantomime

  B. because of their voices either being unattractive or their acting being exaggerated pantomime

  C. with their unattractive voices and exaggerated pantomime

  D. because of their unattractive voices or exaggerated pantomime that didn't require sound

  E. because either their voices were unattractive or their acting was only exaggerated pantomime

ANSWERS: 7-1 **C**, 7-2 **A**, 7-3 **C**, 7-4 **B**, 7-5 **E**.

If you answered 7-1 **incorrectly, go to 8-1.**
If you answered 7-1 **correctly, go to 8-2.**

If you answered 7-2 **incorrectly, go to 8-1.**
If you answered 7-2 **correctly, go to 8-3.**

If you answered 7-3 **incorrectly, go to 8-2.**
If you answered 7-3 **correctly, go to 8-4.**

If you answered 7-4 **incorrectly, go to 8-3.**
If you answered 7-4 **correctly, go to 8-5.**

If you answered 7-5 **incorrectly, go to 8-4.**
If you answered 7-5 **correctly, go to 8-5.**

8-1. When President Lyndon Johnson signed the Voting Rights Act in 1965, he used 50 pens, handing them out as souvenirs to a joyous gathering in the President's Room of the Capitol, where Abraham Lincoln had signed the Emancipation Proclamation on January 1, 1863. When President Reagan signed an extension of the Voting Rights Act in 1982, he spoke affectionately of "the right to vote," signed with a single pen, and then concluded the four-minute ceremony by rising from his desk, announcing, "It's done."

If the passage above is true, which of the following is most probably true?

  A. The Voting Rights Act did not require an extension.

  B. The Voting Rights Act is not significantly related to the Emancipation Proclamation.

GO ON TO THE NEXT PAGE

C. President Reagan saw himself as more like Lincoln than did Johnson.

D. President Reagan did not regard the extension of the act as an occasion for fanfare.

E. President Reagan objected strenuously to an extension of the Voting Rights Act.

8-2. Don't spend the night tossing and turning! Take Eezy-Zs for a sound, restful sleep . . . you'll wake up refreshed, energized, with no drugged-up hangover. Remember . . . Eezy-Zs when you need that sleep!

Which of the following is not a claim of Eezy-Zs?

A. a good night's sleep

B. added energy

C. no aftereffects

D. quickly falling asleep

E. a restful slumber

8-3. Which of the following most logically completes the passage at the blank below?

In a civilized society, members of the community will often defer to others, even against their own better judgment. This situation may occur in public, in gatherings with strangers, or in the household with one's family or friends. It is a sign of a more sophisticated culture that one's immediate interests are thought to be secondary to those of another. On first examination this may seem to be selflessness, but _____.

A. actually it is not; it is just ignorance

B. rather it may take many names

C. actually it is

D. to some extent it does serve the ends of the individual concerned

E. sometimes it can harbor animosities and hostility

8-4. Which of the following most logically completes the passage at the blank below?

The English language, lacking the rigidity of most European tongues, has been bent and shaped in at least as many ways as there are countries or regions where it is spoken. Though purists often argue that "standard" English is spoken only in certain high-minded enclaves of the American northeast, the fact is that it is the most widely used language in the world and is not likely to yield that distinction for a very long time, if ever. Nevertheless _____.

A. it remains one of the most widely spoken languages throughout the world

B. it can be understood in just about every corner of the globe

C. even making allowances for regional peculiarities, English as it is spoken has been much abused in recent times

D. though we may be proud of these facts, English remains one of the most difficult languages to master

E. English, as it is spoken, lacks the rigidity of the classical and more historic European languages

8-5. Of all the petty little pieces of bureaucratic arrogance, it's hard to imagine one smaller than that of the city schools in not admitting a British subject whose father is working—as a legal alien—for a nearby petrochemical company. Someone apparently decided that if the boy had been an illegal alien, a recent U.S. Supreme Court decision in a Texas case would have required the district to admit him, but since he is legal, there is no such requirement. That is nonsense.

Which of the following best expresses the point of the author's argument?

A. The city schools outside of Texas should not base decisions on a precedent set in Texas.

B. The stability of a parent's job should have no bearing on the educational opportunity offered his or her child.

C. Bureaucratic arrogance has resulted in unsound legal interpretation.

D. Legal sense and nonsense are sometimes indistinguishable.

E. Both legal and illegal aliens should receive equal treatment.

ANSWERS: 8-1 D, 8-2 D, 8-3 D, 8-4 C, 8-5 C.

Check your answers and continue to the next reading passage.

Read the following passage and answer Questions 9–12.

In economics, demand implies something slightly different from the common meaning of the term. The layperson uses the term to mean the amount that is de-
(5) manded of an item. Thus, if the price were to decrease and individuals wanted more of an item, it is commonly said that demand increases. To an economist, demand is a relationship between a se-
(10) ries of prices and a series of corresponding quantities that are demanded at these prices. If one reads the previous sentence carefully, it should become apparent that there is a distinction between
(15) the quantity demanded and demand. This distinction is often a point of confusion. Demand is a relationship between price and quantities demanded, and therefore suggests the effect of one
(20) (e.g., price) on the other (e.g., quantity demanded). Therefore, knowledge of the demand for a product enables one to predict how much more of a good will be purchased if price decreases. But the
(25) increase in quantity demanded does not mean that demand has increased, since the relationship between price and quantity demanded (i.e., the demand for the product) has not changed. Demand
(30) shifts when there is a change in income, expectations, taste, etc., such that a different quantity of the good is demanded at the same price.

In almost all cases, a consumer wants
(35) more of an item if the price decreases. This relationship between price and quantity demanded is so strong that it is referred to as the "law of demand." This "law" can be explained by the income
(40) and substitution effects. The income effect occurs because price increases

GO ON TO THE NEXT PAGE

Verbal Section

reduce the purchasing power of the individual and, thus, the quantity demanded
of goods must decrease. The substitution
(45) effect reflects the consumer's desire to
get the "best buy." Accordingly, if the
price of good A increases, the individual
will tend to substitute another good and
purchase less of good A. The negative
(50) correlation between price and quantity
demanded is also explained by the law
of diminishing marginal utility.
According to this law, the additional
utility the consumer gains from consum-
(55) ing a good decreases as successively
more units of the good are consumed.
Because the additional units yield less
utility or satisfaction, the consumer is
willing to purchase more only if the
(60) price of the good decreases.

9. Which of the following is an instance
   of a shift in demand as it is understood
   by economists?

   I. A market is selling two pounds of
      coffee for the price it usually
      charges for one pound; the *de-
      mand* for coffee has increased.

   II. The success of a television pro-
       gram featuring cartoon turtles has
       increased the *demand* for an oat
       cereal in turtle shapes.

   III. Because of the rail strike,
        California lettuce costs more in
        Chicago, and the *demand* for let-
        tuce has fallen.

   A. I only

   B. II only

   C. III only

   D. I and III only

   E. I, II, and III

10. According to the passage, a change in
    demand, as economists use the term,
    would occur in which of the following
    situations?

    A. The gasoline price increases,
       resulting in the increased sale of
       compact cars (whose price
       remains stable).

    B. The gasoline price increases,
       resulting in the increased sale of
       compact cars (which go on sale in
       response to increased gas prices).

    C. The gasoline price decreases on
       the same day that a new 43-mpg
       car enters the market.

    D. A federal order imposes a price
       ceiling on gasoline.

    E. A federal order lifts price
       regulations for gasoline.

11. Assume that firms develop an orange-
    flavored breakfast drink high in vita-
    min C that is a good substitute for
    orange juice but sells for less. Based
    upon assertions in the passage, which
    of the following would occur with re-
    spect to the demand for orange juice?

    A. Health food stores would
       resurrect the law of diminishing
       marginal utility.

    B. Assuming that the price of fresh
       orange juice remained constant,
       more orange juice would be
       consumed.

    C. The law of demand would prevail.

    D. Assuming that the price of fresh
       orange juice remained constant,
       the demand would not change.

    E. There is not enough information
       in the passage to answer this
       question.

12. The purpose of the passage is to

   A. introduce several important definitions.

   B. outline the theory of supply on demand.

   C. correct the layperson's economic misapprehensions about prices.

   D. introduce a student to a theory of marketing.

   E. question a popular misunderstanding of "demand."

ANSWERS: 9 **B**, 10 **A**, 11 **C**, 12 **A**.

If you answered **none** of the four reading questions **correctly, go to 13-1.**

If you answered **one** of the four reading questions **correctly, go to 13-2.**

If you answered **two** of the four reading questions **correctly, go to 13-3.**

If you answered **three** of the four reading questions **correctly, go to 13-4.**

If you answered **all four** of the reading questions **correctly, go to 13-5.**

13-1. To the Chair:

At the October 7 meeting it was decided that no two officers would hold positions on the same committee. It has recently come to my attention that both Charles S. Smith and Arnold Krunkle will be serving in some capacity on the Building and Maintenance Committee, and both have been nominated for officer status. As you know, this is in direct disregard for the rules as voted by the membership last October 7. I would hope that sufficient action will be taken by the Disciplinary

Committee (on which committee both of the above are members) so that this problem will be remedied.

Sincerely, Irving H. Fortnast

Which of the following is the essential flaw that the writer of the letter fails to notice?

   A. Smith and Krunkle are already serving together on the Disciplinary Committee.

   B. The Chairman has no power in the matter.

   C. The membership cannot pass rules limiting members.

   D. Smith and Krunkle are not yet officers.

   E. Building and Maintenance is actually two committees.

13-2. Socrates believed that virtue is the outcome of knowledge and that evil is fundamentally ignorance. This is an early instance of the belief that the intellectual or rational is dominant in man and morally superior.

Socrates' point of view, as described in the passage, implies which of the following conclusions about evil people?

   A. They are ignorant.

   B. They are unable to achieve complete self-knowledge.

   C. They are inherently virtuous but incapable of showing it.

   D. They are often either ignorant or irrational.

   E. They often dominate those who are morally superior.

GO ON TO THE NEXT PAGE

13-3. To the Chair:

At the October 7 meeting it was decided that no two officers would hold positions on the same committee. It has recently come to my attention that both Charles S. Smith and Arnold Krunkle will be serving in some capacity on the Building and Maintenance Committee, and both have been nominated for officer status. As you know, this is in direct disregard for the rules as voted by the membership last October 7. I would hope that sufficient action will be taken by the Disciplinary Committee (on which committee both of the above are members) so that this problem will be remedied.

Sincerely, Irving H. Fortnash

Which of the following most completely and reasonably describes actions that may occur in the near future?

A. Fortnash resigns his membership.

B. Either Smith or Krunkle resigns his membership.

C. Krunkle resigns his committee post on the Building and Maintenance Committee.

D. Smith resigns his position on the Building and Maintenance Committee.

E. One of the two (Smith or Krunkle) resigns his position on the Building and Maintenance Committee, and the other resigns his position on the Disciplinary Committee.

13-4. All race-car lovers enjoy classical music.

No backgammon players enjoy classical music.

All those who enjoy classical music also enjoy fine wine.

If each of the above statements is true, which of the following must also be true?

A. Everyone who plays backgammon enjoys fine wine.

B. No one who enjoys fine wine plays backgammon.

C. No backgammon players are race-car lovers.

D. No backgammon players enjoy fine wine.

E. No race-car lover enjoys fine wine.

13-5. It has been proven that the "lie detector" can be fooled. If one is truly unaware that one is lying, when in fact one is, then the "lie detector" is worthless.

Without contradicting his or her own statements, the author might present which of the following arguments as a strong point in favor of the lie detector?

A. The methodology used by investigative critics of the lie detector is itself highly flawed.

B. Law-enforcement agencies have purchased too many detectors to abandon them now.

C. Circumstantial evidence might be more useful in a criminal case than is personal testimony.

D. The very threat of a lie-detector test has led a significant number of criminals to confess.

E. People are never "truly aware" that they are lying.

ANSWERS: 13-1 **D**, 13-2 **A**, 13-3 **E**, 13-4 **C**, 13-5 **D**.

If you answered 13-1 **incorrectly, go to 14-1.**
If you answered 13-1 **correctly, go to 14-2.**

If you answered 13-2 **incorrectly, go to 14-1.**
If you answered 13-2 **correctly, go to 14-3.**

If you answered 13-3 **incorrectly, go to 14-2.**
If you answered 13-3 **correctly, go to 14-4.**

If you answered 13-4 **incorrectly, go to 14-3.**
If you answered 13-4 **correctly, go to 14-5.**

If you answered 13-5 **incorrectly, go to 14-4.**
If you answered 13-5 **correctly, go to 14-5.**

14-1. On a swimming team:

All freestyle swimmers are Olympic winners.

No blue-eyed swimmer is an Olympic winner.

All Olympic winners go on to lucrative professional careers.

If it is determined that all of the above are true, then which of the following must also be true about the swimming team?

A. All those who go on to professional careers are freestyle swimmers.

B. Only freestyle swimmers go on to professional careers.

C. Some blue-eyed swimmers go on to lucrative professional careers.

D. No blue-eyed swimmer is a freestyle swimmer.

E. Only blue-eyed swimmers don't go on to lucrative careers.

14-2. A researcher has concluded that women are just as capable as men in math but that their skills are not developed because society expects them to develop other and more diverse abilities.

Which of the following is a basic assumption of the researcher?

A. Ability in math is more important than ability in more diverse subjects.

B. Ability in math is less important than ability in more diverse subjects.

C. Women and men should be equally capable in math.

D. Women might be more capable than men in math.

E. Women tend to conform to social expectations.

14-3. The census showed a sharp rise during the last decade in the number of Americans living together as unmarried couples, but a more recent increase in the marriage rate this year, the first of this decade, suggests that matrimony will make a comeback over the next ten years.

Which of the following best refutes the argument above?

A. One of the causes of more marriages is that people have waited until they were older to marry.

B. Although information about this year's marriage rate is not complete, most analysts consider it to be reliable.

GO ON TO THE NEXT PAGE

C. Many of those marrying this year were couples who had lived together during the previous decade.

D. The number of Americans living together did not rise at a consistent rate during the previous decade.

E. The marriage rate increased dramatically ten years ago and fell even more dramatically in following years.

14-4. The census showed a sharp rise during the last decade in the number of Americans living together as unmarried couples, but a more recent increase in the marriage rate this year, the first of this decade, suggests that matrimony will make a comeback over the next ten years.

With which of the following would the author be likely to agree?

A. Americans should not live together as unmarried couples.

B. Matrimony is preferable to living together.

C. Economic circumstances have made matrimony attractive as a way of paying less income tax.

D. The attitudes of young people now are altogether different from the attitudes of young people during the last ten years.

E. Prevailing attitudes toward marriage tend to persist for more than one year.

14-5. Money talks as never before in state and local elections, and the main cause is TV advertising. Thirty seconds can go as high as $5,000. Political fundraising is one of the few growth industries left in America. The way to stop the waste might be for television to be paid by state and local government, at a standard rate, to provide air time to all candidates to debate the issues. This might be boring at first. But eventually candidates might actually brush up their debating skills and electrify the TV audience with content, not style.

Which of the following presuppositions is (are) necessary to the argument above?

I. Candidates spend too much money on television advertising.

II. Television can be used to educate and inform the public.

III. The freedom of speech doesn't abridge the freedom to spend.

A. I only

B. II only

C. III only

D. I and II only

E. I, II and III

15-1. The public soon became outraged at the Cabinet member whom betrayed the public trust, and they demanded his ouster by the prime minister.

A. the Cabinet member whom betrayed the public trust

B. the untrustworthy Cabinet member

C. the Cabinet member with whom they betrayed the public trust

D. the Cabinet member who, after betraying the public trust

E. the Cabinet member who betrayed the public trust

15-2. Arthur was sorry he had agreed to employ his cousin's law firm, because at first meeting with the lawyer, the lawyer seemed indecisive.

A. at first meeting with the lawyer, the lawyer seemed indecisive

B. at first meeting, the lawyer seemed indecisive

C. at first meeting the lawyer seems indecisive

D. at first meeting, he seemed an indecisive lawyer

E. at first meeting the lawyer, he seems indecisive

15-3. The most recent National Conference of Mathematics Teachers addressed the problem of convincing students who rely on calculators that the ability to calculate mentally or with pencil and paper is important.

A. The most recent National Conference of Mathematics Teachers addressed the problem of convincing students who

B. The most recent problem faced by the National Conference of Mathematics Teachers was convincing students who

C. The most recent National Conference of Mathematics Teachers addressed the problem of convincing students whom

D. Most recently, the National Conference of Mathematics Teachers addressed the problem of convincing students who

E. The most recent National Conference of Mathematics Teachers addressed those students who

15-4. No matter what experience you have had with forest fires, if you would have witnessed the fire roaring down through the canyon, you would have been terrified.

A. if you would have witnessed

B. if you witnessed

C. if you could witness

D. if you had witnessed

E. when you witnessed

GO ON TO THE NEXT PAGE

15-5. Recounting a painful childhood experience, the woman remembered that her father was very angry when she failed the fifth grade because she could see him shaking with anger.

A. Recounting a painful childhood experience, the woman remembered that her father was very angry when she failed the fifth grade because she could see him shaking with anger.

B. Recounting a painful childhood experience, the woman recounted that her father was shaking with anger when she failed the fifth grade.

C. Painfully, the woman remembered when she failed the fifth grade and when her father was shaking with anger.

D. The failure of the fifth grade and her father's anger were painful for the woman recounting the experience.

E. The woman described her father's shaking with anger when he learned that she had failed the fifth grade.

ANSWERS: 15-1 E, 15-2 B, 15-3 A, 15-4 D, 15-5 E.

If you answered 15-1 **incorrectly**, go to 16-1.
If you answered 15-1 **correctly**, go to 16-2.

If you answered 15-2 **incorrectly**, go to 16-1.
If you answered 15-2 **correctly**, go to 16-3.

If you answered 15-3 **incorrectly**, go to 16-2.
If you answered 15-3 **correctly**, go to 16-4.

If you answered 15-4 **incorrectly**, go to 16-3.
If you answered 15-4 **correctly**, go to 16-5.

If you answered 15-5 **incorrectly**, go to 16-4.
If you answered 15-5 **correctly**, go to 16-5.

16-1. Some Detroit car manufacturers promise to give rebates to new customers between June 1 and June 30, granting the returned money during June but not thereafter.

A. granting the returned money during June but not thereafter

B. during June but not thereafter

C. but not thereafter

D. no money after that

E. denying those who purchase before or after June

16-2. Ella was unable to attend her son's basketball games because she worked the night shift, arriving at 10 p.m. and leaving at 6 a.m.

A. arriving at 10 p.m. and leaving at 6 a.m.

B. having arrived at 10 p.m. and leaving at 6 a.m.

C. she arrived at 10 p.m. and left at 6 a.m.

D. with an arrival at 6 and a departure at 10

E. from 10 p.m. to 6 a.m.

16-3. Every year the banker warned his borrowers that planning a career in business is often easier than to pursue it.

A. planning a career in business is often easier than to pursue it

B. to plan a career in business is often easier than pursuing it

C. planning a business career is often easier than pursuing it

D. the planning of a business career is often easier than its pursuit

E. a business career plan is often easier than a business career

16-4. <u>After having read through the stack of bills laying on my desk</u>, I began wondering whether to file for bankruptcy or to try to consolidate my debts by taking out a new loan.

A. After having read through the stack of bills laying on my desk

B. Having read through the stack of bills lying on my desk

C. Reading through the stack of bills littering my desk

D. The stack of bills lying on the desk, after I had read them

E. After having read through the stack of bills lying on my desk

16-5. <u>According to statistics, one in every two marriages ends in divorce, most often involving married couples not wealthy enough to "buy" each other's love</u>.

A. According to statistics, one in every two marriages ends in divorce, most often involving married couples not wealthy enough to "buy" each other's love.

B. Statistically, 50 percent of marriages are divorces, often caused by people not wealthy enough to "buy" each other's love.

C. According to statistics, half of all marriages ends in divorce, often because the partners are not wealthy enough to "buy" each other's love.

D. Statistics tell half of all marriages that they will end in divorce, often because the partners are not wealthy enough to "buy" each other's love.

E. Those who cannot "buy" each other's love are destined for divorce in at least half the cases, according to statistics.

ANSWERS: 16-1 **C**, 16-2 **C**, 16-3 **C**, 16-4 **B**, 16-5 **C**.

If you answered 16-1 **incorrectly**, go to 17-1.
If you answered 16-1 **correctly**, go to 17-2.

If you answered 16-2 **incorrectly**, go to 17-1.
If you answered 16-2 **correctly**, go to 17-3.

If you answered 16-3 **incorrectly**, go to 17-2.
If you answered 16-3 **correctly**, go to 17-4.

If you answered 16-4 **incorrectly**, go to 17-3.
If you answered 16-4 **correctly**, go to 17-5.

If you answered 16-5 **incorrectly**, go to 17-4.
If you answered 16-5 **correctly**, go to 17-5.

17-1. Though the receptions at the embassy were usually formal and uneventful, to everyone's surprise a fight broke out when the foreign ambassador <u>took a joke serious and punched the jokester hardly</u>.

A. took a joke serious and punched the jokester hardly

B. took a joke seriously and hardly punched the jokester

C. hardly took a joke and seriously punched the jokester

D. took a joke seriously and punched the jokester hard

E. gave a hard punch to a serious jokester

GO ON TO THE NEXT PAGE

17-2. Although there was no contest for senator or governor and voters were expected to be apathetic, the referenda proved so controversial that 90% <u>of those registered showed up at the polls</u>.

   A. of those registered showed up at the polls

   B. of the registered showed up at the polls

   C. of the registered voters showed up at the polls to vote

   D. were registered to vote

   E. who were not showed up at the polls

17-3. With pennants waving and the band playing, <u>the huge crowd at the football game cheered the players making the touchdown from the stands</u>.

   A. the huge crowd at the football game cheered the players making the touchdown from the stands

   B. the huge crowd from the stands at the football game cheered the players making the touchdown

   C. making the touchdown, the huge football game crowd cheered the players from the stands

   D. the huge crowd at the football game cheered from the stands as the players made the touchdown

   E. cheers arose from the stands as the football game players made the touchdown

17-4. According to the employers, the new union contract forbade <u>working overtime past regular hours, and those who did not comply to this</u> were severely censured.

   A. working overtime past regular hours, and those who did not comply to this

   B. working overtime, and those who did so

   C. working after hours, and those not compliant

   D. overtime, and those who did not comply to this

   E. noncompliance with the antiovertime clause

17-5. Because Carla has always been careful to treat all her daycare children affectionately and <u>she likes everyone as much as him</u>, he does not feel special.

   A. she likes everyone as much as him

   B. she likes everyone as much as she

   C. she has a liking for everyone equal to him

   D. she has a liking for everyone equal to he

   E. everyone she likes is equal to him

ANSWERS: 17-1 D, 17-2 A, 17-3 D, 17-4 B, 17-5 A.

Check your answer and continue to the next reading passage.

Read the following passage and answer Questions 18–21.

Each method of counting bacteria has advantages and disadvantages; none is 100 percent accurate. Cell counts may be made with a counting chamber, a
(5) slide marked with a grid to facilitate counting of cells and to determine the volume of liquid in the area counted. Counts are made under a microscope and calculations made to determine the
(10) number of cells per ml of the original culture. Electronic cell counters can be used to count cells suspended in a liquid medium which passes through a hole small enough to allow the passage of
(15) only one bacterial cell at a time. Smear counts are similar to cell counts: A known volume of culture is spread over a known area (1 cm^2) of a slide and then stained. Counts are made from several
(20) microscope fields, and calculations are made. In membrane filter counts, a known volume of a culture is passed through a filter, which is then examined microscopically for cells. The advantage
(25) of cell counts, smear counts, and membrane filter counts is that they are quickly accomplished with little complicated equipment; however, both living and dead cells are counted.

(30) The serial-dilution method involves the making of a series of dilutions, usually by a factor of 10, into a nutrient medium. The highest dilution producing growth gives a rough indication of the
(35) population of the original culture; for example, if the highest dilution to produce growth is the 1:100 dilution, the original culture had between 100 and 1,000 cells per ml.

(40) Plate counts are made by making serial dilutions (usually in sterile tap water or an isotonic solution) of the original culture. Samples of known volume of the

dilutions are transferred to petri dishes
(45) and mixed with nutrient agar. After a suitable incubation period, the colonies on the plates with between 30 and 300 colonies are counted. Because each colony is assumed to have arisen from a
(50) single cell, calculations can be made to determine the original population size. Plate counts have the advantage of not including dead cells, and they can be used when the population is so low as to
(55) make other methods impractical, but they require more time than direct counts, and they detect only those organisms that can grow under the conditions of incubation; the development of
(60) one colony from more than one cell is also a source or error.

18. The author's purpose in this passage is to

  A. argue for the development of a fully accurate counting method.

  B. discuss the advantages of several methods of counting cells.

  C. show that new counting methods have surpassed those used in the past.

  D. give instruction in the performance of cell counts.

  E. describe a variety of methods of counting bacteria.

19. We can infer that no method of bacteria counting is wholly accurate because

  I. the number of cells is likely to be so large.

  II. the cells are microscopic in size.

  III. both living and dead cells are counted.

GO ON TO THE NEXT PAGE

A. II only

B. I and II only

C. I and III only

D. II and III only

E. I, II, and III

20. If we know the total bacteria cell volume in a sample, to determine the bacteria cell count we must also know

   I.   the volume of a single cell.

   II. the volume of the nutrient culture.

   III. the volume of the calibrated centrifuge tube.

   A. I only

   B. II only

   C. III only

   D. I and II only

   E. II and III only

21. Which of the following best describes the audience to which this passage is probably addressed?

   A. advanced students in microbiology

   B. casual readers of a scientific magazine

   C. elementary school students

   D. introductory college biology students

   E. high school mathematics students

ANSWERS: 18 E, 19 B, 20 A, 21 D.

If you answered **none** of the four reading questions **correctly, go to 22-1.**

If you answered **one** of the four reading questions **correctly, go to 22-2.**

If you answered **two** of the four reading questions **correctly, go to 22-3.**

If you answered **three** of the four reading questions **correctly, go to 22-4.**

If you answered all **four** of the reading questions **correctly, go to 22-5.**

22-1. Most citizens of nineteenth-century London believed that remaining respectable was more important and more difficult than <u>to question</u> the virtues of the age.

   A. to question

   B. questioning

   C. the question of

   D. a question over

   E. all

22-2. Opinions about the ballot issue, of course, <u>varies according with the ethnic and economic status</u> of each voter, and for this reason, the poll of a small sample of voters is of no use.

   A. varies according with the ethnic and economic status

   B. varies according to ethnic and economic status

   C. changes with ethnicity and the economy

   D. vary according to the ethnic and economic status

   E. vary according to ethnic and economical status

22-3. While declaring his support for a nuclear weapons freeze, <u>a small bomb exploded some distance from the Cabinet minister, who was startled but unharmed</u>.

A. a small bomb exploded some distance from the Cabinet minister, who was startled but unharmed

B. a small bomb startled the Cabinet minister, but did not harm him

C. a small bomb startled the Cabinet minister from a distance, but did not harm him

D. the Cabinet minister was startled by a bomb that exploded some distance from him, but unharmed

E. the Cabinet minister was startled but unharmed by a small bomb that exploded some distance from him

22-4. Having given up hope of influencing the vote, several disgruntled visitors had left the board meeting <u>before it had considered the new municipal tax cut</u>.

A. before it had considered the new municipal tax cut

B. before it considered the new municipal tax cut

C. before the members considered the new municipal tax cut

D. with the consideration of the new municipal tax cut yet to come

E. previous to the new municipal tax cut

22-5. <u>Not gaining sufficient legislative approval, thousands of women vowed to keep the Equal Rights Amendment alive by continuing their protests</u>.

A. Not gaining sufficient legislative approval, thousands of women vowed to keep the Equal Rights Amendment alive by continuing their protests.

B. Not gaining sufficient legislative approval, the Equal Rights Amendment had thousands of women vowing to keep it alive with their protests.

C. Thousands of women vowed to keep the Equal Rights Amendment alive in spite of failure to gain legislative approval.

D. After the Equal Rights Amendment did not gain sufficient legislative approval, thousands of women vowed to keep it alive by continuing their protests.

E. Not gaining sufficient legislative approval, protests continued by women who vowed to keep the Equal Rights Amendment alive.

ANSWERS: 22-1 **B**, 22-2 **D**, 22-3 **E**, 22-4 **C**, 22-5 **D**.

If you answered 22-1 **incorrectly, go to 23–1.**
If you answered 22-1 **correctly, go to 23–2.**

If you answered 22-2 **incorrectly, go to 23–1.**
If you answered 22-2 **correctly, go to 23–3.**

If you answered 22-3 **incorrectly, go to 23–2.**
If you answered 22-3 **correctly, go to 23–4.**

If you answered 22-4 **incorrectly, go to 23–3.**
If you answered 22-4 **correctly, go to 23–5.**

If you answered 22-5 **incorrectly, go to 23–4.**
If you answered 22-5 **correctly, go to 23–5.**

GO ON TO THE NEXT PAGE

23-1. Revisionist historians <u>have argued that the entry of the United States into</u> World War II was favored by the Chief Executive and his closest advisors.

    A. have argued that the entry of the United States into

    B. arguing about the United States entry into

    C. entering an argument about the United States and

    D. had been having an argument that the entry of the United States into

    E. claim that the entry of the United States into

23-2. Gerrymandering <u>is when a voting area is unfairly divided</u> so that one political party gains advantage, and historically both the Democrats and Republicans have used the gerrymander.

    A. is when a voting area is unfairly divided

    B. divides a voting area unfairly

    C. makes fair voting unfair

    D. occurs when a voting area is unfairly divided

    E. is when a voting area is divided unfairly

23-3. None of the applicants could file all of the forms in time because the job application did not state <u>to whom to be sent the personal references.</u>

    A. to whom to be sent the personal references

    B. to who the personal references should be sent

    C. to whom to send the personal references

    D. to whom the personal references will be sent

    E. to whom to send the personal references to

23-4. Though the chief appeal of their program was their disagreement, <u>movie critics Gene Siskel and Roger Ebert often praised distinguished performances even when they were new to the screen.</u>

    A. movie critics Gene Siskel and Roger Ebert often praised distinguished performances even when they were new to the screen

    B. movie critics Gene Siskel and Roger Ebert, praising distinguished performances that were new to the screen

    C. even distinguished performances that were new to the screen were praised by movie critics Gene Siskel and Roger Ebert

    D. movie critics Gene Siskel and Roger Ebert often praised distinguished performances, even those by actors new to the screen

    E. with distinguished performances in mind, movie critics Gene Siskel and Roger Ebert often praised even new screen actors

23-5. In *Charlotte's Web*, Wilbur is awarded the blue ribbon not because <u>his appearance is superior to the other pigs but also with reference to the belief that he possesses</u> some sort of "supernatural" power.

    A. his appearance is superior to the other pigs but also with reference to the belief that he possesses

B. he looked better than the other pigs but because he was thought to possess

C. of his superior appearance but as far as the belief that he possessed

D. he looks better than that of the other pigs but because of a belief

E. he looks better than the other pigs but because he is thought to possess

---

ANSWERS: 23-1 A, 23-2 B, 23-3 C, 23-4 D, 23-5 E.

If you answered 23-1 **incorrectly**, go to **24-1**.
If you answered 23-1 **correctly**, go to **24-2**.

If you answered 23-2 **incorrectly**, go to **24-1**.
If you answered 23-2 **correctly**, go to **24-3**.

If you answered 23-3 **incorrectly**, go to **24-2**.
If you answered 23-3 **correctly**, go to **24-4**.

If you answered 23-4 **incorrectly**, go to **24-3**.
If you answered 23-4 **correctly**, go to **24-5**.

If you answered 23-5 **incorrectly**, go to **24-4**.
If you answered 23-5 **correctly**, go to **24-5**.

24-1. <u>After having finished the marathon,</u> both the winner and the losers felt proud of their having completed the course of more than 26 miles.

A. After having finished the marathon

B. Having finished the marathon

C. Having been finished after the marathon

D. Finishing the marathon

E. The marathon finished

24-2. If a police officer were to mistake the citizen's friendly intentions, <u>and supposes her to be dangerous,</u> he might draw his revolver or call for backup assistance.

A. and supposes her to be dangerous

B. and supposed her to be dangerous

C. and supposes danger from her

D. and suspect her to be dangerous

E. and suspected her to be dangerous

24-3. Frank Buck, "the great white hunter," was always portrayed on film as <u>fearless and having great skill in hunting dangerous animals,</u> such as lions, leopards, and Cape buffalo.

A. fearless and having great skill in hunting dangerous animals

B. fearless and very skillful in hunting dangerous animals

C. having no fear and having great skill in hunting dangerous animals

D. fearless and with skill in hunting dangerous animals

E. hunting dangerous animals without fear and with skill

24-4. Unaffected by both rising inflation and high interest rates <u>were that type of enterprising American able to create a product</u> adaptable to shifting public tastes.

A. were that type of enterprising American able to create a product

B. was that type of enterprising American able to create a products

GO ON TO THE NEXT PAGE

Verbal Section

C. were the productions of American enterprise

D. were enterprising Americans who were able to create products

E. enterprising Americans creating products

24-5. <u>Success in school, according to many of the more cynical critics of public education, is like playing marbles</u>: Distinguished achievement depends not upon talent but upon luck.

A. Success in school, according to many of the more cynical critics of public education, is like playing marbles:

B. Criticizing success in public education cynically, many compare successful schooling to a successful marble game:

C. School is a game of marbles, according to many of the more cynical critics of public education

D. The more cynical critics of public education say that success in schools is like playing marbles:

E. Many of the more cynical critics of public education say that succeeding in school is like playing marbles:

ANSWERS: 24-1 **B**, 24-2 **D**, 24-3 **B**, 24-4 **D**, 24-5 **E**.

If you answered 24-1 **incorrectly**, go to 25-1.
If you answered 24-1 **correctly**, go to 25-2.

If you answered 24-2 **incorrectly**, go to 25-1.
If you answered 24-2 **correctly**, go to 25-3.

If you answered 24-3 **incorrectly**, go to 25-2.
If you answered 24-3 **correctly**, go to 25-4.

If you answered 24-4 **incorrectly**, go to 25-3.
If you answered 24-4 **correctly**, go to 25-5.

If you answered 24-5 **incorrectly**, go to 25-4.
If you answered 24-5 **correctly**, go to 25-5.

25-1. The term "articulation disorder" refers to the difficulty an individual has when he uses the speech sounds of the language spoken around him. No communication dysfunction is more familiar to the speech pathologist than the problem of misarticulation. Articulation disorders represent over two thirds of the speech clinician's caseload; a rather sizable percentage when one considers that voice, rhythm, and language disorders also fall under this professional's review.

The passage implies that one of the factors contributing to the importance of articulation disorders is

A. the speech clinician's practice of treating nonserious disorders.

B. the lack of organic causes of such disorders.

C. the tendency of many children to "outgrow" the disorder.

D. the high incidence of such disorders.

E. the stress placed on such disorders by hospital administrators.

25-2. "The sum of behavior is to retain a man's dignity without intruding upon the liberty of others," stated Sir Francis Bacon. If this is the case, then not intruding upon another's liberty is impossible.

The conclusion strongly implied by the author's arguments is that

- **A.** retaining one's dignity is impossible without intruding upon another's liberty.
- **B.** retaining dignity never involves robbing others of liberty.
- **C.** dignity and liberty are mutually exclusive.
- **D.** there is always the possibility of a "dignified intrusion."
- **E.** B.F. Skinner's *Beyond Freedom and Dignity* takes its cue from Bacon.

25-3. The fish *Alpha splendes* usually lives in a lake where there are dissolved alkalies. Lake Huron contains the dissolved alkalies soda and potash. There are no *Alpha splendes* in Lake Huron.

Which of the following could logically complete an argument with the premises given above?

- I. Therefore, *Alpha splendes* needs alkalies other than soda and potash.
- II. Therefore, there may not be sufficient dissolved alkalies in the lake.
- III. Therefore, there will be no *Alpha splendes* living in this lake.

- **A.** I only
- **B.** II only
- **C.** III only
- **D.** I and II only
- **E.** II and III only

25-4. "The sum of behavior is to retain a man's dignity without intruding upon the liberty of others," stated Sir Francis Bacon. If this is the case, then not intruding upon another's liberty is impossible.

The author's argument would be weakened if it were pointed out that

- I. Bacon's argument has been misinterpreted out of context.
- II. neither liberty nor dignity can be discussed in absolute terms.
- III. retaining dignity always involves a reduction of liberty.

- **A.** I only
- **B.** III only
- **C.** I and II only
- **D.** II and III only
- **E.** I, II, and III

25-5. The dance tonight is a ball, and my child's toy is a ball. Therefore, in addition to the fact that they are called by the same name, there is a way in which the dance and my child's toy are like each other.

Which of the following statements would explain why the conclusion of the argument does not follow from the premises?

- I. The dance tonight may not be a ball.
- II. Something which is neither a dance nor a toy may be a ball.
- III. The dance tonight and my child's toy are not each a ball in the same sense of the word.
- IV. A ball cannot be anything except a dance or a toy.

GO ON TO THE NEXT PAGE

327

A. II only

B. III only

C. I and II only

D. II and IV only

E. I, II, and IV only

ANSWERS: 25-1 D, 25-2 A, 25-3 B, 25-4 C, 25-5 B.

If you answered 25-1 **incorrectly**, go to **26-1.**
If you answered 25-1 **correctly**, go to **26-2.**

If you answered 25-2 **incorrectly**, go to **26-1.**
If you answered 25-2 **correctly**, go to **26-3.**

If you answered 25-3 **incorrectly**, go to **26-2.**
If you answered 25-3 **correctly**, go to **26-4.**

If you answered 25-4 **incorrectly**, go to **26-3.**
If you answered 25-4 **correctly**, go to **26-5.**

If you answered 25-5 **incorrectly**, go to **26-4.**
If you answered 25-5 **correctly**, go to **26-5.**

26-1. Flamo Lighters when you need them! Always reliable, always dependable. In all weather, with ten-year guarantee. Don't get caught without a light— keep a Flamo in your pocket wherever you go!

All of the following are claims made or implied by Flamo Lighters EXCEPT

A. convenience

B. dependability

C. longevity

D. winter-proof

E. all-purpose

26-2. In parts of the world where the life spans are short, 40 may be regarded as an advanced age. People who live longer are believed to possess special powers. These elders are sometimes treated with a deference based on fear rather than love.

The final statement in the passage is based on which of the following assumptions?

A. Deference is normally accorded based on love.

B. Few elders are treated with deference.

C. People who live shorter lives have no special powers.

D. People with special powers are not loved.

E. A deference based on fear is stronger than one based on love.

26-3. All acts have consequences. Given this fact, we may wish to play it safe by never doing anything.

The speaker implies that

A. we may prefer to live safely.

B. all acts have consequences.

C. consequentiality is not safe.

D. doing nothing has lesser consequences.

E. not doing anything is not an act.

26-4. All acts have consequences. Given this fact, we may wish to play it safe by never doing anything.

What conclusion about consequences must we accept if we accept the speaker's statement?

A. Consequences are significant only for active people.

B. All consequences are dangerous.

C. There are some acts that do not produce consequences.

D. Consequences have moral force.

E. Inaction has moral force.

26-5. The evolution of the various forms of life from biochemical mass must not be considered a linear progression. Rather, the fossil record suggests an analogy between evolution and a bush whose branches go every which way. Like branches, some evolutionary lines simply end, and others branch again. Many biologists believe the pattern to have been as follows: Bacteria emerged first and from them branched viruses, red algae, blue-green algae, and green flagellates. From the latter branched green algae, from which higher plants evolved, and colorless rhizoflagellates, from which diatoms, molds, sponges, and protozoa evolved. From ciliated protozoa (ciliophora) evolved multinucleate (syncytial) flatworms. These branched into five lines, one of which leads to the echinoderms and chordates. The remaining lines lead to most of the other phyla of the animal kingdom.

Which of the following best expresses the analogy between evolution and a bush?

A. Species is to evolution as bush is to branching.

B. Species is to branching as bush is to evolution.

C. Evolution is to species as bush is to branch viruses.

D. Evolution is to species as bush is to branches.

E. Evolution is to species as branches is to bush.

> **ANSWERS: 26-1 E, 26-2 A, 26-3 E, 26-4 B, 26-5 D.**

Check your answer and continue to the next reading passage.

Read the following passage and answer Questions 27–30.

A growing body of research on sharks and their relatives portrays these creatures as behaving in ways far more sophisticated and complex than was
(5) thought possible. Scientists are documenting elaborate social behaviors among these fish, including never-before-witnessed mating rituals that seem to be based on electrical signals.

(10) Compared to other fishes, sharks have huge brains. But because sharks are so difficult to study—they are dangerous, far-ranging, and usually inhabit murky waters—scientists only recently have
(15) accumulated enough data to even hint at their behavioral and sensory complexity. In one of the most surprising findings, a researcher discovered a new sense organ, located on top of certain sharks'
(20) heads. The organ is a sort of light-gathering "third eye," known in some prehistoric fishes, the lantern fishes, and at least one living reptile, the tuatara of New Zealand. Its precise function in the

GO ON TO THE NEXT PAGE

(25) six-gilled shark is still uncertain, though sensing light at the deep depths to which they dive is most likely.

Sharks are literally covered in sense or-
(30) gans. Over the last two decades, re-
searchers have found no fewer than four separate sensory systems to detect chemicals in the water. Past researchers have documented that sharks also have good vision and can see in color; they
(35) have directional hearing, and although they cannot hear notes much above mid-dle C, they can hear sounds below the threshold of human hearing.

But perhaps the most astounding sense
(40) possessed by sharks is their ability to sense electric fields. Elasmobranchs—sharks, skates, and rays—can detect fields so weak they cannot be measured by standard laboratory equipment. All
(45) live organisms, immersed in water, have a weak bioelectric field, a current gener-ated between biological membranes and the surrounding water. Elasmobranch fishes use electroreception to locate
(50) prey. Some scientists suspect that sharks, skates, and rays, sensing and in-terpreting the much larger voltage po-tentials created by salt-water currents moving through the earth's magnetic
(55) field, use this information to navigate.

Electroreception may also play a key role in the mating system of sharks and the one thousand other fishes in the same taxonomic group. The females use
(60) electroreception for some sort of social cues. Receptive females may be adver-tising their availability by congregating in large, highly visible, unburied piles; but unreceptive females, perhaps al-
(65) ready pregnant, may use electrorecep-tion to locate other buried females to hide from amorous males in buried ag-gregation. Field strength intensifies

when the fishes open their mouths.
(70) Literally, "heavy breathing" could en-hance a female's attraction.

27. The complexity of the shark has been underestimated for which of the following reasons?

  I. Sharks are a very ancient life form.

  II. Sharks are dangerous.

  III. Sharks rarely live in clear waters.

  A. II only

  B. I and II only

  C. I and III only

  D. II and III only

  E. I, II, and III

28. It can be inferred from the passage that female sharks hiding in groups from male sharks

  A. could not be found if they were buried in the sand.

  B. could be discovered by a male shark using his "third eye."

  C. would emit no bioelectrical signals.

  D. would be easier to detect by electroreception than a female shark hiding alone.

  E. would open their mouths as often as possible.

29. According to the passage, sharks may use their electroreceptive ability for all of the following EXCEPT to

  A. locate prey.

  B. navigate.

  C. gather light.

D. locate other sharks.

E. locate breeding partners.

30. Which of the following is most relevant to the research described in the passage?

A. Certain birds communicate by emitting cries pitched two octaves above middle C.

B. Certain migrating birds determine their location by detecting variations in the strength of the earth's magnetic field.

C. Migrating herds of wildebeest can reach their destination in spite of major changes in landscape from one year to the next.

D. Some migrating birds and insects appear to arrive at the same place on exactly the same day year after year.

E. Dogs are capable of hearing sounds at pitches inaudible to human ears.

ANSWERS: 27 **D**, 28 **D**, 29 **C**, 30 **B**.

If you answered **none** of the four reading questions **correctly, go to 31-1.**

If you answered **one** of the four reading questions **correctly, go to 31-2.**

If you answered **two** of the four reading questions **correctly, go to 31-3.**

If you answered **three** of the four reading questions **correctly, go to 31-4.**

If you answered **all four** of the reading questions **correctly, go to 31-5.**

31-1. <u>Irregardless of her physical beauty</u>, the judges did not vote for her to represent their state in the Miss America Pageant, but chose the candidate with superior musical abilities.

A. Irregardless of her physical beauty

B. In spite of her physical beauty

C. While her physical beauty was superb

D. No matter how extraordinary her physical appearance

E. Regardless how beautiful her physical appearance

31-2. <u>The defendant's refusal to discuss his whereabouts completely convinced the jury of his guilt</u>, even though so many other facts surrounding the crime indicated not only that he was entirely innocent but also that he had been "framed" by members of a local syndicate.

A. The defendant's refusal to discuss his whereabouts completely convinced the jury of his guilt

B. Refusing to completely discuss the defendant's whereabouts, the jury was completely convinced of his guilt

C. The defendant's refusal to complete a discussion of his whereabouts convinced the jury of his guilt

D. The defendant's refusal to discuss his complete whereabouts convinced the jury that he was guilty

E. Guilty in the eyes of the jury because his whereabouts had not been completely discussed.

GO ON TO THE NEXT PAGE

31-3. According to a report in the gossip columns, <u>the actor, along with his butler, bodyguard, chauffeur, two maids, and four dogs, are on board</u> the train bound for Cannes.

    A. the actor, along with his butler, bodyguard, chauffeur, two maids, and four dogs, are on board

    B. the actor and his butler and also his chauffeur, together with two maids and including four dogs, are on board

    C. the actor, along with his butler, bodyguard, chauffeur, two maids, and four dogs, is on board

    D. the actor, along with his butler, bodyguard, chauffeur, two maids, and four dogs are climbing onto

    E. the actor's butler, bodyguard, chauffeur, two maids, and four dogs are on board

31-4. Though the Foreign Office claimed the troops were sent to protect innocent civilians, <u>the principle reason for the British invasion was because</u> the sovereignty of British territory had been challenged.

    A. the principle reason for the British invasion was because

    B. the principle reason for the British invasion was that

    C. the principal reason for the British invasion was that

    D. the British invaded because

    E. principally, the British staged an invasion because

31-5. Most television is escapist, but <u>reading modern novels continually reminds many people</u> that we live in an age of lost faith and growing anxiety.

    A. reading modern novels continually reminds many people

    B. reading modern novels frequently reminds many people

    C. those who read modern novels continually realize

    D. those who continually read modern novels realize

    E. the reading of modern novels is what continually reminds many people

---

ANSWERS: 31-1 B, 31-2 A, 31-3 C, 31-4 C, 31-5 D.

If you answered 31-1 **incorrectly, go to 32-1.**
If you answered 31-1 **correctly, go to 32-2.**

If you answered 31-2 **incorrectly, go to 32-1.**
If you answered 31-2 **correctly, go to 32-3.**

If you answered 31-3 **incorrectly, go to 32-2.**
If you answered 31-3 **correctly, go to 32-4.**

If you answered 31-4 **incorrectly, go to 32-3.**
If you answered 31-4 **correctly, go to 32-5.**

If you answered 31-5 **incorrectly, go to 32-4.**
If you answered 31-5 **correctly, go to 32-5.**

32-1. <u>Because nuclear weapons had been scorned by so many liberal activists with the power to destroy the world,</u> both of the superpowers began to consider both the limitation and the reduction of their arsenals.

    A. Because nuclear weapons had been scorned by so many liberal activists with the power to destroy the world

B. World-destroying nuclear weapons had been scorned by many liberal activists

C. With the power to destroy the world, liberal activists had scorned nuclear weapons

D. Because nuclear weapons with the power to destroy the world had been scorned by so many liberal activists

E. Liberal activists scorning nuclear weapons

32-2. I'll never forget the tranquil desert resort <u>where having golfed, while I vacationed, in winter, when I was younger</u>.

A. where having golfed, while I vacationed, in winter, when I was younger

B. where I golfed, while having had vacationed in winter when I was younger

C. where I golfed while wintering, when I was younger

D. where I having had golf, while I vacationed in winter when I was younger

E. where I golfed while I vacationed in winter when I was younger

32-3. <u>Neither the director nor the investors in the second sequel predicts</u> that it will earn less money than the other two films, but they are disturbed by the box-office receipts on its opening weekend.

A. Neither the director nor the investors in the second sequel predicts

B. Neither the investors in the second sequel nor its director predicts

C. The director of the second sequel, along with its investors, predict

D. Neither the investors nor the directors of the second sequel predicts

E. About the second sequel, neither the director nor the investors predict

32-4. <u>By composing at the keyboard, the poetry of this century often illustrates a more purposeful alignment of lines and letters made possible by the machine itself.</u>

A. By composing at the keyboard, the poetry of this century often illustrates a more purposeful alignment of lines and letters made possible by the machine itself.

B. The poets of this century who compose at the keyboard often take advantage of the machine to arrange lines and letters more purposefully.

C. The keyboards of the poets of this century align lines and letters more purposefully.

D. With the keyboard as their means of composition, the poets of this century often align lines and letters more purposefully than the poets before the machine.

E. With the more purposeful alignment of lines and letters, the poets of this century rely on their machine often.

GO ON TO THE NEXT PAGE

333

32-5. <u>I will not object to him joining the fraternity</u> if he is willing to accept its social and academic obligations, to pay his fees on time, and to play on house athletic teams.

- A. I will not object to him joining the fraternity
- B. I do not object to his joining the fraternity
- C. I will make no objection to him joining the fraternity
- D. I do not object to him joining the fraternity
- E. I will not object to his joining the fraternity

ANSWERS: 32-1 **D**, 32-2 **E**, 32-3 **B**, 32-4 **B**, 32-5 **E**.

If you answered 32-1 **incorrectly, go to 33-1.**
If you answered 32-1 **correctly, go to 33-2.**

If you answered 32-2 **incorrectly, go to 33-1.**
If you answered 32-2 **correctly, go to 33-3.**

If you answered 32-3 **incorrectly, go to 33-2.**
If you answered 32-3 **correctly, go to 33-4.**

If you answered 32-4 **incorrectly, go to 33-3.**
If you answered 32-4 **correctly, go to 33-5.**

If you answered 32-5 **incorrectly, go to 33-4.**
If you answered 32-5 **correctly, go to 33-5.**

33-1. Beginning this fall, Latino and Asian students will not be allowed to transfer out of bilingual classes (that is, a program in which courses are given in a student's native language) until they pass strict competency tests in math, reading, and writing—as well as spoken English. The board and its supporters say this will protect children from being pushed out of bilingual programs before they are ready. They have hailed this as a victory for bilingual education.

The argument above would be most strengthened if the author were to explain

- A. how efficient the bilingual program is.
- B. how well staffed the bilingual program is.
- C. whether the community supports the bilingual program.
- D. whether any board members do not support the bilingual program.
- E. how the students feel about the bilingual program.

33-2. According to a recent study by the National Academy of Public Administration, postal patrons are regularly affronted by out-of-order stamp vending machines, branch post office lobbies locked at night, and 33-cent letters that take as long to get there as 8-cent letters did long ago.

Which of the following transitions probably begins a sentence critical of the argument in the passage?

- A. However
- B. In addition
- C. Despite
- D. In reality
- E. Therefore

33-3. Consumers are not so easily manipulated as they are often painted. They may know what they want, and what they want may be greatly different from what other people believe they need.

Which of the following statements, if true, most weakens the above argument?

A. Most people continue to buy the same brand of a product year after year.

B. Companies that advertise the most sell the most products.

C. Store shelves packed with a variety of different brands have the potential to confuse the consumer.

D. Most consumers know which brand they are going to buy before entering a store.

E. People who shop with others rarely argue with their companions.

33-4. Voltaire once said, "Common sense is not so common."

Which of the following most nearly parallels Voltaire's statement?

A. God must have loved the common man; he certainly made enough of them.

B. The common good is not necessarily best for everyone.

C. Jumbo shrimp may not actually be very big.

D. Good people may not necessarily have good sense.

E. Truth serum cannot contain the truth.

33-5. Beginning this fall, Latino and Asian students will not be allowed to transfer out of bilingual classes (that is, a program in which courses are given in a student's native language) until they pass strict competency tests in math, reading, and writing—as well as spoken English. The board and its supporters say this will protect children from being pushed out of bilingual programs before they are ready. They have hailed this as a victory for bilingual education.

Which of the following, if true, is the strongest criticism of the position of the board?

A. A foreign student may be quite competent in math without being competent in English.

B. Some native students already in English-speaking classes are unable to pass the competency tests.

C. Most foreign students require many months of practice and instruction before mastering English skills.

D. Many students prefer to transfer out of bilingual classes before they have achieved competency in English.

E. Holding back students will double the number of students in bilingual classes—twice as many Latino and Asian children isolated from the English-speaking mainstream.

ANSWERS: 33-1 **A**, 33-2 **A**, 33-3 **B**, 33-4 **C**, 33-5 **E**.

If you answered 33-1 **incorrectly, go to 34-1.**
If you answered 33-1 **correctly, go to 34-2.**

If you answered 33-2 **incorrectly, go to 34-1.**
If you answered 33-2 **correctly, go to 34-3.**

If you answered 33-3 **incorrectly, go to 34-2.**
If you answered 33-3 **correctly, go to 34-4.**

If you answered 33-4 **incorrectly, go to 34-3.**
If you answered 33-4 **correctly, go to 34-5.**

If you answered 33-5 **incorrectly, go to 34-4.**
If you answered 33-5 **correctly, go to 34-5.**

GO ON TO THE NEXT PAGE

34-1. *Senator:* Serving a few months as a Capitol page can be an exciting and enriching experience for high school students from around the country.

Student: If the circumstances are right.

The student's response suggests which of the following?

A. belligerence

B. acquiescence

C. skepticism

D. disbelief

E. ignorance

34-2. *Speaker 1:* The holy passion of friendship is of so sweet and steady and loyal and enduring a nature that it will last through a whole lifetime.

Speaker 2: If not asked to lend money.

The two speakers represent which of the following contrasting attitudes?

A. faith and despair

B. idealism and cynicism

C. idealism and optimism

D. socialism and capitalism

E. friendship and enmity

34-3. The shortsightedness of our government and our scientists has virtually nullified all of their great discoveries because of their failure to consider the environmental impact. The situation is far from hopeless, but our government agencies must become better watchdogs.

This argument fails to place any blame on

I. consumers who prefer new technology to clean air.

II. the ability of government to actually police industry.

III. legal loopholes which allow industry abuse of government regulations.

A. I only

B. II only

C. III only

D. I and III only

E. I, II, and III

34-4. Every speech intended to persuade either argues for a proposition or argues against a proposition. Any speech which argues for a proposition either presents all of the facts or presents a few of the facts, and any speech which argues against a proposition either presents all of the facts or presents a few of the facts. No speech which presents either all of the facts, a few of the facts, or just one fact is uninformative.

If the statements made in the passage above are true, it follows that

A. every speech presents either all of the facts or a few of the facts.

B. every speech intended to persuade presents many of the facts of the argument.

C. every uninformative speech presents none of the facts.

D. some uninformative speeches present either all of the facts or a few of the facts.

E. some speeches intended to persuade present neither all of the facts nor a few of the facts.

34-5. Every speech intended to persuade either argues for a proposition or argues against a proposition. Any speech which argues for a proposition either presents all of the facts or presents a few of the facts, and any speech which argues against a proposition either presents all of the facts or presents a few of the facts. No speech which presents either all of the facts, a few of the facts, or just one fact is uninformative.

Which of the following statements represents a valid conclusion based upon the passage above?

- **A.** No speech intended to persuade presents some of the facts.

- **B.** No informative speech both intends to persuade and contains a few of the facts.

- **C.** No informative speech both argues against a proposition and contains all of the facts.

- **D.** No informative speech is intended to persuade.

- **E.** No speech is both intended to persuade and uninformative.

ANSWERS: 34-1 C, 34-2 B, 34-3 D, 34-4 C, 34-5 E.

Check your answer and continue to the next reading passage.

Read the following passage and answer Questions 35–38.

Economic growth involves both benefits and costs. The desirability of increasing production has frequently been challenged in recent years, and some have
(5) even maintained that economic growth is merely a quantitative enlargement that has no human meaning or value.

However, economic growth is an increase in the capacity to produce goods
(10) and services that people want. Since the product of economic growth can be measured by its value to someone, it is important to ask whose standard of valuation counts.

(15) In the United States, the value of a product is what purchasers pay for it. This is determined by the purchasers' preferences combined with conditions of supply, which in turn reflect various other
(20) factors, such as natural and technological circumstances at any given time and the preferences of those who supply capital and labor. The value by which we measure a product synthesizes all
(25) these factors. Gross National Product (GNP) is the market value of the nation's total output of goods and services.

Gross National Product is not a perfect measure of all the activities involved in
(30) economic output. It does not account for deteriorations or improvements in the environment, even when they are incidental results of the production process. On the other hand, it does not count as
(35) "product" many benefits provided as side effects of the economic process; it does not include productive but unpaid work (such as that done by a homemaker); and it does not reckon with such
(40) other factors as the burdensomeness of work, the length of the work week, and so forth.

Nonetheless, the GNP concept makes an important contribution to our under-
(45) standing of how the economy is working. While it is not a complete measure of economic productivity and even less so of "welfare," the level and rate of increase of the GNP are clearly and posi-
(50) tively associated with what most people

GO ON TO THE NEXT PAGE

337

throughout the world see as an improvement in the quality of life. In the long run, the same factors result in a growing GNP and in other social benefits: size

(50) and competence of population, state of knowledge, amount of capital, and the effectiveness with which these are combined and utilized.

35. The main purpose of the passage is to

A. define the limitations of using GNP to measure the nation's well-being.

B. contrast the American and the European GNPs.

C. argue for the value of increased economic output.

D. explain the disadvantages of measuring the quality of life using a scale of material affluence.

E. define Gross National Product.

36. The rhetorical purpose of the third paragraph of the passage (beginning on line 28) is to

I. anticipate objections to what the GNP fails to take into account.

II. cite examples of "products" the GNP ought to include.

III. develop the definition of paragraph two with specific details.

A. I only

B. II only

C. III only

D. I and II only

E. I, II, and III

37. We can infer from the passage that of the following, the factor that does NOT influence the growth of the GNP is

A. the condition of the population.

B. a dependence on spiritual values.

C. the capital available in the country.

D. knowledge related to production of goods and services.

E. the efficiency of the production process.

38. A critic of the limitations of the measurements of the GNP might cite its failure to consider all of the following EXCEPT

A. the steady increase in American workers' leisure time.

B. cooperative baby-sitting projects among parents with young children.

C. the widespread existence of chemicals in American rivers.

D. the value of the time a salaried stock broker spends on research.

E. the valuation of family household management.

ANSWERS: 35 E, 36 A, 37 B, 38 D.

If you answered **none** of the four reading questions **correctly, go to 39-1.**

If you answered **one** of the four reading questions **correctly, go to 39-2.**

If you answered **two** of the four reading questions **correctly, go to 39-3.**

If you answered **three** of the four reading questions **correctly, go to 39-4.**

If you answered all **four** of the reading questions **correctly, go to 39-5.**

39-1. The typical holiday shopper, although seduced by row upon row of novelty gifts, tend to purchase more practical items these days because he or she realizes that frivolous gadgets are often cheaply made.

- **A.** The typical holiday shopper, although seduced by row upon row of novelty gifts, tend to purchase more practical

- **B.** As a typical holiday shopper, the tendency to purchase row upon row of novelty gifts is won over by the purchase of more practical

- **C.** Typically, the holiday shopper who is attracted to novelty gifts tends to remain practical with

- **D.** The typical holiday shopper, although seduced by row upon row of novelty gifts, tends to purchase more practical

- **E.** The typical holiday shopper, although seduced by row upon row of novelty gifts, tends to purchase the more practical

39-2. The All-Star Game signals the middle of the baseball season and reminds the losing teams that the time for them to improve their playing is running out.

- **A.** The All-Star Game signals the middle of the baseball season

- **B.** With double significance, the All-Star Game occurs midway through

- **C.** The baseball season is divided in half by the All-Star Game

- **D.** The baseball All-Star Game signals the middle of the season

- **E.** With the All-Star Game, half the season is over

39-3. Contrary to the popularly held opinion, painting is a multifaceted, versatile, and a field in which a great deal of artistic diversity is possible.

- **A.** multifaceted, versatile, and a field in which a great deal of artistic diversity is possible.

- **B.** field in which a lot of multifaceted, versatile artistry is possible

- **C.** multifaceted field with versatility and diversity also possible

- **D.** multifaceted, versatile, and artistically diversified field

- **E.** field of multifaceted versatility and diversified artistry.

39-4. On arriving at Dulles International Airport, his friends met him and took him immediately to his speaking engagement in Springfield.

- **A.** On arriving at Dulles International Airport, his friends met him and took him immediately to his speaking engagement

- **B.** Arriving at Dulles International Airport, his friends who met him immediately took him to his speaking engagement

- **C.** When he arrived at Dulles International Airport, his friends met him and took him immediately to his speaking engagement

- **D.** When he arrived at Dulles International Airport, he was taken immediately to his speaking engagement.

- **E.** After arriving at Dulles International Airport, he was immediately taken to his speaking engagement.

GO ON TO THE NEXT PAGE

39-5. <u>We who graduated from high school in the Unites States in the early '60s were</u> caught in the middle of the crisis in education created by the Soviet Union's "Sputnik" success.

    A. We who graduated from high school in the United States in the early '60s were

    B. We, who graduated from high school in the United States in the early '60s, were

    C. We who then graduated high school in the United States in the early '60s were

    D. Those of us who then graduated from high school in the United States in the early '60s were

    E. We high school graduates who were in the United States in the early '60s were

---

ANSWERS: 39-1 **D**, 39-2 **A**, 39-3 **D**, 39-4 **C**, 39-5 **A**.

If you answered 39-1 **incorrectly, go to 40-1.**
If you answered 39-1 **correctly, go to 40-2.**

If you answered 39-2 **incorrectly, go to 40-1.**
If you answered 39-2 **correctly, go to 40-3.**

If you answered 39-3 **incorrectly, go to 40-2.**
If you answered 39-3 **correctly, go to 40-4.**

If you answered 39-4 **incorrectly, go to 40-3.**
If you answered 39-4 **correctly, go to 40-5.**

If you answered 39-5 **incorrectly, go to 40-4.**
If you answered 39-5 **correctly, go to 40-5.**

40-1. By leaving camp an hour before sunrise, the tourists in the Land Rover were able to catch sight of a lion and his mate <u>laying low in the tall jungle grass</u> waiting for the opportunity to capture an unwary antelope.

    A. laying low in the tall jungle grass

    B. the tall jungle grass concealing their low-lying bodies,

    C. that laid low in the tall jungle grass

    D. lying low in the tall jungle grass

    E. was laying in the tall jungle grass

40-2. When the Republican Party was the minority party, <u>its ability to win a presidential election was determined by the number of Democratic and independent voters it attracts</u>.

    A. its ability to win a presidential election was determined by the number of Democratic and independent voters it attracts

    B. its ability to win a presidential election is determined by the number of Democratic and independent voters it attracts

    C. its ability to win a presidential election has been determined by the number of Democratic and independent voters it attracts

    D. the number of Democratic and independent voters it attracts determines its ability to win a presidential election

    E. the number of Democratic and independent voters it attracted determined its ability to win a presidential election

40-3. The boundaries of the Pleasant Valley School District <u>have and will continue to include</u> the small cities of Millerton, Cedarville, Granite, and Homersfield.

   A. have and will continue to include

   B. have included and will continue to include

   C. has included and will continue to include

   D. has and will continue to include

   E. include and will include

40-4. One question haunted the swindled, penniless investor: <u>What should his fortune have been if he had not been lured into that last, fateful investment?</u>

   A. What should his fortune have been if he had not been lured into that last, fateful investment?

   B. What will his fortune have been if he were not lured into that last, fateful investment?

   C. What would his fortune have been if he had not been lured into that last, fateful investment?

   D. What could his fortune have been had not he been lured into that last, fateful investment?

   E. What would his fortune be if he had only resisted the lure of that last fateful investment?

40-5. The desert <u>canyon, which in spring had appeared lush with scrub oak and blooming cacti, but grew</u> brown and sere as the hot August winds continued.

   A. canyon, which in spring had appeared lush with scrub oak and blooming cacti, but grew

   B. canyon had appeared lush with scrub oak and blooming cacti and grew

   C. canyon which in spring had appeared lush with scrub oak and blooming cacti grows

   D. canyon in the spring appeared lush with scrub oak and blooming cacti, but has grown

   E. canyon, which in spring had appeared lush with scrub oak and blooming cacti, grew

ANSWERS: 40-1 D, 40-2 E, 40-3 B, 40-4 C, 40-5 E.

If you answered 40-1 **incorrectly, go to 41-1.**
If you answered 40-1 **correctly, go to 41-2.**

If you answered 40-2 **incorrectly, go to 41-1.**
If you answered 40-2 **correctly, go to 41-3.**

If you answered 40-3 **incorrectly, go to 41-2.**
If you answered 40-3 **correctly, go to 41-4.**

If you answered 40-4 **incorrectly, go to 41-3.**
If you answered 40-4 **correctly, go to 41-5.**

If you answered 40-5 **incorrectly, go to 41-4.**
If you answered 40-5 **correctly, go to 41-5.**

GO ON TO THE NEXT PAGE

Verbal Section

41-1. Which of the following most logically completes this passage?

Several of the survivors discussed their dilemma. They could remain on the island and attempt to survive as best they knew how. Or they could attempt to escape, using the resources available to them. None of the group wished to venture away from their uncertain sanctuary, but all of them knew that help would be a long time coming. Their discussions were thus _____.

   A. futile, arbitrary, and capricious

   B. limited by their imagination and resolve

   C. dampened by a sense of impending doom

   D. possible, but by no means successful

   E. courageous and honorable

41-2. Aristotle said that art represents "general truths" about human nature. Our city councilman is arguing in favor of the artistry—a giant mural in front of a Jeep dealership, portraying a variety of four-wheel-drive vehicles. He cites Aristotle's conception of art as his support.

The passage above raises which of the following questions?

   A. Can a city councilman understand Aristotle?

   B. Which general truths about human nature does a four-wheel-drive mural NOT represent?

   C. Could Aristotle have predicted a modern society filled with sophisticated machines?

   D. To what extent are four-wheel-drive vehicles representative of a general advance in modern technology?

   E. What "general truth" about human nature does a mural of four-wheel-drive vehicles represent?

41-3. Unfortunately, only 11 percent of the driving public uses regular seat belts. Automatic restraints are the answer, and the quicker they are required, the sooner highways deaths will be reduced.

The author's conclusion is based upon which of the following assumptions?

   A. Only 11 percent of the driving public cares about passengers' lives.

   B. The use of restraints reduces highway deaths.

   C. Regular seat belts are inadequate safety devices.

   D. It is unfortunate that 89 percent of the driving public does not use regular seat belts.

   E. Highway deaths occur often enough so that reducing them is a necessity.

41-4. The $464 million "reserve" in the budget adopted by the legislature in June turns out to have been based mainly on wishful thinking. Because of tax cuts approved by voters on the June ballot, along with the continuing economic slump and other events affecting income and expenses, the actual reserve in prospect may be as low as $7 million.

The author is probably leading to which of the following conclusions?

A. These facts warrant an investigation into who squandered $457 million.

B. A reserve in the budget is not so necessary as we might wish it to be.

C. The legislature would be wise not to add any new spending to the budget adopted in June.

D. The economic slump will probably not last much longer, but while it does the legislature must adjust the budget accordingly.

E. Legislative budgets are typically careless and unheeding of variable factors which may affect their accuracy.

41-5. According to a recent study by the National Academy of Public Administration, postal patrons are regularly affronted by out-of-order stamp vending machines, branch post office lobbies locked at night, and 33-cent letters that take as long to get there as 8-cent letters did long ago.

Which of the following, if true, would weaken the implication of one of the writer's observations.

A. Most out-of-order vending machines are located in rundown neighborhoods.

B. Late-night vandalism has plagued post offices nationwide.

C. Although postage rates have risen, the cost of first class mail is still cheaper in the United States than anywhere else.

D. As a public corporation, the Postal Service has increased its capital assets by $3 billion.

E. When stamps cost 8 cents, most letters reached their destination within 24 hours.

ANSWERS: 41-1 **C**, 41-2 **E**, 41-3 **B**, 41-4 **C**, 41-5 **E**.

Verbal Section

IF YOU FINISH BEFORE TIME IS CALLED, CHECK YOUR WORK ON THIS SECTION ONLY. DO NOT WORK ON ANY OTHER SECTION IN THE TEST.

CHARTING AND ANALYZING YOUR TEST RESULTS

The first step in analyzing your results is to chart your answers. Use the charts on the following pages to do so and to spot your strengths and weaknesses. Complete the process of evaluating your essays and analyzing problems in each area for the practice test. Reexamine your results for trends in types of errors (repeated errors) or poor results in specific subject areas. This reexamination and analysis is of tremendous importance in helping you maximize your score. Be sure also to carefully read the answers and explanations that follow these charts.

Analytical Writing Assessment

Analyze your responses using the following charts. Then estimate your score. (See the explanation of characteristics of responses at each score level in the chapter on The Analytical Writing Assessment, Part II.)

Analysis of an Issue

Questions	Completely	Partially	No
1. Does the response focus on the assigned topic and cover all of the tasks?			
2. Does the response show an understanding of the complexity of the issue?			
3. Does the response show cogent reasoning and logical position development?			
4. Are there sufficient relevant persuasive supporting details?			
5. Is the response well organized?			
6. Does the response show a command of standard written English?			

Analysis of an Argument

Questions	Completely	Partially	No
1. Does the response focus on the assigned topic and cover all of the tasks?			
2. Does the response carefully analyze the important weaknesses of the argument?			
3. Does the response show cogent reasoning and logical development?			
4. Are there sufficient relevant supporting details of the critique?			
5. Is the response well organized?			
6. Does the response show a command of standard written English?			

Score	Level
6	excellent
5	good
4	competent
3	limited
2	weak
1	poor

Quantitative Section

On the chart that follows, draw a small square around the problems you answered correctly and a small circle around the ones you missed. As you follow the path of your problems, be sure to mark the right/wrong box to the left of each question. (You may wish to use a highlighter to graphically follow your path.)

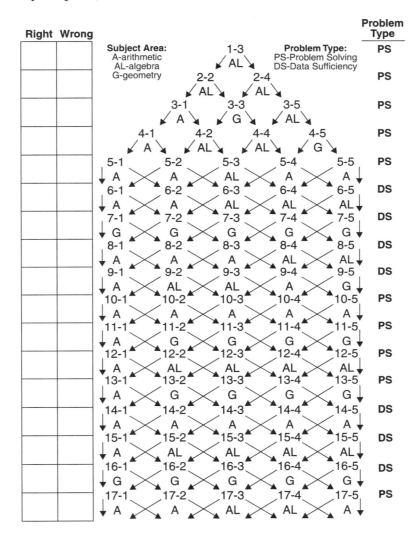

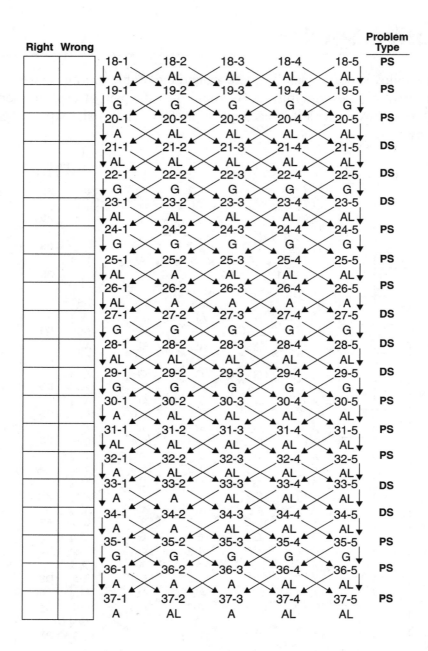

Now that you have completed charting your path, you can tally your responses and review and analyze the results with the following charts.

Average Level Correct

Although the GMAT CAT uses very precise measures to calculate your score, the following calculations will give you a very general approximation of the average level you got right. It is important that you try to finish all 37 questions, and the following score chart assumes that you have done so.

Number Correct	×	Level of Difficulty
Level 1 _____	×	1 = _____
Level 2 _____	×	2 = _____
Level 3 _____	×	3 = _____
Level 4 _____	×	4 = _____
Level 5 _____	×	5 = _____

Total = _____ ÷ 37 = _____
(Average Level)

Type of Problem Missed

Identifying the type of problem you most often miss will help you use your study time efficiently.

	Problem Solving		Data Sufficiency	
	Right	Wrong	Right	Wrong
Arithmetic				
Algebra				
Geometry				
Totals				

Verbal Section

On the chart that follows, draw a small square around the questions you answered correctly and a small circle around the ones you missed. As you follow the path of your questions, be sure to mark the right/wrong box to the left of each question. (You may wish to use a highlighter to graphically follow your path.)

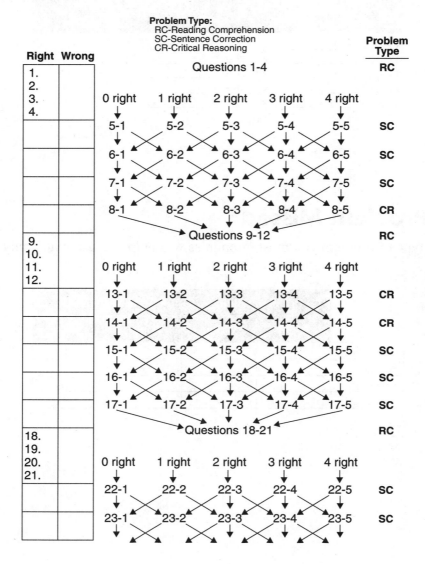

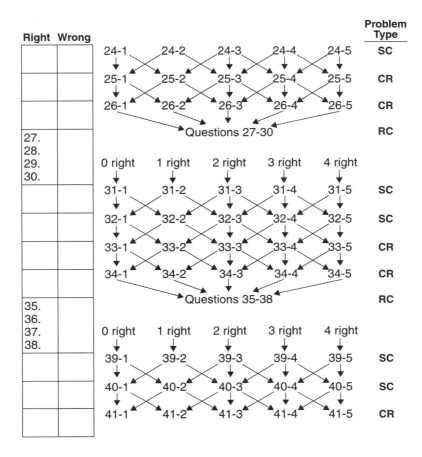

Right	Wrong
27.	
28.	
29.	
30.	
35.	
36.	
37.	
38.	

Now that you have completed charting your path, you can tally your responses and review and analyze the results with the following charts.

Average Level Correct

Although the GMAT uses very precise measures to calculate your score, the following calculations will give you a very general approximation of the average level you got right.

Note: Count all Reading Comprehension questions as Level 3 questions.

It is important that you try to finish all 41 questions, and the following score chart assumes that you have done so.

	Number Correct	×	Level of Difficulty	
Level 1	_____	×	1 =	_____
Level 2	_____	×	2 =	_____
Level 3	_____	×	3 =	_____
Level 4	_____	×	4 =	_____
Level 5	_____	×	5 =	_____
			Total = _____ ÷ 41 =	_____
				(Average Level)

Type of Question Missed

Identifying the type of question you most often miss will help you use your study time efficiently.

	Possible	Right	Wrong
RC	20		
SC	13		
CR	8		
Totals	41		

Where to Go from Here

Now that you have completed the chart and analyzed your results, you should return to the simulated computer-adaptive test and work all of the problems in an organized manner. First work all of the problems at the 1 level, that is 4-1, 5-1, 6-1, 7-1, and so on. Review the answer to each problem after you work it. Having attempted and reviewed the simpler problems, next work and review all of the Level 2 problems, that is, 4-2, 5-2, 6-2, 7-2, and so on.

Continue this process until you have worked all of the problems available on this simulated exam. Starting with the easier problems helps you build a basis for your review. Following this process also helps you prepare to attack the more difficult problems.

ANSWERS AND EXPLANATIONS FOR THE PRACTICE TEST

Quantitative Section

1-3. **B.** Let x be the number of $4 Frisbees. Then $64 - x$ is the number of $3 Frisbees. This gives the equation $3(64 - x) + 4(x) = 204$. Solving gives

$$192 - 3x + 4x = 204$$
$$192 + x = 204$$
$$x = 12$$

Therefore, the fewest number of $4 Frisbees is 12. Note that you could also work from the answers by substituting in each possibility.

2-2. **B.** Solving the first equation for x,

$$\tfrac{2}{x} = 4$$
$$2 = 4x$$
$$\tfrac{2}{4} = x$$

Therefore, $\tfrac{1}{2} = x$

Now solving the second equation for y

$$\tfrac{2}{y} = 8$$
$$2 = 8y$$
$$\tfrac{2}{8} = y$$

Therefore, $\tfrac{1}{4} = y$

Substituting these values for $x - y$ gives,

$$\tfrac{1}{2} - \tfrac{1}{4} = \tfrac{2}{4} - \tfrac{1}{4} = \tfrac{1}{4}$$

Therefore, $x - y = \tfrac{1}{4}$, and the correct answer is **B.**

2-4. **D.** Set up the equation as follows:

Let t be the length of time it will take the plane to overtake the bus; then $t + 4$ is the time that the bus has traveled before the plane starts. The distance that the bus has traveled by 1 p.m. is $50(t + 4)$, since distance equals rate times time ($d = rt$). The distance the plane will travel is $300t$. Now setting these two equal to each other (they will have to travel the same distance for one to overtake the other) gives $50(t + 4) = 300t$. Solve the equation as follows:

$$50(t + 4) = 300t$$
$$50t + 200 = 300t$$

$$200 = 250t$$

Therefore, $\frac{4}{5} = t$

$\frac{4}{5}$ of an hour ($\frac{4}{5} \times 60$) is 48 minutes. Therefore, it will take 48 minutes for the plane to overtake the bus, and since the plane is starting at 1 p.m., it will overtake the bus at 1:48 p.m.

3-1. **E.** Since this is an approximation, round off

$\dfrac{\text{Venus weight of 182}}{\text{Earth weight of 207}}$ to $\dfrac{180}{200}$, which is 90%

3-3. **D.** If cube A has side 2, then the surface area is 24 square units, since the area of one face is 2×2, or 4, and there are 6 equal faces to a cube. If cube B has side 1, then the surface area is 6 square units, since the area of one face is 1×1, or 1, and there are 6 faces. Therefore, the ratio could be 24:6, or 4:1.

3-5. **B.** If each could save $7,200, then all three could save $21,600. Let x stand for the amount each of the five business people invests. Then the difference between the five and three investments would be

$$5x - 3x = 21,600$$
$$2x = 21,600$$
$$x = 10,800$$

Therefore, each of the five invests $10,800, and the total investment is $5 \times 10,800$, or $54,000.

Note that answers **C**, **D**, and **E** are not reasonable. You can also use one of the original investor's savings and work from the equation $\left(\frac{1}{3}x\right) - \left(\frac{1}{5}x\right) = 7,200$.

4-1. **C.** This problem is most easily completed by rearranging and approximating as follows:

$$\frac{69.28 \times 0.004}{0.03} \cong 69 \times \frac{0.004}{0.03} \cong 69 \times 0.1 = 6.9$$

which is the only reasonably close answer to 9.2.

4-2. **D.** This problem is most easily answered by dividing 318 by 3 to get 106, which must be the middle number; therefore, the largest is 108. You can also use the equation

smallest	middle	largest
(2x)	+ (2x + 2)	+ (2x + 4) = 318

and work from there.

4-4. **C.** Let x be the amount invested at 5%. Then $1,000 - x$ is the amount invested at 6%. This gives the equation $5(x) + 6(1,000 - x) = 5,300$. Solving gives

$$5x + 6,000 - 6x = 5,300$$
$$6,000 - x = 5,300$$
$$-x = -700$$

$$x = 700$$

Therefore, $700 was invested at 5%.

Note that answers **A, D,** and **E** are not reasonable.

4-5. **D.** Since *ABCD* is a rhombus, all sides are equal; therefore, $BC = CD = 6$, and $BC + CD = 12$. $AB = 6$, minus $AE \cong 4$ leaves $6 - 4 \cong 2$, which is the approximate length of *BE*. Adding $12 + 2 = 14$ gives the distance around the rhombus that will be traveled. Now using the formula for circumference of a circle $= 2\pi r$ or πd leaves 6π as the circumference of the complete circle. Because the inscribed angle is 45°, arc *DE* is 90° (an inscribed angle is half of the arc it intercepts). This 90° will not be traveled because it is in the interior of the figure; therefore, only 270° of the 360° in the complete circle will be traveled, or ¾ of the circle. $¾ \times 6\pi = 9\pi/2$. This added to the original 14 gives answer **D:** $14 + (9\pi/2)$, or $14 + {}^9\!/_2\pi$.

5-1. **C.** There are eight different arrangements, as follows:

red-red-red	green-green-green
red-green-green	green-red-green
green-green-red	green-red-red
red-green-red	red-red-green

5-2. **C.** Since two-thirds of the students are boys, you have $\frac{2}{3}(36) = 24$ boys in the class.

Out of the 24 boys in the class, three-fourths of them are under 6 feet tall or $\frac{3}{4}(24) = 18$ boys under 6 feet tall.

5-3. **C.** Using the formula,

$$\binom{n}{r} = \frac{n!}{r!(n-r)!}$$

where *n* is the total number of individuals and *r* is the number needed in each group, you can solve for $n = 6$ and $r = 3$:

$$\binom{6}{3} = \frac{6!}{3!(3!)} = \frac{6 \times 5 \times 4 \times 3 \times 2 \times 1}{3 \times 2 \times 1 \times 3 \times 2 \times 1} = 20$$

Thus there are 20 possible combinations: 123, 124, 125, 126, 134, 135, 136, 145, 146, 156, 234, 235, 236, 245, 246, 256, 345, 346, 356, 456.

5-4. **C.** The maximum number of combinations is $3 \times 3 \times 2 = 18$. However, because the woman won't wear her pink blouse and green skirt with either of the two pairs of shoes, two of the combinations are excluded. She could wear $18 - 2 = 16$ different combinations.

5-5. **B.** If only 9 are picked out, it is possible to get 3 of each color. Thus the tenth is necessary to be sure of four pairs.

6-1. **D.** Either statement enables you to calculate the required precipitation, *P*.

(1) $P = 35 - 33$

(2) $P = 35(1 - 0.943)$

6-2. **E.** The first statement implies that a tock equals 30 minutes, but the duration of a tick is indefinite.

6-3. **A.** The first statement translates to $Y = X - 1$ and $Z = \frac{1}{2}X$. Given that $X + Y + Z = 19$, substitution yields $X + X - 1 + \frac{1}{2}X = 19$, so $X = 8$. From statement (1), $Y = 7$ and $Z = 4$.

6-4. **B.** From statement (2), let x equal the number of adults and $3x$ equal the number of children.

$$3x + x = 24$$

$$4x = 24$$

$$x = 6 = \text{number of adults needed}$$

Statement (1) gives a ratio between boys and girls, but no exact numbers can be determined, so the number of adults cannot be determined.

6-5. **E.** The problem offers no information concerning the number of patients who stayed more than one hour and were seen by only one doctor.

7-1. **B.** Since $\overline{AO}$ is perpendicular to $\overline{OB}$, AOB is a right angle.

7-2. **B.** Since the three angles sum to a straight angle, $c = 180° - 131° = 49°$.

7-3. **A.** Because vertical angles are equal, $a = d$. From statement (1) you can find that angle $a = 41°$. In the figure, angles a and e are supplementary, so angle $e = 180 - 41 = 139°$.

7-4. **A.** Area $BCDE$ equals triangle ACD minus triangle ABE. From the sketch it is clear that the two triangles are similar because their respective sides are parallel. From statement (1) you can determine that the base and height of ABE are half of those of ACD; therefore, the area of ABE is one quarter that of ACD. Consequently, the area $BCDE$ is three times the area of ABE.

7-5. **D.** The definition of a rhombus stipulates the equality of its four sides. The first statement reveals that the two triangles are equilateral, so all the angles must be 60°. From the second statement, angle $CBD = 60°$ (by alternate interior angles); triangle BCD is isosceles with $BC = CD$ (from the definition of a rhombus), so angle $BDC = CBD = 60°$; subtracting those angles from 180° leaves 60° for angle BCD.

8-1. **C.** Statement (1) implies that the three cameras sell for a total price of $3 \times \$172 = \$516$. Statement (2) implies that two of the cameras each sell for $\frac{1}{2}(\$332) = \$166$. The third camera must sell for $\$516 - \$332 = \$184$.

8-2. **E.** To calculate the average, you require the sum of the ten numbers. Statement (1) offers the sum of nine. You do not know whether the number cited in statement (2) is one of those nine.

8-3. **A.** Because the average is the sum divided by 5, the sum must be the average times 5. Therefore, the sum is zero.

8-4. **E.** From statement (1), $x < 5$, and from statement (2), $y < 6$, so $xy < 30$. Therefore, the product may or may not exceed 27.

8-5. **D.** The first statement implies that x is a positive number but less than 1. The second statement yields $x < \frac{1}{3}$. Either statement answers the question that, yes, x is less than 2.

9-1. **A.** From statement (1), Toni types $3,150/60 = 52\frac{1}{2}$ words per minute.

9-2. **C.** The problem may be solved using both statements. Emily and Joan's joint rate of counting is $\frac{1}{26}$ of the books per hour. If y is Emily's rate, then Joan's rate is $2y$, twice as fast. The individual rates sum to the joint rate:

$2y + y = \frac{1}{26}$

$y = \frac{1}{78}$ Emily's rate

$2y = \frac{1}{39}$ Joan's rate

Because rates are the reciprocals of the times, *and conversely,* it would take Joan 39 hours (the reciprocal of her rate) to tally the books alone.

9-3. **C.** Remember that rate = 1/time, so Sue's rate = $1/s$, where s is the time for her to paint the room. Since

$$\begin{array}{ccccc} \text{Sue's rate} & + & \text{Bob's rate} & = & \text{joint rate} \\ \dfrac{1}{s} & + & \dfrac{1}{3\frac{1}{4}} & = & \dfrac{1}{2} \end{array}$$

which can be solved for $s = 5.2$ hours.

9-4. **C.** To solve the problem, it is necessary to know the *total* number of beverage cans manufactured in both 1990 and 1995. Graph (1) has the data for aluminum cans, and graph (2) has the data for steel cans. The data from the two graphs must be added together.

9-5. **C.** In the trapezoid, $\overline{BC}$ is evidently parallel to $\overline{AD}$. The first statement reveals that triangle ACD is a 6-8-10 right triangle, with angle $ADC = 90°$. Because $\overline{BC}$ is parallel to $\overline{AD}$, angle BCD must also equal 90°. Consider triangle ABC with base $\overline{BC}$. The altitude to vertex A equals $\overline{CD}$ because $\overline{CD}$ is perpendicular to $\overline{BC}$. Then the area = $\frac{1}{2}bh = \frac{1}{2}(\overline{BC})(\overline{CD}) = \frac{1}{2} \times 7 \times 6 = 21$.

10-1. **C.** Since the reduction was approximately 13 percent, the 195 professors are 87 percent of the original number.

$195 = 0.87n$

$n = \dfrac{195}{0.87} \cong 224$

10-2. **C.** In this type of problem (weighted average), you must multiply the number of students times their respective scores and divide this total by the number of students as follows:

$$\begin{array}{rl} 15 \times 80\% = & 1,200 \\ \underline{10 \times 90\% =} & \underline{\ \ \ 900} \\ 25 & 2,100 \end{array}$$

Now divide 25 into 2,100. This gives an average of 84%; therefore, the correct answer is **C.**

10-3. **C.** If the average of 9 numbers is 7, then the sum of these numbers must be 9×7, or 63.

If the average of 7 numbers is 9, then the sum of these numbers must be 7×9, or 63.

The sum of all 16 numbers must be $63 + 63$, or 126.

Therefore, the average of all 16 numbers must be

$126 \div 16 = {}^{126}/_{16} = 7^{14}/_{16} = 7^{7}/_{8}$

Notice that answers **A** and **E** are not reasonable.

10-4. **C.** Look at total percentage points.

$(.20)(.80) + (.50)(.60) + (.30)(.40) = .5800 = 58\%$

$.1600 \quad + \quad .3000 \quad + \quad .1200 \quad = .5800 = 58\%$

Notice that answers **A** and **B** are not reasonable.

10-5. **B.** Begin by using an arbitrary number, say 100, for the total number of students in the class. Therefore, there are 40 men and 60 women. Of the 60 women, 30%, or 18, are science majors. Since non-science majors make up 80% of the class, then there are 80 non-science majors and 20 science majors. You already know that 18 science majors are women, so the remaining 2 science majors must be men. Among the 40 men, there are 2 science majors, so 5% of the men are science majors.

11-1. **E.** First change 2 hours into 120 minutes. (Always get a common unit of measurement.)

Then dividing 120 by ⅔ gives

$^{60}\cancel{120} \times \dfrac{3}{\cancel{2}_{1}} = 180$

The correct answer is **E,** 180 items. Notice that choices **A** and **B** are not reasonable.

11-2. **D.** Since the large square has side 4 cm, then its area must be 16. By careful grouping of areas, you can see that there are four unshaded smaller squares and four shaded smaller squares (match the shaded parts to four squares). Therefore one half of the area is shaded, or 8 sq cm.

11-3. **C.** The area of triangle $MNP = \frac{1}{2}bh = \frac{1}{2}(MP)(MN)$.

Since triangle MNP is a right triangle, the Pythagorean theorem says

$$c^2 = a^2 + b^2$$
$$(NP)^2 = (MP)^2 + (MN)^2$$
$$26^2 = 24^2 + (MN)^2$$
$$676 = 576 + (MN)^2$$
$$(MN)^2 = 100$$
$$MN = \sqrt{100} = 10$$

So the area of $MNP = \frac{1}{2}(MN)(MP)$

$$= \frac{1}{2}(10)(24)$$
$$= 120$$

11-4. B. The following diagram shows Manny's bicycling path and Irv's walking path.

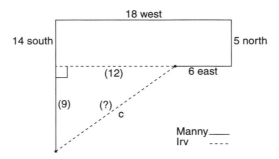

Manny traveled 43 miles at 10 miles per hour, so it took him 4.3 hours. The distance Irv travels is calculated by subtracting travel in opposite directions and using the Pythagorean theorem. 6 east and 18 west leaves 12 west, while 5 north and 14 south leaves 9 south. The right triangle has legs of 9 and 12. Therefore, the hypotenuse must be 15 (3:4:5 ratio), or using the theorem,

$$a^2 + b^2 = c^2$$
$$9^2 + 12^2 = c^2$$
$$81 + 144 = c^2$$
$$225 = c^2$$
$$15 = c$$

Irv must travel 15 miles at 5 miles per hour, or 3 hours. Since they both start at the same time, Irv arrives over one hour earlier than Manny.

11-5. B. Since the surface area of side *ABFE* is 16, then each side is 4. Now use the Pythagorean theorem to find the length of the diagonal that is also the length of the rectangle.

$$4^2 + 4^2 = AH^2$$
$$16 + 16 = AH^2$$
$$32 = AH^2$$
$$\sqrt{32} = AH$$

Simplifying

$$\sqrt{32} = \sqrt{16 + 2} = \sqrt{16} \times \sqrt{2} = 4\sqrt{2}$$

Now multiplying length times width gives

$$4 \times 4\sqrt{2} = 16\sqrt{2}$$

Notice that you might recognize the ratio of 45°:45°:90° triangle as $1 : 1 : \sqrt{2}$ and find the diagonal quickly using $4 : 4 : 4\sqrt{2}$.

12-1. E. First simplify 3^3, which is $3 \times 3 \times 3 = 27$. Then simplify $(\frac{1}{3})^2$, which is $\frac{1}{3} \times \frac{1}{3} = \frac{1}{9}$. Now divided 27 by $\frac{1}{9}$, which is the same as $27 \times \frac{9}{1} = 243$.

12-2. A. You solve for y as follows:

$$x = \frac{1+y}{y}$$
$$xy = 1+y$$
$$xy - y = 1$$
$$y(x-1) = 1$$
$$y = \frac{1}{x-1}$$

12-3. E. Since the five choices all have a number of 1, the denominator of the correct choice times $(x-4)$ will equal $(2x^2 - 10x + 8)$. That denominator may be found by dividing polynomials:

$$
\begin{array}{r}
2x - 2 \\
x - 4 \overline{)\,2x^2 - 10x + 8} \\
\underline{2x^2 - 8x} \\
-2x + 8 \\
\underline{-2x + 8}
\end{array}
$$

12-4. E. Factoring both numerator and denominator of the left side gives

$$\frac{\overset{1}{\cancel{(x+2)}}(x+3)}{\underset{1}{\cancel{(x+2)}}(x-2)} = \frac{3}{2}$$

Thus $\dfrac{x+3}{x-2} = \dfrac{3}{2}$

Cross multiplying gives

$$2(x+3) = 3(x-2)$$
$$2x + 6 = 3x - 6$$
$$6 = x - 6$$
$$12 = x$$

12-5. D. If one root of the equation is 10, then the factored form of $x^2 - 5x + m = 0$ is $(x - 10)(x + ?) = 0$. Since the middle term of the quadratic is $-5x$, then ? must be 5. So the factored version is $(x - 10)(x + 5)$. To check this, multiply the means and extremes together and add them:

$$\overbrace{(x - 10)\underbrace{(x}_{-10x} + 5)}^{+5x}$$

Therefore, m has the value of -10×5, or -50. But the problem asks for $m + 3$, which is $-50 + 3$, or -47.

13-1. **D.** The net profit is 25%, since $12 is 25% of $48. Now add in 15% for overhead and you have 25% + 15% = 40%.

13-2. **E.** First find the area of the shaded region. The difference of the outer rectangle (6 × 12 = 72) and the inner rectangle (2 × 3 = 6) is 66 square feet. Since it takes 24 2-inch x 3-inch tiles to cover one square foot, the correct answer is 24 × 66 = 1,584.

13-3. **E.** The horizontal length of x cannot be determined because there is no indication of the overlapping length of the rectangle to the left of x. If x cannot be determined, then $x + y$ cannot be determined.

13-4. **A.** Ratio of diameters = ratio of radii.

$$\frac{d_1}{d_2} = \frac{r_1}{r_2} = \frac{30}{100} = \frac{3}{10}$$

Ratio of area = (ratio of radii)^2.

$$\frac{A_1}{A_2} = \left(\frac{r_1}{r_2}\right)^2$$

$$\frac{A_1}{A_2} = \frac{9}{100}$$

So the area of circle R, is 9/100, or 9%, of the area of circle S.

13-5. **B.** In the right triangle, if $c = 2a$, then angle $a = 30°$ and $c = 60°$. Since angle f is supplementary to angle c, angle f must be 120°. If angle f is 120°, then there are 60° left to be divided between angles d and b (remember, there are 180° in a triangle). Since $d > 2b$, then b must be less than 30°; therefore, the correct answer is **B**—angle a (30°) is greater than angle b (less than 30°).

Notice the way you can mark the diagram to assist you.

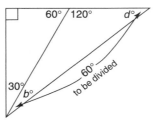

14-1. **C.** From statement (2), the refrigerators cost 112 × $186 = $20,832. Subtraction from the sale revenue in statement (1) leaves a gross profit of $12,228.

14-2. **B.** Statement (2) is sufficient. Since 84 payments of $1,124 each are still to be paid, simply multiply 84 times 1,124 to find the principal and interest still owed.

14-3. **B.** The month is uniquely determined only if there were no deposits or withdrawals from the account. Otherwise, any month is possible. With the restriction, the account exceeded $1,100 first on October 31, when the interest credited brought the account up to $1,104.62.

14-4. **E.** No exact dollar amounts are given for the individual bills. Had the Dufaas paid ½ of each of the bills, 50% would be the answer, but since they paid different fractional amounts of some of the bills, with each bill potentially a different dollar amount, the percent paid of the total amount can differ, depending upon the relative amounts of the different bills. (For example, if the Dufaas' annual trash bill were significantly larger than the other bills, the total percent paid on all the bills would be closer to 75% than 25%.)

14-5. **E.** The information is insufficient to determine the number of workers at the plant. Statement (1) is inadequate without the average salary of the remaining workers. Statement (2) is inadequate because the extra employees may not earn the same average salary as the original employees.

15-1. **A.** The product of the factors is 105. N must be an integer that is an odd multiple of 105. The very mention of factors in statement (1) implies that N is an integer.

15-2. **E.** From statement (2), the product cg is positive; therefore, c and g have the same sign. Note that f could be either positive or negative. Assume all three numbers are positive, and from statement (1) $cf > cg$. However, if you assume c and g are positive but f is negative, then from statement (1) $cf < cg$. The contradiction makes the problem indeterminate.

15-3. **D.** No, x is not prime. From the first statement you know that x is even, or divisible by 2. From the second statement you can deduce that $x = y + 3y = 4y$, so 4 is a factor of x.

15-4. **C.** From the second statement, $3m^2 = 27$, $m^2 = 9$, and $m = \pm 3$. But from both statements, since n is positive, so must be m.

15-5. **D.** Substituting $n = 20$ into the equation $m = n + 2$, you find that $m = 22$. You can then substitute that value into the quadratic expression:

$$m^2 - 4m + 4 = (22)^2 - 4(22) + 4 = 400$$

Statement (2) gives two values for m (+22, −18), each of which when substituted into the expression $m^2 - 4m + 4$ yields 400, so either statement (1) or (2) alone is sufficient.

16-1. **D.** From the first statement, $x = y = 47°$, for vertical angles are equal. From the second statement, the interior angle adjacent to z is 70°, because that angle and z sum to a straight angle. Since the interior angles of a triangle add to 180°, you can write the equation $x + 63° + 70° = 180°$, permitting the determination of x.

16-2. **E.** The area of the right triangle equals half the product of the two legs, AE and CE. The length of AE is given (1). But point E is not on the circle, so CE is less than ½(BD), the diameter (2). Lacking the length of CE, you cannot calculate the area.

16-3. **B.** From the Pythagorean theorem you know that $AD^2 + BD^2 = AB^2$, so $BD^2 = 16 + 121$, and $BD = \sqrt{137}$. The second statement tells you that the base and height of the triangle are equal, so $A = \frac{1}{2}bh = \frac{1}{2}\sqrt{137} \times \sqrt{137} = \frac{137}{2}$.

16-4. **C.** In the rectangle, $BA = CD = 3$ inches. So two sides of right triangle BAE are known, and with the Pythagorean theorem you can find the length of side AE to be 4 inches. Since point E is the midpoint of AD, the length of the rectangle is twice AE, or 8 inches. The area of the right triangle BCD is half the product of the sides adjacent to the right angle:

$A = ½bh = ½(8)(3) = 12$ sq. inches

16-5. **D.** The radius BC must be perpendicular to the tangent AB, so ABC is a right triangle. The second statement implies it is a 6-8-10 right triangle, so the radius is 6. You can solve from the first statement with the Pythagorean theorem:

$$(AC)^2 = (AB)^2 + (BC)^2$$
$$(4 + r)^2 = 8^2 + r^2$$
$$16 + 8r + r^2 = 64 + r^2$$
$$r = {}^{48}\!/_8 = 6$$

17-1. **E.** The given sequence more than doubles at each step, so it is fundamentally a geometric (multiplicative) sequence rather than an arithmetic (additive) sequence. Each term is two more than double the preceding term. The next number in the sequence would be $2 + 2(94) = 190$.

17-2. **C.** A 6% annual interest rate, compounded semiannually (every half year) is the same as a 3% semiannual interest rate. At the end of the first half of the year: Interest on $2,000 at 3% = $2,000 × 0.03 = $60. So the new balance at the end of the first half of the year = $2,000 + $60 = $2,060. At the end of the first full year: Interest on $2,060 at 3% = $2,060 × 0.03 = $61.80 ≅ $62. So the new balance at the end of the first full year = $2,060 + $62 = $2,122.

17-3. **D.** The only reasonable answer is $5^5\!/_9$, since 85¢ per pound is slightly closer to 93¢ per pound than 75¢ per pound. Then slightly more than half of the 10 pounds must be 93¢ per pound.

Algebraically, let x stand for the pounds of 93¢ tea. Then $10 - x$ is the 75¢ tea. This leads to the equation

$$0.93x + 0.75(10 - x) = 0.85(10)$$

Solving gives

$$93x + 750 - 75x = 850$$
$$18x = 100$$
$$x = {}^{100}\!/_{18}$$

Therefore, $x = 5^5\!/_9$

17-4. **B.** Since 100 plus 120 is 220, there must be 20 students who study both languages. Thus, of the 100 who study French, 80 do not study Spanish. 80 is 40% of the total of 200.

17-5. **D.** Only 19 cannot be weighed. To get 13, place 10 and 4 on one side and 1 on the other. To get the 15, place the 10, 4, and 1 on one side. To get the 17, place the 10 and 7 on one side. To get the 21, place the 10, 7, and 4 on one side.

18-1. **B.** Percent change is found by using the formula

$$\text{percent decrease or increase} = \frac{\text{change}}{\text{starting point}}$$

The change was $75 - 60 = 15$. (Notice that rounding off is possible.) The starting point was 75. Thus, ${}^{15}\!/_{75} = {}^1\!/_5 = 20\%$.

18-2. **C.** Let x be the length of time Mr. Dinkle travels. Then $x + \frac{1}{2}$ is the time Mr. Smitherly travels. This gives the equation $50(x + \frac{1}{2}) = 60x$, to see when they will meet. Solving gives

$$50x + 25 = 60x$$
$$25 = 10x$$
$$2.5 = x$$

Therefore, it will take Mr. Dinkle 2½ hours to overtake Mr. Smitherly. Since Mr. Dinkle starts at 8:30 a.m., he will overtake Mr. Smitherly at 11:00 a.m.

Note that answers **A, D,** and **E** are not reasonable.

18-3. **C.** Average speed is *total distance/total time*. The total distance is 360 miles. Time for the first 150 miles is 150/30 = 5 hours. The time for the remaining 210 miles is 210/35 = 6 hours. Thus the average speed is $360/(5 + 6) = 360/11 = 32\frac{8}{11}$ mph.

18-4. **B.** Average speed is *total distance/total time*. The total distance is $2x$. Time going is $x/8$. Time coming back is $x/12$. Thus the average speed is

$$\frac{2x}{x/8 + x/12} = \frac{2x}{3x/24 + 2x/24}$$
$$= \frac{2x}{5x/24} = \frac{2x}{1} \cdot \frac{24}{5x} = \frac{48}{5} = 9.6$$

Notice that answers **C, D,** and **E** are not reasonable.

18-5. **C.** You can set up the following chart

	D	=	R	×	T
Up	D		16		$\frac{D}{16}$
Down	D		24		$\frac{D}{24}$

Since the time is 10 hours for the whole trip,

$$\frac{D}{16} + \frac{D}{24} = 10$$

Multiply by 48, and you get $3D + 2D = 480$

$$5D = 480$$
$$D = 96$$

19-1. **C.** If the radius of a circle is 1, and it is reduced by 20%, it becomes 0.8. Since the area formula squares the radius, the original factor remains 1, but the new factor becomes 0.64, which is a 36% decrease.

19-2. **A.** The shaded area is the difference between the entire rectangle (with an area of $6 \times 8 = 48$) and the white triangle (with an area of $(6 \times x)/2 = 3x$). Thus, $48 - 3x$.

19-3. **B.** Since the perimeter of the square is 32, each side of the square is 8.

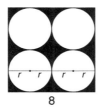

8

Area of square $= 8^2 = 64$

Note that $4r = 8$ or $r = 2$

Area of 1 circle $= \pi r^2$

$= \pi \times 2^2$

$= 4\pi$

Area of 4 circles $= 4 \times$ (area of 1 circle)

$= 4(4\pi)$

$= 16\pi$

Then shaded area $=$ (area of square) $-$ (area of 4 circles)

$= 64 - 16\pi$

19-4. **E.** The circumference of the large circle is 64π.

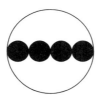

Since circumference $= 2\pi r$

$64\pi = 2\pi r$

$32 = r$

Radius of large circle $= 32$

Diameter of 2 small circles $= 32$

So diameter of 1 small circle $= 16$

Radius of small circle $= 8$

Area of small circle $= \pi r^2$

$= \pi \times 8^2$

$= 64\pi$

So area of 4 small circles $= 4 \times$ (area of 1 small circle)

$= 4(64\pi)$

$= 256\pi$

19-5. **C.** The area of any square equals one-half the product of its diagonals. Thus, the area of square $ABCD = \frac{1}{2}(2)(2) = 2$. The area of circle O equals $\pi r^2 \cong 3 \times 1 = 3$. The shaded area = the area of circle O minus the area of square $ABCD$, or $3 - 2 = 1$. Notice that to find the area of square $EFGH$, you may move the radius as follows:

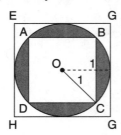

Thus the sides of square $EFGH$ are each 2, so its area is $2 \times 2 = 4$. Therefore, the shaded area is approximately 1 out of 4, or 25% of square $EFGH$. You may also simply eliminate choices **A, B, D,** and **E** by inspection. Every choice except **C** is not reasonable. Be aware that this type of elimination by inspection is possible only if the diagram is drawn close to scale and if the answer choices are far enough apart to allow approximating.

20-1. **B.** First note that $\frac{1}{4}$ of $\frac{3}{5} = \frac{3}{20}$. You then have: $\frac{3}{20}$ is what percent of $\frac{3}{4}$?

$$\frac{\text{is number}}{\text{of number}} = \frac{\text{percent}}{100}$$

$$\frac{\frac{3}{20}}{\frac{3}{4}} = \frac{P}{100}$$

Cross multiplying gives

$$\frac{3}{4}P = \frac{3}{\overset{}{\underset{1}{20}}}(\overset{5}{100})$$

$$\frac{3}{4}P = 15$$

$$P = \frac{4}{\overset{}{\underset{1}{3}}}(\overset{5}{15})$$

$$P = 20$$

Thus **B,** 20%, is the correct answer.

20-2. **A.** The desired weekly income is $600. $600 − $150 (weekly salary) = $450 (amount to be made up from commission). Let x = number of dollars in sales for one week. Since the sales representative earns 15% on all sales, this gives the equation

$$0.15x = 450$$
$$x = \frac{450}{0.15}$$
$$x = 3,000$$

Therefore, she must make sales totaling $3,000.

20-3. **D.** Begin with an arbitrary number of items sold, say 10, for a gross income of $1,000. By reducing the price 10% to $90, the owners sell 20% more items, or now 12. Now their gross income is $12 \times \$90 = \$1,080$. The percent increase is 80/1,000, or 8%.

20-4. **C.** The best way to solve this problem is by using simple numbers. If the recliners originally sold at $100 each, then a 20% reduction leaves a price of $80 each. If the owner sold 50% more recliners, it would be the same as $40 more for each original sale. This total is $120, ($80 + $40), which is 20% more than $100 per recliner.

An alternate method is to let $\frac{3}{2}$ represent a 50% increase. Then $\frac{3}{2} \times 80\% = 120\%$, which is a 20% increase over the original 100%.

20-5. **C.** If x is increased by 50%, you can represent it by $\frac{3}{2}x$. You need to multiply this by $\frac{2}{3}y$ in order to keep the product equal to xy. Since ⅔ is a ⅓ reduction, answer **C** is the correct response. You can also try using some values for x and y.

21-1. **B.** Whether m is positive or negative, m^2 must be positive. So the sign of n determines the sign of the product.

21-2. **D.** The sole solution is $m = 1 = 1 \times 1 = 1 \times 1 \times 1$ and so m is positive. Note that $-1 \neq (-1)(-1) \neq (-1)(-1)(-1)$.

21-3. **E.** Neither statement permits the calculation of $x + y + z$. Especially, the second statement cannot be inverted to obtain ¾, because the summation of fractions requires a common denominator:

$$\frac{yz + xz + xy}{xyz} = \frac{4}{9}$$

21-4. **C.** The question can be answered with both pieces of information. With $x < y$ and $y < 0$, then $(x - y)$ is negative. With $y < 0$ and $z < 0$, then the product yz is positive. Given both statements, $(x - y)$ is less than yz.

21-5. **D.** If $b < a$, according to statement (1), then $(a - b) > 0$ and, for any c, $(a - b)^c$ is positive. Incidentally, if $c = 0$, the entire exponential quantity equals 1, by definition. Also, if $c = 2a$, as in statement (2), then c is an even integer and the entire exponential quantity is positive, even if $(a - b)$ is negative.

22-1. **E.** Volume is the product of three dimensions. For the can, volume equals its base area (two dimensional) times its height; but the height is not stated.

22-2. **D.** From the first statement, $x + 4 = 4x - 2$, because opposite sides of a rectangle are equal. So $x = 2$ and the width $x + 4 = 6$. Or you can use the area of the second statement, since width = area/length = ⁴⁸⁄₈ = 6.

22-3. **C.** The first statement implies that the diagonal divides the field into two 30°-60° right triangles, with sides in the ratio $1 : 2 : \sqrt{3}$. Employing that ratio to find the width with a length of 173 feet, the width equals 100 feet. Then the area equals 17,300 square feet.

22-4. **D.** This problem may be solved swiftly with knowledge of the principle that for quadrilaterals of equal area, the square has the shortest perimeter. Then the farmer would need less fencing for the stubbier configuration, approaching a square. Statement (2) yields that information immediately. Since the area of 3,000 equals the length times the width, statement (1) implies that lot X would be 75×40 and lot Y would be 60×50. From either statement, lot Y would have the shorter perimeter.

22-5. **A.** Angle *ABC*, inscribed on a diameter, is necessarily 90°, so the second statement adds nothing new. But the first statement implies that the triangle has an altitude equal to the circle's radius, 6. So the shaded area equals the area of the semicircle, $(\frac{1}{2} \times \pi \times 6^2)$ minus the area of the triangle $(\frac{1}{2}bh = \frac{1}{2} \times 12 \times 6 = 36)$.

23-1. **C.** Since there are two unknowns, you need two equations to solve for *p* and *r*. From statement (2), $p = r + 5$. Substituting that *p* in statement (1) yields $2r + 10 + 3r = 11$, or $r = \frac{1}{5}$. Since $p = r + 5$, $p = \frac{1}{5} + 5 = \frac{26}{5}$.

23-2. **A.** From the first statement, $m^2/s^3 = 3$, and squaring each side, $m^4/s^6 = 9$. Substituting into the original expression, $14(m^4/s^6) = 14 \times 9 = 126$.

23-3. **E.** Making substitutions from both statements yields the expression $9 - 2y < 17$. To solve for *y*, you first subtract 9 from both sides and then divide by −2; the latter operation reverses the sense of the inequality. The solution $y > -4$ records that *y* may be positive, zero, or negative (between 0 and −4).

23-4. **A.** From statement (1), $3c$ and $8d^3$ have opposite signs. Hence, *c* and d^3 have opposite signs. With the odd exponent, the sign of *d* will be the same as d^3. So statement (1) is sufficient to answer the question, even though the answer is "no."

23-5. **B.** You cannot solve the first equation by elementary methods. The second equation implies $x = 1$. Hence, $x^3 - 2x^2 + 7 = 6$.

24-1. **B.** In triangle *ABD*, the sum of ∠*A*, ∠*B*, and ∠*BDA* is 180°. If ∠*B* = 90° and ∠*BDA* = 50°, then ∠*A* = 40°. Since ∠*A* = $x° + 15°$, you have

$$40° = x° + 15°$$

$$25° = x°$$

Therefore, $x = 25$

24-2. **D.** Perimeter of triangle *MNP* = $\frac{1}{2}$(perimeter of triangle *XYZ*)

$$= \frac{1}{2}(XY + YZ + XZ)$$

$$= \frac{1}{2}(10 + 15 + 17)$$

$$= \frac{1}{2}(42)$$

Perimeter of triangle *MNP* = 21

24-3. **D.** From the figure and using the Pythagorean theorem, you can determine that the radius is 13 inches.

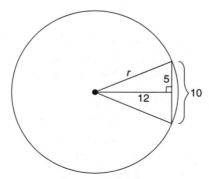

$$5^2 + 12^2 = r^2$$
$$25 + 144 = r^2$$
$$169 = r^2$$
$$13 = r$$

Alternate method: If you recognized the 5-12-13 right triangle, you could quickly find r to be 13.

24-4. **D.** Let

$$5x = \text{first angle}$$
$$2x = \text{second angle}$$
$$5x - 2x = 3x = \text{third angle}$$

Since the sum of the angles in any triangle is 180°, you have

$$5x + 2x + 3x = 180°$$
$$10x = 180°$$
$$x = 18°$$

Therefore,

$$5x = 90°$$
$$2x = 36°$$
$$3x = 54°$$

The smallest angle has a measure of 36°.

24-5. **E.** From the figure, you can use the Pythagorean theorem and find the missing side, x, is 12 inches. Thus, **E** is correct.

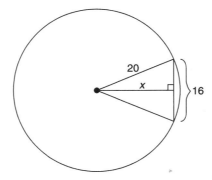

$$a^2 + b^2 = c^2$$
$$16^2 + x^2 = 20^2$$
$$256 + x^2 = 400$$
$$x^2 = 400 - 256$$
$$x^2 = 144$$
$$x = 12$$

25-1. D. When $N + 1$ is divided by 5, the remainder is 4. When N (which is one less than $N + 1$) is divided by 5, the remainder should be 3 (which is one less than 4).

25-2. A. The two-digit numbers whose remainder is 1 when divided by 10 are: 11, 21, 31, 41, 51, 61, 71, 81, and 91. When divided by 6, the remainder is 5 for the numbers 11, 41, and 71. Therefore, 3 numbers satisfy the conditions of the problem.

25-3. B. Set up the problem as follows

$$\frac{x+2}{x+5+(2)} = \frac{7}{12}, \text{ or } \frac{x+2}{x+7} = \frac{7}{12}$$

By observation $x = 5$ since $\frac{5+2}{5+7} = \frac{7}{12}$

Substituting into the original fraction $\frac{x}{x+5}$ gives

$$\frac{5}{5+5} = \frac{5}{10} = \frac{1}{2}$$

A simpler method is

$$\frac{7-2}{12-2} = \frac{5}{10} = \frac{1}{2}$$

25-4. D. Begin by choosing a simple fraction, say 100/100. If the numerator is tripled and the denominator is doubled, the resulting fraction is 300/200, or 1½. So the new fraction represents a 50% increase over the original fraction.

25-5. B. The @ of $2 = (2)(5) - 2 = 8$. So 2 is the largest positive integer n such that @ of n will be less than 10.

26-1. C. If x represents the cost of the book, then you have the following equation:

$$x + 0.20x = \$12.00$$
$$1.2x = \$12.00$$
$$x = \$10.00$$

26-2. E. Since the chart does not distinguish how many houses are 3 years old or 4 years old, the answer cannot be determined.

26-3. E. Simply continue the chart as follows, adding 40¢ for each two years to Product A and 15¢ for each two years to Product B:

Products	1998	2000	2002	2004	2006
A	$6.60	$7.00	$7.40	$7.80	$8.20
B	$7.20	$7.35	$7.50	$7.65	$7.80

It is evident that the correct answer is 2006.

26-4. C. The total price of toy A is $5.0227 [$2.5796 + $2.4431], and the total price of toy B is $5.0080 [$2.5768 + $2.4312]. Toy A exceeds toy B by $0.0147; therefore 10,000 of each must be manufactured to have a $147.00 difference.

26-5. B. Mr. Talbot's charge for the call

Mr. Talbot's charge for the call	$14.09
Cost of first 3 minutes of a person-to-person call	− $4.35
Cost of additional minutes	$9.74
Cost of additional minutes	$9.74
Cost of each additional minute	$0.46

$\cong 21$ minutes

Total length of call = first 3 minutes + additional minutes

$$= 3 + 21 = 24 \text{ minutes}$$

27-1. C. The number of tiles would equal the area of the kitchen divided by the area of one tile, or $(120 \times 84)/48 = 210$ tiles.

27-2. B. The amount of wallpaper can be measured in square feet, the area of the two largest walls. Each large wall has an area equal to the length of the room times the height of the room. The total amount of wallpaper required is $2 \times 24 \times 9 = 432$ square feet.

27-3. B. The central angle MON must be 96°, twice the inscribed angle NPM. Further, the triangle MNO has two radii as sides, so it is isosceles, and angle $OMN = MNO$. Therefore, $2(MNO) + 96° = 180°$, and one may solve for $MNO = 42°$.

27-4. D. Either statement suffices to determine MN to be 7½. Because of similar triangles, $MN{:}OQ = MP{:}QP$. From the Pythagorean theorem, $OP = 13$. By addition, $NP = ON + OP = 6½ + 13 = 19½$; also $MP = 18$. Therefore, $MN{:}5 = 18{:}12 = 19½{:}13$ and you can solve for MN.

27-5. E. Since P is not now touching the ground, all you know is that the wheel has traveled more than 5 circumferences but less than 5¼. So, $5\pi d < 36 < 5¼\pi d$. Therefore, the diameter is uncertain, somewhere in the range 2.18 to 2.29 feet.

28-1. B. The sale price equaled the list price L minus 30%. So $140 = 0.7L$, and $L = 140/0.7 = \$200$.

28-2. D. To solve the first expression, you add 5 to both sides and divide by 4. The second expression is solved by collecting terms on the left, $m^2 - 6m + 9 = 0$, and factoring, $(m - 3)^2 = 0$. From either expression, $m = 3$.

28-3. E. No relationship can be determined between x and y, since the two equations are the same. (Multiply the second equation by 4.)

28-4. E. The first statement reveals only that c and a have the same sign. From the initial proportion and the second statement, $ac = b^2 = 32$, but the sign of c is indeterminate.

28-5. A. The first five perfect cubes are 1, 8, 27, 64, and 125. Therefore, $C = 64$.

29-1. C. If the box is cubical, then each side is square. An edge of the box would be the square root of the side, or 4 inches. The volume equals the edge cubed, or 64 cubic inches.

29-2. E. The first statement lists two points through which the circle passes, but many circles could pass through any two points. Knowing the diameter would still not yield a unique circle.

29-3. E. Combining both statements, all you know is that the line passes through the point $(5, -3)$, and the orientation is unspecified.

29-4. B. Necessarily, the diagonal equals the sides times $\sqrt{2}$, so from the second statement, $d = \sqrt{8} \times \sqrt{2} = \sqrt{16} = 4$, a rational number.

29-5. A. The shaded part equals the area of the large circle minus the areas of the two small circles. For any circle, $A = \pi r^2$, so you can ascertain the radii of the circles from statement (1) alone. The small circles are of equal size, with radii of $2\frac{1}{2}$. Because the small circles are equal, their diameter is the radius of the large circle. Shaded area = $25\pi - 2(25/4)\pi = (25/2)\pi$.

30-1. C.

$$\frac{\overset{1}{\cancel{7}}}{10_2} \times \frac{14}{1} \times \frac{\overset{1}{\cancel{5}}}{1} \times \frac{1}{\cancel{28}_4} \over \frac{\overset{2}{\cancel{10}}}{\cancel{17}_1} \times \frac{\overset{1}{\cancel{3}}}{\cancel{5}_1} \times \frac{1}{\cancel{6}_2} \times \frac{\overset{1}{\cancel{17}}}{1}} = \frac{\frac{14}{8}}{\frac{2}{2}} = \frac{\frac{7}{4}}{1} = \frac{7}{4}$$

30-2. C. Having spent $\frac{2}{5}$ of her money on clothes, Mary has $\frac{3}{5}$ of her money left. Then $\frac{1}{2}$ of $\frac{3}{5}$, or $\frac{3}{10}$, is placed in her savings account. She has now spent $\frac{2}{5} + \frac{3}{10} = \frac{7}{10}$ of her money. Thus, she has $\frac{3}{10}$ remaining. If m is the money she started with, and she has only $21 left, you have the equation

$$(\tfrac{3}{10})m = 21$$
$$m = 21(\tfrac{10}{3})$$
$$m = 70$$

30-3. A. Set up two equations.

$$5A + 2B = 6B + 5C \qquad 1A + 4C = 2A + 4B$$
$$5A = 4B + 5C \qquad\qquad 4C = A + 4B$$
$$\qquad\qquad\qquad 4C - A = 4B$$

Substitute $4C - A$ for $4B$ in the other equation.

$$5A = 4C - A + 5C$$
$$6A = 9C$$
$$A = \tfrac{9}{6}C$$
$$= \tfrac{3}{2}C$$

30-4. D. Since Felix earns 30% more than Oscar, let x = Oscar's salary and $1.3x$ = Felix's salary. If Felix's salary is reduced by 10%, he is now earning $1.3x - 0.13x = 1.17x$. If Oscar's salary is increased 10%, he is now earning $1x + 0.1x = 1.1x$. Felix is now earning $(0.07x/1.1x) = 6.36\%$ more than Oscar.

30-5. A. Let x equal 1995's amount used; let y equal 1995's rate. Therefore, $xy = $ 1995's water expenditure. For 1996, instead of y, use $1.5y$ for the new rate, and let p equal the new fraction of x (water used) to set up the equation:

expenditure in 1995 = expenditure in 1996

$$xy = (px)(1.5y)$$
$$xy = xy(1.5p)$$
$$1 = 1.5p$$
$$1/1.5 = p$$
$$.66\tfrac{2}{3} = p$$

Since for 1996, the Johnsons must use only $66\tfrac{2}{3}\%$ of 1995's amount, they must reduce their 1995 usage by $33\tfrac{1}{3}\%$.

31-1. E. If y is a positive integer, y could be 1. Choices **A, B, C,** and **D** are all evenly divisible by 1. Only choice **E,** $1\tfrac{1}{2}$, is not divisible by 1.

31-2. C. Two 2-digit numbers, 80 and 88, are each divisible by 8, and the sums of their digits are divisible by 8.

31-3. A. You need to solve the two simultaneous linear equations for both variables.

$3r + s = 17$	The first equation
$\underline{-3r - 6s = -27}$	The second equation times -3
$-5s = -10$	Adding two equations
$s = 2$	Solution for s
$3r + 2 = 17$	Substituting into the first equation
$3r = 15$	
$r = 5$	Solution for r

So r exceeds s by 3.

31-4. E. First rearrange and simplify the first equation as follows:

Add $+12$ and $+6y$ to both sides of the equation $6x - 12 = -6y$ and you get

$$6x - 12 = -\,6y$$
$$\underline{+\,12 + 6y = +\,6y + 12}$$
$$6x + 6y = 12$$

Now dividing through by 6 leaves $x + y = 2$.

Next, rearrange and simplify the second equation as follows:

$5y + 5x = 15$ is the same as $5x + 5y = 15$. Dividing through by 5 leaves $x + y = 3$.

The equations $x + y = 2$ and $x + y = 3$ have no solutions in common because you can't add the same two numbers and get two different answers.

31-5. A. Note that $(x-y)^2 = x^2 - 2xy + y^2$

$$= \underbrace{x^2 + y^2}_{14} - \underbrace{2xy}_{-2(3)}$$

$$= 14 - 6$$

$$= 8$$

32-1. A. Start at the lower right, and add the whole number 2 with the fraction. Change to an improper fraction, invert, and continue.

$$2 + \cfrac{1}{2 + \cfrac{1}{2\frac{1}{2}}}$$

$$2 + \cfrac{1}{2 + \cfrac{1}{\frac{5}{2}}}$$

$$2 + \cfrac{1}{2\frac{2}{5}}$$

$$2 + \cfrac{1}{\frac{12}{5}}$$

$$2 + \frac{5}{12}$$

$$2\frac{5}{12} = \frac{29}{12}$$

32-2. C. Since 21 is 70% of the total, the total must be 30. Thus the team lost 9 matches.

$$21 = 70\% \text{ of } x$$

$$21 = 0.7x$$

$$21/0.7 = x$$

$$30 = x$$

$$30 - 21 = 9$$

Notice that answers **A** and **B** are not reasonable.

32-3. C. Calculate the rates of production per day. Two of the factories each make 100,000/15 $\cong$ 6,667 hubcaps per day. The third plant makes $1.3 \times 6,667 \cong 8,667$ hubcaps per day. The total production rate is $8,667 + 2(6,667) = 22,001$ hubcaps per day. At that rate it would take 45.5 days to produce a million hubcaps.

32-4. A. Since it takes Dan 15 hours to complete the job, then in 9 hours he will be able to do only $\frac{9}{15}$, or $\frac{3}{5}$, of the job. This leaves $\frac{2}{5}$ of the job to be finished by Fred. Since Fred takes 10 hours to do the *whole* job by himself, to do only $\frac{2}{5}$ of the job, it would take Fred $\frac{2}{5} \times 10 = 4$ hours.

32-5. C. Since machine A worked for 2 hours and could do the entire job in 8 hours, machine A must have done $\frac{1}{4}$ of the job. You then have the following formula in which the value of x represents the time actually worked.

$$\underset{\text{A}}{\frac{2}{8}} + \underset{\text{B}}{\frac{x}{10}} + \underset{\text{C}}{\frac{x}{12}} = 1$$

$$\frac{x}{10} + \frac{x}{12} = \frac{3}{4}$$

$$6x + 5x = 45$$

$$11x = 45$$

$$x = 4\frac{1}{11}$$

9:00 a.m. $+\ 4\frac{1}{11}$ hours $\cong$ 1:00 p.m.

33-1. C. The question asks how far the car can travel, and the answer is $\frac{50}{8} \times 100 = 625$ kilometers. Remember that liters measure volume and kilometers measure distance.

33-2. A. Since Ethyl, Dora, and Carl are consecutive, Grace and Bill must be in the remaining adjacent seats.

33-3. E. The question is indeterminate because many different combinations of the two cone prices can sum to $209.15. The question could be answered if you also knew *either* the number of Generous cones *or* the number of all cones.

33-4. B. Let g be the fraction of gasoline. Then the fraction of alcohol is $1 - g$. So for the mixture, $1.09g + 1.81(1 - g) = 1.22$, and you can solve for $g = 0.82$. Gasohol 99 is 82% gasoline and 18% alcohol.

33-5. E. The question cannot be answered, even with both statements, because any burnt-out bulb could have its switch either ON or OFF.

34-1. E. The second statement means that the Emporium sold a total of 2,568 shoes. You cannot assume from the first statement that one-quarter of those shoes were black, because some shoes are neither black nor brown.

34-2. C. The radiator requires 60% antifreeze in its 3 gallons, or 1.8 gallons antifreeze.

34-3. E. The two statements may be translated into the equations

(1) $M + 2 = 2b$

(2) $S = (M + B)/2$

Because two equations are insufficient to determine three variables, Mary's age is indeterminate.

34-4. B. The first statement translates to the equation $A + 1 = \frac{1}{2}(M + 1)$, which has two unknowns and cannot be solved for A. But the second statement means $A + 5 = 2(A - 10)$, and you can solve for Anne's age, 25 years.

34-5. A. Symbolize the first number as f and the second as s. The main clause of the first sentence of the question yields the equation $f = 5 + \frac{1}{2}s$, and statement (1) is the equation $f = s - 1$. Those two linear equations with two unknowns can be solved for both the first number ($f = 11$) and the second number ($s = 12$).

35-1. C. The six faces of the cube each have an area of $10 \times 10 = 100$ square feet. That is a total of 600 square feet. Since it takes one quart for each 20 square feet, you need 30 quarts. Take $30 \times \$3.20 = \$96.00$.

35-2. B. Notice that in triangle *BCE* the angle *B* equals 94°. Therefore, any perpendicular dropped from *C* to line *AB* must be less than 3 (see diagram below). Since the area of a parallelogram = base × height, then the area of parallelogram *AECD* = 8 × (a height less than 3) = an area less than 24.

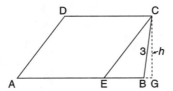

35-3. D. Points *A*, *B*, and *P* form a 30°-60°-90° triangle, the sides of which are in a $1 : \sqrt{3} : 2$ relationship. A proportion can therefore be established:

$$\frac{120}{\sqrt{3}} = \frac{?}{1}$$

Solving:

$$\frac{120}{\sqrt{3}} = \frac{x}{1}$$

$$x = \frac{120}{\sqrt{3}}$$

$$x = \frac{120}{\sqrt{3}} \cdot \frac{\sqrt{3}}{\sqrt{3}} = \frac{120\sqrt{3}}{3} = 40\sqrt{3}$$

35-4. C. Since the perimeter of rectangle *ABCD* is 22 and *DC* = 7, you have

$$22 = 2(AD) + 2(7)$$
$$22 = 2(AD) + 14$$
$$8 = 2(AD)$$
$$4 = AD$$

Next note that triangle *ADE* is a 30°-60°-90° triangle with side ratios $1 : \sqrt{3} : 2$. Since the side across from 30° is 4, the side across from 60° is $4\sqrt{3}$. Thus $DE = 4\sqrt{3}$. Also note that triangle *DEF* is a 45°-45°-90° triangle with side ratios $1 : 1 : \sqrt{2}$. Since $DE = 4\sqrt{3}$, then $EF = 4\sqrt{3}$. Then the area of *DEF*

$$= \tfrac{1}{2}(EF)(DE)$$
$$= \frac{1}{2}\left(4\sqrt{3}\right)\left(4\sqrt{3}\right)$$
$$= \tfrac{1}{2} \times 16 \times 3$$
$$= 24$$

35-5. **D.** Since arc AC is 120°, then arc AE equals 60°. Therefore, $\angle AOE$ is 60°, and triangle AOD is a 30°-60°-90° triangle, and its sides are in the proportion $1:\sqrt{3}:2$. Since AO is 2, AD equals $\sqrt{3}$, and OD is 1. So the base of triangle ABC is $2\sqrt{3}$, and its height is $1 + 2 = 3$. So the area of $ABC = \frac{1}{2}bh = \frac{1}{2}(2\sqrt{3})(3) = 3\sqrt{3}$.

36-1. **D.** The most the trip will cost is when gas costs $1.12 and the mileage is 16 mph. Thus $1.12 \times (480/16) = 33.60. The least would be $0.96 \times (480/24) = 19.20. The difference is $14.40.

36-2. **E.** The ferry can transport the maximum number of cars when they are all the minimum weight, 1,800 pounds. Each of those cars weighs $1,800/2,000 = 0.9$ tons. The number of those automobiles that the ferry can transport is its capacity divided by the weight of one car: $78/0.9 = 86.67$ automobiles.

36-3. **C.** Focussing on the water part of the mixture, you have ⅔ of 2 quarts = ⁴⁄₃ quarts, and ⅜ of 3 quarts = ⁹⁄₈ quarts. These add together to give 2¹¹⁄₂₄, which is very close to 50% of 5 quarts.

36-4. **C.** Set up an equation for the amount of salt.

10% of 10 plus 0% of x equals 7% of $(10 + x)$

$$1 \quad + \quad 0 \quad = \quad (0.7 + 0.07x)$$

$$1 = 0.7 + 0.07x$$

$$0.3 = 0.07x$$

$$\frac{0.3}{0.07} = x$$

$$\frac{30}{7} = x$$

Solving for x, you get 4²⁄₇.

36-5. **B.** Since there are 8 pints per gallon, the volume of punch is 60 pints. If you call the amount of orange juice J, then the amount of buttermilk is $2J$ and the amount of brandy is $J/3$. All the ingredients add to 60 pints.

$$J + 2J + \frac{J}{3} = 60$$

$$\frac{3J + 6J + J}{3} = 60$$

$$3J + 6J + J = 180$$

$$10J = 180$$

$$J = 18 \text{ pints of orange juice}$$

37-1. **B.** Solve this problem by plugging in simple numbers. Start with 1, an odd integer.

$$(1 + 1) \quad \text{times} \quad (2 \cdot 1) + 1 \quad =$$

$$(2) \quad \text{times} \quad (2 + 1) \quad =$$

$$2 \quad \times \quad 3 \quad = 6 \text{ Not odd}$$

Now try 2, an even integer.

$$(2 + 1) \quad \text{times} \quad (2 \cdot 2) + 1 \quad =$$
$$(3) \quad \text{times} \quad (4 + 1) \quad =$$
$$3 \quad \times \quad 5 \quad = 15 \quad \text{Odd}$$

37-2. D. Examining each choice,

A. $(x + 3)(x + 5)$ Since x is even, both $x + 3$ and $x + 5$ are odd; then (odd)(odd) = odd.

B. $x^2 + 5$ Since x is even, x^2 is even, and $x^2 + 5$ is odd.

C. $x^2 + 6x + 9$ Since x is even, x^2 is even and $6x$ is even; then (even) + (even) + (odd) = (odd).

D. $3x^2 + 4$ Since x is even, $3x^2$ is even; then (even) + (even) = *even*.

E. $5(x + 3)$ Since x is even, $x + 3$ is odd; then (odd)(odd) = odd.

37-3. B. If the annual bonus were normally $100, tripled it would be $300. Therefore, the increase ($200) is ⅔ of the new bonus ($300). Two-thirds is 66⅔%.

37-4. E. Any number of members is possible as long as the number of dollars per member is two more than the number of members.

37-5. C. Let c = cost of each brick. Let M = total money. Thus $M = 45c$ and $M = 50(c - 10)$.

Therefore, $45c = 50(c - 10)$

$$45c = 50c - 500$$
$$500 = 5c$$
$$100 = c$$

Thus $M = 4,500$ cents, or $45.00.

Verbal Section

1. **C.** The first paragraph supports answers **A, B, D,** and **E.** One of the points of the experiments described is to show that people will change their opinions *without* being given good reasons to do so.

2. **C.** The passage concludes that a change of judgment is likely to be based on a change of knowledge or assumptions about the topic.

3. **A.** Though the passage refers to ideas in choices **B, C,** and **D,** only **A** is the main point of the *whole* passage.

4. **D.** The passage gives us no information on the author's views of men as opposed to women. Answer **D,** referring to both men and women, is clearly implied by the last paragraph.

5-1. **B.** Choice **B** correctly supplies the plural *know,* which agrees with *ecologists.* The subject closest to the verb determines the number of the verb in this case. Choice **B** also retains the necessary *neither . . . nor.*

5-2. **B.** Choice **B** corrects the verb agreement problem in the original wording. The verbs must both be past tense or both be present tense. No other choice uses proper tense without introducing a subject-verb agreement error.

5-3. **E.** Choice **E** best expresses the parallel form called for in this sentence (*neglect, house-cleaning, lack*—all nouns). The other choices contain the same "unparallel" structure of the original wording.

5-4. **A.** The original is better than any of the alternatives. All other choices are less direct, create ambiguities, or change the meaning of the original.

5-5. **D.** Choice **D** clarifies whose physical examination is in question—Marvin's or the doctor's. Choice **C** is straightforward and concise, also leaving no doubt as to whose examination it is; however, the *doctor* is not mentioned, and because one cannot assume that all physical examinations are administered by a doctor, this information must be included.

6-1. **B.** Choice **B** contains the correct verb form *are* for the *neither . . . nor* construction. The verb in this case should be plural to match *friends,* which is the closer of the two subjects to the verb. Choice **D** correctly uses *are* but changes the meaning of the original.

6-2. **D.** In the original sentence, the adjective *quick* is used incorrectly to modify an *action,* signing. Actions are modified by adverbs—in this case, *quickly.* This is the only necessary change.

6-3. **C.** In order to indicate that participation in the debate precedes voter understanding, the verb *had* must replace *would have.* None of the other choices retains the original meaning clearly and fully.

6-4. **D.** Choice **D** correctly states the comparison by adding *those.* The alternative wordings do not clearly express the comparison. Choice **B** is wordy and imprecise, and **C** changes the meaning of the original sentence.

6-5. **E.** Choice **E** best simplifies the awkward wording of the original sentence. Choices **C** and **D** change the meaning slightly by eliminating the notion of *consider,* and choice **B** is not idiomatic.

7-1. **C.** The original is constructed so that "a train" seems to be "working as an engineer." Also, the phrase "according to legend" repeats information supplied later in the sentence. Choice **C** is both economical and clearly constructed.

7-2. **A.** The original wording is the best expression of this idea. Choice **E** changes the meaning slightly. The other choices are either stylistically awkward or ungrammatical.

7-3. **C.** The original is extremely wordy, filled with repetitious phrases (for instance, "understanding . . . with comprehension" and "class members . . . were students"). All choices except **C** retain some of the original wordiness or are grammatically unacceptable.

7-4. **B.** Two major errors weaken the original. (1) Faulty parallelism—"enjoying the beauty" is not parallel in structure with "clarity" and "brilliance." (2) Vague wordiness—"and along with it" might suggest that the diamond and the painting are being perceived together, but the more logical meaning is that they are phenomena that are generally similar to one another. **B** is syntactically and logically correct and retains the intended meaning of the original.

7-5. **E.** *Either* is misplaced in the original so that it does not refer to *voices* as well as *acting*. **E** corrects this error, eliminates the repetitive term *speaking,* and changes *consisted of* to *was* to produce a more economical, parallel structure.

8-1. **D.** Choices **B** and **E** are contradicted by the passage, and the passage does not support the probability of **A** or **C.** Choice **D** is reasonable, plausible, and probable, given the information in the passage.

8-2. **D.** The commercial either explicitly states or implies all but **D.** It makes no reference to how long it will take to fall asleep or how quickly the drug works. It does, however, claim to provide a restful, good night's sleep, with added energy and no aftereffects the next morning.

8-3. **D.** The passage sets up the thesis that sometimes individuals yield to others' interests. Choices **A** and **E** are unsubstantiated or not mentioned in the passage; **C** does not fit the structure of the sentence; **B** could possibly be the correct answer, but **D** more nearly completes the thought of the passage and is neatly juxtaposed with the first part of the incomplete sentence.

8-4. **C.** The transitional word *nevertheless* establishes a juxtaposition of the phrases immediately before and after it. Therefore, **A** and **B** are incorrect. Choice **D** may be a good answer, but **C** is better, as it addresses a concern initially introduced in the paragraph and brings the passage full circle.

8-5. **C.** Geographic location and employment status are irrelevant issues, so **A** and **B** should be eliminated. **D** and **E** are too general and vague. Only **C** makes explicit the point of the author's argument, that interpretation of the Texas law is arrogant and unsound.

9. **B.** Demand, as economists use the word, requires the relationship between price and the quantity demanded to remain unchanged. In both statements I and III, the price has changed, rising in statement III and falling in statement I.

10. **A.** Initially, the passage emphasizes a distinction between *demand* and *quantity demanded,* concluding that "demand shifts when there is a change in income, expectations, taste, etc., such that a different quantity of the good is demanded at the same price." This statement fits **A** precisely. All other choices include or allow for a changing price.

11. **C.** This situation establishes a relationship between price and quantity that parallels the paragraph's explanation of the *law of demand.* This section discusses "the consumer's desire to get the 'best buy'" and goes on to say that "if the price of a good A increases, the individual will tend to substitute another good and purchase less of good A." Since the appearance of a lower-priced breakfast drink makes orange juice more "expensive" in relation, the law of demand as so described would prevail.

12. A. The passage defines a number of important economic terms. Though it does not question a popular misunderstanding **E,** it does so only in the first paragraph. The passage does not deal with supply **B** or marketing **D.**

13-1. D. The letter fails to note that the decision concerns *officers,* and Smith and Krunkle have been merely nominated to be officers and are not yet such. The other choices are either not stated in the letter or are not essential to the argument.

13-2. A. This question draws from a simple, explicit statement: "Socrates believed . . . that evil is fundamentally ignorance." Each of the other choices is an unwarranted complication or extension of this statement.

13-3. E. Answers **B, C,** and **D** are only partial descriptions and, although they may be correct, are not as complete a description of possible future action as answer **E.** Nothing in the letter would imply the action stated in **A.**

13-4. C. All race-car lovers enjoy classical music. Since there are no backgammon players who enjoy classical music, then none of the backgammon players are race-car lovers. **D** is false because the third statement does not necessarily exclude those who don't enjoy classical music from enjoying fine wine.

13-5. D. Only this choice both represents a *strong* point *and* is not contradictory. **A, C,** and **E** contradict the argument, and **B** is not a relatively strong point.

14-1. D. Since no blue-eyed swimmer is an Olympic winner, then no blue-eyed swimmer may be a freestyle swimmer, since *all* freestyle swimmers are Olympic winners. **B** and **E** are false because they exclude other possibilities that may, in fact, exist.

14-2. E. The researcher concluded that women could be just as capable as men in math but that they develop other abilities because of social pressures. Thus, the researcher assumes that women do conform to social expectations.

14-3. E. Choices **A, C,** and **D** are irrelevant to the argument, and **B** actually strengthens the argument. **E** suggests that the evidence from one year cannot reliably predict a long-term trend.

14-4. E. This is implied in the final sentence. Each of the other choices requires assumptions or beliefs extraneous to the passage.

14-5. D. The argument presupposes both that candidates are spending too much on television advertising ("the waste") and that television can be used to inform the public ("provide air time to all candidates to debate the issues"). Statement III is irrelevant to the argument.

15-1. E. The correct pronoun in this case is *who,* the subject of *betrayed.*

15-2. B. Choice **B** is correct because it is both concise and clear. The other choices are ambiguous or unnecessarily change the past tense of the original to the present tense. Choice **D** is a less direct, more wordy way to express what choice **B** does more concisely.

15-3. A. The original is more correct, clear, and logical than any of the other choices.

15-4. D. Choice **D** supplies the correct verb form *had witnessed* called for by the original sentence.

15-5. **E.** The original suggests that she failed the fifth grade possibly because of her father's shaking. **B** is clearer in this respect but repetitious with its use of both *recounting* and *recounted.* Choice **E** is the clearest and most economical of the choices. The fact that such an experience would be painful is obvious, and since the experience happened in the fifth grade, it is clearly a childhood experience. The sentence is not harmed by the lack of these details.

16-1. **C.** "Granting the returned money during June" is repetitious, and of the choices offered, **C** is the clearest and most economical expression.

16-2. **C.** With the semicolon, the second part of the original sentence is a fragment; so are choices **B, D,** and **E.**

16-3. **C.** The original is flawed by faulty parallelism. *Planning* is not parallel to *to pursue* (the former a gerund, the latter an infinitive). Choice **C** corrects this problem; *planning* is parallel to *pursuing.*

16-4. **B.** The original contains two errors. "After having read" is redundant (*having read* already contains the *after* meaning), and *laying* (which means *putting*) is incorrect (*lying* is correct).

16-5. **C.** The original is not the best choice here because it is not as economical and clear as **C.** Each of the other choices is either too wordy, vague, or illogical.

17-1. **D.** Both errors in the original result from a confusion of adjectives and adverbs. *Seriously,* an adverb, correctly modifies the verb *took; hard,* used as an adverb meaning *with strength,* correctly modifies *punched.* Choices **B, C,** and **E** significantly change the meaning of the original.

17-2. **A.** The original is better than any of the alternatives.

17-3. **D.** The phrase *from the stands,* in the original, is a misplaced modifier suggesting that the players made the touchdown from the stands, which is impossible. Choice **E** leaves *crowd* out of the sentence (a significant omission), and all other choices except **D** contain misplaced modifiers.

17-4. **B.** The original contains two important errors. *Overtime* and *past regular hours* are repetitious, and *comply to this* is both vague and nonidiomatic. Choice **B** corrects both of these weaknesses. **D** is a correct expression but retains the vague pronoun *this,* which possibly refers to either the contract or the overtime.

17-5. **A.** The original is correct. This sentence abbreviates "She likes everyone as much as *she likes* him." All other choices are either ungrammatical or change the meaning of the sentence.

18. **E.** Though the passage alludes to the advantage of one method, the excerpt as a whole is concerned with describing several methods used to count bacteria.

19. **B.** Though some methods count both living and dead cells, one method that is described counts only living cells.

20. **A.** If you know the total volume of the bacteria cells and the volume of one cell, you can divide the former by the latter to determine the total number of cells.

21. D. The passage is too advanced for options **B** or **C** but not so technical as you would expect for advanced students **A**. The subject of the passage is not mathematics **E**.

22-1. B. *To question* is not parallel with *remaining;* only **B** corrects this problem.

22-2. D. The original contains two errors. *Varies* does not agree with the plural subject, *opinions,* and *according with* is not idiomatic. **C** is a correct phrase but changes and obscures the meaning of the sentence.

22-3. E. The introductory phrase is a dangling modifier, corrected by following *freeze* with *the Cabinet minister* to make clear to whom the introductory phrase refers. Choice **D** is not best because *but unharmed* is left in an awkward position.

22-4. C. The original contains two errors. *It* suggests that the meeting, not the members, does the considering, and *had considered* is a verb tense simultaneous with *had left* and does not indicate that considering the tax cut occurred after the visitors had left. Choice **D** is unnecessarily wordy and leaves unsaid who did the considering.

22-5. D. The introductory phrase is a dangling modifier, making it seem as if the *women* did not gain legislative approval. Only choice **D** both clarifies the relationship between the Equal Rights Amendment and legislative approval and indicates that the failure of the amendment precedes the protests logically and chronologically.

23-1. A. The original is better than any of the alternatives.

23-2. B. *Is when* is not acceptable because *gerrymandering* is not a time; choice **E** repeats this error. **D** is not best because it leaves vague whether gerrymandering is synonymous with unfair division. **C** is very general and vague.

23-3. C. Choice **C** best corrects the awkward wording in the original sentence. Choice **D**, although grammatically correct, changes the meaning of the original.

23-4. D. The pronoun *they* is not used clearly in the original; it is illogical to conclude that *they* refers to "distinguished performances" because all performances are "new to the screen." (Each performance is done only once even though it may be shown many times.) New *performers* (as opposed to veteran actors) may be new to the screen, however, and the use of *actors* in choice **D** provides this clear, logical reference.

23-5. E. The conventions of standard written English dictate that *but also* be preceded by *not only,* which is not the case in the original here. Additionally, the underlined portion illogically compares *appearance* to *other pigs* and relies on a vague, wordy phrase, "with reference to the belief." Choice **E** remedies all of these problems by simplifying the structure and clarifying the diction. **B** is not a good choice because it employs the past tense. The original is in present tense, and there is no reason to change it because present tense is appropriate when one discusses "timeless" works of art and literature.

24-1. B. *Having finished* expresses the past tense by itself, so *after* is repetitious (its meaning is already implied in *having finished*). None of the other choices expresses the past tense both economically and clearly.

24-2. D. *Supposes* is not the correct verb tense; in order to be parallel with *to mistake,* the verb in the underlined portion must also connect idiomatically with *to. Suspect* is the only possible choice.

24-3. B. The original is flawed by faulty parallelism. *Fearless* is not parallel to *having great skill*. Choice **B** corrects this problem. *Fearless* is parallel to *skillful*. **C** and **E** are both unnecessarily wordy.

24-4. D. In the original, the verb *were* does not agree with the subject, *type*. **B** is incorrect because it uses the plural *products* with *a*. **E** is incorrect because it results in a sentence fragment. **D** is an economical and clear choice that retains the meaning of the original.

24-5. E. The original sentence contains a subtle error in faulty parallelism. The items compared—"success in school" and "playing marbles"—become parallel if *success* is changed to *succeeding*. **E** makes this necessary change and also brings the compared items closer together in order to further clarify their relationship.

25-1. D. The paragraph implies the importance of articulation disorders by mentioning how heavily they contribute to a clinician's caseload.

25-2. A. Bacon advocates retaining dignity without intruding upon liberty. The author implies that retaining dignity is impossible without intruding upon another's liberty by stating that not intruding upon liberty is impossible. **B, C,** and **D** contradict the author's argument, and **E** presents an irrelevant issue.

25-3. B. II only. The only reasonable completion of the argument would be that the alkalies in Lake Huron may be insufficient to support *Alpha splendes*.

25-4. C. I and II only. The author both relies on an interpretation of Bacon's statement and discusses liberty and dignity in absolute terms; statements I and II subvert such reliance. Statement III supports, reiterates in fact, the author's argument.

25-5. B. III only. The same word may have more than one meaning, each of which may be completely different from the others. In this case, the word *ball* means two different things.

26-1. E. Flamo Lighters claim to be convenient ("in your pocket wherever you go"), have longevity ("ten-year guarantee"), be winter-proof ("all-weather"), and be dependable ("always reliable, always dependable"). They do not profess to be all-purpose, however.

26-2. A. The final statement that elders believed to possess special powers are "sometimes treated with a deference based on fear rather than love" assumes that deference is normally accorded based on love.

26-3. E. Choices **A** and **B** are not implied; they are explicitly stated. **C** is vague; the meaning of *consequentiality* is not clear. **D** is incorrect because the author is arguing that doing nothing has no consequences. Choice **E** is correct. This author says that doing nothing keeps us safe from consequences; this could be true only in light of the implication that doing nothing is not an act.

26-4. B. According to the author, the alternative to experiencing consequences is playing it *safe*. This can mean only that consequences are dangerous.

26-5. D. *Evolution* is to *species* in the same way as *bush* is to *branches*. Just as the branches of a bush reach out every which way in varying lengths, the results of evolution (forms of life, species) have developed in irregular "branches." This is the main point of the paragraph.

27. D. Shark study has been slowed because the sharks are so dangerous and live in murky waters.

28. D. All organisms have a bioelectric field, so the male shark would be able to find many sharks more easily than one. They congregate to make it more difficult for the male to grasp one, not to make detection more difficult.

29. C. The *third eye* is the light-gathering organ.

30. B. The sharks' sensing the voltage created by currents moving through the earth's magnetic field is at least tangentially relevant to choice **B.**

31-1. B. Choice **B** eliminates the *irregardless* of the original wording. *Irregardless* is incorrect in standard written English. Choices **C** and **D** change the original meaning slightly and are therefore wrong. Choice **E** is not idiomatic.

31-2. A. Choice **B** is a dangling phrase. Choice **C** is wordy and changes the meaning. Choice **D** has a misplaced modifier *(complete),* and choice **E** has no grammatical subject.

31-3. C. The verb in this sentence should be *is* (not *are*) to agree with the singular subject, *actor.* A parenthetical phrase enclosed by commas and beginning with words such as *along with, including,* and *as well as* changes the number of neither the subject nor the verb. Choice **B** correctly uses *are* because the subject in this sentence has been made plural; however, the construction is awkward and wordy. Choice **D** retains the incorrect *are* and changes the meaning of the sentence. **E** leaves out the fact that the actor is on the train.

31-4. C. The original contains two errors: *principle* (fundamental truth) is incorrect usage, and *reason . . . was because* is a redundant phrase. Only choice **C** corrects both of these errors and retains the full meaning of the original.

31-5. D. *Continually* is a squinting modifier, unclear because it may refer to either *reading* or *reminds.* Choice **D** clarifies its reference. Choice **E** is vague and wordy.

32-1. D. A misplaced modifier here makes it seem that liberal activists had "the power to destroy the world." Choice **D** logically links nuclear weapons with the power to destroy the world. Although choice **B** is somewhat clearer than the original, it creates a clause incompatible with the rest of the sentence.

32-2. E. Choice **E** corrects the "disjointed" wording of the original sentence.

32-3. B. When subjects are connected with *nor* or *or,* the verb is governed by the subject closest to it; in **A** and **D,** the closer subject does not agree with the verb. **E** is awkward. In **B,** the subject, *director,* agrees with the verb, *predicts.*

32-4. B. The introductory phrase is a dangling modifier and makes the sentence seem to say that the poetry is composing at the keyboard. Choice **B** makes it clear that the poets do the composing, and it does so without significantly altering the meaning of the original.

32-5. C. Choice **E** correctly states *his joining.* The possessive *his* is called for here before the *–ing* verb from *joining.* Choice **D,** although grammatically correct, slightly alters the meaning of the original sentence.

33-1. A. All of the other choices are much less relevant than the issue of how efficiently and effectively the program helps students to achieve competency.

33-2. A. Only this choice necessarily introduces a contrasting statement, one which would probably take issue with the points of the argument. **C** and **D** might possibly begin critical, contrasting statements but may have other uses as well.

33-3. B. This choice suggests that exterior forces, such as advertising, influence consumer choices, and it undercuts the contention that consumers know what they want. Each of the other choices is either irrelevant or strengthens rather than weakens the argument.

33-4. C. Voltaire's statement shows the irony that the descriptive word used *(common)* may not, in reality, be so. Likewise, the adjective describing the shrimp *(jumbo)* indicates that the shrimp are large, though this may not be the case.

33-5. E. Choices **A** and **B** are irrelevant to the argument, and **D** is an illogical criticism. **E** is a logical conclusion that poses a significant problem.

34-1. C. The student's qualification shows that he or she doubts whether the senator's statement is absolutely true, but the response is not so pronounced as to suggest any of the other choices.

34-2. B. The first speaker puts forth a "perfect" view of friendship (idealistic), and the second questions the endurance of friendship (cynicism).

34-3. D. I and III. Neither consumers nor legal loopholes are mentioned in the statement.

34-4. C. If no speech that presents one or more facts is uninformative, any and every uninformative speech must present no facts.

34-5. E. Since all speeches intended to persuade contain few or all facts, such a speech cannot be uninformative, since an uninformative speech is *factless*.

35. E. Though parts of the passage would support the ideas of **A, C,** or **D,** the best answer here is **E.** In questions about the "purpose" of a passage, the best answers apply to almost all of the excerpt, not to just one paragraph.

36. A. The rhetorical purpose is its function in the development of the argument. Though some believe that the GNP ought to include the work described in the third paragraph, the author takes no stand. In any case, statement II is not a rhetorical purpose. Statement III is inaccurate.

37. B. Choices **A, C, D,** and **E** are all listed or implied as growth factors in the passage (end of the last paragraph).

38. D. The GNP does not include "productive but unpaid work." But a salaried stock broker would be paid for time spent doing research.

39-1. D. In the original, the subject, *shopper,* does not agree with the verb, *tend.* Choice **D** corrects this error without making additional, unnecessary changes.

39-2. A. The original is perfectly clear and correct, and none of the other choices is an improvement.

39-3. D. Choice **D** provides the parallel structure needed in this sentence for the three ideas stated in a series. The other choices are structurally wrong or alter the original meaning.

39-4. C. Choice **C** clarifies the ambiguous working of the original sentence. It is clear in **C** who is arriving and who is doing the meeting.

39-5. A. Of the choices given, the original is the best phrasing. The commas in choice **B** change the meaning of the original by making the phrase nonrestrictive. In **C,** the phrase *graduated high school* is not acceptable standard written English. Choice **D** is awkward, and **E** changes the meaning of the sentence.

40-1. D. The verb *lying* (resting—lie, lay, lain) is correct here; *laying* (placing—lay, laid, laid) takes an object.

40-2. E. Choice **E** is the most direct, concise wording of the original sentence. The verbs in these answers are the problem areas. Choice **B,** for example, is incorrect because of the present tense *is* and *attracts.*

40-3. B. Choice **B** corrects the verb problem in the original sentence. "Have and will continue to include" is better expressed as "have included and will continue to include."

40-4. C. Choice **C** supplies the correct verb for this sentence, *would.* The other choices either introduce additional errors or change the original meaning.

40-5. E. Choice **E** eliminates the *but* in the original wording and supplies the correct punctuation for the *which* clause that needs commas to set it off from the rest of this sentence.

41-1. C. The passage establishes that the survivors were caught in a life-and-death "survival" situation. Although **B** may be a possible choice, answer **C** logically follows the sense of their dilemma, clouded by uncertainty and the possibility of death.

41-2. E. This choice raises the question relevant to establishing the mural as art in Aristotelian terms.

41-3. B. The conclusion that highway deaths will be reduced with the advent of automatic restraints is necessarily based upon the assumption that such restraints reduce highway deaths. None of the other choices focuses on the conclusion; **E** is an assumption which could motivate the passage as a whole, rather than just the conclusion.

41-4. C. Each of the other choices requires assumptions and conclusions not supported or implied by the argument. The argument's stress on reduced funds leads logically to the conclusion that further spending is unwise.

41-5. E. This choice weakens the point made by the final observation. Each of the other choices either strengthens points made by the observation or is irrelevant.

PART IV

ANOTHER PRACTICE TEST

General Directions: In this section, you will have a total time of 60 minutes to plan and write two essays, one for each topic given. The specific time allotted for each essay is 30 minutes.

Analysis of an Issue

TIME: 30 Minutes

Directions: This section will require you to analyze and explain your views on the issue given. Consider many points of view as you develop your own position on the issue. There is no right or wrong answer to the question.

Read the statement and directions carefully. Make any notes or do any prewriting on your scratch paper. Then type your response into the computer.

> "The government should enable parents to pay tuition at either a public or private school. If fewer children attend public schools, the state will save money, and healthy competition for students will inevitably lead to an improvement of all schools."

> Do you disagree with this statement? Write a response supporting or opposing a voucher system to support education. Use your readings or personal experience to develop your argument.

GO ON TO THE NEXT PAGE

Analysis of an Argument

TIME: 30 Minutes

Directions: This section will require you to critique the argument given. Questioning underlying assumptions, finding alternative explanations or counterexamples, and delineating evidence to strengthen or weaken an argument are some possible approaches.

Read the argument and directions carefully. Make any notes or do any prewriting on your scratch paper. Then type your response into the computer.

The following appeared as an editorial in a city newspaper:

"Only thirty-eight percent of the city's registered voters turned out to cast ballots on the proposed increase in the public school tax assessment, and the measure was defeated by a wide margin. This voter apathy cannot be excused by the bad weather on election day. It demonstrates all too clearly the city's indifference to education and to the well-being of the next generation."

Write an essay in which you discuss how convincing you find this argument. Your essay should consider its line of reasoning and how well it uses evidence. You may wish to discuss any doubtful assumptions and how other possible explanations could affect its conclusions. Your essay may also consider how the argument could be made more persuasive and its conclusion more convincing.

IF YOU FINISH BEFORE TIME IS CALLED, CHECK YOUR WORK ON THIS SECTION ONLY. DO NOT WORK ON ANY OTHER SECTION IN THE TEST.

QUANTITATIVE SECTION

TIME: 75 Minutes

37 Questions

General Directions: Your score on the quantitative section will be based on how well you do on the questions presented and also on the number of questions you answer. You should try to pace yourself so that you have sufficient time to consider every question. If possible, answer all 37 questions in this section. Guess if you need to. Select the best answer choice for each question.

Use the scratch paper given for any necessary calculations.

Note: Some problems may be accompanied by figures or diagrams. These figures are drawn as accurately as possible except when it is stated in a specific problem that the figure is not drawn to scale. The figure is meant to provide information useful in solving the problem or problems. Unless otherwise stated or indicated, all figures lie in a plane. All numbers used are real numbers.

Data Sufficiency Directions: Each of the problems below consists of a question and two statements, labeled (1) and (2), in which certain data are given. You must decide whether the data given in the statements are sufficient to answer the question. Using the data given in the statements plus your knowledge of mathematics and everyday facts (such as the number of days in July or the meaning of "counterclockwise"), you are to choose oval

- **A.** if statement (1) ALONE is sufficient, but statement (2) alone is not sufficient to answer the question asked;

- **B.** if statement (2) ALONE is sufficient, but statement (1) alone is not sufficient to answer the question asked;

- **C.** if both statements (1) and (2) TOGETHER are sufficient to answer the question asked, but NEITHER statement ALONE is sufficient;

- **D.** if EACH statement ALONE is sufficient to answer the question asked;

- **E.** if statements (1) and (2) TOGETHER are NOT sufficient to answer the question asked, and additional data specific to the problem are needed.

Problem Solving Directions: Solve each problem in this section by using the information given and your own mathematical calculations. Then select the correct answer of the five choices given.

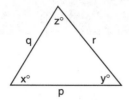

Note: Figure not drawn to scale

1. In the triangle above, which is greatest, *p, q,* or *r*?

   (1) The side with length *q* is the shortest side of the triangle.

   (2) $z = x + y$

   A. Statement (1) ALONE is sufficient, but statement (2) alone is not sufficient.

   B. Statement (2) ALONE is sufficient, but statement (1) alone is not sufficient.

   C. BOTH statements (1) and (2) TOGETHER are sufficient, but NEITHER statement ALONE is sufficient.

   D. EACH statement ALONE is sufficient.

   E. Statements (1) and (2) TOGETHER are NOT sufficient.

2. If *m* and *n* are positive integers, what is the value of *p*?

   (1) $p = 4^{(m + n)}$

   (2) $m = 15 - n$

   A. Statement (1) ALONE is sufficient, but statement (2) alone is not sufficient.

   B. Statement (2) ALONE is sufficient, but statement (1) alone is not sufficient.

C. BOTH statements (1) and (2) TOGETHER are sufficient, but NEITHER statement ALONE is sufficient.

D. EACH statement ALONE is sufficient.

E. Statements (1) and (2) TOGETHER are NOT sufficient.

3. Currently, 30% of The Flower Company's total revenue comes from sales through the Internet. Internet-based sales are projected to increase by 150% in the next three years at The Flower Company. If the projected increase turns out to be accurate, what will be The Flower Company's Internet-based revenue in three years?

   (1) In three years, The Flower Company's total revenue will be $10,000.

   (2) Currently, The Flower Company's total revenue is $6,000.

   A. Statement (1) ALONE is sufficient, but statement (2) alone is not sufficient.

   B. Statement (2) ALONE is sufficient, but statement (1) alone is not sufficient.

   C. BOTH statements (1) and (2) TOGETHER are sufficient, but NEITHER statement ALONE is sufficient.

   D. EACH statement ALONE is sufficient.

   E. Statements (1) and (2) TOGETHER are NOT sufficient.

4. When $x - p$ is divided by $p + 1$, the quotient is n and there is no remainder. Which of the following must be the value of x?

A. $n(p + 1)$

B. $n(p - 1)$

C. $p(n + 1)$

D. $p(n + 1) + n$

E. $n(p + 1)(p - 1)$

5. Is x divisible by 9?

(1) x is divisible by 3.

(2) When x is divided by 6, the remainder is 3.

A. Statement (1) ALONE is sufficient, but statement (2) alone is not sufficient.

B. Statement (2) ALONE is sufficient, but statement (1) alone is not sufficient.

C. BOTH statements (1) and (2) TOGETHER are sufficient, but NEITHER statement ALONE is sufficient.

D. EACH statement ALONE is sufficient.

E. Statements (1) and (2) TOGETHER are NOT sufficient.

6. Ralph bought a stereo priced at $120. If the total price he paid at the counter was $133.50, which included the price of the stereo plus x percent sales tax, which of the following is the best estimate of x?

A. less than 5

B. between 5 and 9

C. between 9 and 12

D. between 12 and 15

E. more than 15

7. What is the value of $(x + 3)^2$?

(1) $|x| = 3$

(2) $|x| + x = 0$

A. Statement (1) ALONE is sufficient, but statement (2) alone is not sufficient.

B. Statement (2) ALONE is sufficient, but statement (1) alone is not sufficient.

C. BOTH statements (1) and (2) TOGETHER are sufficient, but NEITHER statement ALONE is sufficient.

D. EACH statement ALONE is sufficient.

E. Statements (1) and (2) TOGETHER are NOT sufficient.

8. In a high school, some students have single majors while all others have double majors. How many more students have double majors than single majors?

(1) 60 percent of the students in the high school have double majors.

(2) There are 200 students in the high school.

A. Statement (1) ALONE is sufficient, but statement (2) alone is not sufficient.

B. Statement (2) ALONE is sufficient, but statement (1) alone is not sufficient.

C. BOTH statements (1) and (2) TOGETHER are sufficient, but NEITHER statement ALONE is sufficient.

D. EACH statement ALONE is sufficient.

E. Statements (1) and (2) TOGETHER are NOT sufficient.

9. A store reduced the price of all items in the store by 10% on the first day and by another 10% on the second day. The price of items on the second day was what percent of the price before the first reduction took place?

A. 80.0

B. 80.9

C. 81.0

D. 81.1

E. 81.9

10. If $N = 16 \times 10^{-p}$ and $-4 < p < 4$, how many different integer values of p will make N a perfect square?

A. 0

B. 2

C. 3

D. 5

E. 7

11. Joe's average (arithmetic mean) test score across 4 equally weighted tests was 80. He was allowed to drop his lowest score. After doing so, his average test score improved to 85. What is the lowest test score that was dropped?

A. 20

B. 25

C. 55

D. 65

E. 80

12. What was Joe's average (arithmetic mean) test score for the semester if there were 4 tests in the semester that were equally weighted?

(1) Joe's total score for the semester was 324.

(2) Joe's average score for the first two tests was twice the average score for the last two tests.

A. Statement (1) ALONE is sufficient, but statement (2) alone is not sufficient.

B. Statement (2) ALONE is sufficient, but statement (1) alone is not sufficient.

C. BOTH statements (1) and (2) TOGETHER are sufficient, but NEITHER statement ALONE is sufficient.

D. EACH statement ALONE is sufficient.

E. Statements (1) and (2) TOGETHER are NOT sufficient.

13. Is x greater than y?

(1) $x^2 > y^2$

(2) x and y are positive integers

A. Statement (1) ALONE is sufficient, but statement (2) alone is not sufficient.

B. Statement (2) ALONE is sufficient, but statement (1) alone is not sufficient.

C. BOTH statements (1) and (2) TOGETHER are sufficient, but NEITHER statement ALONE is sufficient.

D. EACH statement ALONE is sufficient.

E. Statements (1) and (2) TOGETHER are NOT sufficient.

14. In a manufacturing plant, it takes 36 machines 4 hours of continuous work to fill 8 standard orders. At this rate, how many hours of continuous work by 72 machines are required to fill 12 standard orders?

A. 3

B. 6

C. 8

D. 9

E. 12

15. Ann is 5 years older than Sue, and Jill is twice as old as Ann. If S is Sue's age and J is Jill's age, what is the relationship between S and J?

A. $J = S + 10$

B. $J = 2S + 10$

C. $J = 2S + 5$

D. $J = 2S - 10$

E. $J = 2S - 5$

16. The water level in a reservoir has been dropping at the rate of 14 inches per day. Exactly 5 days ago, the water level was at w inches. What will be the water level exactly 4 days from now if the rate at which the level is dropping remains the same?

A. $w - 126$

B. $w - 56$

C. $w - 14$

D. $w + 14$

E. $w + 126$

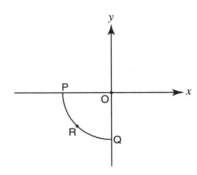

17. In the x-y coordinate plane shown above, point R is at the center of the quarter-circle arc PQ. What is the x-coordinate of point R if the radius of the quarter circle is 2?

A. $-\sqrt{3}$

B. $-\sqrt{2}$

C. $\dfrac{-\sqrt{2}}{2}$

D. $-\dfrac{1}{2}$

E. $\sqrt{2}$

18. If $x + 3y - 3 = 0$, what is the value of x?

   (1) $3x + 9y = 9$

   (2) $2x + 6y = 6$

   A.   Statement (1) ALONE is sufficient, but statement (2) alone is not sufficient.

   B.   Statement (2) ALONE is sufficient, but statement (1) alone is not sufficient.

   C.   BOTH statements (1) and (2) TOGETHER are sufficient, but NEITHER statement ALONE is sufficient.

   D.   EACH statement ALONE is sufficient.

   E.   Statements (1) and (2) TOGETHER are NOT sufficient.

19. Company P's profit this year was what percent of its profit last year?

   (1)   Company P's total profit for this year and last year combined was $15,000.

   (2)   This year, Company P's profit was $5,000.

   A.   Statement (1) ALONE is sufficient, but statement (2) alone is not sufficient.

   B.   Statement (2) ALONE is sufficient, but statement (1) alone is not sufficient.

   C.   BOTH statements (1) and (2) TOGETHER are sufficient, but NEITHER statement ALONE is sufficient.

   D.   EACH statement ALONE is sufficient.

   E.   Statements (1) and (2) TOGETHER are NOT sufficient.

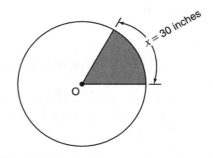

20. What is the radius, in inches, of Circle O?

   (1)   Arc x is $\frac{1}{16}$ of the circumference.

   (2)   Area of the shaded region is $\frac{3,600}{\pi}$ square inches.

   A.   Statement (1) ALONE is sufficient, but statement (2) alone is not sufficient.

   B.   Statement (2) ALONE is sufficient, but statement (1) alone is not sufficient.

   C.   BOTH statements (1) and (2) TOGETHER are sufficient, but NEITHER statement ALONE is sufficient.

   D.   EACH statement ALONE is sufficient.

   E.   Statements (1) and (2) TOGETHER are NOT sufficient.

21. If 1.001×10^k is exactly 1,000 times greater than p, what is the value of p?

   A. $1.001 \times 10^{k/3}$

   B. $1.001 \times 10^{k-3}$

   C. 1×10^k

   D. 1.001×10^{-3}

   E. 1.001×10^{1000k}

22. During the first two weeks of January, the total rainfall in Springdale was 15 inches. If the rainfall during the second week was 1.5 times the rainfall during the first week, what was the rainfall during the *second* week of January?

    A.   5 inches

    B.   6 inches

    C.   9 inches

    D.   10 inches

    E.   12 inches

23. On a number line, integer C is between integers A and B. What is the value of C if the value of A is 1?

    (1)   The distance between A and C is twice the distance between C and B.

    (2)   The distance between A and B is 9 units.

    A.   Statement (1) ALONE is sufficient, but statement (2) alone is not sufficient.

    B.   Statement (2) ALONE is sufficient, but statement (1) alone is not sufficient.

    C.   BOTH statements (1) and (2) TOGETHER are sufficient, but NEITHER statement ALONE is sufficient.

    D.   EACH statement ALONE is sufficient.

    E.   Statements (1) and (2) TOGETHER are NOT sufficient.

24. On Saturday, the original price of a shirt was discounted by 20%. On Monday, the price of the shirt was marked up p percent so that the new price on Monday was 20% more than the original price before the discount. What is the value of p?

    A.   20%

    B.   30%

    C.   33⅓%

    D.   40%

    E.   50%

25. Train A is traveling at 40 miles per hour and Train B is traveling on a parallel track in the same direction at 60 miles per hour. Currently, Train A is 15 miles ahead of Train B. How many minutes will it take Train B to catch up with Train A?

    A.   45

    B.   60

    C.   75

    D.   80

    E.   90

26. Profit ratio is defined as the ratio of the profit in dollars to the investment in dollars. Was Bill's profit ratio greater than Jack's profit ratio?

   (1) Bill invested $4,000 and his profit was $1,500.

   (2) Jack's profit was 12 cents per dollar that he invested.

   A. Statement (1) ALONE is sufficient, but statement (2) alone is not sufficient.

   B. Statement (2) ALONE is sufficient, but statement (1) alone is not sufficient.

   C. BOTH statements (1) and (2) TOGETHER are sufficient, but NEITHER statement ALONE is sufficient.

   D. EACH statement ALONE is sufficient.

   E. Statements (1) and (2) TOGETHER are NOT sufficient.

27. The area of one square is $x^2 + 10x + 25$ and the area of another square is $4x^2 - 12x + 9$. If the sum of the perimeters of both squares is 32, what is the value of x?

   A. 0

   B. 2

   C. 2.5

   D. 4.67

   E. 10

28. If p is a positive integer and $r = p(p + 1)(p + 2)$, then which of the following could *not* be a value of r?

   A. 6

   B. 36

   C. 116

   D. 156

   E. 180

29. Sue has only pennies, dimes, and nickels in a jar. The jar has at least 1 but no more than 4 pennies. If the jar has at least 1 nickel and 1 dime, which of the following could NOT be the total amount of money in the jar?

   A. 51 cents

   B. 53 cents

   C. 55 cents

   D. 57 cents

   E. 59 cents

30. Compound P contains just three chemicals — X, Y, and Z. The three chemicals are required to be in the following ratio: 5 grams of X, 15 grams of Y, and z grams of Z. If 25 grams of X and a proportional amount of Y are added to the compound, what is the weight of Z that must also be added to maintain the required overall proportion?

   (1) The weight of Compound P is always three times the weight of Z.

   (2) The weight of Z is always twice the weight of X.

   A. Statement (1) ALONE is sufficient, but statement (2) alone is not sufficient.

B. Statement (2) ALONE is sufficient, but statement (1) alone is not sufficient.

C. BOTH statements (1) and (2) TOGETHER are sufficient, but NEITHER statement ALONE is sufficient.

D. EACH statement ALONE is sufficient.

E. Statements (1) and (2) TOGETHER are NOT sufficient.

31. The password for a computer account has to consist of exactly eight characters. Characters can be chosen from any of the following: letter of the alphabet, numerical digits from 0 to 9, a hyphen, or the exclamation mark. Upper-case letters (e.g., *A*) are considered different from lower-case letters (e.g., *a*), and characters can be repeated. Given these rules, how many different passwords are possible?

A. 2^9

B. 2^{14}

C. 2^{18}

D. 2^{40}

E. 2^{48}

32. For any real number *x*, the operator α is defined as:

$\alpha(x) = x(1 - x)$

If $p + 1 = \alpha(p + 1)$, then $p =$

A. -1

B. 0

C. 1

D. 2

E. 3

33. What is the cost of wallpaper needed to cover all four walls of a square room if each wall is 10 feet high?

(1) The floor has a surface area of 144 square feet.

(2) Each square foot of wallpaper costs 60 cents.

A. Statement (1) ALONE is sufficient, but statement (2) alone is not sufficient.

B. Statement (2) ALONE is sufficient, but statement (1) alone is not sufficient.

C. BOTH statements (1) and (2) TOGETHER are sufficient, but NEITHER statement ALONE is sufficient.

D. EACH statement ALONE is sufficient.

E. Statements (1) and (2) TOGETHER are NOT sufficient.

34. There are how many 4-digit even numbers if the first digit cannot be a zero?

A. 3,600

B. 3,645

C. 4,500

D. 4,999

E. 5,000

35. When positive integer *x* is divided by 6, the remainder is 1. Which of the following must be true?

    I. *x* is a prime number

    II. *x* is odd

    III. *x* is divisible by 7

  A. I only

  B. II only

  C. III only

  D. I and II only

  E. II and III only

36. What is the greatest integer in a set of five different positive integers if 1 is the smallest integer in the set?

  (1) The average (arithmetic mean) of all integers is 4 and the median of the set is also 4.

  (2) The set contains only 1 even number.

  A. Statement (1) ALONE is sufficient, but statement (2) alone is not sufficient.

  B. Statement (2) ALONE is sufficient, but statement (1) alone is not sufficient.

  C. BOTH statements (1) and (2) TOGETHER are sufficient, but NEITHER statement ALONE is sufficient.

  D. EACH statement ALONE is sufficient.

  E. Statements (1) and (2) TOGETHER are NOT sufficient.

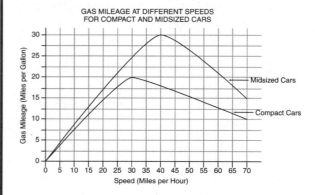

37. The figure above shows gas mileage at different speeds for all compact and midsize cars. John drove a compact car at 30 miles per hour for 1 hour and at 50 miles per hour for 30 minutes. Jill drove a midsize car at 40 miles per hour for 1 hour and at 60 miles per hour for 30 minutes. The total amount of fuel consumed by Jill's car is approximately what percent of the total amount of fuel consumed by John's car?

  A. 80%

  B. 90%

  C. 110%

  D. 140%

  E. 145%

VERBAL SECTION

TIME: 75 Minutes

41 Questions

General Directions: Your score on the verbal section will be based on how well you do on the questions presented and also on the number of questions you answer. Try to pace yourself so that you have sufficient time to consider every question. If possible, answer all 41 questions in this section. Guess if you need to. Select the best answer choice for each question. You will encounter three kinds of questions in this section: Sentence Correction, Reading Comprehension, and Critical Reasoning.

Sentence Correction Directions: Some part of each sentence is underlined; sometimes the whole sentence is underlined. Five choices for rephrasing the underlined part follow each sentence; the first choice repeats the original, and the other four are different. If the first choice seems better than the alternatives, choose that answer; if not, choose one of the others.

For each sentence, consider the requirements of standard written English. Your choice should be a correct and effective expression, not awkward or ambiguous. Focus on grammar, word choice, sentence construction, and punctuation. If a choice changes the meaning of the original sentence, do not select it.

Reading Comprehension Directions: A reading passage will be followed by questions based on its content. After reading the passage, choose the best answer to each question (select the corresponding oval on the computer screen). Answer all questions about the passage on the basis of what is *stated* or *implied* in the passage. You may refer back to the passage.

Critical Reasoning Directions: You will read a brief passage and determine the passage author's line of reasoning using only commonsense standards of logic. No knowledge of formal logic is required. Then choose the best answer, realizing that several choices may be possible, but only one is best.

GO ON TO THE NEXT PAGE

1. Opponents argue that physician-assisted suicide would be disproportionately chosen <u>by the poor, by those who were undereducated, and those people</u> fearful of the high cost of their illness.

   A. by the poor, by those who were undereducated, and those people

   B. by the poor, by those who were undereducated, and by those people

   C. by the poor, those who were undereducated, and by those

   D. by the poor, by the undereducated and by those

   E. by the poor, the undereducated, and those

Read the following passage and answer Questions 2–5.

Nothing is sure but death and taxes, and of course that north is north and south is south, and thus it has always been, so they say. But they'd be wrong. You can
(5)   perhaps be sure about death and taxes, but you might want to reconsider the rest of it. In fact, at many times in our planet's history, north has become south and south has become north, in a
(10) process called magnetic reversal.

Paleogeologists have discovered the existence of these mysterious phenomena (in a field of study known as paleomagnetism) by investigating rocks. When
(15) rocks are being formed from magmas, atoms within their crystals respond to the earth's magnetic field by "pointing" toward the magnetic north pole. By age dating the rocks and noting their mag-
(20) netic alignment, scientists can determine where on earth the north pole was located at that time because as the rocks solidified, they trapped that information within them. The study of ancient lava
(25) flows has revealed that at certain periods

in the earth's history magnetic north was directly opposite its present location. In fact, it has been determined that the north/south reversal has occurred on av-
(30) erage every 500,000 years and that the last reversal took place about 700,000 years ago. Scientists call those periods of "normal" polarity (the magnetic orientation of our modern era) and "reversed"
(35) polarity (the magnetic orientation of the reverse situation) by the name "magnetic chrons."

Although the fact of such reversals is clear, why and how they happen and
(40) their effects on the planet are subjects of considerable debate. Because no one knows precisely how the earth's magnetic field is produced, it becomes difficult to say how it might be reversed.
(45) Among explanations proposed are a reversal of the direction of convection currents in the liquid outer core of the earth and a collision between the earth and a meteorite or comet. And while the pre-
(50) cise effects of a reversal are not known, there can be little doubt that the earth would receive during the process a great deal more damaging ultraviolet radiation than it now does and that such
(55) occurrences have been correlated with the extinction of certain species in the geologic past.

2. The main purpose of the passage is to

   A. explain what is meant by "normal" polarity and its relationship to "magnetic chrons."

   B. present opposing hypotheses concerning the earth's magnetic field and argue that one of them is adequate.

   C. explain the process of magnetic reversal and how it was discovered.

D. discuss the difference between "normal" and "reversed" polarities and how the difference affects convection currents in the earth's outer core.

E. set forth a time table for magnetic reversal.

3. "Magnetic reversal" refers to

A. the atoms in rock crystals pointing toward the magnetic north pole.

B. north becoming south and south becoming north.

C. the reversal of direction in ancient lava flows.

D. a reversal of the direction of convection currents in the outer core of the earth.

E. a disturbance in the regular 500,000 year cycle of the magnetic field.

4. According to the passage, which of the following was crucial to the discovery of magnetic reversal?

A. solidification of rocks formed from magmas

B. the extinction of certain species 700,000 years ago

C. the rapid change from "normal" to "reversed" polarity

D. the change in the direction of convection currents in the earth's outer core

E. lava flows "pointing" to magnetic north

5. It is reasonable to infer from the passage that

A. in spite of past reversals, "normal" polarity is now firmly established.

B. if the earth collides with a meteorite, the magnetic field will be reversed.

C. the earth's magnetic field was produced about 700,000 years ago.

D. reversal of the direction of convection currents would signal a magnetic reversal.

E. a magnetic reversal could present a danger to humans.

6. It is hardly strange that all societal people possess something in common, no matter how different they consider themselves. For in the act of acquiring and rejecting objects they all acquire a social identity. This identity stems from a person's unwillingness to possess objects that may not be socially acceptable and a person's unwillingness to reject certain objects that are necessary for social acceptance.

The above argument assumes that

A. People who are not materialistic may not have social identities.

B. All people live in societies.

C. People who are willing to possess socially unacceptable objects will not have social identities.

D. All societal people engage in the acquisition and rejection of objects.

E. People who are willing to reject socially unacceptable objects will have social identities.

GO ON TO THE NEXT PAGE

Verbal Section

7. The mummies discovered in the caves have been hidden for so long that no other traces of their civilization remain, <u>which leaves many questions anthropologists cannot answer</u>.

   A. which leaves many questions anthropologists cannot answer.

   B. and this leaves many questions that anthropologists cannot answer.

   C. a gap that leaves many questions anthropologists cannot answer.

   D. and it raises many unanswered questions for anthropologists.

   E. this leaving many unanswered questions for anthropologists.

8. Unlike London, where the bus and underground systems make travel throughout the city simple and affordable, <u>visitors to Los Angeles soon discover that a car is indispensable</u>.

   A. visitors to Los Angeles soon discover that a car is indispensable.

   B. Los Angeles visitors discovering soon that a car is indispensable.

   C. Los Angeles makes a car indispensable, as visitors soon discover.

   D. a car is indispensable in Los Angeles, as visitors soon discover.

   E. visitors soon discover that a car is indispensable in Los Angeles.

9. During the first six months of life, infants tend to babble using velar consonants. From six to nine months, infants use alveolar sounds more than velar consonants. Labial sounds, an essential part of spoken English, are present throughout the first year but are never the most common sound in infant babbling. Based on these findings, one can conclude that infants have the complete physical ability to produce the sounds of words long before they use language.

   If true, which of the following statements would most strengthen the conclusion in the passage?

   A. Fricatives, a basic unit of speech, have not been observed in infant babbling.

   B. Computer speech synthesizers rely exclusively on alveolar, labial, or velar sounds.

   C. Exposure to language as an infant affects a person's later verbal ability.

   D. Infants have the mental capacity to do many things their bodies are not ready to perform.

   E. Alzheimer patients eventually lose the ability to use language but can still generate basic sounds.

10. Humans have a longer stride than dogs, but the frequency of their steps <u>is much slower</u>.

    A. is much slower.

    B. is much more slowly.

    C. are much slower.

    D. are much more slowly.

    E. are much less frequent.

Read the following passage and answer Questions 11–14.

A cyclone, which can cover an area of thousands of square miles, is made up of circulating winds, spiraling inward toward the center, in an atmospheric low-pressure system. Cyclonic winds travel

(5)

clockwise in the Southern Hemisphere and counterclockwise in the Northern Hemisphere. A tornado is a relatively small but extremely powerful and po-
(10) tentially dangerous type of cyclone.

The name tornado is derived from the Spanish tronado (thunderstorm) and the Latin tonare (thunder), as this weather phenomenon is usually accompanied by
(15) storms and precipitation. Tornadoes, also called twisters, most often form along a front and accompanying squall line where dry, cool, northern air meets water-laden, warm, southern air flowing
(20) in below, weather conditions most often found in the United States from April though June. As the warm air quickly rises along this line, more warm air rushes in to fill the void, and the classic
(25) funnel-shaped cloud begins to form, hanging down from the dark, heavy cumulonimbus storm clouds above. The funnel is visible because of its content of water droplets and the load of dust
(30) and debris rising with the violent updraft at its center.

Much that is known about tornadoes comes from inference from measurement of accompanying phenomena
(35) (since a tornado can destroy any measurement device in its path). Radar, particularly Doppler radar, has been used extensively to study these storms. Radar picks up an echo from storm clouds and
(40) precipitation, producing an analyzable image on the radarscope. The classic image associated with tornadoes is the echo resembling a "hook." The diameter of a tornado may vary from a few feet to
(45) well over a mile. Although forward speed averages from 10 to 25 mph, rotation speeds are often more than 200 mph and, in the case of an extremely strong storm, can reach 500 mph or
(50) more, and the updraft speed can reach

200 mph or better. While these storms can occur at any time and travel in any direction, they most often arise from midafternoon to early evening and most
(55) often move from the southwest to the northeast.

These storms can and do occur worldwide, but the United States is beset by more and more-violent tornadoes each
(60) year than is any other country. Of the states, Texas averages the most per year, followed by Florida, Oklahoma, Kansas, Nebraska, and Iowa. Obviously, these storms center on the Great Plains, with
(65) the exception of the high incidence in Florida, where tornadoes are often associated with hurricanes.

11. The main purpose of the passage is to

   A. contrast weather phenomena.

   B. explain the difficulty of measuring tornadoes.

   C. present detailed information about tornadoes.

   D. explain terminology related to tornadoes.

   E. provide an example of a general observation about tornadoes.

12. The funnel shape of a tornado is the result of

   A. the presence of water droplets and debris in cumulonimbus storm clouds.

   B. the "hook" of the tornado's rotation.

   C. the slow forward speed (10 to 25 mph) of the tornado.

GO ON TO THE NEXT PAGE

Verbal Section

D.   a rapid updraft of warm air filling a void left by rising warm air.

E.   the meeting of dry, warm air with wet, cool air.

13. Which of the following can be inferred about tornadoes from the information in the third paragraph?

    A.   The strength of a tornado arises from its rotation and updraft speeds as opposed to its forward speed.

    B.   The diameter of a tornado is dependent on the amount of debris and water droplets it contains.

    C.   Although it is the only method available, Doppler radar is inadequate for studying tornadoes.

    D.   The radar image of a tornado looks like a hook because of the tornado's large diameter.

    E.   A tornado's strength varies depending on the time of day it occurs and the direction it moves.

14. The most likely reason that more violent tornadoes appear to occur in the United States than in other countries is that

    A.   the Great Plains in the United States is the topography most conducive to violent tornadoes.

    B.   weather conditions in the United States are particularly conducive to the formation of violent tornadoes.

    C.   the population of the United States is significantly less dense than it is in other countries.

    D.   tornadoes can move only from the southwest to the northeast.

    E.   recording methods for tornadoes are more sophisticated and precise in the United States than in other countries.

Read the following passage and answer Questions 15–17.

The citizen must indeed be happy and good, and the legislator will seek to make him so; but very rich and very good at the same time he cannot be, not,
(5) at least, in the sense in which the many speak of riches. For they mean by "the rich" the few who have the most valuable possessions, although the owner of them may quite well be a rogue. And if
(10) this is true, I can never assent to the doctrine that the rich man will be happy—he must be good as well as rich. And good in a high degree, and rich in a high degree and the same time, he cannot be.
(15) Some one will ask, why not? And we shall answer—Because acquisitions which come from sources which are just and unjust indifferently are more than double those which come from just
(20) sources only; and the sums which are expended neither honorably nor disgracefully are only half as great as those which are expended honorably and on honorable purposes. Thus, if the one
(25) acquires double and spends half, the other who is in the opposite case and is a good man cannot possibly be wealthier than he. The first—I am speaking of the saver and not of the spender—is not al-
(30) ways bad; he may indeed in some cases be utterly bad, but, as I was saying, a good man he never is. For he who receives money unjustly as well as justly, and spends neither justly nor unjustly,
(35) will be a rich man if he be also thrifty. On the other hand, the utterly bad is in general profligate, and therefore very poor; while he who spends on noble objects, and acquires wealth by just means
(40) only, can hardly be remarkable for riches, any more than he can be very poor. Our statement, then, is true, that the very rich are not good, and, if they are not good, they are not happy. But the

(45) intention of our laws was that the citizens should be as happy as may be and as friendly as possible to one another. Therefore, as we have said not once but many times, the care of riches should
(50) have the last place in our thoughts.

15. The premise behind the argument in this passage is that

    A. to be happy, a man must be good.

    B. the drive to achieve wealth is greater than the drive to achieve goodness.

    C. a man who spends his money honorably is rarer than a man who spends his money disgracefully.

    D. it is better to be good than to be either rich or happy.

    E. if a man is a saver rather than a spender, he will be both good and wealthy.

16. The passage makes all of the following points EXCEPT

    A. A man will be richer if he doesn't insist on acquiring money only in honorable ways.

    B. Generally, a man who behaves wickedly will not be thrifty with his money.

    C. If a man acquires more than he spends, he is not necessarily bad, but neither is he good.

    D. Generally, poverty is a sign of a man's goodness.

    E. Donating money to worthy causes doesn't make a man good.

17. Which of the following best describes the method the author uses to make his point in this passage?

    A. providing concrete examples that lead to a generalization

    B. presenting a series of statements leading to a logical conclusion

    C. showing the weakness of opposing views

    D. listing exceptions to a generally accepted premise

    E. making a general statement and illustrating it with a particular case

18. Woven in bright blues, reds, and purples, <u>the mid-Asian tribes wore clothes remarkably similar</u> to those made by the ancestors of the Celts in Europe.

    A. the mid-Asian tribes wore clothes remarkably similar

    B. the tribes of mid-Asia wore clothes remarkably similar

    C. the mid-Asian tribes' clothes were remarkable in similarity to

    D. clothes were worn by the mid-Asian tribes that were remarkably similar

    E. clothes worn by mid-Asian tribes were remarkably similar

19. The hypoglossal canal, which carries the nerve complex required for speech, is as large in the skulls of Neanderthals <u>as modern humans which may indicate</u> an ability to speak.

    A. as modern humans which may indicate

    B. as modern humans, a fact that may indicate

    C. as modern humans, and this may indicate

GO ON TO THE NEXT PAGE

D. as in modern humans which may indicate

E. as in modern humans, a fact that may indicate

20. According to aerial reconnaissance, the bombers struck supply centers and airfields, <u>destroyed more than half of the enemy's fighter planes</u> and most of the oil supply lines.

A. destroyed more than half of the enemy's fighter planes

B. destroying more than half of the enemy's fighter planes

C. and destroyed more than half of the enemies fighter planes

D. and this destroyed more than half of the enemy's fighter planes

E. having destroyed more than half of the enemy's fighter planes

21. <u>In view of the fact that few voters could except her ideas</u> about immigration, her articles had little effect on the state elections.

A. In view of the fact that few voters could except her ideas

B. Due to few voters excepting her ideas

C. Because few voters accepted her ideas

D. Her ideas having been accepted by few voters

E. Voters having accepted few of her ideas

22. It really isn't necessary to eat a balanced diet of meat, breads, vegetables, and dairy products. After all, with the wide variety of vitamins on the market today, one can simply eat the foods one likes the most and take vitamins to balance one's diet and provide the missing nutrients.

Which of the following supports the conclusion in the passage above?

A. Excess vitamin intake can lead to many health problems that can range from minor infections to serious diseases.

B. The four food groups—meats, dairy products, breads and vegetables—are essential to maintaining a nutritional diet and a healthy body.

C. Studies have shown that three meals a day and the proper proportions of the four food groups are required in order to insure a strong immune system resistant to diseases.

D. Of the four food groups, each one provides certain nutrients that when combined together help to build a strong healthy body.

E. In order to maintain a healthy diet, only the nutrients derived from food intake are required; other elements such as proteins and carbohydrates are not necessary.

23. A variety of portable camcorders are now available which reproduce lifelike video and audio for playback on home televisions. Tapes used by these camcorders are available on two formats: VHS-C and 8mm. VHS-C tapes can be played in standard VHS video recorders through the use of an included adapter, but 8mm tapes require purchasing cables and installing them. The 8mm camcorders produce higher quality images

than VHS-C. Therefore, sales of the VHS-C are likely to be considerably greater than the 8mm format.

The argument above logically depends on which of the following assumptions?

A. VHS-C camcorders are superior to 8mm camcorders in all respects, providing excellent overall performance.

B. Due to their easy portability and capacity for reproducing pictures and sound, VHS-C camcorders are an ideal choice for people who wish to capture those once-in-a-lifetime moments.

C. The cost and inconvenience of additional cables required for playback by the 8mm format outweighs the customer's desire for picture clarity.

D. In recent years, manufacturers have reduced both the size and the weight of VHS-C and 8mm camcorders making them handheld marvels weighing a little over a pound.

E. Both 8mm and VHS-C camcorders are widely available in most electronics and department stores.

24. Along with guarantees of immediate elections to determine the future of the province, United Nations negotiators in the region are calling for an immediate cease-fire.

A. United Nations negotiators in the region are calling

B. United Nations negotiators are calling in the region

C. in the region, United Nations negotiators are calling

D. United Nations negotiators in the region calling

E. United Nations negotiators regionally called for

25. Radial Keratonomy (RK) is a new technology giving visually-impaired people the opportunity to attain perfect vision. RK can free people from the burden of wearing glasses or having to maintain contact lenses. The risks of this delicate operation have decreased significantly since the procedure's creation, and success rates have risen such that seven out of every ten people undergoing RK surgery can achieve perfect vision. Although the cost of the procedure is high ($3,000 per eye), all visually-impaired individuals should take advantage of RK to attain the perfect vision that everyone deserves, and thus improve their quality of life.

Which of the following assumptions underlies the passage above?

A. The benefits of perfect vision are numerous, and visually-impaired individuals should undergo RK surgery.

B. Visually-impaired individuals cannot improve their sight unless RK surgery is used to correct their disability.

C. RK technology will decrease in cost in the future.

D. The possibility of achieving perfect vision outweighs the costs and risks of RK surgery.

E. RK provides perfect vision for all individuals, regardless of their genetic background and visual disabilities.

GO ON TO THE NEXT PAGE

26. Scientists have performed numerous studies in order to determine the effects of irregular sleep patterns on health. Most have concluded that if one does not maintain a consistent sleeping schedule, the odds of becoming sick increase tremendously.

    All of the following support this conclusion EXCEPT:

    A. Daily activities such as eating and sleeping help to maintain the human body's biological clock which governs such functions as the immune system.

    B. Sleeping at the same time every day for a minimum number of hours contributes to overall good health and increases immunity to sickness.

    C. Since sleep is cumulative, taking numerous naps any time during the day will provide sufficient energy and resistance to sickness.

    D. The immune system functions most efficiently when the body is accustomed to resting a specific number of hours at the consistent time on a daily basis.

    E. To maintain a healthy body, a lifestyle that includes a balanced diet and regular sleeping patterns is essential.

27. The best actress award will probably go <u>in a film from a major studio starring an older performer with large profits here and overseas.</u>

    A. in a film from a major studio starring an older performer with large profits here and overseas.

    B. to an older performer starring in a major studio film with large profits here and overseas.

C. to a film with an older actress starring with large profits here and overseas.

D. to an older film actress starring in a major studio film with large profits here and overseas.

E. to a film with large profits here and overseas starring an older performer from a major studio.

28. It's clear that plants are ultimately dependent on animals for their survival. Because plants depend on carbon dioxide to make their food, and because animals are producers of carbon dioxide, if all animals died, then plants would eventually starve.

    Which of the following statements, if true, would most seriously weaken the argument that plants are ultimately dependent on animals?

    A. Plants can propagate without the help of humans or other animals.

    B. Chemical reactions in the troposphere produce carbon dioxide.

    C. Animals destroy plants by eating them.

    D. Virtually all of the earth's carbon dioxide comes from the respiration of animals.

    E. Plants can get food from the soil without converting carbon dioxide to sugar.

29. It is not so much the continuing threat of food shortages <u>but instead it is</u> the danger of cholera that worries the rescue workers.

    A. but instead it is

    B. but

C. but it is

D. as it is

E. as

30. After the absentee ballots had been counted, the total of authorized votes cast in the election <u>were one third less than was predicted</u>.

A. were one third less than was predicted.

B. were one third fewer than was predicted.

C. were one third less than had been predicted.

D. was one third less than had been predicted.

E. was one third fewer than predicted.

31. Traveling to new places may introduce vacationers to different people and foreign sites that they may possibly find uninteresting, yet it also provides opportunities for novel experiences and insights. Thus, vacationers to a new destination will return from the trip intellectually broadened.

Which of the following supports the conclusion above?

A. Most people will likely not find foreign destinations and people to be interesting.

B. New experiences and insights broaden a person's intellect.

C. Anyone who wants to take a vacation has the opportunity to do so.

D. Vacationers will not go to a new destination if it is interesting.

E. Most people go on vacation to become intellectually broadened.

32. <u>Unlike those in the James Bond movies,</u> the British Secret Service is made up chiefly of men and women with advanced degrees in mathematics.

A. Unlike those in the James Bond movies,

B. Unlike the James Bond movies,

C. Unlike the organization in the James Bond movies,

D. Different from those in the James Bond movies,

E. Different than the one in the James Bond movies,

33. The iridescent nature of opals is a result of water trapped inside silica material. With time, this water will escape. Unlike advice given for most precious stones, experts advocate frequent handling of opals, which transmits body oils to the stones and helps them maintain their water content.

Which of the following can be inferred from the passage above?

A. Opals will eventually lose their color if left alone.

B. Fire opals are most commonly found in Mexico.

C. Body oils give opals their iridescent colors.

D. An opal rarely maintains its value for longer than a century.

E. Opals require the same care as most precious stones.

GO ON TO THE NEXT PAGE

413

Verbal Section

Read the following passage and answer Questions 34–36.

The modern mania for psychological testing springs directly from some dark need of the psyche of certain humans to name, to label, to thus stereotype and
(5) thereby control. The testing tidal wave began building from little contributory wavelets early in the twentieth century when Alfred Binet and Theodore Simon, French psychologists, introduced their
(10) Binet-Simon intelligence scale. To be sure, these scientists' intent was admirable, to assure that French children would not unfairly be denied an education. But we all know just what road, ac-
(15) cording to folk wisdom, is paved with good intentions, don't we?

The wavelets began building to stormier seas over the decades. Robert Woodworth, to satisfy the mili-
(20) tary's hunger to know how their soldiers might fare under the combat conditions of World War I, developed one of the first of what were eventually known as "personality inventories." Inventories—
(25) as though one could cunningly separate elements of the marvelously coherent and complex human mind, wrap them up and ribbon them, and stock them on convenience store
(30) shelves. Many more tests came hard on the heels of Woodworth's. Aptitude tests, achievement tests, personality tests, intelligence tests, the California Achievement Tests, the Rorschach
(35) inkblot test, and the Wechsler scale.

Who knows what aptitudes humans will discover in themselves tomorrow, or next week, or next year, or when they're ninety-five? How can we measure
(40) achievement with a few multiple-choice questions? Who says if I see Mom's apple pie in the inkblot I've got an Oedipus

complex? How can we measure intelligence when no one knows exactly what
(45) intelligence is? And what do we get for the money and time spent on all this nonsense? We get labels, pigeonholes to conveniently deposit people in. We get to say, "Johnny isn't capable of doing
(50) that," so we never expect Johnny to do that, so probably he won't.

34. What is the primary reason that the author objects to psychological testing?

   A. It is dangerously biased.

   B. It is a waste of money and time.

   C. It favors the least imaginative people.

   D. It pigeonholes and stereotypes people.

   E. It cannot be validated.

35. According to the author, Binet and Simon

   A. helped French children get an education.

   B. started a dangerous trend.

   C. were admirable but ineffective.

   D. introduced Robert Woodworth to intelligence testing.

   E. believed in intelligence testing but not in personality testing.

36. Based on the passage, all of the following are reasonable inferences EXCEPT

   A. No multiple choice test can examine all aspects of a human being's intelligence and personality.

   B. Interpretations of many psychological tests are subjective.

C. No definition of intelligence has been set forth that is agreed upon by all experts.

D. Personality inventories are more valid than intelligence tests.

E. A person's performance is often influenced by the expectations of others.

37. The orchestra director urged the student musicians to concentrate on the works of Bach, <u>the composer who, to him, represented the greatest achievement of the eighteenth century</u>.

A. the composer who, to him, represented the greatest achievement of the eighteenth century.

B. a composer whose achievement represented the greatest in the eighteenth century to him.

C. whose eighteenth century achievement was the greatest.

D. who, among composers, to him in the eighteenth century represented the greatest achievement.

E. the greatest achiever as a composer in the eighteenth century to him.

38. Candidates for office usually <u>campaign for the vacant seats and visit cities</u> with an expected high voter turnout.

A. campaign for the vacant seats and visit cities

B. campaign for the vacant seats by visiting cities

C. campaigns for the vacant seats, and they visit cities

D. for the vacant seats campaign in visits to cities

E. in campaigns for vacant seats visit cities

39. Whenever I need to study but feel sleepy, all I do is take a few of those caffeine pills, and I'm completely awake. According to the label, these pills are perfectly safe to use, since I could get the same amount of energizing caffeine by drinking a few cups of coffee.

Which of the following statements weakens the argument expressed in the passage?

A. Pills that can help prevent drowsiness often contain caffeine, a natural substance that can increase "awakeness" and provide the user with a sudden boost of energy.

B. Since caffeine is a natural substance found in many common foods such as chocolate, pills that are caffeine-based may be just as safe.

C. One subconsciously limits intake of caffeine through its method of intake; for example, most people can only drink a few cups of coffee before they feel full.

D. Many students tend to pull "all nighters" in school, and caffeine pills are an ideal way to reduce drowsiness and study through the night.

E. In the last decade, many pharmaceutical companies have released caffeine-based pills which have been widely sold over the counter in drug stores.

GO ON TO THE NEXT PAGE

40. If people want to begin a vegetable garden in the Rocky Mountains before the spring equinox, they must first sprout the seeds indoors and then transplant them to fertilized soil outdoors once the plants reach three inches. However, carrots and turnips can never be sprouted indoors.

If the statements above are true, which of the following statements must also be true about growing a garden in the Rocky Mountains?

A. Plants that are not yet three inches tall should be brought indoors before equinox.

B. Carrots can be planted outdoors before equinox.

C. Spring equinox is approximately the time the soil thaws in the Rocky Mountains.

D. Turnips can never be sprouted before equinox.

E. Gardens in Colorado have a shorter growing season than those in Georgia.

41. <u>Although it is required for admission,</u> many candidates have not completed three advanced courses in chemistry.

A. Although it is required for admission,

B. Although required for admission,

C. Although they are requirements for admission,

D. Although required,

E. Required for admission,

IF YOU FINISH BEFORE TIME IS CALLED, CHECK YOUR WORK ON THIS SECTION ONLY. DO NOT WORK ON ANY OTHER SECTION IN THE TEST.

CHARTING AND ANALYZING YOUR TEST RESULTS

The charts on the following pages should be used to carefully analyze your results and spot your strengths and weaknesses. The complete process of evaluating your essays and analyzing individual problems in each subject area should be completed for each practice test. These results should then be reexamined for trends in types of errors (repeated errors) or poor results in specific subject areas. **This reexamination and analysis is of tremendous importance in helping you maximize your score.**

Analytical Writing Assessment

Analyze your responses using the following charts. Then estimate your score by referring to the explanation of characteristics of responses at each score level in the chapter on The Analytical Writing Assessment in Part II.

Analysis of an Issue

Questions	Completely	Partially	No
1. Does the response focus on the assigned topic and cover all of the tasks?			
2. Does the response show an understanding of the complexity of the issue?			
3. Does the response show cogent reasoning and logical position development?			
4. Are there sufficient relevant persuasive supporting details?			
5. Is the response well organized?			
6. Does the response show a command of standard written English?			

Score	Level
6	excellent
5	good
4	competent
3	limited
2	weak
1	poor

Analysis of an Argument

Questions	Completely	Partially	No
1. Does the response focus on the assigned topic and cover all of the tasks?			
2. Does the response carefully analyze the important weaknesses of the argument?			
3. Does the response show cogent reasoning and logical development?			
4. Are there sufficient relevant supporting details of the critique?			
5. Is the response well organized?			
6. Does the response show a command of standard written English?			

Analysis: Tally Sheet for Problems Missed

One of the most important parts of test preparation is analyzing WHY you missed a problem so that you can reduce the number of mistakes. Now that you have taken the practice test and corrected your answers, carefully tally your mistakes by marking them in the proper column.

REASON FOR MISTAKE

	Total Missed	Simple Mistake	Misread Problem	Lack of Knowledge
QUANTITATIVE SECTION				
VERBAL SECTION				
Total Verbal and Quantitative				

Reviewing this data should help you determine WHY you are missing certain problems. Now that you have pinpointed the types of errors you have made, you can focus on avoiding your most common type.

ANSWERS AND EXPLANATIONS FOR THE PRACTICE TEST

Quantitative Section

1. **B.** In a triangle, the side opposite the greatest angle is the longest, and the side opposite the smallest angle is the shortest. Statement (1) does not tell us whether side p is shorter or longer than side r. Hence, it is not sufficient. Statement (2) tells us that angle z is the largest angle in the triangle (only then could it equal the sum of the other two angles), which means that the opposite side—side p—must be the greatest.

2. **C.** If we rearrange statement (2), we get: $m + n = 15$. If we substitute this value of $m + n$ in statement (1), we get $p = 4^{15}$, which can be solved for p.

3. **B.** If t is the current total revenue, Internet-based revenue is $.3t$. If this increases by 150%, the Internet-based revenue in three years will be $2.5(.3t) = .75t$.

   From statement (1), we can write

   $$.75t + \text{NI} = 10,000$$

   where NI stands for non-Internet-based sales in three years.

   Notice that this doesn't help us solve for $.75t$, which is what we need to find. Hence, statement (1) alone is not sufficient.

   From statement (2), we know that current Internet-based revenue is $.3 \times 6,000 = 1,800$. If this increases by 150%, we can find the total Internet-based revenue in three years.

4. **D.** If we get n when we divide $(x - p)$ by $(p + 1)$, then, when we multiply $(p + 1)$ by n, we should get $(x - p)$.

   That is, $(p + 1)n = (x - p)$

   $$np + n = x - p$$

   $$np + n + p = x$$

   By factoring out p, we get

   $$p(n + 1) + n = x$$

5. **E.** The first statement tells us that x is a multiple of 3. Not all multiples of 3 are multiples of 9 (e.g., 6, 12, 15, etc.) and so the first statement is not sufficient.

   The second statement tells us that x is 3 more than a multiple of 6. However, not all such numbers are multiples of 9. For example, if you divided 15 by 6, the remainder would be 3, and 15 is not a multiple of 6. On the other hand, if, say, you divided 27 by 6, you'd get a remainder of 3, and 27 is a multiple of 9. Hence, statement (2) is not sufficient.

Notice that statement (2) adds nothing new to the first statement because 3 plus a multiple of 6 is always divisible by 3. Hence, even when we combine statements (1) and (2), we don't have enough information to solve the problem.

6. **C.** The price of the stereo was 120. If the tax were 10%, the total price would be $120 + .1(120) = 120 + 12 = 132$. If the tax were 12%, the total price would be $120 + .12(120) = 120 + 14.40 = 134.40$. Hence, the tax must be between 10 and 12 percent, which means choice **C** is the best answer.

7. **C.** The first statement tells us that x can either be 3 or -3. This statement, by itself, is not sufficient to find the value of $(x + 3)^2$.

   The second statement tells us that x has to be either 0 or some negative number. (If x is a positive number, $|x| + x$ will always be greater than 0.) Hence, the second statement, by itself, is not sufficient.

   By combining the two statements, we see that $x = -3$. Hence, we can find the value of $(x + 3)^2$.

8. **C.** Once we know the total number of students in the school from statement (2), we can find the number of students who have double majors from statement (1). The remaining students have single majors. We can then determine how many more students have double majors than single majors.

9. **C.** If, for example, the original price of an item was 100, on the first day, the price was $100 - 10\% = 100 - 10 = 90$.

   On the second day, the price was $90 - 10\% = 90 - 9 = 81$. Hence the price on the second day, 81, was 81% of the original price.

10. **C.** Note that p can have values $-3, -2, -1, 0, 1, 2$, and 3.

    If $p = -3$, $N = 16 \times 10^{-(-3)} = 16 \times 10^3 = 16,000$

    If $p = -2$, $N = 16 \times 10^{-(-2)} = 16 \times 10^2 = 1,600$

    If $p = -1$, $N = 16 \times 10^{-(-1)} = 16 \times 10^1 = 160$

    If $p = 0$, $N = 16 \times 10^{-(0)} = 16 \times 1 = 16$

    If $p = 1$, $N = 16 \times 10^{-(1)} = 16 \times .1 = 1.6$

    If $p = 2$, $N = 16 \times 10^{-(2)} = 16 \times .01 = .16$

    If $p = 3$, $N = 16 \times 10^{-(3)} = 16 \times .001 = .016$

    Of these, the perfect squares are 1,600, 16, and .16.

11. **D.** If the average of 4 tests was 80, their total was $80 \times 4 = 320$. After dropping the lowest score, the average (of 3 tests) was 85. The total of the three tests was $85 \times 3 = 255$. Hence, the dropped test was $320 - 255 = 65$.

12. **A.** The average score is the total score divided by the number of tests. Hence, statement (1) is sufficient. Statement (2) only tells us the relationship between scores on the first two and the last two tests without giving us the actual scores.

13. C. The first statement is not sufficient because x could be negative (e.g., -4) and y could be positive (e.g., 3) in which case $x < y$, but $x^2 > y^2$.

The second statement is also not sufficient because we don't know whether x is smaller than, greater than, or equal to y.

However, when we combine both statements, we know that x and y are both positive integers and $x^2 > y^2$. This can be true only if x is greater than y.

14. A. It takes 36 machines 4 hours to fill 8 orders. If we have 72 machines, they can fill the same number of orders (8) in half the time, that is, in 2 hours. To go from 8 orders to 12 orders is $1\frac{1}{2}$ times as much work and so it will take $1\frac{1}{2}$ times as long. Hence time taken is $1\frac{1}{2} \times 2 = 3$ hours.

15. B. Ann is 5 years older than Sue. That is,

$$A = 5 + S$$

Jill is twice as old as Ann. That is,

$$J = 2A$$

Substituting the value of A from the first equation into the second, we get

$$J = 2(5 + S) = 10 + 2S$$

16. A. If, five days ago, the water level was w, the level today must be $w - 5(14)$ (because it drops 14 inches each day). Four days from now, the drop will be $4 \times 14 = 56$ inches. Hence the water level will be $w - 5(14) - 56 = w - 70 - 56 = w - 126$.

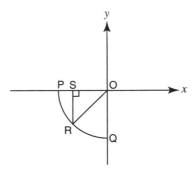

17. B. From R, draw RS perpendicular on OP. Then, because R lies at the center of arc PQ, OS = RS. We know that OR, the radius, is 2. Then, using the Pythagorean theorem, we can write:

$$(OR)^2 = (OS)^2 + (RS)^2$$
$$2^2 = 2(RS)^2$$
$$2 = (RS)^2$$
$$\sqrt{2} = RS$$

The x-coordinate of R will be $\sqrt{2}$ units to the left of the origin, and so its value is $-\sqrt{2}$.

18. E. Given the equation $x + 3y - 3 = 0$, it appears as if any other equation with x and y in it should be sufficient to find the value of x because we will then have two unknowns and two equations. However, notice that statements (1) and (2) are not independent equations. That is, if we take the given equation $x + 3y - 3 = 0$ and multiply each term by 3, we get the equation in (1), and if we multiply it by 2, we get the equation in (2). In other words, all three equations are the same and so this problem is not solvable for x.

19. C. From statements (1) and (2), we know that profit last year was $15,000 - $5,000 = $10,000. Thus we know the profits for both years and can answer the question.

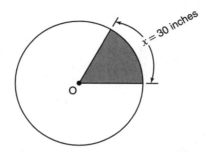

20. D. From statement (1), if x is $1/16$ of the circumference and we know that $x = 30$, then the circumference of the circle is $16 \times 30 = 480$. If we plug this value in the formula for the circumference of a circle (circumference = $2\pi r$), we can find the radius.

From statement (2), we know that the area of the shaded region is $\dfrac{3600}{\pi}$ square inches.

In the circle, we can write the following proportion:

$$\frac{\text{area of shaded region}}{\text{area of entire circle}} = \frac{\text{circumference of shaded region}}{\text{circumference of entire circle}}$$

$$\text{Or, } \frac{3600/\pi}{\pi r^2} = \frac{30}{2\pi r}$$

$$\text{Or, } \frac{3600}{\pi^2 r^2} = \frac{15}{\pi r}$$

$$\text{Or, } \frac{3600}{\pi r} = \frac{15}{1}$$

If we simplify, we can find the radius.

21. B. If 1.001×10^k is 1,000 times greater than p, then $1,000 \times p$ must be equal to 1.001×10^k. That is,

$$1000p = 1.001 \times 10^k$$

$$\text{Or, } p = \frac{1.001 \times 10^k}{1,000}$$

$$\text{Or, } p = 1.001 \times 10^k \times 10^{-3}$$

$$\text{Or, } p = 1.001 \times 10^{k-3}$$

22. C. If the rainfall during the first week was f, then rainfall during the second week, s, can be written as:

$$s = 1.5f$$

We know that the total rainfall was 15 inches. That is,

$s + f = 15$

Substituting the value of s as $1.5f$, we get

$1.5f + f = 15$

$2.5f = 15$

$f = {}^{15}\!/_{2.5} = {}^{150}\!/_{25} = 6$

If $f = 6$, then $s = 1.5(6) = 9$ inches.

23. E. We can map points A, B, and C as follows, where A = 1.

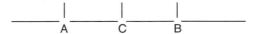

From statement (1), we know that AC is twice CB. If CB is x, then AC is $2x$. That is,

Notice that this statement by itself is not sufficient to find the value of C.

From statement (2), we know that AB is 9. Because A is 1, B could be 10, but this statement by itself is not sufficient to find the value of C.

If we combine both statements, our figure becomes:

This implies that $x = 3$ and $2x = 6$. That is, because A = 1, C = 1 + 6 = 7. However, nothing in the problem suggests that we can't have the number line as shown below, where A is 1 and points B and C are to the left of A. If so, C would be 6 units to the left of A with a value of −5.

Therefore, we do not know whether C is 7 or −5.

24. E. Assume that the original price of the shirt was $100. Then, after the 20% discount, the price on Saturday was $80. The price of the shirt was marked up to be 20% more than the original price. Therefore, the price after the markup was $120. That is, the price was increased from $80 to $120.

That is, $p = \dfrac{120 - 80}{80} \times 100$

$p = \dfrac{40}{80} \times 100$

$p = 50$

25. A. The chart below shows the current position of the two trains, where x is the distance traveled when both trains meet.

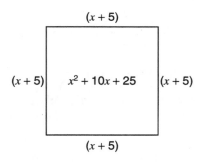

When Train B catches up with Train A, it will have traveled x miles and Train A will have traveled $x - 15$ miles. If h is the number of hours traveled by Train B before catching up with Train A, then $x = 60h$ (because distance = speed × time). Since Train A is traveling at 40 miles per hour, $40h = x - 15$. Substituting the value of x as $60h$, we get $40h = 60h - 15$.

That is, $20h = 15$, or $h = {}^{15}\!/_{20} = \frac{3}{4}$ hour = 45 minutes.

Alternate explanation: Since B travels 20 miles per hour faster than A, it catches up at the rate of 20 miles per hour. In order to make up the 15-mile difference, it would take ${}^{15}\!/_{20} = \frac{3}{4}$ hour, which is 45 minutes.

26. C. Bill's profit ratio was $\dfrac{1{,}500}{4{,}000}$.

Jack's profit ratio was $\dfrac{12}{1}$.

Combining both these items, we can solve the problem.

27. B. The area of the first square is $x^2 + 10x + 25$. This can be factored to get $(x + 5)(x + 5)$, which means that the square is of side $x + 5$. Then, the perimeter of the square is $4(x + 5) = 4x + 20$.

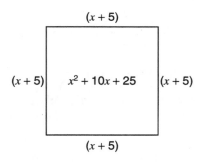

The area of the second square is $4x^2 - 12x + 9$. This can be factored to get $(2x - 3)(2x - 3)$, which means that the square is of side $2x - 3$. The perimeter of this square is $4(2x - 3) = 8x - 12$.

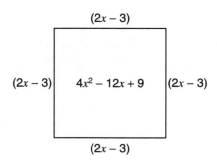

The sum of the two perimeters of $4x + 20 + 8x - 12 = 12x + 8$. We know that the perimeter is 32. Then,

$$12x + 8 = 32$$
$$12x = 24$$
$$x = 2$$

28. **C.** If p is a positive integer, note that r will always be a multiple of 3 because $p(p + 1)(p + 2)$ represents 3 consecutive integers, one of which will always be a multiple of 3. Hence, r must be a multiple of 3. Among the answer choices, 6, 36, 156, and 180 are all multiples of 3. Only 116 is not a multiple of 3.

29. **C.** If she has only 1 penny, the numerical value of the total amount of money must end in either a 1 (e.g., 51 cents) or a 6 (e.g., 56 cents). If she has 2 pennies, the total amount must end in either a 2 or a 7. If she has 3 pennies, the total amount must end in either a 3 or an 8. And, if she has 4 pennies, the total amount must end in either a 4 or a 9. Notice that it's not possible for her total amount to end in a 5. Hence, her jar cannot have 55 cents.

30. **D.** Initial composition of Compound P is: 5 grams of X, 15 grams of Y and z grams of Z. If 25 grams of X is added, the weight of Y that is added is 75 grams (because 5 times the initial weight of X was added, the amount of Y to be added should also be 5 times the initial weight).

The initial weight of P is

5 grams of X + 15 grams of Y + z = 20 + z

From statement (1), we know that P = 3 times the weight of Z. That is, because 20 + z was the original weight of P, we can write:

$$20 + z = 3z$$

This gives us the original weight of z. If we multiply it by 5, we can find the weight of Z that must be added.

From statement (2), we know that Z is always twice the weight of X. Then, the initial weight of P is:

5 grams of X + 15 grams of Y + 10 grams of X = 30 grams.

Because X and Y make up 20 grams, initial weight of Z is 10 grams. And, because the weight of each chemical added to the compound is 5 times the initial weight, we can find the weight of Z required.

31. **E.** Each character can consist of 26 lower-case letters, 26 upper-case letters, any numerical digit from 0 to 9, a hyphen, or the exclamation mark. That is, each character is to be chosen from $26 + 26 + 10 + 2 = 64$ possibilities. Since there are to be 8 such characters in the password, the total number of possibilities is $(64)^8 = (2^6)^8 = 2^{48}$.

32. A. The operation $\alpha\,(x) = x(1 - x)$.

To find the value of $\alpha\,(p + 1)$, we can substitute "$p + 1$" for x in the above equation. Then we get

$$\alpha\,(p + 1) = (p + 1)[1 - (p + 1)]$$
$$= (p + 1)(1 - p - 1)$$
$$= (p + 1)(-p)$$
$$= -p^2 - p$$

We're also given that $p + 1 = \alpha\,(p + 1)$. Substituting this value, we get

$$p + 1 = -p^2 - p$$
$$p^2 + 2p + 1 = 0$$
$$(p + 1)^2 = 0$$

Hence, $p = -1$.

33. C. The first statement is required to find the length of the walls, which can be used to find the total surface area of the walls. Statement (2) gives us the cost for each square foot of the wallpaper. If you multiply the total square footage of the walls by 60, you will get the cost of the wallpaper. Hence, both (1) and (2) are required.

34. C. Because we're looking for an even number, the last digit has to be 0, 2, 4, 6, or 8. That is, there are 5 possibilities for the last digit.

Because the first digit cannot be a 0, 9 possibilities remain for the first digit (1 through 9). For the second and third digits, there are 10 possibilities each (0, 1, . . . 9).

Hence, the total number of possibilities is

$$9 \times 10 \times 10 \times 5 = 4,500$$

35. B. x is not always a prime number. For example, if x is 55, then x divided by 6 gives a remainder of 1 and x is not a prime number. Any number divisible by 6 is also divisible by both 2 and 3, which means only even numbers are divisible by 6. So, if a number is 1 more than a multiple of 6, that number must be odd. Hence statement II must be true. Statement III is not true; for example, x could be 13. When 13 is divided by 6 the remainder is 1, but it is not divisible by 7. Only statement II must be true.

36. C. From the first statement, we know that, if we arrange the numbers in the set in an increasing order, the number in the middle, i.e., the median, is 4. Because the first number is 1, the set can be written as:

$$1 \_ 4 \_ \_$$

Because the average is 4 and there are 5 numbers, the sum of all 5 numbers is $5 \times 4 = 20$. The first and third numbers add up to $1 + 4 = 5$, and so the other three numbers must add up to $20 - 5 = 15$.

In the second slot, we must have either 2 or 3 (because the third number, 4, must be greater than the second number). If we have 2 in the second slot, the sum of the three numbers is $1 + 2 + 4 = 7$, which means the fourth and fifth numbers must add up to $20 - 7 = 13$. The fourth and fifth numbers could be 5 and 8 or 6 and 7. Hence, statement (1) is not sufficient to find the greatest number in the set.

According to statement (2), the set contains only 1 even number. This by itself is not sufficient to find the greatest number in the set.

If we combine the two statements, we can extend the logic from the first statement and get, as a possible set,

1 _ 4 _ _

The second slot cannot be 2 because there is only 1 even number (4) in the set. Hence, the second slot has to be a 3. Then, we have

1 3 4 _ _

The sum of the three numbers is 8, which means the last two must add up to $20 - 8 = 12$. The last two numbers must also be greater than 4. The only possibility is:

1 3 4 5 7

Hence, statements (1) and (2) are both required.

37. B. Jill drove for 1 hour at 40 mph. This means she drove 40 miles. At that speed, her midsize car gives 30 miles per gallon. So, the amount of fuel consumed to travel 40 miles is $^{40}\!/_{30} = {}^4\!/_3$ gallons.

Jill drove at 60 mph for 30 minutes, which means she drove 30 miles. At that speed, her car gives 20 miles per gallon. Amount of fuel consumed to travel 30 miles is $^{30}\!/_{20} = {}^3\!/_2$ gallons.

Fuel consumed by Jill $= {}^4\!/_3 + {}^3\!/_2 = {}^{8 + 9}\!/_6 = {}^{17}\!/_6$

John drove for 1 hour at 30 miles per hour, which means he drove 30 miles. At that speed, his mileage was 20 miles per gallon. Hence, amount of fuel consumed is $^{30}\!/_{20} = {}^3\!/_2$ gallons.

At 50 miles per hour, John drove for 30 minutes. That is, he drove 25 miles. At this speed, his mileage was 15 miles per gallon. Therefore, amount of fuel consumed is $^{25}\!/_{15} = {}^5\!/_3$ gallons.

Fuel consumed by John $= {}^3\!/_2 + {}^5\!/_3 = {}^{9 + 10}\!/_6 = {}^{19}\!/_6$

Therefore, total fuel consumed by Jill's car as a percent of fuel consumed by John's car is:

$^{17}\!/_6 \div {}^{19}\!/_6 \times 100 = {}^{17}\!/_6 \times {}^6\!/_{19} \times 100 = {}^{17}\!/_{19} \times 100 = 89.5\%$

The closest approximation is 90%.

Verbal Section

1. **E.** The question is testing parallelism in a series. In the best answer, all three elements will have a structure as nearly alike as possible. Options **A** and **C** use the preposition *by* inconsistently. The parallelism is better in options **B** and **D**, but **E,** by not repeating the preposition, is not so wordy.

2. **C.** The passage's central concern is explaining magnetic reversal and how it was recognized. **A** and **E** are both incomplete; in addition, although the passage does touch on the number of years between reversals, it certainly does not present a time table. **B** is incorrect; the passage mentions hypotheses but does not argue either for or against them (lines 41–49). **D** is simply incorrect. Therefore, **C** is the best choice.

3. **B.** See lines 8–10. **A** might seem tempting, but the pointing of atoms in rock crystals was only the *means* by which magnetic reversal was shown to have occurred. The passage does not consider a change in the direction of lava flows (**C**) or convection currents (**D**). The passage does state that it is believed that magnetic reversal occurs on average every 500,000 years; magnetic reversal is not a disturbance in some other undefined 500,000 year cycle of the magnetic field, as indicated in **E**.

4. **A.** See lines 18–24. Had the rocks not solidified, the information about the magnetic field would not have been available for scientists to discover. Although the extinction of certain species has been correlated with magnetic reversal, the extinction was not the key to the discovery, ruling out **B**. There is no "rapid" change between polarities, so **C** is incorrect, and a reversal of convection currents is offered as a possible explanation of magnetic reversal, not the means by which it was discovered, eliminating **D**. **E** is incorrect because the *direction* of lava flows is not considered in the passage.

5. **E.** In lines 49–57, the passage mentions that little doubt exists that a magnetic reversal would produce a great deal more "damaging" ultraviolet radiation; there is a suggestion that such radiation could be responsible for extinction of species. **A** is incorrect; although a magnetic reversal occurs on average every 500,000 years, and it has been 700,000 years since the last reversal, the assumption cannot be made that no future reversal will occur. **B** is incorrect; a collision with a meteorite is only one hypothesis as to the cause of magnetic reversal. The same is true of **D**. **C** is incorrect; in lines 41–43, the passage makes it clear that no one knows the source of the earth's magnetic field; 700,000 years is the last time a magnetic reversal occurred.

6. **D.** An assumption typically precedes a conclusion and may or may not be explicitly stated. In this argument, the logic goes as follows:

   All societal people have something in common: In the act of acquiring and rejecting objects they all acquire a social identity.

   Therefore the passage assumes that all societal people both acquire and reject objects.

7. **C.** The major problem in this sentence is the use of pronouns (*which, this*, and *it*) with no specific antecedents. Only in **C** does the pronoun (*that*) have a specific antecedent (*a gap*).

8. **C.** The sentence begins with *Unlike London*. The main clause of the sentence must begin with a subject that is a city, not *visitors* or *a car*. Although **B** begins with *Los Angeles*, the subject is *visitors*.

9. **B.** Find a statement that strengthens the idea that infants can make the sounds of language long before they learn how to speak. Read through each option and ask yourself, "Does this strengthen the conclusion?" If the answer is no, cross it out and move on. One answer you shouldn't cross out is **B:** Computer speech synthesizers rely exclusively on alveolar, labial, and velar sounds. If this is true, then alveolar, labial, and velar sounds are sufficient for speaking a language. Therefore, infants have all the essential sounds mastered in their first year. They need only put the sounds together in an understandable way, something that we call language.

10. **A.** Options **C, D,** and **E** have agreement errors: the plural *are* with the singular subject *frequency*. **A** rightly uses an adjective (*slower*) to modify this subject.

11. **C.** **C** is the best choice because it presents several facts about tornadoes. **B** and **D** are among the points covered, but neither is the main purpose of the passage. Weather phenomena are not contrasted in the passage, eliminating **A,** nor is a specific example of a tornado presented to illustrate an observation about tornadoes in general, so **E** does not work.

12. **D.** The presence of water and debris in the funnel makes it visible, but notice that answer **A** refers to the cumulonimbus storm clouds, not the funnel cloud. **B** describes the echo image of the tornado, not the cause of the funnel cloud. Neither does the slow forward movement of the tornado cause the funnel cloud as indicated in **C.** Wet, warm air meeting dry, cool air is a condition of a tornado; **E** describes the reverse.

13. **A.** **A** is the only possible inference among the answers; note lines 45–51. Nothing implies that tornado diameter depends on the materials it contains (**B**), nor that the hook image of a tornado is a result of the diameter (**D**). Also, although the passage states that tornadoes cannot be measured directly, it does not imply that Doppler radar is inadequate, eliminating **C.** Also, no connection can be inferred between a tornado's strength and the time it occurs or the direction it moves, so **E** is incorrect.

14. **B.** Passage **B** makes clear that weather conditions, not topography (**A**) or population density (**C**), cause tornadoes. **D** is irrelevant; tornadoes could move in this direction in any country. Nothing in the passage suggests **E.**

15. **A.** See lines 9–12. The passage does not address the *drive* for either wealth or goodness (**B**), nor the rarity of a man who spends his money honorably (**C**). **D** is incorrect because the passage moves from the premise that goodness and happiness are linked. **E** is contradicted in lines 28–32.

16. **D.** **D** is the best answer. Nothing in the passage implies that poverty is a sign of goodness; notice, for example, that the "utterly bad" are "very poor" (lines 36–38). **A** is supported in lines 24–28, **B** in lines 36–38, and **C** in lines 28–32. **E** is supported because the passage makes it clear that it is not only how a man spends his money but also how he earns it that is important.

17. **B.** In **B,** the author makes his arguments through statements that lead to his logical conclusion: that the very rich are not good, and if they are not good, they are not happy. He does not provide concrete examples or exceptions (**A** and **D**), nor does he present a particular case (**E**). Opposing views are not addressed in the passage (**C**).

18. **E.** The participial phrase that begins this sentence will dangle if the main clause does not begin with the word it modifies. Both **D** and **E** have the correct *clothes*, but **E** is the better choice because it is more concise.

19. **E.** The phrase *as large in* requires the parallel *as in*. **E** is better than **D** because its pronoun (*that*) has a specific antecedent (*fact*).

20. **B.** The original sentence is a run-on sentence. It can be repaired either by eliminating the second independent clause by changing the verb to a participle (**B**) or by adding an *and*. **C** rightly adds the *and*, but *enemies'* is a plural, not a possessive.

21. **C.** This is primarily a test of wordiness. Option **C** is the briefest and uses the active voice. The sentence requires the verb *accept*, not the preposition *except*.

22. **E.** If vitamins can maintain one's health by making up for the deficiencies resulting from eating an unbalanced diet, then they must provide everything (nutrients, minerals) that food provides. This choice suggests that food and/or vitamins are capable of providing the nutrients necessary for survival and that no other elements are needed to maintain a healthy body. This is the only choice that in any one way supports the argument in the passage.

23. **C.** Although consumers would likely prefer to have higher picture clarity, the expenses and inconvenience of purchasing extra cables for playback exceed the value the consumer places on quality pictures. Because of these added costs of 8mm format, the consumer is likely to forego picture clarity in favor of the lower price of VHS-C and the convenience of easy playback.

24. **A.** The first version of the sentence is the best choice. It correctly uses a present indicative verb, unlike **D** and **E,** and places the phrase *in the region* in the least awkward position.

25. **D.** Although the costs of RK surgery are high and the risk of failure is still quite significant (30%), the possible benefits of a lifetime of perfect vision outweigh all of these cons and justify the risks. At least that's what you can be sure the author assumes, since the author encourages those visually impaired to undergo the operation.

26. **C.** This passage assumes that consistent sleeping patterns are necessary for good health. This choice contradicts this assumption by stating that good sleep is merely cumulative and that random naps during the day are just as efficient as consistent sleeping patterns.

27. **B.** The original sentence has a idiom error (*go in* should be *go to*). **C** and **E** give the actress award to a *film* rather than to an actress, while **D**, though grammatical, awkwardly repeats the word *film*. The best choice is **B**.

28. **B.** Your job is to find a statement that weakens the argument that plants are ultimately dependent on animals. The argument in the passage is based on the idea that animals provide plants with carbon dioxide, which is essential for their survival. The argument is most seriously weakened by the statement that other sources of carbon dioxide exist besides animals. Choice **B** suggests that carbon dioxide is naturally produced in the troposphere. This would make plants no longer dependent on the carbon dioxide which animals produce, thus weakening the argument.

29. **E.** The correct idiom here is *not so much . . . as*. Option **E** has it right using the fewest words.

30. D. The subject of the sentence is the singular noun *total*. The better adjective with *total* is *less* rather than *fewer.*

31. B. The passage draws a connection between "traveling to new places" and becoming intellectually broadened. The latter conclusion does not directly result from the former observation unless the new experiences of travel challenges and expands the visitor's intelligence.

32. C. The opening phrase should refer to something that is *unlike . . . the British Secret Service.* The plural *those,* used in **A** and **D,** cannot be right. Nor can *movies* (**B**). The phrase *different than* in **E** is unidiomatic.

33. A. Your task here is to pick a statement that would logically follow based on the ideas in the passage. You could go through the statements one by one, but you should quickly see that choice **A** is on the money. First, the passage states that water content gives opals their color. Next, the passage points out, somewhat indirectly, that not handling opals will result in opals losing their water content. When we combine these two ideas, we can infer that opals will eventually lose their color if not handled frequently.

34. D. D is the best choice. Although the author might well agree with the other statements, he is most concerned with the tests' tendency to stereotype and pigeonhole. See the first sentence of the passage.

35. B. The best answer is **B.** The passage does state that Binet and Simon's motivations were undoubtedly admirable, as suggested in **A,** for example, but it is the dangerous trend they began that is the focus of the passage. The passage does not indicate that they were ineffective — quite the contrary (**C**). Neither **D** nor **E** is supported by the passage.

36. D. The passage suggests all of the statements except **D: A** in lines 24–30; **B** in lines 41–43; **C** in lines 43–45; and **E** in lines 48–51.

37. A. None of the subsequent versions retains the full meaning and avoids a misplaced modifier as well as the original.

38. B. The most concise version (without the awkward separation of the subject and verb of **E**) subordinates the second clause by changing *visit* to *visiting.*

39. C. The method of caffeine intake helps to safely limit the amount of caffeine that any person can ingest over a short period of time. For foods such as coffee, one can only drink so much before becoming full from the liquid. Pills, however, can be taken in any quantity without subsequent discomfort, and this can lead to possible problems.

40. D. Because turnips cannot be sprouted indoors, and because everything that is planted before equinox must be sprouted indoors, turnips cannot be planted before equinox. In other words, suppose you want to start growing turnips a week before equinox. The passage says that you can't plant anything out of doors before equinox, so you can rule out choice **B,** planting carrots before equinox. But the passage also says you can't ever sprout turnips indoors. So both indoor sprouting and outdoor planting of turnips before equinox are out of the question.

41. C. The first clause must have a subject, or it will dangle as it does in **B, D,** and **E.** The correct pronoun is the plural *they* to agree with the plural *three courses.*

DATE DUE

DEC 1 3 2010			

HIGHSMITH 45230

FINAL PREPARATIONS

Before the Exam

1. Spend the last week of preparation primarily reviewing already completed problems, some basic skills, strategies, techniques, and directions for each area.

2. Carefully review the sections on taking the GMAT CAT and the general strategies.

3. Do a quick review of each of the question types and the specific strategies.

4. Don't cram the night before the exam. It's a waste of time.

5. Make sure that you are familiar with the testing center location and nearby parking facilities.

6. Gather the things that you need to take to the exam: A valid photo-bearing ID, your score recipient information, your authorization voucher (if you requested one from ETS), and a few pencils.

At the Exam

7. Arrive at the exam location and check in at least 30 minutes before your scheduled testing time.

8. If a problem is too difficult or takes too much time, take your best guess. Try to eliminate one or more of the answer choices before guessing.

9. Take advantage of having the scratch paper. Do calculations, redraw diagrams, note eliminated choices, or simply make helpful notes.

10. Make sure that you are answering "what is being asked" and that your answer is reasonable.

CliffsNotes

LITERATURE NOTES

Absalom, Absalom!
The Aeneid
Agamemnon
Alice in Wonderland
All the King's Men
All the Pretty Horses
All Quiet on the Western Front
All's Well & Merry Wives
American Poets of the 20th Century
American Tragedy
Animal Farm
Anna Karenina
Anthem
Antony and Cleopatra
Aristotle's Ethics
As I Lay Dying
The Assistant
As You Like It
Atlas Shrugged
Autobiography of Ben Franklin
Autobiography of Malcolm X
The Awakening
Babbit
Bartleby & Benito Cereno
The Bean Trees
The Bear
The Bell Jar
Beloved
Beowulf
The Bible
Billy Budd & Typee
Black Boy
Black Like Me
Bleak House
Bless Me, Ultima
The Bluest Eye & Sula
Brave New World
The Brothers Karamazov
Call of the Wild & White Fang
Candide
The Canterbury Tales
Catch-22
Catcher in the Rye
The Chosen
The Color Purple
Comedy of Errors...
Connecticut Yankee
The Contender
The Count of Monte Cristo
Crime and Punishment
The Crucible
Cry, the Beloved Country
Cyrano de Bergerac
Daisy Miller & Turn...Screw
David Copperfield
Death of a Salesman
The Deerslayer
Diary of Anne Frank
Divine Comedy-I. Inferno
Divine Comedy-II. Purgatorio
Divine Comedy-III. Paradiso
Doctor Faustus

Dr. Jekyll and Mr. Hyde
Don Juan
Don Quixote
Dracula
Electra & Medea
Emerson's Essays
Emily Dickinson Poems
Emma
Ethan Frome
The Faerie Queene
Fahrenheit 451
Far from Madding Crowd
A Farewell to Arms
Farewell to Manzanar
Fathers and Sons
Faulkner's Short Stories
Faust Pt. I & Pt. II
The Federalist
Flowers for Algernon
For Whom the Bell Tolls
The Fountainhead
Frankenstein
The French Lieutenant's Woman
The Giver
Glass Menagerie & Streetcar
Go Down, Moses
The Good Earth
Grapes of Wrath
Great Expectations
The Great Gatsby
Greek Classics
Gulliver's Travels
Hamlet
The Handmaid's Tale
Hard Times
Heart of Darkness & Secret Sharer
Hemingway's Short Stories
Henry IV Part 1
Henry IV Part 2
Henry V
House Made of Dawn
The House of the Seven Gables
Huckleberry Finn
I Know Why the Caged Bird Sings
Ibsen's Plays I
Ibsen's Plays II
The Idiot
Idylls of the King
The Iliad
Incidents in the Life of a Slave Girl
Inherit the Wind
Invisible Man
Ivanhoe
Jane Eyre
Joseph Andrews
The Joy Luck Club
Jude the Obscure
Julius Caesar
The Jungle
Kafka's Short Stories
Keats & Shelley
The Killer Angels
King Lear
The Kitchen God's Wife
The Last of the Mohicans

Le Morte Darthur
Leaves of Grass
Les Miserables
A Lesson Before Dying
Light in August
The Light in the Forest
Lord Jim
Lord of the Flies
Lord of the Rings
Lost Horizon
Lysistrata & Other Comedies
Macbeth
Madame Bovary
Main Street
The Mayor of Casterbridge
Measure for Measure
The Merchant of Venice
Middlemarch
A Midsummer-Night's Dream
The Mill on the Floss
Moby-Dick
Moll Flanders
Mrs. Dalloway
Much Ado About Nothing
My Ántonia
Mythology
Narr. ...Frederick Douglass
Native Son
New Testament
Night
1984
Notes from Underground
The Odyssey
Oedipus Trilogy
Of Human Bondage
Of Mice and Men
The Old Man and the Sea
Old Testament
Oliver Twist
The Once and Future King
One Day in the Life of Ivan Denisovich
One Flew Over Cuckoo's Nest
100 Years of Solitude
O'Neill's Plays
Othello
Our Town
The Outsiders
The Ox-Bow Incident
Paradise Lost
A Passage to India
The Pearl
The Pickwick Papers
The Picture of Dorian Gray
Pilgrim's Progress
The Plague
Plato's Euthyphro...
Plato's The Republic
Poe's Short Stories
A Portrait of the Artist...
The Portrait of a Lady
The Power and the Glory
Pride and Prejudice
The Prince
The Prince and the Pauper
A Raisin in the Sun

The Red Badge of Courage
The Red Pony
The Return of the Native
Richard II
Richard III
The Rise of Silas Lapham
Robinson Crusoe
Roman Classics
Romeo and Juliet
The Scarlet Letter
A Separate Peace
Shakespeare's Comedies
Shakespeare's Histories
Shakespeare's Minor Plays
Shakespeare's Sonnets
Shakespeare's Tragedies
Shaw's Pygmalion & Arms...
Silas Marner
Sir Gawain...Green Knight
Sister Carrie
Slaughterhouse-Five
Snow Falling on Cedars
Song of Solomon
Sons and Lovers
The Sound and the Fury
Steppenwolf & Siddhartha
The Stranger
The Sun Also Rises
T.S. Eliot's Poems & Plays
A Tale of Two Cities
The Taming of the Shrew
Tartuffe, Misanthrope...
The Tempest
Tender Is the Night
Tess of the D'Urbervilles
Their Eyes Were Watching God
Things Fall Apart
The Three Musketeers
To Kill a Mockingbird
Tom Jones
Tom Sawyer
Treasure Island & Kidnapped
The Trial
Tristram Shandy
Troilus and Cressida
Twelfth Night
Ulysses
Uncle Tom's Cabin
The Unvanquished
Utopia
Vanity Fair
Vonnegut's Works
Waiting for Godot
Walden
Walden Two
War and Peace
Who's Afraid of Virginia...
Winesburg, Ohio
The Winter's Tale
The Woman Warrior
Worldly Philosophers
Wuthering Heights
A Yellow Raft in Blue Water